T0364999

Living and Active

inspirational readings for college students

Suzanne Penner

WESTBOW
PRESS®
A DIVISION OF THOMAS NELSON
& ZONDERVAN

WestBow Press books may be ordered through booksellers or by contacting:

WestBow Press
A Division of Thomas Nelson & Zondervan
1663 Liberty Drive
Bloomington, IN 47403
www.westbowpress.com
1 (866) 928-1240

ISBN: 978-1-5127-4790-4 (sc)
ISBN: 978-1-5127-4792-8 (hc)
ISBN: 978-1-5127-4791-1 (e)

Library of Congress Control Number: 2016910429

Print information available on the last page.

WestBow Press rev. date: 7/25/2016

ACKNOWLEDGEMENT

All verses of scripture for the devotionals are quoted from the King James Version (KJV) of the Bible and downloaded from the Bible Gateway website: www.biblegateway.com

DEDICATION

For all my family and friends who have
helped me in my walk with the Lord,
I am eternally grateful

PREFACE

Written by a college professor, this book of devotional readings for college students was created in response to a couple of aspects of the modern university environment: the specific habits of college students and the spiritual needs of college students. The hope of this book is that students will be challenged to read the Bible for themselves and become motivated to find out how its truths pertain to their lives today.

Students carry a lot of heavy books around with them all day long and have limited time for lengthy reading outside of assigned course readings. They also use the latest technology as part of daily life, and they like to fill their empty time with information from technology.

The brevity of the devotional readings accommodates the busy lifestyle of modern college students. The inclusion of Scripture passages with each reading emphasizes the importance of the Word of God. The inerrancy of the Word of God is assumed.

Students today face many challenges that are inconceivable to previous generations. Clearly, the need exists for a fresh way to bring the book of hope for the entire world to the generation who represents the future hopes of the world. May the God of grace bless you as you increase in the knowledge of His word. Keep in mind that

the word of God is living and active,
sharper than any two-edged sword,
piercing to the division of soul and spirit,
of joints and marrow,
and discerning the thoughts and intentions of the heart.

Contentment from the Truth

Trust in the Lord with all thine heart; and lean not unto thine own
understanding. In all thy ways acknowledge him, and he shall direct
thy paths. Be not wise in thine own eyes: fear the Lord, and depart
from evil. It shall be health to thy navel, and marrow to thy bones.
—Proverbs 3:5–8

For it is not a vain thing for you; because it is your life:
and through this thing ye shall prolong your days in
the land, whither ye go over Jordan to possess it.
—Deuteronomy 32:47

Our culture places a high value on education at the same time that it acts as
if standards are not very important in almost every other area of life. This
dichotomy causes confusion in the minds of incoming college students because
they are not sure whom to believe: the educators or the culture at large. In order
to prioritize our lives, it is important to look to the Bible, the book that tells the
truth.

We go to college because we think education matters and we think that
a college education will further our plans in life. Learning is important, but
education is not all that comprises a human life. Trusting God means that we
are willing to listen to an opinion that is different from our own. Trusting God
means that we are willing to let the Lord lead us on His path instead of our own
path. Trusting God means that we are willing to forego evil behavior. Trusting
God may also include turning to God to get us through the next four years
financially, academically, and socially.

We cannot fool God, so when we trust God, we reap the consequences: a
sense of well-being and contentment that is not manufactured by anyone except
the Creator who made us. This trust enables us to concentrate our efforts in
the right places. The world sends a message to us that can be summed up in the
motto "Live and learn," but the Bible can be summed up as "Learn and live."
The Creator who made us also knows best the specifics that will serve Him, and
He will best fulfill our needs and interests—at the same time—without conflict
or harm to anyone.

The Creator Who Directs Our Lives

God that made the world and all things therein, seeing that he is
Lord of heaven and earth, dwelleth not in temples made with hands;
Neither is worshipped with men's hands, as though he needed any
thing, seeing he giveth to all life, and breath, and all things; And hath
made of one blood all nations of men for to dwell on all the face of
the earth, and hath determined the times before appointed, and the
bounds of their habitation; That they should seek the Lord, if haply
they might feel after him, and find him, though he be not far from
every one of us: For in him we live, and move, and have our being; as
certain also of your own poets have said, For we are also his offspring.
—Acts 17:24–28

As technology has improved and made more information available on the
Internet, users have learned that any type of information can be found in
cyberspace. Some of us long to learn census data about our grandparents and
great grandparents who came to this country as immigrants. By searching the
Internet, we hope to find significant facts about why or how we arrived to the
place where we are right now. When we forget that the Internet is only a tool, we
may expect it to tell us more about ourselves than it is really capable of doing.

But there is a better way to learn more about ourselves. Do we know what
this way is? Do we understand that we live and move only according to the will of
the Creator who made us? We need God; there is no question about it. He made
the world. He made everything in it. God needs nothing from us, yet the Creator
gives us life and breath and everything else. Even more than that, the Lord has
specifically directed the steps of our forebears and our own to bring us where we
are right now. He figured it out ahead of time—*our time,* that is.

His concern and care for us extend to the minutiae of individual lives: the
nation we live in, the time spans of our lives, the specific neighborhoods in which
we grew up, the exact dwellings we have inhabited, the family in which God
placed us, etc. Every bit of us belongs to Him, so let us reach out to Him because
He is not far from any of us. He has been and is right now with us in this life.

Seek God with thankfulness for what He has already done, with the
understanding that He will continue to lead us according to His good and
perfect will.

Time, Space, and Matter

> In the beginning God created the heaven and the
> earth … And God saw every thing that he had made,
> and, behold, it was very good … Thus the heavens and
> the earth were finished, and all the host of them.
> —Genesis 1:1, 1:31a, 2:1

> For the world is mine, and the fulness thereof.
> —Psalm 50:12b

> [God] Hath in these last days spoken unto us by his Son, whom he
> hath appointed heir of all things, by whom also he made the worlds.
> —Hebrews 1:2

Students may have learned in science class that the universe is comprised of a continuum of time, space, and matter—a very grand way of describing the world we see around us on a daily basis. Since evolution has taken hold of the scientific mind-set, the thought that a god could have created the universe seems to belong more to the realm of science fiction than hard science. Popular television specials promote the idea of evolutionary theory at the expense of creationism. Science no longer thinks of itself as thinking God's thoughts after Him, as Johannes Kepler is once thought to have believed.

But the language we use gives us clues to the truth anyway. The fact that science discovers facts means that the facts are already in plain sight, waiting to be noticed (discovered) by humans. The very word *discover* implies a magnificent Creator who put those facts in front of us so that we cannot miss what He has done for all people.

At the same time, as the creation of the world may appear difficult or unnecessary to comprehend or explain, it may also seem far removed from the biblical story of creation. Yet the first words of Genesis tell us the same message that scientists discovered centuries later and passed on to students: in the beginning (time), God created the heavens (space) and God created the earth (matter).

When we read the Bible as an accurate record of what has occurred, we understand more clearly that the truth has gone out into the world from the Creator who made it. The knowledge that God in heaven created a masterpiece of a planet out of nothing should create in us a deep sense of wonder, awe, gratitude, and determination to do Him proud. Our beliefs and our attitudes about the truth help us reflect His image—to the glory of God.

Forever Friends

A friend loveth at all times, and a brother is born for adversity ...
and there is a friend that sticketh closer than a brother.
—Proverbs 17:17, 18:24b

I am a companion of all them that fear thee,
and of them that keep thy precepts.
—Psalm 119:63

And when he saw their faith, he said unto
him, Man, thy sins are forgiven thee.
—Luke 5:20

College is a time to meet many new people and make many new friends. The uniqueness of these few years that pass so quickly quickens the energy with which we form attachments to others, and this is another blessing from the God who placed us on this campus. We have gladly left one life behind and look forward to the future.

Good friends are important to all of us. We need and value them for numerous reasons. Some listen to us, and some advise us. We spend leisure time with some, and we work with others. Friends explain what we do not understand, they notice what is best about us, and they allow us to let off steam.

Perhaps we still need to consider that the best friend we may ever have is Jesus, the Son of God, who loved us and died for our sins. He is better than the friend who sticks to us through thick and thin, because He is always with us. We cannot see Him, but we can sense His presence with us, indicating that our heavenly friend is always able and willing to help us in difficulties. The stresses of life are numerous and often require immediate attention and interventions. A cheerful friend can help us see the difficulty from another perspective, and sometimes the cheerful attitude matters more than the trial itself.

When we rely upon our heavenly friend first for forgiveness for sins and second for daily friendship, we begin to learn the heavenly perspective, and this type of friendship is what we need most.

The Power of Rest

Let us therefore fear, lest, a promise being left us of entering into his
rest, any of you should seem to come short of it … Seeing therefore
it remaineth that some must enter therein, and they to whom it was
first preached entered not in because of unbelief: Again, he limiteth a
certain day, saying in David, To day, after so long a time; as it is said,
To day if ye will hear his voice, harden not your hearts. For if Jesus
had given them rest, then would he not afterward have spoken of
another day. There remaineth therefore a rest to the people of God.
For he that is entered into his rest, he also hath ceased from his own
works, as God did from his … For the Word of God is quick, and
powerful, and sharper than any twoedged sword, piercing even to
the dividing asunder of soul and spirit, and of the joints and marrow,
and is a discerner of the thoughts and intents of the heart. Neither is
there any creature that is not manifest in his sight: but all things are
naked and opened unto the eyes of him with whom we have to do.
—Hebrews 4:1, 6–10, 12–13

The idea of Sunday as a day of rest began to disappear from our societal
consciousness when retailers began opening their doors on Sundays. The
reasoning is purely economic; one more day of business means one more day
of profits and no business can ever earn too much money, can it? The fact that
business has been booming on Sundays attests to the fact that many people no
longer value the day of rest and worship, yet God clearly desires believers to
enter His rest.

Does this mean that we withdraw from life? Become passive onlookers?
Stop engaging in ordinary activities? No! We need to cease from the workaday
activities because God has made the human body to function best in this way.
Rest gives us the time to reflect on the Creator and our relationship to Him. God
wants us to rest in Him because He rested on the seventh day—after creating
the world in six days.

Did the world stop operating because God was no longer actively overseeing
its operation? No, of course not! The nature of rest resides in the power of God,
not in the absence of activity. When we obey God's command to rest, His power
to rejuvenate us operates in our lives—as surely as it did on the seventh day and
from that day forward to today. How can this be? Resting in Him matters because
the Word of God is so powerful that it discerns what needs to be done and does
it without human aid, without human effort, and without human thought. Relax,
and enjoy the day!

Superhuman Beings

And Jacob went on his way, and the angels of God met him …
And Jacob said, O God of my father Abraham, and God of my
father Isaac, the Lord which saidst unto me, Return unto thy
country, and to thy kindred, and I will deal well with thee: I am
not worthy of the least of all the mercies, and of all the truth,
which thou hast shewed unto thy servant; for with my staff I
passed over this Jordan; and now I am become two bands … And
Jacob was left alone; and there wrestled a man with him until
the breaking of the day. And when he saw that he prevailed not
against him, he touched the hollow of his thigh; and the hollow
of Jacob's thigh was out of joint, as he wrestled with him.
—Genesis 32:1, 9–10, 24–25

Some people dream of an alternate universe in which superhuman beings enter the human world, direct individual lives, wage great battles, and win every time. Of course, in our dreams, we belong to the winning side. As fantastic as it may sound, this otherworldly experience really happened to Jacob. He was a believer, but his decisions revealed shrewdness and cunning; such personal qualities are not always admired. Jacob knew how he had lived his life. He was a conniver who had traded a bowl of stew for the birthright of the firstborn son (that originally belonged to his older-born twin brother, Esau).

The natural grudge of Esau for his brother's trickery caused Jacob to flee hundreds of miles to his uncle's home. Later, he wanted to return home as a successful man with his family, flocks, and herds, but he remained somewhat hesitant and very uncertain of the reception his brother Esau would give him. God left the strong man alone: Jacob wrestled first with his thoughts and then with God. Jacob possessed so much physical strength and endurance that he won the wrestling match, but God possesses all authority so He had the final word, wrenching Jacob's hip to give him a permanent limp.

God humbled the strong man physically to remind him of who is in charge of all situations, even situations in which the believer is at fault. God did not need Jacob's strength then anymore than He needs ours today. God wants us to know that we are able to act only according to His power in us.

Mystery

And Adam knew his wife again; and she bare a son, and
called his name Seth: For God, said she, hath appointed me
another seed instead of Abel, whom Cain slew. And to Seth,
to him also there was born a son; and he called his name
Enos: then began men to call upon the name of the Lord.
—Genesis 4:25–26

Whereby, when ye read, ye may understand my knowledge in the
mystery of Christ) Which in other ages was not made known unto the
sons of men, as it is now revealed unto his holy apostles and prophets
by the Spirit; That the Gentiles should be fellowheirs, and of the same
body, and partakers of his promise in Christ by the gospel: Whereof I
was made a minister, according to the gift of the grace of God given
unto me by the effectual working of his power … To the intent that
now unto the principalities and powers in heavenly places might be
known by the church the manifold wisdom of God, According to
the eternal purpose which he purposed in Christ Jesus our Lord.
—Ephesians 3:4–7, 10–11

Mysteries intrigue most people because of a natural human attraction to
the unknown. Yet once the mystery is clarified, interest may evaporate
even though fresh understandings open up. Do we ever wonder what religion or
worship was like before the church, as we know it today, was established? The
Bible records that our earliest forebears called upon God, but we might also infer
that their worship was not organized in a format familiar to us.

In the human timeline, there was once a time when Jesus Christ, the sinless
One, had not yet died for all sinners. There was once a time when God had not
yet explained that salvation belongs to all who believe. But because of Jesus
Christ, the mystery has been cleared up. We can now live with certainty instead
of confusion, knowledge instead of ignorance, and confidence instead of fear.
The mystery of who may be saved has now been explained. Do we ever stop to
consider that those of us who believe and are not from a Jewish background (most
of us) were once beyond God's saving power? God has blessed the church with
this knowledge so we can pass it on.

The mystery of God's eternal purpose became clear on the cross of Jesus
Christ. The knowledge that God has cared for us so deeply gives us the freedom
and confidence to approach the God who was formerly unapproachable.

What Group Do You Belong To?

Say unto them, Thus saith the Lord God; Behold, I will take the
stick of Joseph, which is in the hand of Ephraim, and the tribes of
Israel his fellows, and will put them with him, even with the stick
of Judah, and make them one stick, and they shall be one in mine
hand ... And David my servant shall be king over them; and they
all shall have one shepherd: they shall also walk in my judgments,
and observe my statutes, and do them ... My tabernacle also shall
be with them: yea, I will be their God, and they shall be my people.
And the heathen shall know that I the Lord do sanctify Israel,
when my sanctuary shall be in the midst of them for evermore.
—Ezekiel 37:19, 24, 27–28

One part of the childhood educational experience from kindergarten to
grade 12 involves the desire to belong to a specific group, yet sometimes a
stronger-willed child prevents us from belonging to it. The effort to break into a
clique or the humiliation of being snubbed from it can create painful memories
during those young years. But it is time to grow up.

The desire to belong to a group is normal, and because God has given us
that desire, He intends to fulfill us. The Word of God tells us that the people of
God form a group of God's own choosing. When we belong to the Lord, we join
an enormous congregation. We should never neglect to seek out the fellowship
of like-minded believers in a God-fearing church.

The Lord brings the body of believers together in a single, cohesive unit.
God changes us and leads us in His will. The friendships we form from our
congregation support us and encourage us daily. Every group needs a leader, and
the leader of the church is Jesus Christ. He is the perfect shepherd, descended
from King David. God made an eternal promise to live among the group. God
wants to dwell with us, to be our companion and leader. Why should God want
us to belong to His group? So that we may enjoy fellowship and friendship and
show the rest of the world what He is like.

Born Again

Jesus answered and said unto him, Verily, verily, I say unto thee,
Except a man be born again, he cannot see the kingdom of God.
Nicodemus saith unto him, How can a man be born when he is
old? can he enter the second time into his mother's womb, and be
born? Jesus answered, Verily, verily, I say unto thee, Except a man
be born of water and of the Spirit, he cannot enter into the kingdom
of God. That which is born of the flesh is flesh; and that which
is born of the Spirit is spirit. Marvel not that I said unto thee, Ye
must be born again. The wind bloweth where it listeth, and thou
hearest the sound thereof, but canst not tell whence it cometh,
and whither it goeth: so is every one that is born of the Spirit.
—John 3:3–8

At a time when the nation, the culture, and the government of Israel were
looking for a better quality of life, Jesus Christ told Nicodemus, a member
of the Jewish ruling council, about a new kind of life, a life that held a completely
different kind of quality. Nicodemus was intrigued and asked a further question,
but he was understandably confused about salvation, just like people today.

How do individuals gain the favor of God? Do they get to heaven by
following rules or rituals? False religions indicate false paths that create spiritual
misunderstanding, so Jesus explained to Nicodemus that the spiritual birth or
regeneration is similar to human birth. Our earthly parents brought us into
the world. Our heavenly father brings us into the kingdom of God. Jesus also
explained that the spiritual birth is different from the human birth. We do not
choose to be born any more than our parents specifically chose us to be their
children, yet God chose us before the foundation of the world to belong to His
family. We must still choose to join Him through repentance.

The choice we make is like the wind. No one can see the wind, but everyone
can see the effects of the wind. One quiet moment, one quiet deliberation, one
quiet decision becomes a real, visible, tangible witness to others of the power of
God to save sinners, even you!

JANUARY 10

Give Credit to God

I saw in the visions of my head upon my bed, and, behold, a watcher and an holy one came down from heaven; He cried aloud, and said thus, Hew down the tree, and cut off his branches, shake off his leaves, and scatter his fruit: let the beasts get away from under it, and the fowls from his branches: Nevertheless leave the stump of his roots in the earth, even with a band of iron and brass, in the tender grass of the field; and let it be wet with the dew of heaven, and let his portion be with the beasts in the grass of the earth: Let his heart be changed from man's, and let a beast's heart be given unto him; and let seven times pass over him. This matter is by the decree of the watchers, and the demand by the word of the holy ones: to the intent that the living may know that the most High ruleth in the kingdom of men, and giveth it to whomsoever he will, and setteth up over it the basest of men ... All this came upon the king Nebuchadnezzar ... The same hour was the thing fulfilled upon Nebuchadnezzar: and he was driven from men, and did eat grass as oxen, and his body was wet with the dew of heaven, till his hairs were grown like eagles' feathers, and his nails like birds' claws.
—Daniel 4:13–17, 28, 33

Do we understand that God gives various gifts to all of us, that none of us can claim our intelligence or skills or strengths as our own? Many people live as self-taught paragons and promote themselves for their own purposes. Hollywood may be the most obvious place to look for such people, but they are everywhere. Take for example King Nebuchadnezzar, whose life prospered tremendously. He chalked up his earthly success to his own greatness, strength, and dominion. He never once saw God as the source of his life, let alone of anything else.

But God resists proud people and dealt with the king in a unique, dramatic, and unforgettable way. Instead of sending a human being to witness to the king, God sent a heavenly messenger to King Nebuchadnezzar to warn him to repent of his sins, but the king paid no attention to the message. As a result, God punished the king by sending him out of his palace and into the wilderness. Nebuchadnezzar lived like a wild animal until he admitted that God was a greater ruler than he was. When Nebuchadnezzar finally gave credit to God, God restored the sanity of his mind and returned the rule of his kingdom to him.

Likewise, God gives us time to give Him credit for what He has done, but if we continue in pride, He deals with us unmistakably. God knows that the best quality of life comes from acknowledging Him in our lives.

Spiritual Heritage

For I speak to you Gentiles, inasmuch as I am the apostle of the
Gentiles, I magnify mine office … And if some of the branches be
broken off, and thou, being a wild olive tree, wert grafted in among
them, and with them partakest of the root and fatness of the olive
tree; Boast not against the branches. But if thou boast, thou bearest
not the root, but the root thee. Thou wilt say then, The branches
were broken off, that I might be grafted in. Well; because of unbelief
they were broken off, and thou standest by faith. Be not highminded,
but fear: For if God spared not the natural branches, take heed lest
he also spare not thee. Behold therefore the goodness and severity
of God: on them which fell, severity; but toward thee, goodness, if
thou continue in his goodness: otherwise thou also shalt be cut off.
—Romans 11:13, 17–22

Some of us take pride in thinking that we come from several generations of
Christian believers in our family. It is certainly true that a spiritual heritage is
valuable, but we should always remember that most of us Christians are believers
by default. God chose the apostle Paul to bring the gospel to the Gentiles
(everyone who is not Jewish). He made it clear that the unbelief of the Jews stood
between them and salvation. Those who were not Jews were then grafted into
the spiritual genealogical tree of salvation.

Nevertheless, we do not live according to our genealogies or genetics; we
live by faith. Faith is still the means of salvation, just as it was for the patriarch
Abraham. The same rules still apply to all humans when it comes to salvation.
The warning not to take our faith for granted should remind us of what we might
have been like without the power of the cross of Jesus Christ. The words of God
should also remind us of all we may become—through the power of the cross
of Jesus Christ.

Let us who are Gentiles by birth be humbled when we think that God not
only wanted us, He accepted us. He was kind to us when we deserved His wrath
and censure. God has let us grow into a more fruitful tree than we could have
produced on our own. Our spiritual heritage really comes from the knowledge
of Him, not our human ancestry.

Questioning the Lord

> O Lord, how long shall I cry, and thou wilt not hear! even cry
> out unto thee of violence, and thou wilt not save! ... Behold ye
> among the heathen, and regard, and wonder marvelously: for I
> will work a work in your days which ye will not believe, though
> it be told you ... Art thou not from everlasting, O Lord my God,
> mine Holy One? we shall not die. O Lord, thou hast ordained
> them for judgment; and, O mighty God, thou hast established
> them for correction ... Behold, his soul which is lifted up is not
> upright in him: but the just shall live by his faith ... But the Lord
> is in his holy temple: let all the earth keep silence before him.
> —Habakkuk 1:2, 5, 12; 2:4, 20

Is it all right to be upset with God, to be really angry with God, to question God? Yes, it is. The prophet Habakkuk was as human as the rest of us, and he complained quite a bit to the Lord. He struggled with the unfairness of the society in which he lived. Society promoted evil, glorified evil, and let evil go unpunished. Habakkuk demanded an answer from the Lord who hates evil.

We need to do the same when the situation at hand is so overwhelmingly beyond human control. God did not reprimand Habakkuk for his attitude. He answered him by telling him to wait and see what would happen next. God wants believers to question Him and wait expectantly for the answers He will give. God reminded Habakkuk that He alone is God, and He alone can accomplish spectacular feats. God wants believers to look for the specific details and the unexpected answers He will bring to a difficult situation.

God's response to Habakkuk was so brutal that Habakkuk was shocked to learn that God would punish sinners so severely. So may we think the same thing; nevertheless, God is holy. He reminds Habakkuk that even when society is decaying, the righteous will always live by faith. No one's behavior goes unnoticed by God. The Lord sits enthroned in his holy temple, so all of us should silence ourselves before Him in awe.

Preparation

The beginning of the gospel of Jesus Christ, the Son of God; As it
is written in the prophets, Behold, I send my messenger before thy
face, which shall prepare thy way before thee. The voice of one crying
in the wilderness, Prepare ye the way of the Lord, make his paths
straight. John did baptize in the wilderness, and preach the baptism
of repentance for the remission of sins. And there went out unto him
all the land of Judaea, and they of Jerusalem, and were all baptized
of him in the river of Jordan, confessing their sins. And John was
clothed with camel's hair, and with a girdle of a skin about his loins;
and he did eat locusts and wild honey; And preached, saying, There
cometh one mightier than I after me, the latchet of whose shoes I
am not worthy to stoop down and unloose. I indeed have baptized
you with water: but he shall baptize you with the Holy Ghost.
—Mark 1:1–8

Think about how much preparation goes into the completion of any task.
It is monumental. When we go to college, we go through all the stuff
of childhood. We keep some, we lose some, and we pack some up for future
reference. Parents take us shopping to buy dorm-sized sheets and room
accessories. Everything we need is packed until the family car is stuffed. Then
we go to the campus, where counselors tell us what courses to take, and they
give us a campus map. We see what a dormitory looks like and we experience the
exhilaration of walking around the college grounds.

College requires a lot of preparation, but we understand that our future lives
depend upon our present preparedness. The atmosphere builds excitement. We
want to go, we want to begin, and we want to finish the course. We engage in a
lot of planning, only to turn around and take orders from advisors and professors
before completing the degree.

God knows that groundwork is a big part of any task, even the task of
salvation of human souls. Jesus did not announce Himself to the world at large,
but to John the Baptist first. John was the final prophet to tell of His imminent
coming. We need to be prepared for repentance and baptism to follow the Lord.
Such a lot of preparation, and it is only the beginning of our walk with the Lord.

Take God All the Way

And Moses sent them to spy out the land of Canaan, and said unto
them, Get you up this way southward, and go up into the mountain:
And see the land, what it is, and the people that dwelleth therein,
whether they be strong or weak, few or many; And what the land
is that they dwell in, whether it be good or bad; and what cities
they be that they dwell in, whether in tents, or in strong holds; And
what the land is, whether it be fat or lean, whether there be wood
therein, or not. And be ye of good courage, and bring of the fruit
of the land. Now the time was the time of the firstripe grapes ...
And they came unto the brook of Eshcol, and cut down from thence
a branch with one cluster of grapes, and they bare it between two
upon a staff; and they brought of the pomegranates, and of the
figs ... And Caleb stilled the people before Moses, and said, Let us
go up at once, and possess it; for we are well able to overcome it.
—Numbers 13:17–20, 23, 30

Whenever we embark upon a new adventure, we plan ahead. We don't know exactly what to expect so we scout out the situation. Today, this may mean an Internet search to gain information, to buy equipment for tasks, or to find the best route. For the Israelites, it meant sending out spies, scouting out the land, seeing what goes on there, and bringing back a report on conditions.

Accurate information helps us to make a better decision, no matter what the decision may be. And while we are gathering and sifting through the relative importance of the bits of information, God is guiding our thoughts so that we will follow His leading.

Twelve spies took God's orders from Moses to check out the Promised Land. All twelve spies shared the same experience, but only two of them gave a favorable report. Why? How do we account for the disparity in their reports? Ten scouts lived by their wits, shrewdness, and personal understanding in order to accomplish the task set before them by God. But the understanding of Joshua and Caleb included taking God at His word that He was on their side, to help them, to prosper them. Trusting God means that we never rely on our own strength or understanding. God is always perfectly able to accomplish His will.

Living with Unbearable Pressure

For we would not, brethren, have you ignorant of our trouble
which came to us in Asia, that we were pressed out of measure,
above strength, insomuch that we despaired even of life: But
we had the sentence of death in ourselves, that we should not
trust in ourselves, but in God which raiseth the dead: Who
delivered us from so great a death, and doth deliver: in whom
we trust that he will yet deliver us; Ye also helping together by
prayer for us, that for the gift bestowed upon us by the means
of many persons thanks may be given by many on our behalf.
—2 Corinthians 1:8–11

Everyone is acquainted with the pressures of modern life—at work, even in
a good working situation, at home, especially in a bad home situation, and
in college, with so many deadlines and a lot less time that we would like for the
tasks. Talk shows and televised counselors offer ways to deal with a variety of
stressful scenarios. These shows enjoy widespread popularity because they strike
a relevant chord in human experience.

The apostle Paul traveled throughout the Mediterranean region, the known
world at the time. The first Christian missionary traveled from Israel in the Near
East, to Turkey, Greece, and Italy in southern Europe, and to islands of the
Mediterranean Sea. In addition to the physical hardships of travel in his century,
the spiritual warfare waged against Paul was severe. Pressure is not a problem
of the modern world. It can come from others because the enemy of our souls
desires our destruction.

Pressure is a tool that God uses to help us rely on Him. We need to realize
how weak we are, how ineffective we are, and how unable we are to accomplish
any task apart from the God who helps us. When we depend on God, He delivers
us from the pressure we feel and gives us hope in Him.

Unfaithfulness

The beginning of the word of the Lord by Hosea. And the Lord
said to Hosea, Go, take unto thee a wife of whoredoms and children
of whoredoms: for the land hath committed great whoredom,
departing from the Lord. So he went and took Gomer the daughter
of Diblaim; which conceived, and bare him a son. And the Lord
said unto him, Call his name Jezreel; for yet a little while, and I will
avenge the blood of Jezreel upon the house of Jehu, and will cause
to cease the kingdom of the house of Israel … And she conceived
again, and bare a daughter. And God said unto him, Call her name
Loruhamah: for I will no more have mercy upon the house of Israel;
but I will utterly take them away … Now when she had weaned
Loruhamah, she conceived, and bare a son … Yet the number of
the children of Israel shall be as the sand of the sea, which cannot
be measured nor numbered; and it shall come to pass, that in the
place where it was said unto them, Ye are not my people, there
it shall be said unto them, Ye are the sons of the living God.
—Hosea 1:2–4, 6, 8, 10

It may be nearly impossible for us to place ourselves in the life, times, and
mind-set of Hosea the prophet. God spoke to him directly, and God clearly
told him to marry a woman was already immoral and who would continue to
commit adultery after her marriage to Hosea. Even more incredible to modern
thinkers is the fact that Hosea obeyed God and married Gomer, a woman with
a bad name and a worse lifestyle. But God does everything for a purpose—His
purpose—so we can learn God's lessons from the situation.

Hosea's marriage teaches us that marriage is good and that everyone desires
to be married, even when they live a life of gross sexual sin. Hosea's wife teaches
us that marriage does not cure the sin of adultery. When the mind believes that
promiscuity is all right, then the act of marriage is secondary and negligible to
the behavior that comes from strongly held beliefs contrary to fidelity. Marriage
represents the union of God with His people, of Christ with His bride, the
church. In the life of Gomer, we see someone who wants God, who wants the
church at the same time as she wants her own sinful life.

When people are conflicted about good and evil, evil will take over. In spite
of deliberate sin, God still loves the sinner, just like Hosea actually loved his wife.
God does everything to woo us back to a right relationship with Him.

Fair Punishment

For the day of the Lord is near upon all the heathen: as thou hast done, it shall be done unto thee: thy reward shall return upon thine own head. For as ye have drunk upon my holy mountain, so shall all the heathen drink continually, yea, they shall drink, and they shall swallow down, and they shall be as though they had not been. But upon mount Zion shall be deliverance, and there shall be holiness; and the house of Jacob shall possess their possessions. And the house of Jacob shall be a fire, and the house of Joseph a flame, and the house of Esau for stubble, and they shall kindle in them, and devour them; and there shall not be any remaining of the house of Esau; for the Lord hath spoken it.
—Obadiah 1:15–18

When Obadiah predicted that Edom would be judged for harassing and attacking the Israelites, Edom was a strong nation—strong in its own strength and strong in the pride of its strength. The Edomites descended from Esau, and the Israelites descended from Jacob, so they were closely related. When Jacob and Esau were twins in the womb, they tussled with each other. When he was a young adult, Esau sold his birthright to Jacob for a bowl of stew, bringing about a long-lasting animosity between twin brothers who could otherwise have been friends. The youthful decision matured.

As landowners, the Edomites (Esau) refused to let the Israelites (Jacob) pass through their country, even when surrounding nations warred against Israel. The fire of the twin brothers' feud was kindled and fanned; it blazed into a fire that seared the national conscience. God uses the relationship between Esau and Jacob to show how the choices of young men reveal attitudes—and attitudes foster specific behavior patterns throughout life. The personal grudge was long gone, but the attitudes and behaviors of sinful thinking remained to blight the family structure.

The importance of making right choices when young cannot be overstated enough. We should always keep in mind that God observes everything we do, and He brings about the appropriate moral outcome to every decision we make. God judges all peoples fairly. Sin cannot win; evil cannot triumph. Although it seemed like an unlikely prediction that Edom would fall and Israel would be delivered, it really did happen several hundred years later.

God is at Work in Us

Being confident of this very thing, that he which hath begun a good
work in you will perform it until the day of Jesus Christ ... For I have
no man likeminded, who will naturally care for your state. For all
seek their own, not the things which are Jesus Christ's ... For indeed
he was sick nigh unto death: but God had mercy on him; and not on
him only, but on me also, lest I should have sorrow upon sorrow.
—Philippians 1:6; 2:20–21, 27

Most endeavors in life require a specific way to begin, a process to follow
through the middle, and an achievable goal to gain as the result. We like to
tick off these steps because they give a sense of concrete progress to life. College
is a lengthy effort that takes four years, and we mark how well we are doing at
the end of every semester. When we turn to Christ, we tend to think we have
reached the end of a road, but new life in Christ is really a beginning that never
ends. It never ends because God is infinite; we can never know all there is to
know about Him. There is always more because He is the highest, the greatest,
and the best—every superlative adjective describes Him.

The best aspect of the Christian life is that we need not struggle through
life anymore. God begins the good work of salvation because the work of Christ
on the cross was efficacious to save us. The Holy Spirit continues the work of
changing us into His likeness. We should aim to live in a way that honors the
Word of God. We can read the Ten Commandments in Exodus, chapter 20, for
a quick summation of godly life principles.

Above all, we can rest in God and let Him finish this life for us. When we
compare our physical life to our spiritual life, we must reason differently. We
cannot judge one by the other. Paul could see the spiritual differences in the life
of Timothy, his assistant in the work of evangelization. He understood that God
is at work even when He sometimes stops us from working.

Who Is Jesus Christ?

Who is the image of the invisible God, the firstborn of every
creature: For by him were all things created, that are in heaven,
and that are in earth, visible and invisible, whether they be thrones,
or dominions, or principalities, or powers: all things were created
by him, and for him: And he is before all things, and by him all
things consist. And he is the head of the body, the church: who
is the beginning, the firstborn from the dead; that in all things
he might have the preeminence. For it pleased the Father that in
him should all fulness dwell; And, having made peace through the
blood of his cross, by him to reconcile all things unto himself; by
him, I say, whether they be things in earth, or things in heaven.
—Colossians 1:15–20

We often notice the similarities between generations. When fathers and sons
share the same profession, we are even more amazed. Family members
who work together remind us of how love can unify a group of people and extend
the blessings of that love to others.

Likewise, the Son of God is the image of the invisible God—like father,
like son. He is the first true man, because He never sinned. The rest of us fall far
short. Jesus Christ created the world we see and the world we cannot see—life
so small it can only be seen with a microscope. This includes creatures who live
in the depths where eyesight cannot penetrate, galaxies so far away they can only
be seen with a telescope, all the unseen denizens of the spiritual realm—those
who love to serve God—and even those who live in rebellion to Him. So much
is hidden from humans that we must take God's word for the reality of it.

Jesus Christ gives authority to and withholds authority from individuals.
No one climbs a political ladder unless Jesus Christ allows it. Jesus Christ holds
the universe together. Neither science nor ideas, neither technology nor people,
holds the world together. Jesus Christ is the best, the first, the top, the supreme
of every superlative. Jesus Christ made peace with God for us, through His blood
shed on the cross. Let us give Him our undivided attention and loyalty so that
we may resemble the heavenly family to which we belong.

Attitude first, Activity second

See that none render evil for evil unto any man; but ever follow
that which is good, both among yourselves, and to all men. Rejoice
evermore. Pray without ceasing. In every thing give thanks:
for this is the will of God in Christ Jesus concerning you.
—1 Thessalonians 5:15–18

This I say then, Walk in the Spirit, and ye
shall not fulfil the lust of the flesh.
—Galatians 5:16

That ye might walk worthy of the Lord unto all pleasing, being
fruitful in every good work, and increasing in the knowledge of God.
—Colossians 1:10

For God hath not called us unto uncleanness, but unto holiness.
—1 Thessalonians 4:7

When we live in our own way, we do what seems best for each moment. Sometimes our activities are all right, but sometimes they are questionable. When we decide to enter the godly way of living, we know we must change ourselves, at least a little.

How to live a Christian life can make us wonder whether or not a complete reversal of general plans is in order. It is easy to see that God has given numerous and diverse gifts to believers, so new believers can become confused about how to live out their newly acquired Christian beliefs. When Christian workers speak to congregations, they may come across as if Christian work is best in life. But if we look at biblical advice, we can see that the best activities in life are not specific professions but specific actions that anyone can do.

Living the Christian life engages the attitudes first, and from right attitudes come activities that please God. We should show respect for church leaders and pastors. We should learn to live in peace instead of anger toward others. We should be glad to work instead of idle away the time. We can give encouragement to others and exercise patience toward them. We can be kind and avoid revenge-based activities toward others. The activities of the Christian life help us to be joyful and thankful. This is what God wants, and every believer can live in the way that pleases God.

Sinners Are Saved

This is a faithful saying, and worthy of all acceptation, that Christ
Jesus came into the world to save sinners; of whom I am chief.
Howbeit for this cause I obtained mercy, that in me first Jesus Christ
might shew forth all longsuffering, for a pattern to them which
should hereafter believe on him to life everlasting. Now unto the
King eternal, immortal, invisible, the only wise God, be honour and
glory for ever and ever. Amen ... For this is good and acceptable in
the sight of God our Saviour; Who will have all men to be saved,
and to come unto the knowledge of the truth. For there is one God,
and one mediator between God and men, the man Christ Jesus;
Who gave himself a ransom for all, to be testified in due time.
—1 Timothy 1:15–17; 2:3–6

Perhaps we belong to a religion that does not believe that human nature is
sinful. Perhaps we never learned anything at all about the topic because
we never went to church. Whatever we may think, we all know that as human
beings, we fall short in many ways. We are so familiar with the sinful nature that
we cannot escape it, but we ought to label it correctly. This knowledge should
not depress us or give us cause to accept the sinful nature as our final destination
in life. The patience of God toward sinners is all we need to become what we
cannot be of our own volition.

The apostle Paul got in touch with this reality when he repented of his sins.
God changed him from a person who persecuted believers in Jesus to a person
who loved Jesus. He learned to speak the simple truth that Jesus Christ saves
sinners. His life is an example to us of how far a person may go from God, yet
God still saves him. Paul has no doubt about the patience of God to forgive great
sinners. He is thankful.

Paul reiterates that God desires salvation for all of us and sent his Son, Jesus
Christ, to be the mediator between God and man. Mediator means "ransom" or
"substitution." We don't need to die for our sins because Jesus Christ already did
it for us, and God accepts the price He paid for our sins.

Good Things in Life

Preserve me, O God: for in thee do I put my trust. O my soul,
thou hast said unto the Lord, Thou art my Lord: my goodness
extendeth not to thee; But to the saints that are in the earth, and
to the excellent, in whom is all my delight ... The Lord is the
portion of mine inheritance and of my cup: thou maintainest my
lot. The lines are fallen unto me in pleasant places; yea, I have a
goodly heritage. I will bless the Lord, who hath given me counsel:
my reins also instruct me in the night seasons ... For thou wilt not
leave my soul in hell; neither wilt thou suffer thine Holy One to see
corruption. Thou wilt shew me the path of life: in thy presence is
fulness of joy; at thy right hand there are pleasures for evermore.
—Psalm 16:1–3, 5–7, 10–11

We don't normally think twice about the source of anything that we call our
own. We are so accustomed to having all our needs met by anonymous
others that we often forget that God is the originator of every good and perfect
gift. We might want to pause our busy lives for a few minutes to think about a
few facts: workers we will never meet assembled the car we drive, seamstresses
unknown to us have stitched the garments we wear, and nameless farmers have
grown the food we eat.

Whereas children understand that their parents take care of them, adults
tend to feel that they are responsible for everything in life. When we enter a
relationship with God, we should eventually revamp our understanding to accept
that everything in this life comes from God. God is truly good to give us all we
have. God graciously gives us every useful and beautiful object in life. With this
insight comes happiness and thankfulness to God. We can take pleasure in the
company of like-minded believers. The knowledge that God has taken care of all
these details gives us a sense of security, leading to confidence and contentment
in Him. God leads us along the path of life.

What God wants for us is always exciting and interesting to us; God makes
us happy. It is important to grow in spiritual understanding because we need
increasing confidence to ask of God for our needs as we expect Him to answer
our prayers.

Freedom of Choice

And Joshua said unto all the people, Thus saith the Lord God of
Israel, Your fathers dwelt on the other side of the flood in old time,
even Terah, the father of Abraham, and the father of Nachor: and
they served other gods. And I took your father Abraham from
the other side of the flood, and led him throughout all the land of
Canaan, and multiplied his seed, and gave him Isaac. And I gave
unto Isaac Jacob and Esau: and I gave unto Esau mount Seir, to
possess it; but Jacob and his children went down into Egypt … Now
therefore fear the Lord, and serve him in sincerity and in truth:
and put away the gods which your fathers served on the other side
of the flood, and in Egypt; and serve ye the Lord. And if it seem
evil unto you to serve the Lord, choose you this day whom ye will
serve; whether the gods which your fathers served that were on the
other side of the flood, or the gods of the Amorites, in whose land
ye dwell: but as for me and my house, we will serve the Lord …
And Joshua said unto the people, Ye cannot serve the Lord: for
he is an holy God; he is a jealous God; he will not forgive your
transgressions nor your sins … And the people said unto Joshua,
The Lord our God will we serve, and his voice will we obey.
—Joshua 24:2–4, 14–15, 19, 24

In every age, God gives human beings freedom of choice. It does not matter
what our life has been or what our parents taught us. Abraham, who is
considered the father of three faiths (Judaism, Christianity, and Islam), began
life as an idol worshipper. No one remembers this part of his life because he
exercised his freedom of choice when God spoke to him personally.

Joshua reminded the Israelites of the father of their faith to help them
understand that they may exercise the same freedom of choice. They may choose
to follow the gods of the Amorites (to their eternal destruction), or they may
choose to serve the living God (unto everlasting life). It is very heartening to hear
the people vociferously assert their allegiance to the Lord their God.

The same choices belong to all of us today: the choice to repent unto eternal
life and the choice to rebel to utter damnation. God holds us to the promises we
make. Whatever way we choose, God accomplishes the outcomes of our goals.
We will always be surprised—for better or for worse—at how our lives turn out.
Choose the Lord today and settle the outcome of life right now.

Sovereignty of God

O clap your hands, all ye people; shout unto God with the voice of
triumph. For the Lord most high is terrible; he is a great King over
all the earth. He shall subdue the people under us, and the nations
under our feet. He shall choose our inheritance for us, the excellency
of Jacob whom he loved. Selah ... The princes of the people are
gathered together, even the people of the God of Abraham: for the
shields of the earth belong unto God: he is greatly exalted ... I will
cry unto God most high; unto God that performeth all things for
me. He shall send from heaven, and save me from the reproach of
him that would swallow me up. Selah. God shall send forth his mercy
and his truth ... From the end of the earth will I cry unto thee, when
my heart is overwhelmed: lead me to the rock that is higher than I.
—Psalm 47:1–4, 9; 51:10–12; 57:2–3; 61:2

God is sovereign; He rules over every aspect of the earth: political,
agricultural, personal, and spiritual. His sovereignty means that no one
else can know more about how to do things right than the One who brought the
world into existence.

When we live in a country that exercises the freedom of voting, this may
seem inaccurate, but the Bible assures that not only does God choose political
leaders, He also chooses individuals like us to serve Him with gladness. God is
in charge of the agriculture of planet earth. He created all animals; therefore, He
owns them, but he allows humans to husband the livestock and farm the land.
In all of this, God fulfills His purpose in numerous individual lives. Not only
does this mean that He has saved us, it also means that He continues to pursue
us with love and faithfulness to keep us true to Himself.

This awesome knowledge gives us cause to clap our hands for joy that
someone else runs the show. It is too big for us to handle anyway. While God is
running the show, He still has time to lead us gently to the great and hard rock
of security that we find only in Him.

Failure

But Peter said unto him, Although all shall be offended, yet will not I. And Jesus saith unto him, Verily I say unto thee, That this day, even in this night, before the cock crow twice, thou shalt deny me thrice. But he spake the more vehemently, If I should die with thee, I will not deny thee in any wise. Likewise also said they all ... And as Peter was beneath in the palace, there cometh one of the maids of the high priest: And when she saw Peter warming himself, she looked upon him, and said, And thou also wast with Jesus of Nazareth. But he denied, saying, I know not, neither understand I what thou sayest. And he went out into the porch; and the cock crew ... And he denied it again. And a little after, they that stood by said again to Peter, Surely thou art one of them: for thou art a Galilaean, and thy speech agreeth thereto. But he began to curse and to swear, saying, I know not this man of whom ye speak. And the second time the cock crew. And Peter called to mind the word that Jesus said unto him, Before the cock crow twice, thou shalt deny me thrice. And when he thought thereon, he wept.
—Mark 14:29–31, 66–68, 70–72

Those of us who prefer to sit on the sidelines also enjoy watching energetic personalities like Peter, one of Jesus's disciples. On one occasion, Peter eagerly jumped into Lake Galilee and actually walked a step or two on the surface of the lake before beginning to drown in the water. We all wish we could be that spontaneous, but we are not cut from the same cloth as Peter. On another occasion, Peter eagerly agreed to stand by Jesus no matter what happened. If we know people who swear they will always or never do something, we know a person like Peter. We probably also know that such volatile eagerness can also indicate reckless overconfidence.

When we believe that the strength of our emotions will enable us to perform excellently, we may be surprised to learn from embarrassing experiences that the opposite is actually true. Peter learned this lesson the hard way. Peter needed to fail in order to learn to trust in God instead of in his emotions. We too need to subjugate our emotions to God.

History reveals that the personality of Peter did not change. God does not want to remove our personalities from us. He wants us to surrender our personalities to Him. Then God works through us as our emotions come under the control of the Holy Spirit. True power and ability come from God, not eager emotion.

Surrender

On the morrow, as they went on their journey, and drew nigh unto
the city, Peter went up upon the housetop to pray about the sixth
hour ... And there came a voice to him, Rise, Peter; kill, and eat.
But Peter said, Not so, Lord; for I have never eaten any thing that
is common or unclean. And the voice spake unto him again the
second time, What God hath cleansed, that call not thou common.
This was done thrice: and the vessel was received up again into
heaven. Now while Peter doubted in himself what this vision
which he had seen should mean, behold, the men which were sent
from Cornelius had made enquiry for Simon's house, and stood
before the gate ... While Peter thought on the vision, the Spirit
said unto him, Behold, three men seek thee ... Then Peter opened
his mouth, and said, Of a truth I perceive that God is no respecter
of persons: But in every nation he that feareth him, and worketh
righteousness, is accepted with him ... But Peter rehearsed the
matter from the beginning, and expounded it by order unto them.
—Acts 10:9, 13–17, 19, 34–35; 11:4

There is no doubt that Peter was a saved believer, but God still needed
his undivided attention. Peter, the new believer, had always equated his
understanding of Scriptures with the truth of Scriptures. We think the same
today. We believe the Bible; therefore, the parts we don't understand must not
matter very much.

Peter behaved according to his limited understanding, but not according
to all that God wanted him to do. Peter had a vision in which God told him
to do something that Peter considered inappropriate and unholy. He could not
understand it, so he didn't do it, but he kept on trying to figure it out. Meanwhile,
Cornelius had sought Peter out and brought him to his home. Cornelius knew
that Peter would bring a message from God to him and his friends. When Peter
faced the group, he finally understood what God had said to him in the vision.

Once Peter understood that his ideas about God were faulty, he gave himself
over to God's perspective. Surrendering his will to God's will enabled Peter to
do God's will. For Peter, this meant preaching, communicating precisely and
accurately the message of the gospel. When we surrender our notions to God,
we make ourselves available to do what God wants us to do.

Perfect Obedience

And in the sixth month the angel Gabriel was sent from God unto
a city of Galilee, named Nazareth, To a virgin espoused to a man
whose name was Joseph, of the house of David; and the virgin's
name was Mary ... And, behold, thou shalt conceive in thy womb,
and bring forth a son, and shalt call his name Jesus. He shall be great,
and shall be called the Son of the Highest: and the Lord God shall
give unto him the throne of his father David: And he shall reign
over the house of Jacob for ever; and of his kingdom there shall be
no end. Then said Mary unto the angel, How shall this be, seeing
I know not a man? And the angel answered and said unto her, The
Holy Ghost shall come upon thee, and the power of the Highest shall
overshadow thee: therefore also that holy thing which shall be born
of thee shall be called the Son of God ... For with God nothing shall
be impossible. And Mary said, Behold the handmaid of the Lord; be
it unto me according to thy word. And the angel departed from her.
—Luke 1:26–27, 31–35, 37–38

Mary is the mother of our Lord and Savior, Jesus Christ. She is generally
thought to have been a young woman in her late teenage years. Instead
of defiance to authority, like so many teenagers today, Mary was obedient to
authority. She calmly accepted the will of God for her life. We cannot imagine her
wearing skimpy clothing, outré hairstyles, or behaving in a questionable manner.

But she was like us, because she was human; she lived and she died. She did
not appear to understand the message fully; nevertheless, she exhibited complete
trust in the angelic messenger Gabriel, who spoke God's message to her. Mary
was so excited at the change in her life that she visited her older cousin Elizabeth,
who was also pregnant. Mary was spiritually minded enough to see a connection
between the out-of-time pregnancy of Elizabeth, the mother of John the Baptist,
and her out-of-this-world pregnancy. She and Elizabeth understood one another,
united by a common bond of the grace of God to each of them.

Mary's song reveals that she was well acquainted with the Bible. Her devout
spiritual grounding prepared her for the ultimate obedience to God when He
changed her body to benefit the rest of the world. Her life reminds us that no
one is too young to obey God.

What Next?

But as many as received him, to them gave he power to become
the sons of God, even to them that believe on his name Which
were born, not of blood, nor of the will of the flesh, nor of the
will of man, but of God. And the Word was made flesh, and
dwelt among us, (and we beheld his glory, the glory as of the
only begotten of the Father,) full of grace and truth ... And
of his fulness have all we received, and grace for grace.
—John 1:12–14, 16

Every human has the sense of being created by God, but apart from the
instruction given in the Bible, getting to know the God who made us
remains a mystery. We can always be glad to learn the truth, and the apostle John
tells us how to get to know God.

To begin with, we receive Jesus Christ. We believe in Jesus Christ as the Son
of God when we repent of our sins. In this way, by this one act of the will—by
a simple and singular decision—God accepts us as His children. We are now
children who are born of God. Mom and Dad have nothing to do with this birth.
The family lineage, the national ties, and the ethnic heritage have no bearing
on this birth. The rapist had nothing to do with this birth either. This birth is a
transaction between the individual and God.

Why can this birth happen? Because Jesus Christ the Son of God, became
a man. He lived a human life among people before dying and returning to life
in heaven with the Father. When we belong to Him and do what He says, we
glimpse the glory that will belong to us in increasing measure as we follow Him.
What happens after we become believers? What can we expect? God grants us
one blessing after another because He is full of grace toward sinners. All good
things come from God, and nothing good exists apart from the truth.

Believers Who Fail

> The woman gave birth to a boy and named him Samson. He grew
> and the LORD blessed him, ... One day Samson went to Gaza,
> where he saw a prostitute. He went in to spend the night with
> her ... Some time later, he fell in love with a woman in the Valley
> of Sorek whose name was Delilah ... Having put him to sleep on
> her lap, she called a man to shave off the seven braids of his hair,
> and so began to subdue him. And his strength left him. Then she
> called, "Samson, the Philistines are upon you!" He awoke from his
> sleep and thought, "I'll go out as before and shake myself free."
> But he did not know that the LORD had left him ... Then Samson
> prayed to the LORD, "O Sovereign LORD, remember me. O God,
> please strengthen me just once more, and let me with one blow get
> revenge on the Philistines for my two eyes" ... Samson said, "Let
> me die with the Philistines!" Then he pushed with all his might,
> and down came the temple on the rulers and all the people in it.
> Thus he killed many more when he died than while he lived.
> —Judges 13:24; 16:1, 4, 19–20, 28, 30

Samson was a child of promise, born to a devout but barren wife. He grew up in a faithful household. He was a believer God set apart to be a judge over Israel. His role as judge was to clear the land of the Philistine population, so Samson waged several successful one-man campaigns that killed many Philistines. This sounds brutal and cutthroat to us, but the Philistines had oppressed Israel for over a decade and ruled over them for another four decades.

The Philistines represent sin, so it is fair to say that Samson knew how to kill sin in his life. God gave Samson superb physical strength, but Samson took it for granted. Like some of us, he assumed that what he had would always be there for him. To his shame, Samson's reckless and sinful behavior caused the Spirit of the Lord to leave him defenseless, but he was so smug and self-absorbed that he didn't even notice the loss. When the Philistines removed the source of his strength—his uncut hair—Samson could not resist them any longer, so he became their prisoner, stooge, and slave. What a victory for the enemies! What a loss to Samson!

Pride caused the man who had killed sin in public life to choose sin in private life. The blinded man had time to think about his life, and God was merciful to him at the end of his life. Samson asked God to perform one last task as judge by collapsing the pagan temple roof upon the assembly, including himself. God allowed it to happen. His life reminds us not to take God for granted or to squander the talents God has given us.

Cultural Values

> Now when they had passed through Amphipolis and Apollonia,
> they came to Thessalonica, where was a synagogue of the Jews: And
> Paul, as his manner was, went in unto them, and three sabbath days
> reasoned with them out of the scriptures, Opening and alleging,
> that Christ must needs have suffered, and risen again from the dead;
> and that this Jesus, whom I preach unto you, is Christ ... And the
> brethren immediately sent away Paul and Silas by night unto Berea:
> who coming thither went into the synagogue of the Jews. These were
> more noble than those in Thessalonica, in that they received the word
> with all readiness of mind, and searched the scriptures daily, whether
> those things were so. Therefore many of them believed; also of
> honourable women which were Greeks, and of men, not a few ... (For
> all the Athenians and strangers which were there spent their time
> in nothing else, but either to tell, or to hear some new thing.)
> —Acts 17:1–3, 10–12, 21

When we think of people from places other than home, we often characterize them with a specific cultural tag. For example, Italians like to cook, Germans are methodical, Latinos are emotional, British are unemotional, and Egyptians love archeology. While these generalizations may identify a generic cultural value, they do not usually hold true for specific individuals. Nevertheless, it is helpful to know cultural characteristics when visiting a foreign location.

The apostle Paul understood these cultural values and adjusted his message to his hearers. Dr. Luke records these notions about others as a way to begin to understand and communicate meaningfully with them. The Bereans were thoughtful, academically inclined, education-oriented people; they cross-referenced every word Paul spoke with the (Hebrew) Scriptures before they would be convinced of the veracity of Paul's gospel message. Apparently, the Thessalonians were less open-minded in their approach. They were more culturally defined, they liked being Jewish, and they wanted to stay that way. The Athenians were educated but unthinking. They liked to discuss every new philosophy and idea of the day, but they didn't care if the new idea was true or practical to daily life in any way.

It is always helpful to recognize wider cultural values in others so that we may gain a greater insight into how to explain God's Word to people who hold values that are different from our own.

We Live in Him

Lord, thou hast been our dwelling place in all generations. Before the
mountains were brought forth, or ever thou hadst formed the earth
and the world, even from everlasting to everlasting, thou art God.
Thou turnest man to destruction; and sayest, Return, ye children
of men. For a thousand years in thy sight are but as yesterday when
it is past, and as a watch in the night. Thou carriest them away as
with a flood; they are as a sleep: in the morning they are like grass
which groweth up. In the morning it flourisheth, and groweth up; in
the evening it is cut down, and withereth ... So teach us to number
our days, that we may apply our hearts unto wisdom ... And let the
beauty of the Lord our God be upon us: and establish thou the work
of our hands upon us; yea, the work of our hands establish thou it.
—Psalm 90:1–6, 12, 17

What does it mean to say that God is the dwelling place of humans? Don't
we live in rooms of houses or apartments, a physical type of residence? We
know that God lives in us who believe, but do we live in Him? To say that God
is our dwelling place harkens back to the days in the Garden of Eden, when God
created Adam from the dust of the earth and then created Eve from Adam's rib.
Yet when we feel our flesh, we think of ourselves as solid, real, and substantial.
The Bible reminds us that we really are as frail as dust.

The type of earth that we call dust is a household problem, and most of
us prefer to live in clean environments. Dust can allow microscopic vermin to
thrive and thereby infect the humans who live in too much of it. Dirty dust can
carry fine pollen granules that clog the lungs, making it difficult to breathe and
stay alive. Dust can be the leftover residue from many manufacturing processes,
and the dust may be metallic or chemical in composition, dangerous to human
health. We have nothing to brag about if we are really made of dirty, earthy dust.
So what can we do about it?

The Bible always has answers to questions. God wants us to maintain our
awareness of what we are and who we are. When we remember our original
source, we lose our sense of superiority and gain a sense of realism about
ourselves. Realism is important because it helps us to recognize that the favor of
the Lord upon our lives is more important than any other quality we could desire.
When we live in Him, God acts in our lives and establishes our competencies for
the job He wants us to do.

Submission or Self-Help?

Such as sit in darkness and in the shadow of death, being bound
in affliction and iron; Because they rebelled against the words of
God, and contemned the counsel of the most High: Therefore he
brought down their heart with labour; they fell down, and there
was none to help. Then they cried unto the Lord in their trouble,
and he saved them out of their distresses. He brought them out
of darkness and the shadow of death, and brake their bands in
sunder. Oh that men would praise the Lord for his goodness,
and for his wonderful works to the children of men! For he hath
broken the gates of brass, and cut the bars of iron in sunder.
—Psalm 107:10–16

This passage of Scripture sounds like the description of the prisoners in Plato's cave of ignorance, only the Bible would say that they are prisoners in a cave of sin. The prisoners in Plato's cave believed that the flickering shadows on the walls of the cave were real—until they were loosed from their chains and led up into the beautiful sunlight.

In the same way, rebellion to God gives people an inaccurate picture of how the world operates. We live in a time when a lot of free advice and self-help is readily available to everyone. Television programming, with its accompanying books and videos, touts for us the benefits of weight loss, financial security, physical fitness, emotional stability, home décor, and outdoor landscaping, to name several popular topics. All of this information intends to "save" people from self-inflicted problems. These experts recognize, as the Bible does, that people can live gloomily, like self-shackled prisoners, when some parts of their lives are unbalanced in comparison to other parts.

Modern society does not seem to have progressed very far from the image of the prisoners in Plato's cave. According to the advice of Plato, education is the answer to the ignorance of the cave dwellers. The idea that education enlightens people enough to solve big problems and make huge progress is still a viable idea on most campuses today. Unlike popular media, the Bible diagnosis the problem as rebellion against the Word of God, requiring a more effective remedy. The result of living in the cave of sin is that God shackles us with our sins—to cause us to return to Him. He wants to save us from the distress we have brought upon ourselves, and He will rescue us when we cry out to Him.

Agreement and Alignment

On the morrow, as they went on their journey, and drew nigh
unto the city, Peter went up upon the housetop to pray about the
sixth hour: And he became very hungry, and would have eaten:
but while they made ready, he fell into a trance, And saw heaven
opened, and a certain vessel descending upon him, as it had been
a great sheet knit at the four corners, and let down to the earth:
Wherein were all manner of fourfooted beasts of the earth, and
wild beasts, and creeping things, and fowls of the air. And there
came a voice to him, Rise, Peter; kill, and eat. But Peter said,
Not so, Lord; for I have never eaten any thing that is common or
unclean. And the voice spake unto him again the second time,
What God hath cleansed, that call not thou common. This was
done thrice: and the vessel was received up again into heaven. Now
while Peter doubted in himself what this vision which he had seen
should mean, behold, the men which were sent from Cornelius
had made enquiry for Simon's house, and stood before the gate.
—Acts 10:9–17

Even today, Peter remains one of the most admired apostles out of the
original twelve. His high points are so high that we wish to emulate him.
The popularity of stunts that we enjoy watching in movies today is enough
knowledge to remind us that we still love to watch and hear about people who
engage in phenomenal feats of derring-do. Peter was just such a man of action.
He eagerly followed Jesus. He jumped into the lake after Him. And he walked
on water, at least a few steps.

Don't we all wish to have some high moments in our lives like that? In
addition to his emotional temperament, he was devoutly religious, he prayed
regularly to God, he lived blamelessly, and he was sure he understood God's
Word. But Peter, the spiritually young believer, was like a lot of believers today.
God clearly disagreed with Peter in some ways because He sent Peter the same
vision three times. Peter saw the large sheet containing unclean animals coming
down from heaven. He knew the vision came from God, but it didn't seem right
to him so he puzzled over the meaning of it. When Peter finally realized the
message of the vision to him—that God accepts all people and never shows
favoritism—he acquiesced to the will of God.

The lesson of this incident is that when people agree with God, they are
empowered to do His will. We always need to pay attention to situations or
persons or circumstances that God forces upon us. This is how we learn from
Him and align ourselves with His will.

Private or Public?

For the ways of man are before the eyes of the Lord, and he
pondereth all his goings. His own iniquities shall take the wicked
himself, and he shall be holden with the cords of his sins. He shall
die without instruction; and in the greatness of his folly he shall
go astray ... Go to the ant, thou sluggard; consider her ways, and
be wise: Which having no guide, overseer, or ruler, Provideth her
meat in the summer, and gathereth her food in the harvest.
—Proverbs 5:21–23, 6:6–8

Privacy seems to be an issue of concern for everyone these days. We know that
Google has taken aerial photos of every square inch of planet earth. When
we look at some of these photos, we can actually see people in them. It is no
longer outside the realm of possibility that we recognize some of those faces. We
also know that security cameras have been installed wherever people congregate,
from the gas station to the shopping malls and the street corners. Our behavior
is always being monitored to see if we are doing anything illegal.

When we think about the surveillance of our lives, we don't like it very much,
but we accept it as an impersonal fact of modern living. Surveillance cameras
should also remind us of God, who watches us unseen. Does it comfort us or
embarrass us to know that a personal God sees everything we do? Whichever
answer we have in mind, we should remember that God always responds to what
He sees us doing by punishing shiftlessness and rewarding diligence. When we
refuse to discipline ourselves in basic ways, we ensnare ourselves in the sin of
laziness and we prevent ourselves from developing the ability to prioritize our
lives.

The watchfulness of God redirects us in order to benefit us. God give us an
example to follow in the precise behavior of ants. God has put orderliness and
discipline into their lives so that they can carry on with their day-to-day activities.
He will do as much for us when we respond to Him.

Purposes and Purity

Counsel in the heart of man is like deep water; but a man of
understanding will draw it out ... The just man walketh in his
integrity: his children are blessed after him ... Who can say, I have
made my heart clean, I am pure from my sin? ... The hearing ear,
and the seeing eye, the Lord hath made even both of them.
—Proverbs 20:5, 7, 9, 12

Lead me, O Lord, in thy righteousness because of mine enemies;
make thy way straight before my face ... And see if there be
any wicked way in me, and lead me in the way everlasting.
—Psalm 5:8, 139:24

I have taught thee in the way of wisdom; I have led thee in right paths.
—Proverbs 4:11

As much as we admire prominent people in the entertainment, political, or business world, we have to ask ourselves what we specifically admire about them. Do they possess specific characteristics or traits that we identify with, making us think that we might do the same if given the opportunity? Or, do we just want to see their photos in the daily newspaper and read a clip about them in a popular blog? Do we cravenly desire to earn the huge amount of money they earn?

It is popular today to believe that a purposeful life is more valuable than other types of lifestyles, so we usually ascribe single-mindedness, clear focus, and a high degree of skill to those we admire most. However, when a prominent person is found to be living in compromising, embarrassing, shameful, or criminal circumstances, it is natural to wonder whether our admiration for them is worth holding on to. We must all eventually decide what to do with our lives, famous or not. Because of the sinful nature, we cannot always understand our own thoughts, intentions, or purposes very well, but others can help us discern our motives, skills, and goals.

When we let the Lord direct our steps, He may use others to give guidance, but He will always guide us truthfully. God never leaves us alone to fend for ourselves.

A Lease on Life

> For the kingdom of heaven is as a man travelling into a far country,
> who called his own servants, and delivered unto them his goods. And
> unto one he gave five talents, to another two, and to another one; to
> every man according to his several ability; and straightway took his
> journey. Then he that had received the five talents went and traded
> with the same, and made them other five talents. And likewise he that
> had received two, he also gained other two. But he that had received
> one went and digged in the earth, and hid his lord's money. After a
> long time the lord of those servants cometh, and reckoneth with them.
> And so he that had received five talents came and brought other five
> talents, saying, Lord, thou deliveredst unto me five talents: behold, I
> have gained beside them five talents more. His lord said unto him, Well
> done, thou good and faithful servant: thou hast been faithful over a
> few things, I will make thee ruler over many things: enter thou into
> the joy of thy lord. He also that had received two talents came and said,
> Lord, thou deliveredst unto me two talents: behold, I have gained two
> other talents beside them. His lord said unto him, Well done, good and
> faithful servant; thou hast been faithful over a few things, I will make
> thee ruler over many things: enter thou into the joy of thy lord ... For
> unto every one that hath shall be given, and he shall have abundance:
> but from him that hath not shall be taken away even that which he hath.
> —Matthew 25:14–23, 29

How often do people express the thought that if they don't finish the task today, there is always tomorrow? Time is the common commodity of this life, and human nature never values abundance; human nature always presumes upon it. When we continue to live daily life with this human perspective, we cheat ourselves of God's best for our lives because the human perspective differs alarmingly from the heavenly perspective.

God tells us that this life is like a journey and that this life is both brief and impermanent. Journeys must also be planned out to the last detail. We make specific choices about the journey, but a lot of the choices as we go along do not belong to us. Journeys involve a certain amount of travel, a change of scenery, and a change of pace. We should get excited to see where the Lord will take us in this life. Journeys are full of activities compressed into short time spans; they never adhere to the daily routine. Even though it seems like time stretches limitlessly in front of us, God loans this life to us for a short time, endowing us with specific talents of His choosing and design.

God gives us freedom of choice to do as we please, and He will call us to account for how we have handled his gifts to us during the time He allots to us.

Questionable Behavior

And Dinah the daughter of Leah, which she bare unto Jacob, went
out to see the daughters of the land. And when Shechem the son
of Hamor the Hivite, prince of the country, saw her, he took her,
and lay with her, and defiled her. And his soul clave unto Dinah the
daughter of Jacob, and he loved the damsel, and spake kindly unto the
damsel. And Shechem spake unto his father Hamor, saying, Get me
this damsel to wife. And Jacob heard that he had defiled Dinah his
daughter: now his sons were with his cattle in the field: and Jacob held
his peace until they were come. And Hamor the father of Shechem
went out unto Jacob to commune with him. And the sons of Jacob
came out of the field when they heard it: and the men were grieved,
and they were very wroth, because he had wrought folly in Israel in
lying with Jacob's daughter: which thing ought not to be done ... And
it came to pass on the third day, when they were sore, that two of the
sons of Jacob, Simeon and Levi, Dinah's brethren, took each man
his sword, and came upon the city boldly, and slew all the males.
—Genesis 34:1–7, 25

We know that ancient cultures held cultural mores that were different from
today, but we also know that human behavior, emotions, and reasoning
remain constant from one millennium to the next. Human nature has never
changed.

It is not clear to modern readers why Dinah, the only daughter of Jacob, and
a daughter from a believing household, visited her neighbors by herself. Did she
wander through the town alone and just happen to stop at the local ruler's palace?
Did she go shopping with girlfriends and deliberately separate herself from the
group? Whatever the reason, her behavior was questionable. Perhaps she assumed
that the status of her wealthy family would protect her from harm. Perhaps she
was seeking to break free from imagined social bonds. Perhaps she was vain
enough to think that family wealth equaled nobility of intention and action.

She presumed upon the grace of God to help her in a tight situation, but
her thought was wrong. Because of her questionable choice, she was physically
violated and her large family took revenge upon Shechem. Sexual sin may
occur in private, but the consequences of that particular sin are very public and
unmistakable. We live in a society that promotes sexual sin in every disgusting
form imaginable, but we cannot escape the harm we do to ourselves by believing
that anyone can do anything to another person, and no one really minds what
is going on.

FEBRUARY 7

God Provides

Those things, which ye have both learned, and received, and
heard, and seen in me, do: and the God of peace shall be with
you ... Not that I speak in respect of want: for I have learned,
in whatsoever state I am, therewith to be content. I know both
how to be abased, and I know how to abound: everywhere and
in all things I am instructed both to be full and to be hungry,
both to abound and to suffer need ... But my God shall supply all
your need according to his riches in glory by Christ Jesus. Now
unto God and our Father be glory for ever and ever. Amen.
—Philippians 4:9, 11–12, 19–20

A lot has been spoken and written regarding the high cost of college tuition
and fees these days, and when people complain in this way, they recall
decades ago when times were supposedly simpler, cheaper, and less complicated.
The world was reputedly less demanding, so college did not represent the
economic advantage of the more technologically advanced society in which we
live today.

When we read the Bible, it makes us question some of the assumptions we
believe as solid fact today. Human needs are always pressing, and this fact is a
constant throughout generations of human existence. All of us, in every age,
share the need for the necessities of life. Psychological theory tells us that once
we satisfy our basic needs like shelter, food, and clothing, we enable ourselves to
focus on the self-development aspects of life.

The Bible speaks differently. The God who made us also sees our needs.
He gives us unmistakable assurance that He will supply them for us. The apostle
Paul, as an itinerant missionary, had many genuine needs. Not all of them could
be met by his tent-making income, so he sometimes lived in dire want—and
at other times in bounteous plenty. He learned about God, the source of his
strength, as much as he learned about God the provider. He accepted what God
gave him as part of the riches that belong to all of us who are in Christ. When
we trust God, He still provides us with what we need today.

Appropriate Worship

And the glory of the Lord came into the house by the way of the gate whose prospect is toward the east. So the spirit took me up, and brought me into the inner court; and, behold, the glory of the Lord filled the house ... Thou son of man, shew the house to the house of Israel, that they may be ashamed of their iniquities: and let them measure the pattern. And if they be ashamed of all that they have done, shew them the form of the house, and the fashion thereof, and the goings out thereof, and the comings in thereof, and all the forms thereof, and all the ordinances thereof, and all the forms thereof, and all the laws thereof: and write it in their sight, that they may keep the whole form thereof, and all the ordinances thereof, and do them.
—Ezekiel 43:4–5, 10–11

In literature class, students are introduced to the concept of representation. Representation means that when we read a story, we expect the literal names, incidents, or locations to convey a figurative (representative) meaning to us. In a memorable story, we remember the message longer because the story formed an image in the mind. The transposition of an idea from the medium of literature into the mentality of the human brain is one of the ways God created the human brain to work.

In a similar fashion, we also transpose strongly held concepts into more concrete forms, like the architecture of a building. For example, the floor plan of a church is sometimes designed in the shape of a cross to remind us of the cross of Jesus Christ. The character of God is also represented in many ways when we worship Him. We understand that the communion bread and wine represent the body and blood of Jesus Christ. The glory of the Lord fills the entire earth, and God wants the body of believers to model holy living in every way.

One way to perceive the holiness of God in Old Testament times was to consider the design of the temple—designed by God and built by men. The arrangement of the temple spaces, even the entrances and exits, forms a part of God's plan of holy worship from holy people. Today, churches understand that the order of worship represents the orderliness of the Creator God. The beauty of worship comes from the adoration of repentant people who are ashamed of their lives. When they come into the house of worship, repentance precedes faithful worship and obedience to God.

FEBRUARY 9

Meaning in Life

The words of the Preacher, the son of David, king in
Jerusalem. Vanity of vanities, saith the Preacher, vanity of vanities;
all is vanity. What profit hath a man of all his labour which he taketh
under the sun? ... And I gave my heart to seek and search out by
wisdom concerning all things that are done under heaven: this sore
travail hath God given to the sons of man to be exercised therewith.
I have seen all the works that are done under the sun; and, behold,
all is vanity and vexation of spirit ... And whatsoever mine eyes
desired I kept not from them, I withheld not my heart from any
joy; for my heart rejoiced in all my labour: and this was my portion
of all my labour ... There is nothing better for a man, than that he
should eat and drink, and that he should make his soul enjoy good
in his labour. This also I saw, that it was from the hand of God.
—Ecclesiastes 1:1–3, 13–14; 2:10, 24

If you tend to be of a negative cast of mind, a quick glance through the book
of Ecclesiastes may appear to be no more than the lengthy complaint of an
older man about the boredom and futility of daily life. King Solomon rants
about meaninglessness in life until we cannot stand to hear anymore about it.
Even a boring life is more interesting that Solomon's view of life in this book.
A pessimistic outlook sees what is heavy and difficult and repetitive and boring.

Pessimism assumes that past, present, and future merge into one long
continuum of monotony and dissatisfaction. To mitigate this tendency, the world
cries out to us today that if we gain more experiences, we will gain greater
satisfaction and meaning in life, but Solomon disagrees.

He was a fabulously wealthy king who denied himself nothing this world
could offer. Money paved the way for him to have as many experiences as
he wanted. Gold was so common during his reign that silver was counted as
worthless. He had a literary sort of mind and wrote many proverbs. He possessed
a scientific kind of mind and recorded a lot of botanical information. He loved
everything he did but still found his life empty and meaningless. Because he
desired to honor God as a young man according to the advice of his father,
David, Solomon understood that there is no meaning or pleasure in life apart
from the God who gives it.

Enduring Love

*Set me as a seal upon thine heart, as a seal upon thine arm: for love
is strong as death; jealousy is cruel as the grave: the coals thereof are
coals of fire, which hath a most vehement flame. Many waters cannot
quench love, neither can the floods drown it: if a man would give all
the substance of his house for love, it would utterly be contemned.*
—Song of Songs 8:6–7

Perhaps we prefer to read romantic stories instead of detective and mystery tales. Maybe we like to watch all the fashion and wedding shows where an underlying theme of love is always apparent. Many television shows and popular movies employ the theme of love to attract increased viewership. Even when the focus of the story line deals with drama or mystery, love is worked into the plot.

Unfortunately, the Hollywood version of love is based on whatever the producer thinks will attract more viewers or sell more copies; it rarely reflects the true nature of genuine love. Such trivialized portrayals of love underscore the real human need for love in our lives. And in spite of the inaccuracies of love on the silver screen, many college students hope to meet a soul mate very soon.

It is critical to look to the Bible for the most accurate definition of love ever written. When our family upbringing has lacked a true love relationship to reflect upon, we can be glad to believe what the Bible has to say about true love. True love cannot stop loving, making it stronger than death. It cannot burn up in a fire. It cannot wash away in a flood; it is permanent. Love puts the other person first—always. Love matters more than material possessions. Love perseveres—it never fails. Love loves the good instead of the evil. Let God guide us to true love as we look for that special soul mate among our new acquaintances.

Pleasing Our Parents

And it came to pass in those days, that Jesus came from Nazareth of
Galilee, and was baptized of John in Jordan. And straightway coming
up out of the water, he saw the heavens opened, and the Spirit like
a dove descending upon him: And there came a voice from heaven,
saying, Thou art my beloved Son, in whom I am well pleased.
—Mark 1:9–11

Some of us come from happier homes where everything we did made our
parents happy with us—as long as it wasn't outright criminal or immoral.
Others of us come from less stable homes where nothing we ever said or did
was ever good enough to please our parents. We hope they are pleased enough
with us to let us finish college with their help, but we may not even be sure about
this right now.

It is easy to forget that Jesus was a son who had a relationship with his father.
We tend to think of His redemptive work as the major effort of his life. So it was,
but Jesus models a perfect child-to-parent relationship pattern for us to follow.
The parent-child relationship should parallel the God-human relationship, but
when it doesn't, we cannot simply discard that relationship. Instead, we can turn
to God the Father in obedience, just as the Son did.

Just as college entry signals the entry into the adult world with its different
rules, we can transition into a more mature spiritual world as we grow in our
relationship with God. God speaks to us directly through His Word, and He
wants us to pay attention to what the Word of God says. When we obey Him, we
become better acquainted with how good fathers behave. This will help us live
better lives than we could without God's help. God is pleased with us when we
obey Him, so look for the signs of His pleasure in your life. Maybe someone has
paid toward your tuition, maybe someone has given you clothes that fit, maybe
someone has hired you. Put God first, please put God first, and He will take care
of all the other details of your life.

The High Cost of Sin

Now Korah, took men: And they rose up before Moses, with
certain of the children of Israel, two hundred and fifty princes of
the assembly, famous in the congregation, men of renown ... And
the Lord spake unto Moses, saying, Speak unto the congregation,
saying, Get you up from about the tabernacle of Korah, Dathan, and
Abiram ... And he spake unto the congregation, saying, Depart, I
pray you, from the tents of these wicked men, and touch nothing
of their's, lest ye be consumed in all their sins. So they gat up from
the tabernacle of Korah, Dathan, and Abiram, on every side: and
Dathan and Abiram came out, and stood in the door of their tents,
and their wives, and their sons, and their little children. And Moses
said, Hereby ye shall know that the Lord hath sent me to do all
these works; for I have not done them of mine own mind. If these
men die the common death of all men, or if they be visited after
the visitation of all men; then the Lord hath not sent me. But if the
Lord make a new thing, and the earth open her mouth, and swallow
them up, with all that appertain unto them, and they go down
quick into the pit; then ye shall understand that these men have
provoked the Lord. ... And there came out a fire from the Lord,
and consumed the two hundred and fifty men that offered incense.
—Numbers 16:2, 23–24, 26–30, 35

God judges individuals for sin, but God also judges groups or communities,
such as cities and towns, for sin as well. This is what happened when 250
councilmen and four leaders insolently rose up against the leadership of Moses.

In today's parlance, we would say that the citizens were trying to exert the will
of the majority to change a bylaw or to restructure the entire municipal system.
But back in ancient times, they thought they could assail the commandments
of God and the integrity of Moses; they thought they could shift the leadership
to others, probably to themselves. They wanted huge structural change to the
government, not minor change.

This was a sin, because God had given the books of the Law to Moses and
expected the newly formed nation to adhere to His commands. God punishes
communal sin. The world today has seen the evidence where cities have been
buried in volcanic ash or submerged under the sea and former landscapes have
become unrecognizable. When humans feel that a group can overpower an
individual, they behave like the people did in the time of Moses or in the time of
the tower of Babel. God crushes collective human pride. In the time of Moses,
fire consumed the 250 councilmen and the four leaders, showing that the wages
of sin is death—the same then as it is now.

How We Ought to Live

For our rejoicing is this, the testimony of our conscience, that in
simplicity and godly sincerity, not with fleshly wisdom, but by the
grace of God, we have had our conversation in the world, and more
abundantly to you-ward ... Now he which stablisheth us with you
in Christ, and hath anointed us, is God; Who hath also sealed us,
and given the earnest of the Spirit in our hearts ... Now thanks
be unto God, which always causeth us to triumph in Christ, and
maketh manifest the savour of his knowledge by us in every place.
—2 Corinthians 1:12, 21–22; 2:14

As much as we like to plan our lives, we cannot imagine every obstacle or
circumstance we will face. Life sometimes throws us unexpected challenges.
When facing those circumstances, we don't know how to behave, so we react.

We always face a choice at such times—the chance to respond according to
either worldly wisdom or God's grace. Because we can never predict the outcome
of a situation, it is more logical and godly to rely on obedience to God as the only
safeguard in difficulty.

God knows both the end and the beginning of the situation that we face.
He honors obedience, and the benefits of obedience are clear. God gives firm
assurance from deep within that Christ holds us in the palm of His hands. He
shows how much He loves us. God has set us apart for His service with a seal of
ownership. He enables us to do the right thing, even in difficult times. He leaves
the Holy Spirit with us, like a deposit on something that has been bought. We
are on His mind constantly. He constantly affirms the truth in us. God knows
that when a dying world sees Christians living by the name of Christ, they get
a glimpse of the beauty of holiness—the reverent fear that comes from the
knowledge of Him. Only the grace of God is sufficient to teach us how to live in
a way that honors Him when we face difficulties.

Love for God

And God spake all these words, saying, I am the Lord thy God, which have brought thee out of the land of Egypt, out of the house of bondage. Thou shalt have no other gods before me. Thou shalt not make unto thee any graven image, or any likeness of any thing that is in heaven above, or that is in the earth beneath, or that is in the water under the earth. Thou shalt not bow down thyself to them, nor serve them: for I the Lord thy God am a jealous God, visiting the iniquity of the fathers upon the children unto the third and fourth generation of them that hate me; And shewing mercy unto thousands of them that love me, and keep my commandments. Thou shalt not take the name of the Lord thy God in vain; for the Lord will not hold him guiltless that taketh his name in vain. Remember the sabbath day, to keep it holy. Six days shalt thou labour, and do all thy work: But the seventh day is the sabbath of the Lord thy God: in it thou shalt not do any work, thou, nor thy son, nor thy daughter, thy manservant, nor thy maidservant, nor thy cattle, nor thy stranger that is within thy gates: For in six days the Lord made heaven and earth, the sea, and all that in them is, and rested the seventh day: wherefore the Lord blessed the sabbath day, and hallowed it.
—Exodus 20:1–11

It is completely logical that the God who made us should tell us how to relate to Him. But when we look at the world today with its multifarious forms of idolatry, we might be tempted to think otherwise. What does God want from us anyway?

First of all, God wants us to avoid idolatry, no mean feat in a society that is glutted with every form of it, both overt and hidden. He wants us to put Him first, because He rescued us from the kingdom of death and set us the kingdom of light. The avoidance of idolatry preserves our family relationships. God wants us to refrain from bad language because we offend His majesty, not to mention the ears of others. When we practice speaking well of others, we begin to understand the goodness of the Creator. God wants us to participate in worship of Him weekly.

The day of rest and worship reminds us that God rested after the work of six days of creation. God blesses us for resting in remembrance of Him. Loving God benefits us in the ways that matter most to us.

Loving Family Relationships

Children, obey your parents in the Lord: for this is right. Honour
thy father and mother; which is the first commandment with
promise; That it may be well with thee, and thou mayest live long
on the earth. And, ye fathers, provoke not your children to wrath:
but bring them up in the nurture and admonition of the Lord.
—Ephesians 6:1–4

Honour thy father and thy mother: that thy days
may be long upon the land which the Lord thy God
giveth thee … Thou shalt not commit adultery.
—Exodus 20:12, 14

According to current statistics about divorce, loving family relationships
escape about half of our nation today. In spite of the high incidence of broken
homes, everyone still desires good, stable, long-lasting family relationships.
When we live in a society where more divorces occur among Christians than
others, even believers wonder how to accomplish the goal of loving relationships
and long-term marriages. We must obey God's Word to establish and maintain
longstanding family relationships.

The Ten Commandments indicate that the two most basic family
relationships occur between husbands and wives and among parents and
children. The foundation of a stable society stems from the stability of individual
families. When we face family situations beyond our power to mend them, we
can turn to God to take care of the situation for us. Long ago, God said simply
that children should honor and respect their parents because it is right. We also
want to mature into accomplished adults, a process that begins in the behavior
patterns of childhood. The flip side of this coin is that adults need to discipline
their children for their good. Since irrational discipline breeds problems, we want
to keep this in mind when we establish our own families.

Long ago, God said that adults should never commit adultery. The
consequences are so deadly that we should never be tempted to walk that path.

FEBRUARY 16

Friendship toward Others

Thou shalt not kill … Thou shalt not steal. Thou shalt not
bear false witness against thy neighbour. Thou shalt not covet
thy neighbour's house, thou shalt not covet thy neighbour's
wife, nor his manservant, nor his maidservant, nor his
ox, nor his ass, nor any thing that is thy neighbour's.
—Exodus 20:13, 15–17

Human friendships form the basis for most of our daily activities throughout life. Depending on what we like to do, we call upon different friends for different reasons. When we enjoy outdoor activities, we like the friends who will go hiking or climbing with us. When we love traveling, we like the friends who will drop everything and go places with us. When we need a sympathetic ear, we like the friends who listen and counsel us. When we miss our families, we like to get together with them for any reason.

The Bible identifies the friends of our lives by the generic term "neighbors," so when we begin to think biblically, we receive a different kind of message from God about the topic of friendship. We value the friendships of our lives. Yet because it is so easy to spoil relationships, God has given us His final Word to make sure we behave the right way toward others. God tells us never to murder or steal or tell lies or covet anything belonging to another. Most of us pat ourselves on the back for exemplary behavior because we never expect to go to jail for murder. Do we then skim over the remaining three commands? Do we long for the goods of another friend? Have we ever gossiped about our friends?

We are sinners, so we must understand that we tend to overlook some of the commandments. Although these commandments are phrased in the negative, they convey to us that the opposite or the positive is the best foundation for friendship toward others. When we speak kind words, we affirm the life-giving qualities of the Creator for His creatures. When we refuse to envy what others have, we affirm that the provision of God is sufficient for us, no matter what it is.

How can we stay true to God's Word? When we fear God more than others and honor God more than self, God the Holy Spirit comes alongside us to keep us from sinning.

47

Save the Environment

Hear the word of the Lord, ye children of Israel: for the Lord hath
a controversy with the inhabitants of the land, because there is no
truth, nor mercy, nor knowledge of God in the land. By swearing,
and lying, and killing, and stealing, and committing adultery, they
break out, and blood toucheth blood. Therefore shall the land
mourn, and every one that dwelleth therein shall languish, with
the beasts of the field, and with the fowls of heaven; yea, the fishes
of the sea also shall be taken away ... My people are destroyed for
lack of knowledge: because thou hast rejected knowledge, I will
also reject thee, that thou shalt be no priest to me: seeing thou hast
forgotten the law of thy God, I will also forget thy children.
—Hosea 4:1–3, 6

The current generation is more familiar with ecological issues than previous
generations. Children are schooled into thinking that a campaign to collect
a lot of money will save the trees, the lions, the estuaries, the salt marshes, the
whales, the eagles, or the elephants. "You name it, we save it" might be a fairly
accurate slogan for all we have been taught.

But is human effort the only way to solve environmental issues? Does God
care about the ecology of the environment He has created, or did He just leave the
earth alone after creating it? Yes, He does care about planet earth, and He actually
has advice to give on the restoration of ecosystems. When people forget God and
no longer acknowledge Him, when personal sins like lying, cursing, and adultery
overtake society, when crimes like murder and stealing reign over city streets, this
means that people are breaking all the beneficial boundaries of human behavior.
The result, according to the Lord, is that the environment is corrupted.

It seems sociologically unsound to draw a connection between human
behavior and ecological results, but God is telling us that such parallels exist
because He made the earth to function in this way. There is a spiritual solution
to an ecological problem—God's solution, not ours. Humans cannot really
understand the connection between the physical world and the creatures God
created, so we are left with working toward the evangelization and missions
emphasis. This is appropriate because when we are in a right relationship with
God, He helps us think His thoughts in the right way, and as a result, we learn
how to institute good practices that will save the environment, not harm it.

Me?—a Missionary?

Now the word of the Lord came unto Jonah the son of Amittai, saying, Arise, go to Nineveh, that great city, and cry against it; for their wickedness is come up before me. But Jonah rose up to flee unto Tarshish from the presence of the Lord, and went down to Joppa; and he found a ship going to Tarshish: so he paid the fare thereof, and went down into it, to go with them unto Tarshish from the presence of the Lord ... Now the Lord had prepared a great fish to swallow up Jonah. And Jonah was in the belly of the fish three days and three nights ... And the Lord spake unto the fish, and it vomited out Jonah upon the dry land. And the word of the Lord came unto Jonah the second time, saying, Arise, go unto Nineveh, that great city, and preach unto it the preaching that I bid thee. And Jonah began to enter into the city a day's journey, and he cried, and said, Yet forty days, and Nineveh shall be overthrown.
So the people of Nineveh believed God, and proclaimed a fast, and put on sackcloth, from the greatest of them even to the least of them. But it displeased Jonah exceedingly, and he was very angry.
—Jonah 1:1–3, 17; 2:10; 3:1–2, 4–5; 4:1

Jonah is noteworthy for being the first missionary recorded in the Bible. God sent him to a foreign country, a land he hated because everyone hated them, and everyone is right, right? He is not a stellar example of a selfless missionary. First, he disobeyed God's direct call. Then, he obeyed God's call instead of losing his life. Finally, he was angry that he obeyed God. He doesn't sound like any missionary who has ever visited my church.

All of us want a purpose in life, but Jonah just didn't want God's purpose in his life. Instead of traveling northwest to obey God's call, Jonah went south to the shipyard and headed west across the Mediterranean Sea. When a violent storm arose, the sailors cast lots and learned that Jonah was responsible for it. He knew he could not escape obedience to God, so he asked the sailors to throw him into the sea. He lived inside a great fish for three days until the fish spit him out onto dry land. He finally obeyed God. The Ninevites repented at his message, and God spared the nation punishment. Jonah was furious. He wanted that horrible nation to be punished.

When we read the Bible, it sometimes seems like God pays more attention to his chosen people that to the rest of humanity. Not true! Jonah reminds us how much God loves and chases after sinners and sinful nations in order to turn their souls to Him.

Does It Matter Where We Come From?

Now these were the sons of David, which were born unto him in Hebron; the firstborn Amnon, of Ahinoam the Jezreelitess; the second Daniel, of Abigail the Carmelitess: The third, Absalom the son of Maachah the daughter of Talmai king of Geshur: the fourth, Adonijah the son of Haggith: The fifth, Shephatiah of Abital: the sixth, Ithream by Eglah his wife. These six were born unto him in Hebron; and there he reigned seven years and six months: and in Jerusalem he reigned thirty and three years.
—1 Chronicles 3:1–4

And hath made of one blood all nations of men for to dwell on all the face of the earth, and hath determined the times before appointed, and the bounds of their habitation; That they should seek the Lord, if haply they might feel after him, and find him, though he be not far from every one of us: For in him we live, and move, and have our being; as certain also of your own poets have said, For we are also his offspring.
—Acts 17:26–28

The Old Testament is replete with genealogical lists, and the lists seem very tedious to us today. If we know our own relatives to three generations back, such limited knowledge is considered a lot. It no longer matters to us who we are or where we come from because we are so accustomed to viewing ourselves as independent entities.

Unlike our own methods of tracking our ancestors, biblical genealogies serve two functions. The first function is to record the generations from the first man, Adam, to the first sinless man, Jesus Christ. The genealogies remind us that the story is true because we can name specific names. They also make us aware of God's long-term, overarching care for all human life. Ultimately, we all come from Adam, so we know that all of us can be saved by the sacrifice of Jesus Christ.

The second function of the genealogies is to record the tribal names that linguists and historians trace as they study the expansion of the world's original population, moving out in concentric waves of immigration to populate the entire earth. We may think of ourselves as South American or Asian or European, but we all come from the same original location. Instead of genealogies, it is now more important for us to know that God chose the exact house, street, town, and family to which we belong. He gave us the specifics of our lives so that we would seek Him out and remember that we belong to Him, both physically and spiritually. Since we know we belong to Him, He commands us to repent and turn to Him.

Stay on Track

Which is come unto you, as it is in all the world; and bringeth forth
fruit, as it doth also in you, since the day ye heard of it, and knew
the grace of God in truth: As ye also learned of Epaphras our dear
fellowservant, who is for you a faithful minister of Christ; Who
also declared unto us your love in the Spirit. For this cause we
also, since the day we heard it, do not cease to pray for you, and to
desire that ye might be filled with the knowledge of his will in all
wisdom and spiritual understanding; That ye might walk worthy of
the Lord unto all pleasing, being fruitful in every good work, and
increasing in the knowledge of God; Strengthened with all might,
according to his glorious power, unto all patience and longsuffering
with joyfulness; Giving thanks unto the Father, which hath made
us meet to be partakers of the inheritance of the saints in light.
—Colossians 1:6–12

As we become more acquainted with the world at large, we become aware that diversity and variety characterize every area of human endeavor. College is a time when we might like to make different choices just because college is a time for change. But we need to ask ourselves upon what basis we form opinions and make decisions. Some opt for emotional decisions only; others steer clear of emotional complications and choose rational decisions only. Neither way of choosing is better than the other, because unless our emotions or reasoning powers are based upon the truth, the decisions we make will fail us.

Philosophies and religions offer us many paths of enlightenment or ways of salvation, so how do we separate true religion from false, true philosophy from empty words, and biblical concepts from human traditions? Only true religion and biblical concepts stand the test of time. When we read the Bible, it becomes clear that the underlying assumption of the entire book is one of truth. Other ideas may have temporary merit, but they change when human ideas change. In order to stay on track with God, we need to read the Bible regularly, apply what it says to daily life, and become thankful for every little thing.

When true Christian understanding and living replace old ways of thinking, hollow and deceptive philosophies find no foothold in our lives. We belong to Christ and represent Him to the world—family, friends, and coworkers. We should always aim to reflect God in our lives.

Working with People of a Different Faith

Thus saith Cyrus king of Persia, The Lord God of heaven hath given me all the kingdoms of the earth; and he hath charged me to build him an house at Jerusalem, which is in Judah. Who is there among you of all his people? his God be with him, and let him go up to Jerusalem, which is in Judah, and build the house of the Lord God of Israel, (he is the God,) which is in Jerusalem. And whosoever remaineth in any place where he sojourneth, let the men of his place help him with silver, and with gold, and with goods, and with beasts, beside the freewill offering for the house of God that is in Jerusalem ... Then stood up Jeshua the son of Jozadak, and his brethren the priests, and Zerubbabel the son of Shealtiel, and his brethren, and builded the altar of the God of Israel, to offer burnt offerings thereon, as it is written in the law of Moses the man of God. And they set the altar upon his bases; for fear was upon them because of the people of those countries: and they offered burnt offerings thereon unto the Lord, even burnt offerings morning and evening ... And they sang together by course in praising and giving thanks unto the Lord; because he is good, for his mercy endureth for ever toward Israel.
—Ezra 1:2–4; 3:2–3, 11a

Most of us prefer to hang out and work daily with people who think similarly to ourselves, and preferences may often include a belief in the same religious precepts. God, however, has different goals for human cooperation.

Consider the situation of the Jews when they were in exile in Babylon and subject to a foreign ruler. God caused the Babylonians to treat them mercifully even though they were different in religion and daily practice. Through this situation, God was helping His people to understand and experience the greatness and power of God when they let Him be in charge of their lives. (Remember that when they had been in charge of their own lives back home, they ignored God and resorted to idolatry.)

It took seventy years for the Jews to learn to trust God again. So when the Persian government gave the go-ahead for them to return to their homeland; the foreign overlords gave support, funding, and supplies to help reconstruct the temple of God in Jerusalem.

There is always a witness from believers to others and from them to us. God uses these differences to remind us of differences between true and false, right and wrong, good and bad. God also uses these differences to His own ends, which no one can foresee ahead of time. But worshipping the one true God is always good, and outsiders cannot help but notice the differences. When God moves believers or nonbelievers to act, it is clear to everyone that God has acted.

The Universe

The heavens declare the glory of God; and the firmament sheweth his handywork. Day unto day uttereth speech, and night unto night sheweth knowledge. There is no speech nor language, where their voice is not heard. Their line is gone out through all the earth, and their words to the end of the world. In them hath he set a tabernacle for the sun, Which is as a bridegroom coming out of his chamber, and rejoiceth as a strong man to run a race. His going forth is from the end of the heaven, and his circuit unto the ends of it: and there is nothing hid from the heat thereof.
—Psalm 19:1–6

When we were little, we probably found it very exciting to walk out into the backyard or onto the rooftop late at night to gaze at the stars in the darkened sky. If we had any curiosity, we probably learned the names of some of the stars and constellations. We may have learned how to locate the North Star in the center of the sky or identify the morning star or the evening star.

The universe is exciting, but not just because the wonder of childhood is attached to our feelings about it. It is exciting because a spectacular Creator created it. When we were little, we probably thought that if we could learn all there was to know about a subject, we would be done with studying it forever. As adults, we begin to think about countless possibilities and the limitless nature of human learning. We know that people have traveled to the moon and orbited the outer spaces of the earth. We know that scientists can smash the atom into even smaller parts than anyone once thought was possible. We know that microsurgery makes formerly major operations become minor procedures. We know that archeologists uncover civilizations of the past.

Every part of this world declares the glory of God and the Creator who made it! We don't read the book of nature as a textbook or an encyclopedia. We discover its laws of operation that come from the Creator. The "voice" that speaks is heard wherever people dwell. The "voice" is visible in something as regular as the sunrise and upon which we all depend every day. God rejoices to give the world in its entirety to us! Let us continue to be glad in it!

Getting Help from God

There shall not any man be able to stand before thee all the
days of thy life: as I was with Moses, so I will be with thee: I
will not fail thee, nor forsake thee … Only be thou strong and
very courageous, that thou mayest observe to do according to
all the law, which Moses my servant commanded thee: turn not
from it to the right hand or to the left, that thou mayest prosper
withersoever thou goest. This book of the law shall not depart out
of thy mouth; but thou shalt meditate therein day and night, that
thou mayest observe to do according to all that is written therein:
for then thou shalt make thy way prosperous, and then thou
shalt have good success. Have not I commanded thee? Be strong
and of a good courage; be not afraid, neither be thou dismayed:
for the Lord thy God is with thee whithersoever thou goest.
—Joshua 1:5, 7–9

The physical journey of the Jewish nation coming out of Egyptian bondage
and making their way to the Promised Land vivifies for all of us the spiritual
journey that we have made. This includes the time when we were slaves to sins,
separated from God and dead to righteousness, to our final destination of living
according to God's Word, practicing the precepts of the Word, and passing the
good news on to the next generation as heirs of holiness.

As we read through the first books of the Old Testament, we see how much
God loves people, how often God speaks to humans, how firmly God deals with
human error, and how clearly God guides those who look to Him. The most
important thing to remember is that God is present with us—both now and
forever. Once we have committed ourselves to His keeping, He commits Himself
to our preservation and well-being. We still don't know what life may hold or
where the journey of life will take us, but the knowledge of God's presence with
us is of paramount comfort.

The second most important thing to know once we have begun the journey
of faith is that we can be strong and courageous because God is with us. We can
now do this because the Lord is in us, and He helps us. Sometimes the future
appears exciting and enticing; sometimes it seems very fearful and foreboding.
Whatever the future holds does not matter as much as the fact that God goes
with us into it.

Appearances Are Deceptive

Truly God is good to Israel, even to such as are of a clean heart. But as for me, my feet were almost gone; my steps had well nigh slipped. For I was envious at the foolish, when I saw the prosperity of the wicked. For there are no bands in their death: but their strength is firm ... They set their mouth against the heavens, and their tongue walketh through the earth. When I thought to know this, it was too painful for me; Until I went into the sanctuary of God; then understood I their end. Surely thou didst set them in slippery places: thou castedst them down into destruction. How are they brought into desolation, as in a moment! they are utterly consumed with terrors. As a dream when one awaketh; so, O Lord, when thou awakest, thou shalt despise their image ... For, lo, they that are far from thee shall perish: thou hast destroyed all them that go a whoring from thee. But it is good for me to draw near to God: I have put my trust in the Lord God, that I may declare all thy works.
—Psalm 73:1–4, 9,16–20, 27–28

It is easy to look with envy upon how much others have that we clearly lack. Others appear handsome or beautiful in their disease-free bodies. Their faces shine with the self-satisfaction of earning a huge salary and spending it as they please. It is easy to envy the ease of a seemingly burden-free life.

Before envy grips our hearts, minds, and souls completely, we should consider the matter from the heavenly perspective. Satan blunts the perceptions of those who refuse the grace of God so that they sincerely appear carefree. Their sincerity conveys a false conviction and convinces us to think incorrectly. The person who ignores God becomes conceited. They feel that they can do anything—right or wrong—because no one stops them. Envy can tell us that it is pointless to live for God, but if we allow ourselves to act upon this thought, we betray the God who is faithful to us. We may even betray our future children if we continue on the path that leads away from God.

We should never forget that everyone moves toward a final destiny that is determined by choices made today, right now, in this life. Destruction is the end of those who refuse the God who made them. They are not worth the envy we are inclined to give them.

FEBRUARY 25

Real Love

And one of the scribes came, and having heard them reasoning
together, and perceiving that he had answered them well, asked him,
Which is the first commandment of all? And Jesus answered him,
The first of all the commandments is, Hear, O Israel; The Lord our
God is one Lord: And thou shalt love the Lord thy God with all
thy heart, and with all thy soul, and with all thy mind, and with all
thy strength: this is the first commandment. And the second is like,
namely this, Thou shalt love thy neighbour as thyself. There is none
other commandment greater than these. And the scribe said unto
him, Well, Master, thou hast said the truth: for there is one God;
and there is none other but he: And to love him with all the heart,
and with all the understanding, and with all the soul, and with all
the strength, and to love his neighbour as himself, is more than all
whole burnt offerings and sacrifices. And when Jesus saw that he
answered discreetly, he said unto him, Thou art not far from the
kingdom of God. And no man after that durst ask him any question.
—Mark 12:28–34

We love ice cream, we love pizza, we love Pepsi, we love the latest gadget,
we love the most stylish clothes, and we love the newest technology. We
love to walk, jog, swim, or play tennis. We love to talk to our friends, neighbors,
and family.

If all of the above is true, why do we get such bad results from all the loves
of our lives? Problems like obesity, budget deficits, feuds, and divorce seem to
plague us a lot. We cannot deny this contradictory love dilemma because many
television shows, movies, state lotteries, self-help books, and programs offer big
solutions to the common problems that arise from love problems. Jesus Christ
says that the most important commandment is to love God first and foremost.
We shouldn't just love Him like we love everything else. We should love Him
above all else. We should love Him with all our heart, all our soul, all our mind,
and all our strength. This is easier to do than we realize.

Once we commit our first love to God, He helps us to do all He wants us to
do, which is above and beyond our limited imaginations. He gives us assurance
that His way is best. Our reliance on God deepens our love toward others and
moderates our love for everything else.

Wonder Kid

> Then took he him up in his arms, and blessed God, and said, Lord,
> now lettest thou thy servant depart in peace, according to thy word:
> For mine eyes have seen thy salvation, Which thou hast prepared
> before the face of all people; A light to lighten the Gentiles, and the
> glory of thy people Israel. And Joseph and his mother marvelled at
> those things which were spoken of him. And Simeon blessed them,
> and said unto Mary his mother, Behold, this child is set for the fall
> and rising again of many in Israel; and for a sign which shall be
> spoken against; (Yea, a sword shall pierce through thy own soul also,)
> that the thoughts of many hearts may be revealed. And there was one
> Anna, a prophetess, the daughter of Phanuel, of the tribe of Aser:
> she was of a great age, and had lived with an husband seven years
> from her virginity … And she coming in that instant gave thanks
> likewise unto the Lord, and spake of him to all them that looked
> for redemption in Jerusalem. And the child grew, and waxed strong
> in spirit, filled with wisdom: and the grace of God was upon him.
> —Luke 2:28–36, 38, 40

Parents love their children and detect signs of genius in them from a very young age. No one (except possibly Grandma) ever agrees with parents, so as children grow up, parents must come down to a more realistic view of their children.

Unlike all other human parents, Joseph and Mary really did raise a wonder kid, a genius who knew everything because He was the Son of God. Their hasty marriage, due to Mary's unexpected conception by the Holy Spirit, drew them together in love. God dealt with both of them in a tender yet unusual way. They were determined to raise Him right, yet it appears they did not yet fully understand who Jesus was. When they consecrated the infant Jesus at the temple, Simeon, the prophet, and Anna, the prophetess, came forward to praise God for the birth of that wonderful baby boy.

The parents stood in awe at the words that were spoken of baby Jesus. Unlike all other earthly parents, they needed to upgrade their view of the Son of God. They kept the personal details of their life private and continued to be good parents to Jesus and His brothers and sisters. The childhood of all their children gave them time to consider the will of God more deeply.

He Is the Same Today

If I have told you earthly things, and ye believe not, how shall ye believe, if I tell you of heavenly things? And no man hath ascended up to heaven, but he that came down from heaven, even the Son of man which is in heaven. And as Moses lifted up the serpent in the wilderness, even so must the Son of man be lifted up: That whosoever believeth in him should not perish, but have eternal life. For God so loved the world, that he gave his only begotten Son, that whosoever believeth in him should not perish, but have everlasting life. For God sent not his Son into the world to condemn the world; but that the world through him might be saved.
—John 3:12–17

And the Lord said unto Moses, Make thee a fiery serpent, and set it upon a pole: and it shall come to pass, that every one that is bitten, when he looketh upon it, shall live.
—Numbers 21:8

Jesus spent a lot of time teaching people about God, about heaven, about how to live, and about many other spiritual matters. His teaching continued a long tradition of rabbinical teaching in local synagogues to local residents. The uniqueness of the teaching of Jesus was its accuracy, its truth, and its power.

It was not just the best a human teacher could offer to a human audience; as the Son of God, He spoke the very words of God. One point of His teaching was that Jesus Christ wanted believers to see the connection between Old Testament times and New Testament times, as we now call them. He gave the example of the time when the Israelites sinned against God and the Lord sent venomous snakes to bite them. What was God's solution to sin? Put a bronze snake on a pole. Anyone who looks on the snake will live and not die.

When we look at Jesus on the cross that was lifted over two other humans on top of a hill, we will not suffer and die for our sins. We will live. Why did God do this? He loves us beyond compare. Even before Jesus lived, died, and came to life again, He loved people beyond compare. As we mature in the Christian faith, we should read the Old Testament and learn to draw connections between it and today. We will find that God is the same, yesterday, today, and forever.

Obedience and Peace

If ye love me, keep my commandments. And I will pray the Father, and he shall give you another Comforter, that he may abide with you for ever; Even the Spirit of truth; whom the world cannot receive, because it seeth him not, neither knoweth him: but ye know him; for he dwelleth with you, and shall be in you. I will not leave you comfortless: I will come to you. Yet a little while, and the world seeth me no more; but ye see me: because I live, ye shall live also. At that day ye shall know that I am in my Father, and ye in me, and I in you. He that hath my commandments, and keepeth them, he it is that loveth me: and he that loveth me shall be loved of my Father, and I will love him, and will manifest myself to him. Judas saith unto him, not Iscariot, Lord, how is it that thou wilt manifest thyself unto us, and not unto the world? … But the Comforter, which is the Holy Ghost, whom the Father will send in my name, he shall teach you all things, and bring all things to your remembrance, whatsoever I have said unto you. Peace I leave with you, my peace I give unto you: not as the world giveth, give I unto you. Let not your heart be troubled, neither let it be afraid.
—John 14:15–22, 26–27

When we embark upon the spiritual journey of this life, we obey God willingly. Obedience is important because it reveals our reverence and love for the one who gave His life so that we may live. Obedience means that we are paying attention to God's Word enough to understand what it says. Obedience also means that we do what the Bible says to do.

We learn a lot from the Bible, God's Holy Word. We learn that God does not want us to live this life on our own terms. God does not want us to live in isolation. God does not want us to live according to our own quirks and interpretations.

Jesus tells us that He has asked God the Father to send the Holy Spirit to be with us, to guide us, to counsel us, to teach us, and to remind us daily to obey God. When we allow the Holy Spirit to work in us, He gives us peace from God. The Holy Spirit also bears witness to His new life in us. The transcendent peace that marks the obedient believer witnesses to the world of the overwhelming love and abundant life of the Savior to others. Others need to see Him in us so that they may also be drawn to Him.

Terrors and Fears

He that dwelleth in the secret place of the most High shall abide under the shadow of the Almighty. I will say of the Lord, He is my refuge and my fortress: my God; in him will I trust. Surely he shall deliver thee from the snare of the fowler, and from the noisome pestilence. He shall cover thee with his feathers, and under his wings shalt thou trust: his truth shall be thy shield and buckler. Thou shalt not be afraid for the terror by night; nor for the arrow that flieth by day ... Because thou hast made the Lord, which is my refuge, even the most High, thy habitation; There shall no evil befall thee, neither shall any plague come nigh thy dwelling ... Because he hath set his love upon me, therefore will I deliver him: I will set him on high, because he hath known my name. He shall call upon me, and I will answer him: I will be with him in trouble; I will deliver him, and honour him. With long life will I satisfy him, and shew him my salvation.
—Psalm 91:1–5, 9–10, 14–16

Even if we rarely read newspapers anymore, we cannot escape learning about what has happened around the world. Think about the content of newspapers, the images of the evening news, and the general conversations heard daily. Most of it is bad.

As a result, people live in fear about all manner of terrifying events happening around them. We want to know where the most dangerous neighborhoods are because we hope we don't live in one of them. We want to know where the most dangerous countries are, and we are glad we don't need to travel in them.

Because we are sinners, it is human to fall prey to many kinds of fears— both rational and irrational. It doesn't matter what kinds of fears we are prone to elevate in our lives, but it matters a lot that we turn to God with all of those fears and hand them over to Him. When we surrender all of them to the Lord, He protects our minds as well as our bodies from the terrors and fears that so easily beset us. Loving and trusting God has other benefits as well. God answers the prayers of the faithful and helps us in every kind of trouble. God delivers us from evil, and His deliverance satisfies us at the point of our deepest need.

MARCH 1

Excellence

O Lord, our Lord, how excellent is thy name in all the earth! who
hast set thy glory above the heavens. Out of the mouth of babes and
sucklings hast thou ordained strength because of thine enemies,
that thou mightest still the enemy and the avenger. When I consider
thy heavens, the work of thy fingers, the moon and the stars, which
thou hast ordained; What is man, that thou art mindful of him?
and the son of man, that thou visitest him? For thou hast made
him a little lower than the angels, and hast crowned him with glory
and honour. Thou madest him to have dominion over the works
of thy hands; thou hast put all things under his feet: All sheep and
oxen, yea, and the beasts of the field; The fowl of the air, and the
fish of the sea, and whatsoever passeth through the paths of the
seas. O Lord our Lord, how excellent is thy name in all the earth!
—Psalm 8:1–9

Unless we live in a monarchy, we do not often use a noun like *excellence* or its
adjective form *excellent*. The word *excellent* implies splendor, magnificence,
and majesty—a grandeur far beyond the ordinary sense of distinction. Kings and
queens who are addressed in the formal way are still human, even though they
are exalted above the rest of the citizens of the country.

When we read unfamiliar vocabulary within a biblical context, we need to
understand what the term means. God has arranged this world and our lives
in a way that will help us think of Him as we ought. God's Word maintains
that because God has an excellent or majestic name, He is worthy of all human
adoration! He is above and beyond us. Children speak His praise to the delight
of listening adults. They are closer to their Creator because they are so young,
and their words prompt us to consider the majestic qualities of God that we
should never forget. The planets remind us how great God is, yet He still cares
about billions of individuals. Humans can barely comprehend how the universe
functions, yet God has made us in His image. The creation tells us He is glorious.
We need to admire His handiwork. Creatures move along the ground. Fish swim
the underwater path. Birds soar high above, along the windy airways.

Yet God delighted to make us in His image. His excellence is supreme, and
we belong to Him!

How to Trust God

Bow down thine ear, and hear the words of the wise, and apply
thine heart unto my knowledge. For it is a pleasant thing if
thou keep them within thee; they shall withal be fitted in thy
lips. That thy trust may be in the Lord, I have made known
to thee this day, even to thee ... That I might make thee
know the certainty of the words of truth; that thou mightest
answer the words of truth to them that send unto thee?
—Proverbs 22:17–19, 21

The Christian life has two parts: getting saved and living a saved life. When
people blithely accept salvation as the only component of the new life in
Christ, they are sometimes prone to think that they are exempt from ordinary
rules because they have been saved from every sin, or they try to live according to
their own ideas instead of letting the Holy Spirit guide them. Apart from trusting
God to live the Christian life, we have no help or knowledge to promote our new
life. To trust in God may be a message that has been hammered away at in our
lives, but the actual practice of it may escape us.

Trusting God involves listening (not just hearing) His words—so far, so
good. Belief in God involves reading God's Word—ditto. Reading God's Word
involves understanding and applying its principles to daily life—not always easy.
Application involves memorizing Scriptures—sometimes difficult and always
time-consuming.

When we are active instead of passive with regard to our new life in Christ,
the Holy Spirit assures us of the certainty of God's word. He moves us where
He wants us to go and prevents us from doing what displeases our Lord. Trust
means sound judgment and reliable decisions that come from being in close
communication with the Lord. All these virtues come from the Lord of truth.

MARCH 3

True Leadership

And God said unto Jacob, Arise, go up to Bethel, and dwell there: and
make there an altar unto God, that appeared unto thee when thou
fleddest from the face of Esau thy brother. Then Jacob said unto his
household, and to all that were with him, Put away the strange gods
that are among you, and be clean, and change your garments: And
let us arise, and go up to Bethel; and I will make there an altar unto
God, who answered me in the day of my distress, and was with me in
the way which I went. And they gave unto Jacob all the strange gods
which were in their hand, and all their earrings which were in their
ears; and Jacob hid them under the oak which was by Shechem. And
they journeyed: and the terror of God was upon the cities that were
round about them, and they did not pursue after the sons of Jacob.
—Genesis 35:1–5

Jacob was the patriarch of an enormous family, clan, or tribal group, yet
within his extended household lived idolaters and worshipers of foreign gods
alongside the believing members. Nevertheless, God planned to bless the world
through the godly lives of Abraham, Isaac, and Jacob—through their future
descendant named Jesus Christ.

In order to maintain the family focus on moral purity, God gave Jacob
specific instructions to accomplish the task of preserving holiness throughout all
generations. Jacob asked his household to get rid of all idols, to purify themselves,
and to change their clothes.

Today, just as in ancient times, we hold on to objects that we prize, but our
favorite stuff holds no more value than worthless idols. The idea that clothing (on
the outside of us) reveals who we are (on the inside) was alive and well understood
in biblical times as much as it is today. Donning fresh garments still makes us feel
better. Cleansing the outside of the body still makes us feel clean on the inside.
Jacob, the believer and household leader, was not afraid to ask the unbelievers
to follow God's laws, proving that God's laws are written in everyone's hearts.
When the family of the patriarch obeyed God en masse, the neighboring towns
recognized the difference in their lives. The neighbors feared God and left Jacob's
family alone in peace.

MARCH 4

An Appearance of God

And I looked, and, behold, a whirlwind came out of the north, a
great cloud, and a fire infolding itself, and a brightness was about it,
and out of the midst thereof as the colour of amber, out of the midst
of the fire. Also out of the midst thereof came the likeness of four
living creatures. And this was their appearance; they had the likeness
of a man. And every one had four faces, and every one had four
wings ... Now as I beheld the living creatures, behold one wheel upon
the earth by the living creatures, with his four faces ... When they
went, they went upon their four sides: and they turned not when they
went. And the likeness of the firmament upon the heads of the living
creature was as the colour of the terrible crystal, stretched forth over
their heads above. And there was a voice from the firmament that
was over their heads, when they stood, and had let down their wings.
—Ezekiel 1:4–6, 15, 17, 22, 25

Today, we have the Bible to tell us what God is like, and God has sent the Holy
Spirit to guide us. But in Old Testament times, believers only had the Law,
a lengthy set of rules that they tended to forget. It is true that God sometimes
spoke to individuals. These spectacular visitations always aroused wonder and
admiration, but they were never the common lot of most believers.

Reading about the appearance of the glory of the Lord to Ezekiel sounds
a lot like an episode from a science-fiction thriller movie where alien creatures
enter the human world. This may not be entirely inaccurate. After all, God is not
human, is He? We are made like Him; He is not made like us. He is so different
from humans that only metaphors can describe Him.

In this passage of Scripture, God resembles an enormous tornado that
flashes lightning, but He is surrounded by brilliant light (instead of the dark and
swirling dustiness of a tornado). Inside the fiery light are four living creatures
with four different faces. Oversized wheels on the ground beside each living
creature move on high rims, and the rims are completely covered with eyes.
Ezekiel knew he was seeing an appearance of the glory of the Lord. When God
confronts a person, there is no doubt or mistake who it is or what comes next.
God spoke personally to Ezekiel just like He does to us today.

The Riches of the Gospel

Unto me, who am less than the least of all saints, is this grace
given, that I should preach among the Gentiles the unsearchable
riches of Christ; And to make all men see what is the fellowship
of the mystery, which from the beginning of the world hath
been hid in God, who created all things by Jesus Christ: To the
intent that now unto the principalities and powers in heavenly
places might be known by the church the manifold wisdom of
God, According to the eternal purpose which he purposed in
Christ Jesus our Lord: In whom we have boldness and access
with confidence by the faith of him. Wherefore I desire that
ye faint not at my tribulations for you, which is your glory.
—Ephesians 3:8–13

Because about three quarters of the national population now lives in cities
instead of rural areas or small towns, few of us can relate to the terms of
agrarian subsistence living. In the urban world, every aspect of our lives comes
from stores. We are surrounded by buildings, which imply that someone had
enough money to build them. Most of us think of riches in concrete terms:
consumer goods, family money, new home, expensive vehicles, Ivy League
education, and discretionary income—a multitude of eye-candy objects. The
concept of spiritual riches may seem to exist outside our frame of reference.

The apostle Paul needed to separate these two types of riches in his own
understanding because he had enjoyed earthly riches and the prestige that
accompanies it when he lived outside of Christ. Only the grace of God made
him realize that true riches are abstract but real, invisible but tangible, and
unfathomable but comprehensible. Only in Jesus Christ can the world see the
riches of God's mercy to sinners.

Our lives portray to others the explanation of what had once been mysterious.
Our lives display the complete wisdom of God in dealing with sinful creatures.
When we look at the life of Jesus Christ, we begin to understand the depth of
riches so unlike any human concept of them. Faith in Jesus Christ lets us come
to God freely and confidently—no more striving after eye candy.

The Testimony of a Changed Life

> Ye worship ye know not what: we know what we worship: for
> salvation is of the Jews. But the hour cometh, and now is, when
> the true worshippers shall worship the Father in spirit and in
> truth: for the Father seeketh such to worship him. God is a Spirit:
> and they that worship him must worship him in spirit and in
> truth ... And many of the Samaritans of that city believed on
> him for the saying of the woman, which testified, He told me all
> that ever I did ... And said unto the woman, Now we believe,
> not because of thy saying: for we have heard him ourselves, and
> know that this is indeed the Christ, the Saviour of the world.
> —John 4:22–24, 39, 42

No matter how we live our lives, the human spirit seeks out God the Creator. We may live a relatively good life or otherwise, according to our lights. The conversation of the Samaritan woman at the well indicates that this desire was just as true a couple of millennia ago as it is true today. When our lives have been embarrassingly frivolous or unspeakably bad, it can be difficult to face the crowd of old neighbors, family, and friends. Will they believe us and accept the change that Jesus Christ has wrought in us?

The woman at the well had had five husbands and was now living with a man to whom she was not married. When we look at religions that depend upon good works or when we look at religions that worship idols (statues and figures that represent a god), we may also be confused about how to worship God, just like the Samaritan woman was. Yet when she was confronted with the truth, she changed her mind, and she changed the minds of others.

Jesus reminds us that our basic nature is spiritual (unseen) and therefore requires a spiritual, supernatural source. When we abandon ourselves to Him, and when we abandon previous misconceptions and sins, the changed lifestyle reveals the nature of God to others. For this reason, anyone who wants to do so may come to Jesus Christ and learn the same.

MARCH 7

Time for College

To every thing there is a season, and a time to every purpose under
the heaven: A time to be born, and a time to die; a time to plant, and
a time to pluck up that which is planted; A time to kill, and a time to
heal; a time to break down, and a time to build up; A time to weep,
and a time to laugh; a time to mourn, and a time to dance; A time
to cast away stones, and a time to gather stones together; a time to
embrace, and a time to refrain from embracing; A time to get, and a
time to lose; a time to keep, and a time to cast away; A time to rend,
and a time to sew; a time to keep silence, and a time to speak; A time
to love, and a time to hate; a time of war, and a time of peace …
He hath made every thing beautiful in his time: also he hath set the
world in their heart, so that no man can find out the work that God
maketh from the beginning to the end … I know that, whatsoever
God doeth, it shall be for ever: nothing can be put to it, nor any thing
taken from it: and God doeth it, that men should fear before him.
—Ecclesiastes 3:1–8, 11, 14

We do not need to look back in time too far to remember that young children
count the days until they are big enough to go to kindergarten. Similarly,
schoolchildren count the years until they are old enough to graduate from high
school. Thinking patterns have not changed, and college students continue to
count the semester progression until they have enough credit hours to graduate.

Time is a free gift from God to us. God gives us time to help us learn to
divide and conquer our efforts. When we block off time slots in our lives, we are
able to resist the nagging voice inside the head that tells us to get going and do
everything at once, or alternatively, to put every task off until the tomorrow that
never arrives. The sense of accomplishment that a college degree confers comes
from the diligence of steady, spaced-out effort. God says it is beautiful. We don't
know exactly what we will do upon graduation, but God does.

We cannot figure out God, but He gives us the gift of this special time to
think about Him and honor Him while we work away at everything else.

Everything We Need

According as his divine power hath given unto us all things
that pertain unto life and godliness, through the knowledge
of him that hath called us to glory and virtue ... And beside
this, giving all diligence, add to your faith virtue; and to virtue
knowledge; And to knowledge temperance; and to temperance
patience; and to patience godliness; And to godliness brotherly
kindness; and to brotherly kindness charity. For if these things be
in you, and abound, they make you that ye shall neither be barren
nor unfruitful in the knowledge of our Lord Jesus Christ. But
he that lacketh these things is blind, and cannot see afar off,
and hath forgotten that he was purged from his old sins.
—2 Peter 1:3, 5–9

It doesn't take too much observation to look around us and see how much effort other people put into their lives in order to succeed. We admire those go-getters and hope to do as much for ourselves. Because we all spend so much time and effort trying to get ahead and provide basic necessities in our lives, it is a dream to think of a world where everything is done for us. But this is how the spiritual world operates, and it is dramatically different from the physical world we inhabit. God is great, and Jesus Christ has proven how powerful He is by coming to life again. This is enough knowledge to help us comprehend that power from God is valuable, reliable, and practical.

The divine power equips us completely for every human need. Does this mean we should all quit working and stop trying? Of course not! It means that we must grow in our faith in order to appropriate the promises of God, to make them real and efficacious in our lives. When we put diligent effort into godly living—goodness, knowledge, self-control, patience, godliness, kindness, and love—we become more like the God who gave us life in the first place.

When God is active in our lives, our lives are effective. The other part of having everything we need is that we continually remember how good God is to cleanse us from our sins.

MARCH 9

Are we Active or Passive?

And he said unto them, Know ye not this parable? and how then
will ye know all parables? … And he said unto them, Is a candle
brought to be put under a bushel, or under a bed? and not to be
set on a candlestick? For there is nothing hid, which shall not be
manifested; neither was any thing kept secret, but that it should
come abroad. If any man have ears to hear, let him hear. And he
said unto them, Take heed what ye hear: with what measure ye
mete, it shall be measured to you: and unto you that hear shall
more be given. For he that hath, to him shall be given: and he
that hath not, from him shall be taken even that which he hath.
—Mark 4:13, 21–25

Do we plan out our time to the last detail? And do we let time wash over us
and get around to daily tasks whenever? Activity or passivity—these are
two extreme ways of handling life, and no one can say that one approach is really
better than the other. God has made both types of people.

Time management is now considered a behavioral science, and we are
aware that factory productivity is closely allied with time management as well as
spatial management. Such a modern topic might seem to exist outside the scope
of ancient civilizations, but our thinking is probably skewed on this topic. After
all, modern society has been built upon the thinking of past civilizations. Have
we ever thought that God wants us to think about our lives—to consider them
carefully—in order to learn from our experiences?

People do not tell didactic stories (teaching lessons) about themselves every
day, but their behavior does tell us and possibly teach us something about their
lives. When we remember that God gives each of us individual personalities and
that He is in charge of all the circumstances of our lives, we need to figure out
what He is trying to teach us. Our thoughtful engagement with daily life helps us
mature spiritually. When God gives the understanding, act on what is understood
and apply it to daily life. God will continue to increase personal understanding
as we relate to Him more and more.

The Brightest and the Best

Who being the brightness of his glory, and the express image of his
person, and upholding all things by the word of his power, when he
had by himself purged our sins, sat down on the right hand of the
Majesty on high: Being made so much better than the angels, as he
hath by inheritance obtained a more excellent name than they ...
How shall we escape, if we neglect so great salvation; which at the
first began to be spoken by the Lord, and was confirmed unto us
by them that heard him ... Thou hast put all things in subjection
under his feet. For in that he put all in subjection under him, he left
nothing that is not put under him. But now we see not yet all things
put under him. But we see Jesus, who was made a little lower than
the angels for the suffering of death, crowned with glory and honour;
that he by the grace of God should taste death for every man.
—Hebrews 1:3–4; 2:3, 8–9

When looking for the first apartment or the first home, a primary
consideration is that the currently empty space is flooded with light. The
future personal space will be more habitable when it is well lit. We probably do
not have a lot of furniture at this point in our lives, so the quality of the living
space matters more than other conditions.

A lot of people today love candles, bright homes, sunlit rooms, and outdoor
spaces, as if the light lifts their spirits. Who can disagree? But if these are the
only lights we know, then we are looking in the wrong places to lift ourselves
out of gloom. When we repent and turn to Jesus Christ the Savior, God forgives
our sins, removes us from the kingdom of darkness, and sets us in the kingdom
of light. Our living conditions have markedly changed from one of darkness to
one of light.

The kingdom of light is a great place to exist, but it is just the beginning of
new life. To grow in the faith, we need to recognize how bright and beautiful the
Son of God truly is. The rest of this world pales in significance next to Him. To
lift our spirits permanently, we must value the Son above all else. Sunshine and
artificial lighting are only pale reminders of true brightness.

How to Be Better than We Are Now

> To the one we are the savour of death unto death; and to the other
> the savour of life unto life. And who is sufficient for these things? …
> And such trust have we through Christ to God-ward: Not that we
> are sufficient of ourselves to think any thing as of ourselves; but
> our sufficiency is of God … But we all, with open face beholding
> as in a glass the glory of the Lord, are changed into the same
> image from glory to glory, even as by the Spirit of the Lord.
> —2 Corinthians 2:16; 3:4–5, 18

One of the effects of living in a media-oriented world is that we see images of apparently perfect people on the screen. Magazine photos airbrush out the flaws of ordinary mortals, and the imperfections are completely hidden. Television and movies edit out the less palatable portions of the show and portray a distorted image of reality. Reality shows appeal to viewers because they capture a slice or reality, but only the Bible gives the entire, unvarnished reality of human life.

The media make us want to be better than we are right now, but the task seems unlikely, if not impossible. When we turn to the Lord, we come into contact with reality in a way that we could never have perceived before. This brush with reality does not come from an airbrush that removes flaws in a superficial way but from the Lord of truth who desires to bring about the best in us. When we turn to the Lord, we may have to reckon with the fact that we are not as competent as we have previously imagined. The Bible tells us we are not equal to any type of task—only God is equal to the task. When we claim the gifts and promises of God as our own—through Jesus Christ, by the power of the Holy Spirit—God gives us the confidence and competence that comes from Him.

God is perfect, and perfection is found nowhere else. As we obey and trust God, we are transformed into His likeness. This is neither a namby-pamby passivity nor an arrogant, holier-than-thou pride. This is the glory of God in us. He is always better than we are, so it is entirely logical and sensible to turn to Him in submission in order to become better than we are now.

Forgiveness for Sin

> When Israel was a child, then I loved him, and called my son
> out of Egypt. As they called them, so they went from them: they
> sacrificed unto Baalim, and burned incense to graven images. I
> taught Ephraim also to go, taking them by their arms; but they
> knew not that I healed them. I drew them with cords of a man,
> with bands of love: and I was to them as they that take off the yoke
> on their jaws, and I laid meat unto them … And my people are
> bent to backsliding from me: though they called them to the most
> High, none at all would exalt him … Therefore turn thou to thy
> God: keep mercy and judgment and wait on thy God continually.
> —Hosea 11:1–4, 7; 12:6

We take it for granted that parents love their children. It is unimaginable that our own flesh and blood will not matter to us dearly. Just as parents love and cherish their young children, so does God love and cherish His children. We ultimately come from Him just as much as our children come from us. We can see our earthly parents and know all they have done for us.

We cannot see our heavenly Father, so we do not always realize how much He has done for us. And God has given us the book that tells us what we cannot know in any other way. When we ignore God or turn away from God or sin against God, we behave as though God the Father does not really exist. We act as though we belong to ourselves, and we surrender to our own ideas about how to live. We tend to believe a lot of lies, but believing in lies does not make them come true.

When we look into the book that tells us how it is, we enable ourselves to return to God through repentance for sins. Because God loves us so much, He nourishes us. He helps us mature, He heals us when we become ill, He leads us tenderly, and He loves us so much all the time that it is easy to take Him for granted. When we go astray, we need to return to the One who loves us best, who blesses us most, who seeks our highest good, and who is the finest. We can always turn back to God and wait for His love and justice in life.

True Contrition

Therefore also now, saith the Lord, turn ye even to me with all your heart, and with fasting, and with weeping, and with mourning: And rend your heart, and not your garments, and turn unto the Lord your God: for he is gracious and merciful, slow to anger, and of great kindness, and repenteth him of the evil. Who knoweth if he will return and repent, and leave a blessing behind him; even a meat offering and a drink offering unto the Lord your God? ... Fear not, O land; be glad and rejoice: for the Lord will do great things.
—Joel 2:12–14, 21

Look around a bit and see how many religions rely on rituals—acts of devotion performed on certain days, in specific ways, or by designated adherents. Rituals appeal to people because they lend order to an otherwise chaotic world. We all want calmness and stability in life, and rituals seem to fill that need. Rituals also let us off the hook from inquiring further about the nature of worship and the character of God. We have been taught to compartmentalize our lives, so we prefer to get on with the rest of our lives.

Rituals can seem like reality to us, but God wants more than ritual from us. He is an emotional being, and He wants a true emotional response from us. This does not mean an overly emotional response bordering on psychological instability but a heartfelt rejoinder from one emotional being to another. Instead of a ritualistic behavior pattern like the tearing of clothing to represent remorse and sorrow for sin, God looks on the human heart. He wants to love the heart that is ripped apart by sin. He wants to love the heart that knows that such severe brokenness is a heart trouble that God heals best. It is best to turn to him in every circumstance. Yes, God is just and punishes sin, but He is also compassionate and forgiving of sin.

When God sees the sorrowful heart broken by sin, He relents, He forgives, and He changes the situation. He may even bless us when we least deserve it! God alone does great things!

The Listener Who Understands Us

> Seeing then that we have a great high priest, that is passed into
> the heavens, Jesus the Son of God, let us hold fast our profession.
> For we have not an high priest which cannot be touched with the
> feeling of our infirmities; but was in all points tempted like as we
> are, yet without sin. Let us therefore come boldly unto the throne
> of grace, that we may obtain mercy, and find grace to help in time
> of need ... Who in the days of his flesh, when he had offered up
> prayers and supplications with strong crying and tears unto him
> that was able to save him from death, and was heard in that he
> feared; Though he were a Son, yet learned he obedience by the
> things which he suffered; And being made perfect, he became
> the author of eternal salvation unto all them that obey him.
> —Hebrews 4:14–16; 5:7–9

If we have been raised in the Catholic or Orthodox tradition, we may be more familiar with the practices of the confessional than most Protestant churches consider necessary. One idea behind the confessional is that the practice of confessing sins to an impartial third party forces us to acknowledge what we have done and take responsibility for the unmentionable deeds of our lives. Before the priest, who is a witness representing the Lord to us, we make ourselves aware that we need forgiveness for sins.

Priests do represent the people before God, but Jesus, the Son of God, has become the ultimate high priest for all believers. He proved His worth by living a human life, by dying on the cross, and by coming to life again. He knows where we are going, and He wants to take us with Him. During His, life, He was tempted to sin, but He never capitulated to sin. When life becomes lonely and it seems like no one cares about us, we should remember that the Son of God cares about us very much.

Jesus Christ listens to us. We may place all confidence and confession in Him, and we may expect mercy and grace in return.

Stillness and Silence

> Behold, is it not of the Lord of hosts that the people shall labour
> in the very fire, and the people shall weary themselves for very
> vanity? For the earth shall be filled with the knowledge of the
> glory of the Lord, as the waters cover the sea … But the Lord is
> in his holy temple: let all the earth keep silence before him.
> —Habakkuk 2:13–14; 2:20

> Be silent, O all flesh, before the Lord: for he is
> raised up out of his holy habitation.
> —Zechariah 2:13

> Be still, and know that I am God: I will be exalted
> among the heathen, I will be exalted in the earth.
> —Psalm 46:10

> If thou hast anything to say, answer me: speak, for I
> desire to justify thee. If not, hearken unto me: hold
> thy peace, and I shall teach thee wisdom.
> —Job 33:32–33

What difference does it make whether a person reads the Bible a lot or a little? Maybe we think of the Bible as just more words, and all of us are already bombarded by a continual barrage of words, noise, and commotion—words of every sort—in every medium. Our minds ring with jingly lines from current advertisements and popular lines of favorite movie characters. We think that because we call ourselves Christian, we automatically think and speak as the Lord would like us to. But we should ask ourselves whether or not this is actually true.

Do we silence ourselves before the Lord, the maker of heaven and earth? Or, do we spend our time in ceaseless but interesting (to us) activity? The days prior to the crucifixion of Jesus Christ and His glorious resurrection are days when many believers take time to be quiet before the Lord, and this good practice can help believers slow down as they ponder the nature of the Lord who came to earth for us. We cannot know what God desires of us when we do not trouble ourselves to read his Holy Word.

When we understand that God frustrates the efforts of those who exhaust themselves apart from the Lord, spending quiet time in the Word of God becomes critical to the effectiveness of daily life.

The Sin of Idolatry

Not unto us, O Lord, not unto us, but unto thy name give glory, for thy mercy, and for thy truth's sake ... Their idols are silver and gold, the work of men's hands. They have mouths, but they speak not: eyes have they, but they see not: They have ears, but they hear not: noses have they, but they smell not: They have hands, but they handle not: feet have they, but they walk not: neither speak they through their throat. They that make them are like unto them; so is every one that trusteth in them ... The Lord hath been mindful of us: he will bless us; he will bless the house of Israel; he will bless the house of Aaron.
—Psalm 115:1, 4–8, 12

Our culture is so saturated with idolatry that we may no longer recognize it as such any more than we are appalled at its perniciousness. Idolatry of physical images like Buddha, idolatry of sun-drenched beaches, idolatry of the human body, idolatry of specific foods, idolatry of clothing, idolatry of lifestyles, idolatry of possessions—the list is endless. We need to pay attention to the Word of God to learn two things: what an idol is and what happens to idolaters.

The first part is easy. Idols are first conceived as human ideas before they are made into a concrete form by human hands. Idols may be made of metal, wood, or stone; they have no breath of life in them. They are blind, they are deaf, they are dumb, and they perceive no sensual experiences. They are fabrications; they are not real.

The second part should frighten all who desire what does not come from God. Idolaters will become like the idols they worship! Does this mean that we will literally lose all our faculties? Probably not, but consider that metaphorical language conveys realistic meanings. An idolater, a person who worships what is not God, will lose the ability to communicate with others. Family members will not speak with one another, and dysfunctional relationships will result. Coworkers will find difficulty communicating with one another, and the job will not be done correctly, if at all. Does anyone really want to lose the ability to communicate or feel or experience for the sake of holding on to idolatry in this life?

We Know Better

> He hath shewed thee, O man, what is good; and what doth the
> Lord require of thee, but to do justly, and to love mercy, and to
> walk humbly with thy God? ... Therefore also will I make thee sick
> in smiting thee, in making thee desolate because of thy sins. Thou
> shalt eat, but not be satisfied; and thy casting down shall be in the
> midst of thee; and thou shalt take hold, but shalt not deliver; and that
> which thou deliverest will I give up to the sword ... For the statutes
> of Omri are kept, and all the works of the house of Ahab, and ye
> walk in their counsels; that I should make thee a desolation, and the
> inhabitants thereof an hissing: therefore ye shall bear the reproach of
> my people ... Who is a God like unto thee, that pardoneth iniquity,
> and passeth by the transgression of the remnant of his heritage? he
> retaineth not his anger for ever, because he delighteth in mercy. He
> will turn again, he will have compassion upon us; he will subdue our
> iniquities; and thou wilt cast all their sins into the depths of the sea.
> —Micah 6:8, 13–14, 16; 7:18–19

All of us have been taught by our parents and our teachers in the formative years, so we carry with us into our college years the sense of what to do and how to do things right. We know when we screw up, and we know when we toe the line.

We are like this because God has written His good laws on every human heart. We know instinctively how to be fair and how to behave kindly toward others. But now, we may need instruction in how to be humble before God. Being on our own means that we answer directly to God now. We should understand that when we live according to the law of sin, sin begins to destroy us slowly. We experience dissatisfaction. We try hard, but our efforts do not avail. We work hard, but we cannot finish the job.

As we persist in forgetting God, He brings about ruin in our lives, hoping that with each step, we will return to Him. God always stands ready to forgive, to forget, to show mercy, to exercise compassion, to trample sins under His feet, and to hurl sins into the ocean depths. We really do know better than to stay stuck in a life of sin.

Why Suicide?

> Now the Philistines fought against Israel; and the men of Israel fled
> from before the Philistines, and fell down slain in mount Gilboa.
> And the Philistines followed hard after Saul, and after his sons; and
> the Philistines slew Jonathan, and Abinadab, and Malchishua, the
> sons of Saul. And the battle went sore against Saul, and the archers
> hit him, and he was wounded of the archers. Then said Saul to his
> armourbearer, Draw thy sword, and thrust me through therewith;
> lest these uncircumcised come and abuse me. But his armourbearer
> would not; for he was sore afraid. So Saul took a sword, and fell upon
> it. And when his armourbearer saw that Saul was dead, he fell likewise
> on the sword, and died. So Saul died, and his three sons, and all his
> house died together … So Saul died for his transgression which he
> committed against the Lord, even against the word of the Lord, which
> he kept not, and also for asking counsel of one that had a familiar
> spirit, to enquire of it; And enquired not of the Lord: therefore he
> slew him, and turned the kingdom unto David the son of Jesse.
> —1 Chronicles 10:1–6, 13–14

When Saul became king, he was chosen by the people because he was tall, handsome, and strong. People had to look up to him, and they equated physical prowess with administrative qualities and godly leadership skills. They were wrong because Saul proved to be vain, ungodly, and self-centered. In spite of a personal encounter with God, Saul refused to obey God's Word; instead, he followed his own way. God let him know He was withdrawing the blessing from his life. Saul was king for forty years, so God gave him decades to repent and turn back to God, but Saul never did.

Abnormal psychology textbooks include a chapter on the subject of suicide. The chapter lists the data about who commits suicide according to gender, age, mode, etc. When a person commits suicide, no one can ask why anymore, so we rely on statistics to help us figure it out. This makes the Bible's comment on Saul important. Saul was unfaithful to God, so God allowed sin to take over in his life, resulting in suicide.

Dealing with the suicide of a loved one is extremely difficult, and even though the Bible offers an answer, it is still a difficult answer. Perhaps the best solution is to determine today to commit fully to the Lord and to not withhold anything from the One who gave it all to us in the first place.

The World and Its Rules

Let no man therefore judge you in meat, or in drink, or in respect of
an holyday, or of the new moon, or of the sabbath days: Which are
a shadow of things to come; but the body is of Christ. Let no man
beguile you of your reward in a voluntary humility and worshipping
of angels, intruding into those things which he hath not seen, vainly
puffed up by his fleshly mind, And not holding the Head, from which
all the body by joints and bands having nourishment ministered, and
knit together, increaseth with the increase of God. Wherefore if ye
be dead with Christ from the rudiments of the world, why, as though
living in the world, are ye subject to ordinances, (Touch not; taste
not; handle not; Which all are to perish with the using;) after the
commandments and doctrines of men? Which things have indeed
a shew of wisdom in will worship, and humility, and neglecting
of the body: not in any honour to the satisfying of the flesh.
—Colossians 2:16–23

Does it surprise us that people who reject God and His laws in their lives often follow an elaborate personal code of conduct anyway? It shouldn't. When sociologists and anthropologists study groups, they notice patterns of conduct and try to figure out the meanings associated with them. For example, extended families sometimes follow unwritten rules of behavior, so when a cousin gets out of line, the rest of the family tells him about it in no uncertain terms.

Ethnic cultures sometimes follow specific daily habits to maintain continuity with the place they came from. Their ideas about clock time or dieting may differ from the norm of the surrounding culture. Companies may enforce dress code policies to ensure a uniformity of appearance to outsiders. Religions may provide steps to follow, words to chant, ideas to hallow as beneficial to spiritual enlightenment. Exercise and diet can follow very harsh regimens.

All of these areas of human endeavor are good, but without submitting human ideas to biblical precepts first, human regulations and rules become empty. They seem to offer a way of self-control or discipline, which is good, but when spiritual values or assumptions are omitted, the outcomes are useless and possibly detrimental.

When We Sin

The yoke of my transgressions is bound by his hand: they
are wreathed, and come up upon my neck: he hath made my
strength to fall, the Lord hath delivered me into their hands,
from whom I am not able to rise up ... The Lord is righteous;
for I have rebelled against his commandment: hear, I pray you,
all people, and behold my sorrow: my virgins and my young
men are gone into captivity ... It is of the Lord's mercies
that we are not consumed, because his compassions fail not.
They are new every morning: great is thy faithfulness.
—Lamentations 1:14, 18; 3:22–23

Come unto me, all ye that labour and are heavy laden, and I
will give you rest. Take my yoke upon you, and learn of me;
for I am meek and lowly in heart: and ye shall find rest unto
your souls. For my yoke is easy, and my burden is light.
—Matthew 11:28–30

The character of God is holy and righteous, and He demands the same
integrity from us. He knows we can obey Him because He gives us the
strength to do it. We have no excuse for sin. We know better, yet we still fall
into sin. When we sin, we yoke ourselves to our sins and we make ourselves into
slaves of sin. This is God's righteous judgment so that we may know and come
to appreciate the freedom we have when we obey God.

With obedience come energy and strength and power, but sin continually
saps our strength. When we persist in sin, God hands us over to the sin. We
never expect the bad results; in fact, we are shocked and mortified to live with
the outcomes of our sinful behavior. God does this to let us know that His hand
is gentle, His yoke is easy, and His burden is light. Even when we have sinned,
God does not destroy us. He knows how frail the human frame is and how easily
weakness is overpowered.

He desires the best for us, so He gives us a different way to think every day,
as long as we keep asking Him for help. God is faithful to us even when we sin,
and this reminds us and shames us to return to Him with renewed appreciation
and true thankfulness.

Mercy in Captivity

This Ezra went up from Babylon; and he was a ready scribe in the
law of Moses, which the Lord God of Israel had given: and the king
granted him all his request, according to the hand of the Lord his
God upon him. And there went up some of the children of Israel,
and of the priests, and the Levites, and the singers, and the porters,
and the Nethinims, unto Jerusalem, in the seventh year of Artaxerxes
the king. And he came to Jerusalem in the fifth month, which was
in the seventh year of the king. For upon the first day of the first
month began he to go up from Babylon, and on the first day of the
fifth month came he to Jerusalem, according to the good hand of his
God upon him. For Ezra had prepared his heart to seek the law of
the Lord, and to do it, and to teach in Israel statutes and judgments.
—Ezra 7:6–10

As believers, we can fall unthinkingly into the snares of sin or the customs of
the surrounding decadent culture. Once ensnared, we become captive to the
thing or idea that we have committed to. We do not always realize that we cannot
turn back apart from repentance. The nation of Israel behaved like some of us
still do today. They believed in God but lived as they pleased. They observed the
laws when required, and they sacrificed to idols when they wanted. When a bad
situation overtakes us, it becomes embarrassing, humiliating, or unendurable; we
hate it. When the situation seems never-ending, we are abased by it. When we
have not caused the bad situation, we have a little consolation.

Unfortunately, when the Israelites lived in captivity in Babylon, they knew
captivity was their own fault. It must have been easy to engage in loathing and
self-pity. At the same time, God used the captivity to captivate their thoughts for
Him and turn them back to the truth. In spite of their backsliding devotion, God
was merciful to the nation. He reserved a man like Ezra to study the Word of
God, to observe the law, and to teach its precepts to the leaders of the returning
exiles. God knew that this was the only way to get the wayward nation back on
track to God.

When we find ourselves in difficulties imposed on us by others—created by
ourselves—and we want out, look to God's Word to take us back to Him. He is
always ready, waiting, and willing to teach us again how to live for Him.

MARCH 22

When Parents Reject Their Children

> The Lord is my light and my salvation; whom shall I fear? the Lord
> is the strength of my life; of whom shall I be afraid? … For in the
> time of trouble he shall hide me in his pavilion: in the secret of his
> tabernacle shall he hide me; he shall set me up upon a rock … When
> my father and my mother forsake me, then the Lord will take me up.
> Teach me thy way, O Lord, and lead me in a plain path, because of
> mine enemies. Deliver me not over unto the will of mine enemies:
> for false witnesses are risen up against me, and such as breathe out
> cruelty. I had fainted, unless I had believed to see the goodness of
> the Lord in the land of the living. Wait on the Lord: be of good
> courage, and he shall strengthen thine heart: wait, I say, on the Lord.
> —Psalm 27:1, 5, 10–14

> And he said unto them, Verily I say unto you, There is no man that
> hath left house, or parents, or brethren, or wife, or children, for
> the kingdom of God's sake, Who shall not receive manifold more
> in this present time, and in the world to come life everlasting.
> —Luke 18:29–30

Some of us learn too early in life that God is the only one we can trust. Perhaps our parents have turned us out of the home because we have turned to the Lord. Such parents do not like this decision of ours, so they throw us out of the house. They do not realize that they have thrown us onto the mercy seat of God, but we should understand as much. Parents may expect us to return to them as we were before we were saved, but this is not the decision of a Christian life, is it?

We may be thankful for any opportunity sent by God to strengthen our faith. God will never forsake us or fail us; it is not in His nature. Life, at the best of times, is fraught with difficulties, but life without parental support adds a burden that young adults cannot easily handle. As believers, we should not worry about this because God shoulders our troubles and keeps us safe from all harm. The phrase "in the secret of his tabernacle" means that He has transferred the life we now live into His dwelling place—a secret place of security from enemies, a secret place of goodness in the face of evil, a secret place of beauty instead of chaos, a secret place of peace instead of strife, and a secret place of healing instead of harm.

When parents reject believing children, life will still be all right in spite of the parents. Let God lead, and let others be amazed at what He does for His beloved children.

Put the Word of God First

Then Joshua built an altar unto the Lord God of Israel in mount
Ebal, As Moses the servant of the Lord commanded the children
of Israel, as it is written in the book of the law of Moses, an altar
of whole stones, over which no man hath lift up any iron: and they
offered thereon burnt offerings unto the Lord, and sacrificed peace
offerings. And he wrote there upon the stones a copy of the law of
Moses, which he wrote in the presence of the children of Israel. And
all Israel, and their elders, and officers, and their judges, stood on
this side the ark and on that side before the priests the Levites, which
bare the ark of the covenant of the Lord, as well the stranger, as he
that was born among them; half of them over against mount Gerizim,
and half of them over against mount Ebal; as Moses the servant of
the Lord had commanded before, that they should bless the people of
Israel. And afterward he read all the words of the law, the blessings
and cursings, according to all that is written in the book of the law.
There was not a word of all that Moses commanded, which Joshua
read not before all the congregation of Israel, with the women, and
the little ones, and the strangers that were conversant among them.
—Joshua 8:30–35

Joshua led the Israelites into the Promised Land. They conquered the city of
Jericho because they followed the Lord's battle plan. They crossed the Jordan
River on dry land because the people and priests observed God's Word to them.
They punished Aachan for refusing to follow God's explicit command about
taking any plunder. They destroyed the city of Ai by following a unique battle
plan from the Lord.

The life of Joshua shows us that everyone benefits from leaders who obey
God. So much success can easily create pride and a sudden downfall, as some
Old Testament stories attest, but Joshua's conduct stands out as exemplary. He
paused for a while and built an altar of uncut stones, like God had instructed. He
copied the Law of Moses onto stone to keep an extra copy handy.

Joshua remembered to put God's Word first in his leadership roles. This
helped everyone else to do the same. God blessed his efforts and honored the
efforts of the people because of Joshua's faith.

Blessedness

Blessed is that man that maketh the Lord his trust, and respecteth
not the proud, nor such as turn aside to lies ... How amiable
are thy tabernacles, O Lord of hosts! My soul longeth, yea, even
fainteth for the courts of the Lord: my heart and my flesh crieth
out for the living God. Yea, the sparrow hath found an house,
and the swallow a nest for herself, where she may lay her young,
even thine altars, O Lord of hosts, my King, and my God. Blessed
are they that dwell in thy house: they will be still praising thee.
Selah ... For a day in thy courts is better than a thousand. I had
rather be a doorkeeper in the house of my God, than to dwell in
the tents of wickedness. For the Lord God is a sun and shield: the
Lord will give grace and glory: no good thing will he withhold
from them that walk uprightly. O Lord of hosts, blessed is the man
that trusteth in thee ... Blessed is the people that know the joyful
sound: they shall walk, O Lord, in the light of thy countenance.
—Psalm 40:4; 84:1–4, 10–12; 89:15

The Bible uses the word "blessed" so many times that we ought to familiar
with its meaning. But it is such an old-fashioned word and so long out of
date that we may not fully appreciate the nuances of meaning because we are so
modern in outlook.

Is blessedness a quality worth understanding and attaining today? Yes, it is.
Blessedness is not a type of holier-than-thou emotion that seems far removed
from everyday living. It is the quality of life represented in a kind of cheerful
happiness that is rooted in the God who created this world. We recognize
blessedness when we hear crickets chirping or birds singing or when we feel
the cool water on a hot day or the warm sun on a chilly day. The best way to
understand blessedness is to reflect upon the natural world.

The physical world that God created hints at the spiritual reality of
blessedness that humans can experience. How do we do this? By seeking God
first, foremost, and sincerely. By finding our strength in Him. By determining to
go with God no matter what else happens. The more we live for God, the more
we find our strength increasing as we live in a state of blessedness that comes
from God.

Hosanna to the King

And when they came nigh to Jerusalem, unto Bethphage and
Bethany, at the mount of Olives, he sendeth forth two of his
disciples, And saith unto them, Go your way into the village over
against you: and as soon as ye be entered into it, ye shall find a
colt tied, whereon never man sat; loose him, and bring him. And
if any man say unto you, Why do ye this? say ye that the Lord
hath need of him; and straightway he will send him hither. And
they went their way, and found the colt tied by the door without
in a place where two ways met; and they loose him. And certain
of them that stood there said unto them, What do ye, loosing the
colt? And they said unto them even as Jesus had commanded: and
they let them go. And they brought the colt to Jesus, and cast their
garments on him; and he sat upon him. And many spread their
garments in the way: and others cut down branches off the trees,
and strawed them in the way. And they that went before, and they
that followed, cried, saying, Hosanna; Blessed is he that cometh in
the name of the Lord: Blessed be the kingdom of our father David,
that cometh in the name of the Lord: Hosanna in the highest.
—Mark 11:1–10

Jesus Christ spent three years teaching his disciples and others from the Law—
the Old Testament Word of God. At the same time, he pointed to Himself
as the fulfillment of the Law. He is the Son of God, the Son of Man, and the
supreme ruler of the universe. Sometimes we learn everything about a topic,
but obvious truths or points still escape us. Principles, ideas, and theories mean
nothing apart from a real situation that requires us to apply what we know
right now.

The early believers suffered from this blindness too. On the day we call
Palm Sunday, Jesus rode into Jerusalem on a young colt of a donkey that God had
reserved for Him to ride. The people recognized Him as their coming King. It
seems like it was about time for them to understand who He was and to finally
"get" the message!

History records that this application of knowledge to reality did not even last
as long as one week. The triumphal entry became the high point of a week that
went steadily downhill, culminating in the crucifixion of the Lord so recently
acclaimed as King. One thing this final week teaches us is that we must always
look beyond (and not accept) the obvious present reality for a future, larger, more
glorious truth. Only in Jesus Christ the King, the risen Savior, do we find hope.

The Grace of God

But there rose up certain of the sect of the Pharisees which
believed, saying, That it was needful to circumcise them, and to
command them to keep the law of Moses. And the apostles and
elders came together for to consider of this matter. And when
there had been much disputing, Peter rose up, and said unto them,
Men and brethren, ye know how that a good while ago God made
choice among us, that the Gentiles by my mouth should hear
the word of the gospel, and believe. And God, which knoweth
the hearts, bare them witness, giving them the Holy Ghost, even
as he did unto us; And put no difference between us and them,
purifying their hearts by faith. Now therefore why tempt ye God,
to put a yoke upon the neck of the disciples, which neither our
fathers nor we were able to bear? But we believe that through the
grace of the Lord Jesus Christ we shall be saved, even as they.
—Acts 15:5–11

Once God had established the church upon the resurrection of Jesus Christ,
church leaders had to clarify and explain exactly what they believed. The
most important doctrine of Christianity is the salvation of the human soul.
Because Christianity comes out of Judaism, many early Christians were converted
Jews who felt that circumcision should still be considered a condition of salvation.
But so many new converts were turning to the Lord from pagan religions or no
religion at all that the church leaders were no longer sure about this.

The first church council met in Jerusalem to settle the matter of the
requirements for salvation. They went over the facts of the faith and the words
of Jesus. They affirmed that Jesus Christ died on the cross to save sinners—
all sinners—completely. They reasoned logically that the addition of other
conditions to the salvation of the human soul means that the grace of God is
not really sufficient to save souls from sin.

When we look for churches to worship in, we want to look for the single
message that Jesus Christ saves from sin.

Explaining the Right Answer

Now in the fifteenth year of the reign of Tiberius Caesar, the Word of God came unto John the son of Zacharias in the wilderness … Then said he to the multitude that came forth to be baptized of him, O generation of vipers, who hath warned you to flee from the wrath to come? Bring forth therefore fruits worthy of repentance, and begin not to say within yourselves, We have Abraham to our father: for I say unto you, That God is able of these stones to raise up children unto Abraham. And now also the axe is laid unto the root of the trees: every tree therefore which bringeth not forth good fruit is hewn down, and cast into the fire. And the people asked him, saying, What shall we do then? He answereth and saith unto them, He that hath two coats, let him impart to him that hath none; and he that hath meat, let him do likewise. Then came also publicans to be baptized, and said unto him, Master, what shall we do? And he said unto them, Exact no more than that which is appointed you. And the soldiers likewise demanded of him, saying, And what shall we do? And he said unto them, Do violence to no man, neither accuse any falsely; and be content with your wages.
—Luke 3:1a, 2b, 7–14

Successful popular speakers target specific audiences, so when we see the current themes on public television or in person, we usually know right away whether or not it is the kind of information we might be interested in hearing. The best kind of speaker has a more universal message that appeals to a broad audience, but even so, the audience represents different outlooks. The skilled speaker adjusts his message to every type of person. John the Baptist was a powerful and gifted speaker. He gave a message of repentance and forgiveness for sins, a universal remedy for a universal problem. Crowds came to listen to this desert-trained man who wore camel's hair clothing and ate locust pods and honey as his dietary staples.

John knew he needed to reach different segments of society in his audience. He spoke to the Jewish segment of his audience first. He referred them to the Old Testament Scriptures, with which they were familiar. John spoke next to individual citizens and inquirers to tell them to share their goods, an antidote to greed. John spoke again to municipal employees to tell them to collect only the required tax and no more, an antidote to the crime of graft. John spoke finally to federal employees to tell them not to abuse their authority by accusing people falsely.

John the Baptist dealt with the sin of greed to four distinct groups of people. He spoke the same message, adapting it for the understanding of every type of hearer.

Believe the Truth

And they sent out unto him their disciples with the
Herodians, saying, Master, we know that thou art true, and
teachest the way of God in truth, neither carest thou for
any man: for thou regardest not the person of men.
—Matthew 22:16

Verily, verily, I say unto you, He that heareth my word, and believeth
on him that sent me, hath everlasting life, and shall not come into
condemnation; but is passed from death unto life. Verily, verily, I
say unto you, The hour is coming, and now is, when the dead shall
hear the voice of the Son of God: and they that hear shall live. For
as the Father hath life in himself; so hath he given to the Son to have
life in himself; And hath given him authority to execute judgment
also, because he is the Son of man ... I can of mine own self do
nothing: as I hear, I judge: and my judgment is just; because I seek
not mine own will, but the will of the Father which hath sent me.
—John 5:24–27, 30

The occult and its evil practices exert an increasing influence in our culture today. The occult wants us to believe that we can communicate with spirits, sort of like crossing over from life to death. But the Son of God has a completely different kind of message.

Jesus tells us how to cross over from death to life. When people forget, ignore, or rebel against the truth, the spiritual side of human nature will seek spiritual fulfillment somewhere else. The occult lures people by preying on human guilt and other emotions. Séances purport to communicate with loved ones who have crossed from life to death. Is this really true? No, it is not, and this false thinking is unacceptable in God's sight. It is more profitable to be concerned about passing from death to life than the other way around.

Only Jesus holds the true answer to meaning in this life. When we pay attention to the Word of God by believing that God sent His Son, Jesus Christ, to be the means by which our sins are forgiven, Jesus assures us that we pass from death to life. God the Father is the source of all life. He shares His life with God the Son. Jesus Christ tells the truth because God is the truth. We should believe only the truth.

Looking Ahead

> These words spake Jesus, and lifted up his eyes to heaven, and
> said, Father, the hour is come; glorify thy Son, that thy Son also
> may glorify thee: As thou hast given him power over all flesh,
> that he should give eternal life to as many as thou hast given him.
> And this is life eternal, that they might know thee the only true
> God, and Jesus Christ, whom thou hast sent. I have glorified
> thee on the earth: I have finished the work which thou gavest me
> to do. And now, O Father, glorify thou me with thine own self
> with the glory which I had with thee before the world was.
> —John 17:1–5

Unlike the rest of us, Jesus Christ knew exactly what was going to happen next in His life. He also knew that He had done exactly what the Father wanted Him to do. Now He waited upon God to continue doing exactly what the Father wanted Him to do. When Jesus prayed for Himself in the Mount of Olives garden, He knew that the time and the hour of His death was fast approaching.

He did not really want to die—no one does—but He willingly gave His life for us. He understood that no one else was either capable or willing to accomplish this feat of human salvation. Jesus also knew that eternal life was at hand for all of us who believe in Him. It is understood that without the shedding of blood, there is no remission of sins, so Jesus Christ gave His life willingly as the final sacrifice for sin, sufficient to save all of us sinners, both now and forever.

Jesus also knew that His glorification was nigh. Because He shares our human nature as the Son of Man, He needed the help of the Father to obey God. Jesus knew that once He did what no one else was qualified to do, we might look ahead with Him to eternal life and fellowship with God in heaven. We cannot know ahead of time, as Jesus did, the events of our lives, but we can trust the future to Him when we go with God all the way, as Jesus did.

The Evil of Sorcery

Then certain of the vagabond Jews, exorcists, took upon them to call
over them which had evil spirits the name of the Lord Jesus, saying,
We adjure you by Jesus whom Paul preacheth. And there were seven
sons of one Sceva, a Jew, and chief of the priests, which did so. And
the evil spirit answered and said, Jesus I know, and Paul I know; but
who are ye? And the man in whom the evil spirit was leaped on them,
and overcame them, and prevailed against them, so that they fled out
of that house naked and wounded. And this was known to all the Jews
and Greeks also dwelling at Ephesus; and fear fell on them all, and the
name of the Lord Jesus was magnified. And many that believed came,
and confessed, and shewed their deeds. Many of them also which used
curious arts brought their books together, and burned them before all
men: and they counted the price of them, and found it fifty thousand
pieces of silver. So mightly grew the Word of God and prevailed.
—Acts 19:13–20

And the seventy returned again with joy, saying, Lord, even
the devils are subject unto us through thy name. And he said
unto them, I beheld Satan as lightning fall from heaven.
—Luke 10:17–18

Philosophy courses often teach the ancient Greek idea that evil and good
are equal and opposite forces. Philosophical thinking like this objectifies
abstract concepts whose corollaries may be all too real in daily life. Thinking like
this also means that God is not really very great or good, and His Word cannot
be entirely true. In this view, Satan and evil spirits are seen as on par with God,
and evil is not considered very bad after all.

Because many forms of sorcery and witchcraft have become a feature
of modern life in our nation, believers may tend to believe this lie about the
similarities between good and evil. It is important to remember that only God is
good and that evil is a corruption of good—a complete and willful rejection of
goodness. What appears to be merely a board game, a leisure time activity, or an
interesting philosophical speculation is just that—an appearance and not a reality.

Satan masquerades as an angel of light. This means that he will use any means
to convince us of both the harmlessness and insignificance of evil and the allure of
its associated practices. We should be aware of the tactics of Satan and firmly reject
all forms of sorcery and witchcraft forever. When we believe the truth, God makes
us aware of sin and how evil it is. The Bible is true; anything less leads us astray.

Quality of Life

It is a good thing to give thanks unto the Lord, and to sing praises
unto thy name, O Most High: To shew forth thy lovingkindness in
the morning, and thy faithfulness every night, Upon an instrument
of ten strings, and upon the psaltery; upon the harp with a solemn
sound. For thou, Lord, hast made me glad through thy work: I
will triumph in the works of thy hands. O Lord, how great are
thy works! and thy thoughts are very deep ... The righteous shall
flourish like the palm tree: he shall grow like a cedar in Lebanon.
Those that be planted in the house of the Lord shall flourish in
the courts of our God. They shall still bring forth fruit in old
age; they shall be fat and flourishing; To shew that the Lord is
upright: he is my rock, and there is no unrighteousness in him.
—Psalm 92:1–5, 12–15

Because this nation experienced a huge baby boom after World War II, the
country now faces a large and aging population. Because technological
and medical advances now make it possible to cure diseases and prolong life,
many grandparents have had to change their preconceived ideas about older life.
Grandchildren may be aware of these significant changes that occurred before
their birth, but they may still wonder how older adults can continue to maintain a
quality of life in spite of advancing age. Quality of life begins when we are young.
We can do nothing about the childhood we were given, but we can do everything
necessary in our adult lives. God gives us a longer stretch of adult life in which
to make godly decisions that affect the rest of our days.

Quality of life begins by praising God for His love, faithfulness, and
goodness to us. We need to think about the specifics of our lives and give thanks
to God for them, whatever they are! We need to search the Word of God so that
we may learn that the thoughts of God are higher and deeper than our own. We
need to be actively involved in the life of our church.

When we place God first in our lives, we stay fresh and seemingly youthful,
because the Lord fills us more than anything else. He gave us physical life first
and spiritual life second. He wants our lives to be happy and useful for His glory
for as long as He sees fit.

APRIL 1

Fooling Around

The fear of the Lord is the beginning of knowledge: but fools despise
wisdom and instruction ... Wisdom hath builded her house, she hath
hewn out her seven pillars ... Whoso is simple, let him turn in hither:
as for him that wanteth understanding, she saith to him ... Forsake
the foolish, and live; and go in the way of understanding ... A
foolish woman is clamorous: she is simple, and knoweth nothing ...
Whoso is simple, let him turn in hither: and as for him that wanteth
understanding, she saith to him ... But he knoweth not that the
dead are there; and that her guests are in the depths of hell.
—Proverbs 1:7; 9:1, 4, 6, 13, 16, 18

This is the day that has been designated as April Fool's Day, a day when our
best friends, who may also be practical jokers, delight to fool others in silly
ways. The unsuspecting coworker, the new teacher, the gullible friend, and the
naïve newcomer must all beware today. We commonly think of fools as gullible
or easily duped, as if they lack enough common sense to figure out what is really
going on. The hallmark of a modern fool is the quality of being taken advantage
of unwittingly while the rest of us laugh a lot at the fool.

According to the Bible, the nature of a fool is quite different. Being a
fool belongs to the sphere of morality more than to the domain of drama. The
Bible also contrasts fools with wise people, so we get an image of the fool by
comparison. Fools are people who hate the wisdom, discipline, and reproof of
the Lord; they live according to their own lights. Wise people are those who
turn to God in obedience; they live according to God's commands, even when
they do not fully understand them. Lady Wisdom and Lady Folly personify how
biblical foolishness works. Lady Wisdom calls out to the dummies (all of us) to
come to her house. Lady Folly does exactly the same thing. Which house will
we choose to enter?

When we flirt with evil, we are fools in God's sight. We choose death,
whether we are cognizant of it or not. When we choose God, we choose life and
the understanding of how to live it. We should not be tempted to be a fool—even
for a day.

From Restlessness to Satisfaction

O give thanks unto the Lord, for he is good: for his mercy
endureth for ever. Let the redeemed of the Lord say so, whom
he hath redeemed from the hand of the enemy; And gathered
them out of the lands, from the east, and from the west, from
the north, and from the south. They wandered in the wilderness
in a solitary way; they found no city to dwell in. Hungry and
thirsty, their soul fainted in them. Then they cried unto the Lord
in their trouble, and he delivered them out of their distresses.
And he led them forth by the right way, that they might go to
a city of habitation. Oh that men would praise the Lord for his
goodness, and for his wonderful works to the children of men!
—Psalm 107:1–8

We live in a more transient world today than twenty or fifty years ago. The reasons for travel are numerous, but the ability to buy a plane ticket to anywhere in the world allows us to wander the earth, if we are so inclined. If we are shrewd enough, we know how to earn enough money in each place we visit to keep ourselves and save up for the next journey.

So how can we understand this psalm about people who wander in desert wastelands today? A solitary person who wanders in a wilderness sounds like a different form of transience than we may imagine. Some people live transitory lives because the job moves them or causes them to travel them around the country frequently. Transience can make the heart ache for permanence because for most of us, a house evokes the quality of permanence by becoming the place where we finally settle down for decades. Some people wander from one type of job to another, trying to find a suitable fit. Working long hours at a string of unfulfilling tasks eventually becomes exhausting and makes the soul hunger and thirst for predictable working hours. In both of these trying circumstances, it can seem like God is against us, but the Bible assures us that God is good and bears long-lasting love and goodwill toward us.

When we acknowledge His sovereignty, He leads us on a straight path—the one He has chosen for us. None of us needs to wander aimlessly through the desert wastelands of life. Let us cry out to Him often.

APRIL 3

Prayer

Hear me when I call, O God of my righteousness: thou hast
enlarged me when I was in distress; have mercy upon me, and
hear my prayer ... But know that the Lord hath set apart him
that is godly for himself: the Lord will hear when I call unto
him ... Offer the sacrifices of righteousness, and put your trust
in the Lord. There be many that say, Who will shew us any good?
Lord, lift thou up the light of thy countenance upon us. Thou
hast put gladness in my heart, more than in the time that their
corn and their wine increased. I will both lay me down in peace,
and sleep: for thou, Lord, only makest me dwell in safety.
—Psalm 4:1, 3, 5–8

Do we ever think that the psalmist was shouting out to God in sheer
exasperation? When words are no more than words on a page, they can
seem very tame and spiritless, but look again. The psalmist is heatedly demanding
an immediate response from the Lord. As soon as he vents his frustration, he
lapses into a holier kind of writing that we associate with pious and prayerful
believers.

Maybe we have an inaccurate idea of prayer. And maybe the psalmist realizes
that it is all right to be human and frustrated as long as we turn to God for final
answers in the end. Does God answer the prayers of everyone? No. He hears the
prayers of those who believe in Him, yet He may not answer immediately. Waiting
is difficult for believers in distress and need, yet God says He has set apart the
godly for His special pleasure.

With that in mind, it may be that getting answers to prayers does not matter
as much as being in a right relationship with God. Whatever stress, turmoil,
problem, or difficulty we face, we can always remember that God keeps us safe,
God shows His goodness to us, and God enables us to rest contentedly and fully
in Him.

Words That Have Hurt Me

A righteous man falling down before the wicked is as a
troubled fountain, and a corrupt spring ... He that hath no
rule over his own spirit is like a city that is broken down,
and without walls ... As the bird by wandering, as the
swallow by flying, so the curse causeless shall not come.
—Proverbs 25:26, 28; 26:2

But I say unto you which hear, Love your enemies, do
good to them which hate you, Bless them that curse
you, and pray for them which despitefully use you.
—Luke 6:27–28

Bless them which persecute you: bless, and curse not.
—Romans 12:14

One of the greatest benefits about growing up and leaving our parents' home is the freedom that comes to us. We can make our own decisions without interference or questioning. Two things happen almost as soon as we step onto the college campus. First of all, there are all kinds of people asking us to engage in all kinds of activities. Second of all, we realize that we have carried preconceived ideas with us, and these ideas can drag us down when we want to succeed.

As young adults, we must deal with both preconceptions. We must take control of both our physical and our emotional lives. Children sometimes bear the scars of deadly, pointed, ill-timed, and maliciously intended words well into their early adulthood years, but this should not happen! Whenever we are faced with a problem, the Bible always tells how to think about it because the Bible is true. To begin with, what kind of person spoke the horrible words—a person without self-control who blurts out anything in anger, under pressure, or at any moment. The person who loomed so large and ugly in childhood is no better than a deserted, tumbledown ghost town, according to the Bible. Did those words sting? Yes, they did. Do those words count? No, they don't.

Unmerited insults do not stay with us. God has assured us that they do not remain with us. God has said so and wants us to put this aspect of childhood to rest immediately. College is time to give ourselves a fresh start for the rest of our lives.

APRIL 5

Gardening

Another parable put he forth unto them, saying, The kingdom of
heaven is like to a grain of mustard seed, which a man took, and
sowed in his field: Which indeed is the least of all seeds: but when
it is grown, it is the greatest among herbs, and becometh a tree, so
that the birds of the air come and lodge in the branches thereof.
—Matthew 13:31–32

And out of the ground made the Lord God to grow every tree that
is pleasant to the sight, and good for food; the tree of life also in the
midst of the garden, and the tree of knowledge of good and evil.
—Genesis 2:9

The righteous shall flourish like the palm tree:
he shall grow like a cedar in Lebanon.
—Psalm 92:12

For the seed shall be prosperous; the vine shall give her fruit, and the
ground shall give her increase, and the heavens shall give their dew;
and I will cause the remnant of this people to possess all these things.
—Zechariah 8:12

Certain sensual sights and experiences always give us hope: planting a small
seed in the soil, watching the birds build nests, smelling the arrival of
springtime, admiring the efforts of a toddler, or listening to the sound of a
waterfall. Springtime is a time of renewal for the earth and all that grows in the
soil.

After a cold winter, everyone loves the sight of tiny sprouts, green flashes
of color, and full-blown foliage that replaces the harsh white of winter and the
dull brown of melt-offs. The air smells sweeter, fresher, and more invigorating.
Those who plant the smallest garden marvel at the growth process. Some seeds,
as fine as dust, germinate into beautiful flowers. Even enormous trees begin with
a tiny, seemingly insignificant seed.

Jesus lets believers know that Christian growth and maturity is as marvelous
as the rest of creation. One small, seemingly unknown and insignificant life takes
root in the soil of God's Word. The initial growth may not be noticeable, but
the continued growth is so strong that others benefit from one person. Never
overlook the importance of individual obedience.

The Lord's Prayer

And he said unto them, When ye pray, say, Our Father which art
in heaven, Hallowed be thy name. Thy kingdom come. Thy will be
done, as in heaven, so in earth. Give us day by day our daily bread.
And forgive us our sins; for we also forgive every one that is indebted
to us. And lead us not into temptation; but deliver us from evil.
—Luke 11:2–4

Bless the Lord, O my soul: and all that is within me, bless his holy
name. Bless the Lord, O my soul, and forget not all his benefits:
Who forgiveth all thine iniquities; who healeth all thy diseases.
—Psalm 103:1–3

The Lord's Prayer, or the Pater Noster, is a familiar prayer, but we should not treat it familiarly. Jesus was giving us a formulaic way to remember some basic facts about our faith, so memorizing the prayer is still beneficial to us when we face trials. To assure His hearers that He taught nothing new, Jesus spoke in agreement with Old Testament precepts that had already been promulgated.

God is our Father. If we have no father or if we have a horrible father, we may need to figure out the opposite qualities in order to draw closer to God the Father. God is holy. If we are more familiar with profanity, filth, and sin, we need to put these things out of our minds and lives. We can hang around godly believers to learn what holiness acts like so we can do the same. God provides for us. If we grew up with poverty or with attitudes of self-sufficiency, we must learn to always remember that God has granted life, health, and skills to us and our families to enable them to provide for the well-being of the immediate family. He continues to do the same for us now.

God forgives our sins and keeps us away from temptation when we ask Him. None of us can survive on our own, so this prayer helps us acknowledge the powerful presence of God who loves us and takes care of every aspect of life.

The Road to Success

And when his brethren saw that their father loved him more than
all his brethren, they hated him, and could not speak peaceably unto
him ... Then there passed by Midianites merchantmen; and they drew
and lifted up Joseph out of the pit, and sold Joseph to the Ishmeelites
for twenty pieces of silver: and they brought Joseph into Egypt ...
And Joseph was brought down to Egypt; and Potiphar, an officer of
Pharaoh, captain of the guard, an Egyptian, bought him of the hands
of the Ishmeelites, which had brought him down thither ... And it
came to pass from the time that he had made him overseer in his
house, and over all that he had, that the Lord blessed the Egyptian's
house for Joseph's sake; and the blessing of the Lord was upon all that
he had in the house, and in the field ... And Joseph's master took him,
and put him into the prison, a place where the king's prisoners were
bound: and he was there in the prison ... The keeper of the prison
looked not to any thing that was under his hand; because the Lord
was with him, and that which he did, the Lord made it to prosper.
—Genesis 37:4, 28; 39:1, 5, 20, 23

A recent and popular musical portrayed the biblical Joseph as a young man
who saw opportunity, grabbed it, and succeeded against all odds. We like
this kind of story, but when it comes to real life, we need to separate fact from
fiction.

Popular thinking portrays the road to success as one of upward mobility,
slowly but steadily achieving the pinnacle of personal success. We may have
read about personal success stories just like this, but most of us are unlikely to
personally know someone like this. The story of Joseph tells a tale of success, but
it is the opposite of what we admire and hope for. From a distance of more than
two millennia of time, it seems clear that God had great plans for Joseph, but at
the time, it is doubtful that Joseph would have agreed. We hope his childhood
was happy. We know his teenage and young adult years teeter-tottered between
love and hate, freedom and imprisonment, honor and disrespect. We should try
to imagine the difficult psychological trauma of such wide swings of lifestyles
and emotions in a span of about twenty years, from late teens to late thirties.

When thinking about what has occurred in our lives, we can learn from
Joseph to give God credit for everything. God clearly blessed Joseph for his
obedience and patience. He will do as much for us when we look to him as well.

Talking to God

And he said unto me, Son of man, stand upon thy feet, and I
will speak unto thee. And the spirit entered into me when he
spake unto me, and set me upon my feet, that I heard him that
spake unto me. And he said unto me, Son of man, I send thee
to the children of Israel, to a rebellious nation that hath rebelled
against me: they and their fathers have transgressed against
me, even unto this very day ... And thou shalt speak my words
unto them, whether they will hear, or whether they will forbear:
for they are most rebellious ... Behold, I have made thy face
strong against their faces, and thy forehead strong against their
foreheads ... So the spirit lifted me up, and took me away, and
I went in bitterness, in the heat of my spirit; but the hand of the
Lord was strong upon me. Then I came to them of the captivity
at Telabib, that dwelt by the river of Chebar, and I sat where they
sat, and remained there astonished among them seven days.
—Ezekiel 2:1–3, 7; 3:8, 14–15

There may be times when we wish we could have a personal, sit-down, face-to-face conversation with the Lord, but we know that God has arranged our communication with Him differently today. The Holy Spirit indwells believers, and He prays for us with groans that words cannot express; God the Holy Spirit gets our deepest feelings and needs across to God the Father. Before Jesus ascended to heaven after His death and resurrection, God did sometimes speak directly to believers when He wanted them to carry out a specific task.

A conversation with God is an overwhelming and exhausting transaction. God is holy, and no human can feel anything but inadequate by comparison. Ezekiel was chosen by God for such a unique communication. God gave instructions to Ezekiel one bit of information at a time. First, God told Ezekiel to whom he would minister. It didn't sound too difficult to minister to his own kind of people, but Ezekiel knew how far from God they had strayed. He knew that they lived in exile because of rebellion and sin. Yet God has a solution for every difficulty. He made Ezekiel just as unyielding and as hardened as Ezekiel's congregation. This made Ezekiel bitterly angry, even though he knew that God was with him. To digest this information from God, Ezekiel went down to the river and sat there for seven days, overwhelmed.

We can learn from Ezekiel that God gives all of us time to understand what He wants us to do.

APRIL 9

The Source of Power

> John answered and said, A man can receive nothing, except it be
> given him from heaven ... For he whom God hath sent speaketh
> the words of God: for God giveth not the Spirit by measure unto
> him ... Then answered Jesus and said unto them, Verily, verily, I say
> unto you, The Son can do nothing of himself, but what he seeth the
> Father do: for what things soever he doeth, these also doeth the Son
> likewise ... For the Father judgeth no man, but hath committed all
> judgment unto the Son: That all men should honour the Son, even
> as they honour the Father. He that honoureth not the Son honoureth
> not the Father which hath sent him ... I can of mine own self do
> nothing: as I hear, I judge: and my judgment is just; because I seek
> not mine own will, but the will of the Father which hath sent me.
> —John 3:27, 34; 5:19, 22–23, 30

When we watch the televised Olympics or when a presidential election is underway, we start thinking about power—big power. More power than most of us ever expect to possess. But we wonder about power in the lives of those larger-than-life figures who dominate the news media for a few months. The desire to achieve more, to be a better person, or to live an upwardly mobile life exerts its grasp on most of us.

Because we are made in God's image, our brains always think that something bigger and better exists out there—somewhere. We are actually right, but where is that power found, and how do we appropriate it for ourselves? Most of us know that we will never compete as world-class athletes or get elected to the highest national office. Still, power comes from the God who created the heavens and earth. God gives this power through the Holy Spirit—without limit. This means that God wants us to live powerful lives, but in His way, not in the human way. God subjects everything to His Son, Jesus Christ, yet Jesus Christ can only imitate the Father, and He wants only to please the Father.

So the human desire for power needs to be subjugated to God through Jesus Christ and the Holy Spirit, because God has ordained the power sources of the universe in this way. The closer we get to God, the more power our lives will have from Him.

Pay Attention to God

Keep thy foot when thou goest to the house of God, and be more
ready to hear, than to give the sacrifice of fools: for they consider
not that they do evil. Be not rash with thy mouth, and let not thine
heart be hasty to utter any thing before God: for God is in heaven,
and thou upon earth: therefore let thy words be few ... Suffer not
thy mouth to cause thy flesh to sin; neither say thou before the angel,
that it was an error: wherefore should God be angry at thy voice,
and destroy the work of thine hands? For in the multitude of dreams
and many words there are also divers vanities: but fear thou God.
—Ecclesiastes 5:1–2, 6–7

We don't really need statistics to tell us that we all watch too much media, do we? Unless we have made a deliberate decision to avoid the media, we are influenced by it. We live in such a media-oriented time that any face emblazoned before us becomes very big in our eyes. The self-centered and antisocial nature of the media makes us want to be like that visual image. Pro athletes, pop singers, and actors seem larger than life. It is easy to desire the big name that we will never possess. In light of the world in which we live, reading the Bible and paying attention to what it says becomes more of a necessity because of the multitude of distractions that contend for our time and attention.

Do we think God is as big as those popular people in our minds? Or do we relegate Him to a very small, dark, corner in the back of our thoughts? Even though the Bible remains the best-selling book of all time, God is still not popular in the current sense of the word. But He is ever-present, and the Bible assures us that God watches us and listens to us. God is always paying attention to us, so we should pay attention to Him.

When we refuse to let other faces compete for our attention and when we knock others down a few pegs on the scale of importance in our lives, we are on our way to standing in awe of God, and this is where He wants us to be.

The Beauty of the Truth

But was rebuked for his iniquity: the dumb ass speaking with
man's voice forbad the madness of the prophet. These are wells
without water, clouds that are carried with a tempest; to whom
the mist of darkness is reserved for ever. For when they speak
great swelling words of vanity, they allure through the lusts of the
flesh, through much wantonness, those that were clean escaped
from them who live in error. While they promise them liberty,
they themselves are the servants of corruption: for of whom a
man is overcome, of the same is he brought in bondage. For if
after they have escaped the pollutions of the world through the
knowledge of the Lord and Saviour Jesus Christ, they are again
entangled therein, and overcome, the latter end is worse with them
than the beginning. For it had been better for them not to have
known the way of righteousness, than, after they have known it,
to turn from the holy commandment delivered unto them.
—2 Peter 2:16–21

Many religions offer countless fine words about how to live or how to attain
godliness. But the quality of the Bible is superior to any other religious
or spiritual information because it tells the truth. The Bible is not a clever story
invented by human beings; it is a historical account of how God has intervened
in human history and how Jesus Christ lived, died, and came to life again in the
presence of hundreds of reliable witnesses.

The Bible is not a confusing message spoken in a vague way by men or
women; the New Testament both confirms and amplifies the message of the
Old Testament prophets. The Bible is not a dark message that urges us to join
in with the worst of this bad world; it is the glorious light that explains how to
escape all the badness by coming to God in truth. The Bible is not a private
human interpretation with a godly message; it is a cohesive message from God.

The Bible was written by over forty writers who lived in different centuries.
They dwelled in different countries and spoke different languages. Only the Holy
Spirit can carry men along in the mind of God to tell us where we have come
from and where we ought to be going.

Who Is Jesus?

And king Herod heard of him; (for his name was spread abroad:) and
he said, That John the Baptist was risen from the dead, and therefore
mighty works do shew forth themselves in him. Others said, That
it is Elias. And others said, That it is a prophet, or as one of the
prophets ... And there was a cloud that overshadowed them: and a
voice came out of the cloud, saying, This is my beloved Son: hear him.
—Mark 6:14–15; 9:7

Some people refuse to believe in Jesus or anything in the Bible unless science
can prove it is true. This is a very vague and inaccurate way to talk. When
it comes to proof, only two kinds of proof are admissible, and each type serves
different purposes. Scientific proof uses repetition of the same conditions to
"prove" a fact. Historic proof uses eyewitness accounts or the testimony of
witnesses to "prove" that an event that has truly happened. So trying to prove
anything about Jesus by science does not really make sense.

There is no historical doubt that Jesus lived in a specific time, a specific
place, and a specific culture, yet most people continue to think that His identity
is up for grabs. Whoever or whatever we think He is or was seems like a good
answer for us, isn't that right? The trouble with believing any old thing is that it
may not be true.

King Herod and others faced this same quandary, and they were trying
to figure out who Jesus is. How do we know what is true? We believe a reliable
authority to ascertain historical truth. Some religions today still believe that Jesus
Christ is only a prophet. This means that He was a good and holy man. Some
religions believe in Jesus as a good teacher whose lessons still apply to us today.
Some religions think of Jesus as a man or superman, but definitely human. He
did great deeds, He said fine words, and Jesus is just a little or maybe a lot better
than the rest of us.

But we should always remember that the Bible is the truth and that God the
Father speaks only the truth. This book is the only reliable authority that we can
believe in without any doubt. Jesus is the Son of God, whom the Father God loves
very much. What will we do with this truth? Turn to Him in repentance? Ignore
Him? Listen to Him? He will change the life that turns to Him.

Follow God Closely

And I commanded Joshua at that time, saying, Thine eyes have seen all that the Lord your God hath done unto these two kings: so shall the Lord do unto all the kingdoms whither thou passest. Ye shall not fear them: for the Lord your God he shall fight for you. Now therefore hearken, O Israel, unto the statutes and unto the judgments, which I teach you, for to do them, that ye may live, and go in and possess the land which the Lord God of your fathers giveth you. Ye shall not add unto the word which I command you, neither shall ye diminish ought from it, that ye may keep the commandments of the Lord your God which I command you ... Only take heed to thyself, and keep thy soul diligently, lest thou forget the things which thine eyes have seen, and lest they depart from thy heart all the days of thy life: but teach them thy sons, and thy sons' sons ... And he declared unto you his covenant, which he commanded you to perform, even ten commandments; and he wrote them upon two tables of stone.
—Deuteronomy 3:21–22; 4:1–2, 9, 13

When we follow God closely, He leads us with the certainty and strength that come from Him. Moses was the greatest leader of the Israelites, but because he had displeased God, the Lord forbade him from entering the Promised Land. As the giver of the Law, Moses understood the justice of God; he could not excuse his fault. So he encouraged Joshua and the nation to follow God closely. He told them to observe all His laws because God would fight for them. His leadership faltered at times, but his inability to enter the Promised Land strengthened his commitment to follow God exactly.

His life shows us how important it is to continue to live a godly life all the way to the end. We must obey God's commands. We should not add more rules to God's commands any more than we should ignore (subtract from) them. God's Word is completely sufficient on its own. We should remember the events and circumstances by which God had led us to the events of today. We can write them down and figure out how to explain them to others.

Experience and age will give us the knack of explaining them to our children. Let us obey the Ten Commandments, maintain a close relationship with God, enjoy good family relationships, and get along with others when we follow the Ten Commandments.

Like Light Shining in the Darkness

For God, who commanded the light to shine out of darkness,
hath shined in our hearts, to give the light of the knowledge of
the glory of God in the face of Jesus Christ. But we have this
treasure in earthen vessels, that the excellency of the power may
be of God, and not of us ... For we which live are always delivered
unto death for Jesus' sake, that the life also of Jesus might be made
manifest in our mortal flesh ... For all things are for your sakes,
that the abundant grace might through the thanksgiving of many
redound to the glory of God. For which cause we faint not; but
though our outward man perish, yet the inward man is renewed
day by day ... While we look not at the things which are seen, but
at the things which are not seen: for the things which are seen
are temporal; but the things which are not seen are eternal.
—2 Corinthians 4:6–7, 11, 15–16, 18

The spiritual life shares some features with the physical life, but like all comparisons, they fall short of the reality. When we first turn to the Lord in repentance, we feel a sense of wonder that God lifted us up to Him. Soon, ordinary life gets going around us, and it becomes easy to forget that God's light shines out of us in the darkness of the world. It becomes easy for the spiritual life and the physical life to become more similar than different.

The new life we live in Christ is really a death to the sinful self. Death sounds horrible, but when we think of how incomparably great and glorious our God truly is, there is no question which life is better: the old or the new.

Dying to self and losing ourselves in Him is the way God helps us to be more like Him. The world does not need us or our talents; the world needs God. This means that others need to see that the quality of life we now live is completely different from theirs. When we focus on the aspects of life that cannot be seen by the naked eye, others see the hidden side of life that is perceived by the human spirit. All of life is a gift from God—this life, the saved life. When His grace permeates this life, God is preparing us to live in His presence forever.

Seeking Good for All

For thus saith the Lord unto the house of Israel, Seek ye me,
and ye shall live … Seek good, and not evil, that ye may live:
and so the Lord, the God of hosts, shall be with you, as ye
have spoken. Hate the evil, and love the good, and establish
judgment in the gate: it may be that the Lord God of hosts will
be gracious unto the remnant of Joseph … But let judgment
run down as waters, and righteousness as a mighty stream.
—Amos 5:4, 14–15, 24

Our society today separates social conduct from spiritual welfare, which is a terrible mistake because the two are closely linked in God's mind. He created all humans, so He ought to know, shouldn't He? When a society forgets God, they tend to enact laws to suit the accepted mores of the day. Sound familiar?

The thinking goes like this: many people drink, cohabit, use drugs, gamble, have unwanted pregnancies, and wish to die; therefore, we should make a law to say that the behavior is really legal. As a result, drinking is acceptable, living together is standard, drug usage is rising, gambling is all right, out-of-wedlock pregnancies are normal, and euthanasia is a personal right. The majority rules, but is it really a majority? If these standards were really as widely held as our society would like us to think, this nation would have died already.

God is the only majority vote we should listen to. He has given us the laws of good conduct for all people. Follow His laws, and God blesses the nation. God's laws remind us that laws should serve the public good, not personal preferences. When we seek the good standards of God, we seek a good quality of life for everyone.

National Judgment

The burden of Nineveh. The book of the vision of Nahum the
Elkoshite. God is jealous, and the Lord revengeth; the Lord
revengeth, and is furious; the Lord will take vengeance on his
adversaries, and he reserveth wrath for his enemies. The Lord is slow
to anger, and great in power, and will not at all acquit the wicked:
the Lord hath his way in the whirlwind and in the storm, and the
clouds are the dust of his feet. He rebuketh the sea, and maketh it
dry, and drieth up all the rivers: Bashan languisheth, and Carmel,
and the flower of Lebanon languisheth. The mountains quake at
him, and the hills melt, and the earth is burned at his presence,
yea, the world, and all that dwell therein. Who can stand before his
indignation? and who can abide in the fierceness of his anger? his
fury is poured out like fire, and the rocks are thrown down by him.
—Nahum 1:1–6

Ancient Nineveh was the city of sin where God sent Jonah, the reluctant
missionary. Much to his surprise and outrage, Nineveh heeded the stern
message from Jonah that they would be overthrown in forty days if they did not
turn to God in repentance for sin.

They actually believed the message from God, and God blessed them for
their faith. They honored God for about two hundred years before returning to
their sinful ways. At that later date in time, God judged the nation. The seemingly
invincible nation fell to the Babylonians and the Medes.

One message is clear from the history of Nineveh. When civilizations
advance in skills, technology, goods, business, population, and trade, they begin
to feel secure in their own abilities. This is always an inaccurate picture of human
ability because only God gives various abilities to individuals, as He chooses. This
means that groups of individuals who belong to the nation (companies, families,
etc.) possess God-given gifts too. Self-sufficiency is always sinful because it
forgets the source of power, the wellspring of life, and the giver of every gift.
Nations are only as strong as their individual citizens—citizens who humble
themselves before the God who created them.

Teach Others the Right Way

> And David went up, and all Israel, to Baalah, that is, to Kirjathjearim,
> which belonged to Judah, to bring up thence the ark of God the
> Lord, that dwelleth between the cherubims, whose name is called
> on it. And they carried the ark of God in a new cart out of the
> house of Abinadab: and Uzza and Ahio drave the cart. And David
> and all Israel played before God with all their might, and with
> singing, and with harps, and with psalteries, and with timbrels,
> and with cymbals, and with trumpets. And when they came unto
> the threshingfloor of Chidon, Uzza put forth his hand to hold the
> ark; for the oxen stumbled. And the anger of the Lord was kindled
> against Uzza, and he smote him, because he put his hand to the
> ark: and there he died before God … And David was afraid of God
> that day, saying, How shall I bring the ark of God home to me?
> —1 Chronicles 13:6–10, 12

As a tremendously successful leader, commander, and king, no one usually questioned the decisions of David. When David became king, he decided to move the Ark of God from the private residence of Abinadab to Jerusalem, the new capital city. This seemed like a good idea to everyone, so they began the task.

The problem was that in King Saul's time, no one had ever consulted the Ark of God for guidance, so no one remembered the rules from God about how to handle it in a way that honors God. David and the Israelites were asking for trouble, but they were so ignorant of God's holy word that serious trouble took them completely by surprise. They had forgotten that only the Levites were tasked by God to carry the ark because God chose them to minister before Him. When the oxen that were transporting the ark stumbled, Uzzah touched the ark to steady it. This seems like a noble gesture, but it wasn't. The moving plan was wrong from the beginning, and God struck Uzzah so that he died before the Lord.

We retain the same human tendency today—the tendency to do God's will in our own particular way. We must remember to be careful to obey God in every particular lest we find ourselves guilty of the damning ignorance of the next generation.

Unity and Diversity

Mortify therefore your members which are upon the earth;
fornication, uncleanness, inordinate affection, evil concupiscence,
and covetousness, which is idolatry: For which things' sake the wrath
of God cometh on the children of disobedience: In the which ye also
walked some time, when ye lived in them. But now ye also put off
all these; anger, wrath, malice, blasphemy, filthy communication out
of your mouth. Lie not one to another, seeing that ye have put off
the old man with his deeds; And have put on the new man, which is
renewed in knowledge after the image of him that created him: Where
there is neither Greek nor Jew, circumcision nor uncircumcision,
Barbarian, Scythian, bond nor free: but Christ is all, and in all. Put on
therefore, as the elect of God, holy and beloved, bowels of mercies,
kindness, humbleness of mind, meekness, longsuffering; Forbearing
one another, and forgiving one another, if any man have a quarrel
against any: even as Christ forgave you, so also do ye. And above
all these things put on charity, which is the bond of perfectness.
—Colossians 3:5–14

During the last few decades, our culture has emphasized the value of diversity—racial, religious, ethnic, and social—often at the expense of social and cultural unity. Many wonder if it is even possible to honor differences yet maintain unity. According to the Bible, it is possible, but only when the categories of similar and different are defined. The Bible views people in only two categories: those who obey God and those who don't.

The Bible is a leveler of persons because it makes us realize that most differences are external. Diversity fails when it focuses on the outward expression of who we are—human conceptions of race, religion, social practices we adhere to, ethnic habits and assumptions, or social strata. The externals of our lives vary widely, and for the most part, we have little control over them. But internal qualities belong to all of us. They make us human and unique. By them, we reveal our personalities. When we live according to the law of sin, we engage in sinful deeds. When we live according the law of God, we exercise virtue in all our behavior. Suddenly, specifics no longer matter.

The love that comes from God changes us internally first, then outwardly next. In Christ, human barriers of race, religion, ethnicity, or social strata disappear. Lasting unity comes from the love of God and nowhere else.

The Best Teacher

And it came to pass, when the Lord would take up Elijah into
heaven by a whirlwind, that Elijah went with Elisha from Gilgal. ...
And it came to pass, when they were gone over, that Elijah said
unto Elisha, Ask what I shall do for thee, before I be taken away
from thee. And Elisha said, I pray thee, let a double portion of
thy spirit be upon me. And he said, Thou hast asked a hard thing:
nevertheless, if thou see me when I am taken from thee, it shall
be so unto thee; but if not, it shall not be so. And it came to pass,
as they still went on, and talked, that, behold, there appeared a
chariot of fire, and horses of fire, and parted them both asunder;
and Elijah went up by a whirlwind into heaven. And Elisha saw it,
and he cried, My father, my father, the chariot of Israel, and the
horsemen thereof. And he saw him no more: and he took hold of
his own clothes, and rent them in two pieces ... And when the
sons of the prophets which were to view at Jericho saw him, they
said, The spirit of Elijah doth rest on Elisha. And they came to
meet him, and bowed themselves to the ground before him.
—2 Kings 2:1, 9–12, 15

Elisha began his ministry as a young attendant, a prophet-in-training under
the great Old Testament prophet Elijah. Elijah spoke the truth from God
while the world looked on in either dismay or awe. When Elijah spoke the word,
no rain fell from the sky for three years. When Elijah stayed with a destitute
widow and her son, they ate a meal every night during a time of severe famine.

When Elijah told wicked King Ahab of Israel how evil his life was, Ahab
tried to kill him many times and failed. When Elijah challenged the prophets
of Baal to a showdown, only the true God could make a blazing fire out of the
water-soaked wood. When Elijah spoke, a small cloud became a heavy downpour
and ended the drought. When Queen Jezebel, the horrible consort of wicked
King Ahab, tried to kill Elijah, God helped Elijah run a day's journey into the
desert and sent an angel to feed him. The strength of that holy food enabled him
to travel forty more days and nights to Mount Horeb.

Very few of us will ever have such a superior teacher as Elisha had in Elijah,
but he still wanted all that Elijah had and more. Because God granted this request
of Elisha, we know his desire was not self-centered; he was not power-hungry.
Elisha understood that holiness is more powerful than any other earthly gift. He
wanted more spiritual power than Elijah in order to serve the Lord effectively.

A Beautiful Person

I was in the Spirit on the Lord's day, and heard behind me a great
voice, as of a trumpet … And I turned to see the voice that spake
with me. And being turned, I saw seven golden candlesticks; And
in the midst of the seven candlesticks one like unto the Son of
man, clothed with a garment down to the foot, and girt about the
paps with a golden girdle. His head and his hairs were white like
wool, as white as snow; and his eyes were as a flame of fire; And
his feet like unto fine brass, as if they burned in a furnace; and his
voice as the sound of many waters. And he had in his right hand
seven stars: and out of his mouth went a sharp twoedged sword:
and his countenance was as the sun shineth in his strength. And
when I saw him, I fell at his feet as dead. And he laid his right hand
upon me, saying unto me, Fear not; I am the first and the last.
—Revelation 1:10, 12–17

In Sunday School, children learn a song that tells them that heaven is a beautiful
place filled with glory and grace. The ditty is simple enough for children to
understand, but not complete enough for adults to be satisfied with. John, the
beloved apostle, received a vision of heaven when "in the Spirit." His vision
teaches us more completely that in the center of the beautiful place is a beautiful
person. On the Lord's Day, when John was "in the Spirit," he heard a voice from
behind, as unmistakable as a trumpet sound. When he turned around, he saw
the most beautiful sight anyone can behold.

The profusion of light from the lamps revealed to him a man who looked
human, but not quite. A fresh clean robe emphasized the beauty of his face, and
a golden sash sparkled around his torso. His hair was so white that it looked
pure, not old. His piercing eyes blazed out of the lamplight that made known
His beauty. The feet like bronze were so polished that John knew he was seeing
perfection in human form. The voice that spoke sounded like a rushing waterfall.
Everyone can hear the noise, and the tongue speaks words that cut to the chase
like a double-edged sword. The beautiful person held seven stars aloft in a
glittering gesture of sovereignty.

The face of the beautiful person shone with matchless brilliance from
within and from without. No wonder John fell as her feet as if he were dead.
If he had not been comforted and assisted to his feet, we would not now have
been given the beautiful image of that beautiful person, the Savior, whom we
will also someday meet.

Branching Out

I am the true vine, and my Father is the husbandman. Every branch
in me that beareth not fruit he taketh away: and every branch that
beareth fruit, he purgeth it, that it may bring forth more fruit. Now
ye are clean through the word which I have spoken unto you. Abide
in me, and I in you. As the branch cannot bear fruit of itself, except
it abide in the vine; no more can ye, except ye abide in me. I am
the vine, ye are the branches: He that abideth in me, and I in him,
the same bringeth forth much fruit: for without me ye can do
nothing. If a man abide not in me, he is cast forth as a branch, and
is withered; and men gather them, and cast them into the fire, and
they are burned. If ye abide in me, and my words abide in you, ye
shall ask what ye will, and it shall be done unto you. Herein is my
Father glorified, that ye bear much fruit; so shall ye be my disciples.
—John 15:1–8

All of us know that we were once tiny infants weighing from 5–9 pounds and stretching less than 24" long. We have grown steadily upward, and with our height has come increasing girth to fill out our frames. Sometimes we like to compare spiritual growth with physical growth because we know we mature spiritually. As believers, we are already in Christ. This means that we already possess all we need for future growth.

John tells us that we are now branches, and branches grow differently than human bodies grow. At the tip of the branch is the place of growth. Tiny buds begin to swell; they grow into longer shoots that produce leaves and eventually flowers and fruit. The growth of vines reminds us that often God stretches us to our extreme limits to achieve growth. Our heavenly father, the gardener, may also cut off some previous activities or habits—the dead growth of our formerly dead lives. Pruning is beneficial to us. The buds draw their nourishment from water in the soil through the branches all the way out to the extreme end.

Just as branches cannot bear fruit by themselves, neither can we grow spiritually by ourselves. Let us drink of the living water to nourish our souls for spiritual growth.

Building a Solid Life

Except the Lord build the house, they labour in vain that build it:
except the Lord keep the city, the watchman waketh but in vain. It
is vain for you to rise up early, to sit up late, to eat the bread of
sorrows: for so he giveth his beloved sleep. Lo, children are an
heritage of the Lord: and the fruit of the womb is his reward. As
arrows are in the hand of a mighty man; so are children of the youth.
Happy is the man that hath his quiver full of them: they shall not
be ashamed, but they shall speak with the enemies in the gate.
—Psalm 127:1–5

When we enter college, we generally think of our lives as comprising three parts: the career we would like to establish, the family we would like to raise, and the place we intend to live. All areas of our lives require a solid foundation in order to endure longer than our four years of studying for a degree. King Solomon gives good advice on how to achieve success in the civic, family, and professional arenas. He should know, because even though he possessed enormous wealth, limitless human power, and unrestricted privileges, Solomon did not always follow God's laws as carefully as He should have.

According to Solomon, the Lord builds family life when the parents trust God. Solomon married so many foreign wives (seven hundred of them) and concubines (three hundred of them) that he turned to idolatry later on in life. He set a bad example for his family. God caused enemies to attack the nation, and the nation also split into two parts. The king also writes that the Lord protects the city when the residents obey His Law. Solomon honored God in public life. Solomon asked God for wisdom and discernment to govern the people under him, and God gave the king more than he requested. Solomon acknowledged that the Lord blesses professional efforts when adults recognize the giver of their skills. Solomon gave thanks to God for the completion of the temple structure—it took twenty years to build. He knew that God had helped him do it.

The Lord is the foundation of a solid life. We should not let prosperity convince us otherwise, because God does not owe us what He has given us; prosperity is temporary gift.

What to Do and Where to Go

All these are the twelve tribes of Israel: and this is it that their father
spake unto them, and blessed them; every one according to his blessing
he blessed them ... my might, and the beginning of my strength,
the excellency of dignity, and the excellency of power ... Unstable as
water, thou shalt not excel; because thou wentest up to thy father's
bed; then defiledst thou it: he went up to my couch ... instruments of
cruelty are in their habitations ... he whom thy brethren shall praise:
thy hand shall be in the neck of thine enemies; thy father's children
shall bow down before thee ... shall dwell at the haven of the sea;
and he shall be for an haven of ships; and his border shall be unto
Zidon ... shall judge his people, as one of the tribes of Israel ... a
troop shall overcome him: but he shall overcome at the last ... his
bread shall be fat, and he shall yield royal dainties ... a hind let loose:
he giveth goodly words ... a fruitful bough, even a fruitful bough by a
well; whose branches run over the wall ... shall ravin as a wolf: in the
morning he shall devour the prey, and at night he shall divide the spoil.
—Genesis 49:28, 3–5, 8, 13, 16, 19–22, 27

And hath made of one blood all nations of men for to dwell
on all the face of the earth, and hath determined the times
before appointed, and the bounds of their habitation.
—Acts 17:26

Do we have a sense of control over the destiny of our lives? Do we consider it
solely our choice what to do or where to go in life? Do we choose where to live?
Or, does God choose where we live? It may be challenging to transpose God's choice
of Israel and her individual territories to the specific locations we live in, have lived
in, or plan to live in. It may be thought provoking to compare the various gifts God
gave to the individual sons of Jacob to the talents God has placed in our lives today.
Travel today is relatively easy and safe. We can pack a suitcase and fly anywhere in
the world. This makes us feel that we may live anywhere and do anything we please.

When we think in this autonomous way, we dethrone the Lord from the
throne of the universe, at least in our own minds. Jacob spoke a blessing to his
sons on his deathbed that indicated their future places of residence, their personal
aptitudes, and their God-given skills: power, violence, wise counsel, living by the
ocean, bad judgment, superior judgment, cunning, gourmet cooks, physical beauty,
stable leadership, and greed. The variety still astounds readers today. Likewise,
God reminds us that he has also made specific and detailed choices for us today.

It is worth considering the claim God has on every aspect of our lives, even
upon our skill sets and our choices of residence. He still lets us know today what
He want to do and where He wants us to go.

Death Is Not the End

> And it was the third hour, and they crucified him. And the
> superscription of his accusation was written over, The King Of
> The Jews. And with him they crucify two thieves; the one on
> his right hand, and the other on his left. And the scripture was
> fulfilled, which saith, And he was numbered with the transgressors.
> And they that passed by railed on him, wagging their heads, and
> saying, Ah, thou that destroyest the temple, and buildest it in
> three days, Save thyself, and come down from the cross. Likewise
> also the chief priests mocking said among themselves with the
> scribes, He saved others; himself he cannot save ... And Jesus
> cried with a loud voice, and gave up the ghost. And the veil of
> the temple was rent in twain from the top to the bottom.
> —Mark 15:25–31, 37–38

The life of Jesus Christ bridges the crossroads of human history. Our dating system reflects His life. The abbreviation BC means *before Christ*. The abbreviation AD means *anno Domini* or "in the year of our Lord." We reckon human history by the life of the Son of God. Some people are trying to change this to BCE, meaning *before the Common Era*, but even the non-biblical abbreviations imply that the commonality of historical dating is the birth of Jesus Christ. Whether we believe in Him or not, He has forever changed human history.

The date of the year 0 means that the calendar system acknowledges that Jesus Christ is the most important person who ever lived. A similar mixture of belief and unbelief occurred at the cross of Jesus Christ. Pilate ordered a sign to be placed over the cross of Christ, bearing the sign: "the king of the Jews." Pilate let the world know the truth even though it does not seem that he actually believed in the truth himself. Others, standing near the cross, had less faith than Pilate. The Jewish priests and teachers of the law mocked the very idea that Jesus could save anyone let alone Himself. The criminals, justly crucified alongside Jesus, insulted Him as if He were as criminal as they were.

From the vantage point of about 2,000 years later, it is easy to see that unbelief looks at the moment only, no further. None of those unbelievers saw beyond the horror of the crucifixion. If they had, they would have seen resurrection—to all who believe—hope for all who believe—and eternal life to all who believe in Jesus Christ, the Son of God. The resurrection confirms that His life is the most important fact to know.

The Rock

There is none holy as the Lord: for there is none beside
thee: neither is there any rock like our God.
—1 Samuel 2:2

The Lord liveth; and blessed be my rock; and exalted
be the God of the rock of my salvation.
—2 Samuel 22:47

For their rock is not as our Rock, even our enemies
themselves being judges ... And he shall say, Where
are their gods, their rock in whom they trusted.
—Deuteronomy 32:31, 37

Moreover, brethren, I would not that ye should be ignorant,
how that all our fathers were under the cloud, and all passed
through the sea; And were all baptized unto Moses in the cloud
and in the sea; And did all eat the same spiritual meat; And
did all drink the same spiritual drink: for they drank of that
spiritual Rock that followed them: and that Rock was Christ.
—1 Corinthian 10:1–4

Those of us who live in the rockier parts of this country and those of us who have climbed mountains hold a concrete image in our minds about the hardness and immovability of rock. The enduring qualities of rock and stone appeal to the side of human nature that desires something firm, solid, and long-lasting in this life. This physical characteristic of rock has a parallel in spiritual life, and we can understand the parallels from the lives of some biblical personages.

Joseph endured slavery and mistreatment because of his brothers' unjustified jealousy. He thought he was doing all right until Potiphar's wife wrongly accused him of sexual misconduct. He learned that he could trust only the Lord. The Rock of Israel steadied Joseph through his trials and eventually honored him above all Egyptians except the Pharaoh himself. David spent more than a decade fleeing King Saul who had become his enemy. He learned that God was keeping him alive, and David praised God for his safekeeping. Moses led the Israelites across the desert and mountains for forty years. God used this time to teach Moses the difference between gods made of rocks and the God who is a Rock of refuge.

The apostle Paul enlightens us centuries later that the rock that accompanied the Israelites through the wilderness was none other than the person of Jesus Christ. It is worth reflecting on our lives to figure out the way in which God has become a rock to us as individuals. God does not change, and His immutability, the rock-like quality that we all desire, needs to be acknowledged in our lives.

What We Plant

Either make the tree good, and his fruit good; or else make the tree
corrupt, and his fruit corrupt: for the tree is known by his fruit. O
generation of vipers, how can ye, being evil, speak good things? for
out of the abundance of the heart the mouth speaketh. A good man
out of the good treasure of the heart bringeth forth good things:
and an evil man out of the evil treasure bringeth forth evil things.
But I say unto you, That every idle word that men shall speak, they
shall give account thereof in the day of judgment. For by thy words
thou shalt be justified, and by thy words thou shalt be condemned.
—Matthew 12:33–37

Some of us love to visit the local orchards throughout the growing season and
pick our own tree-ripened fruit. We don't care whether the day is hot or wet;
we don't care whether the ground is lumpy or slippery with squashed fruit. The
orchard smells sweet and wonderful. We like to plan how we will use the fruit
we have picked with our own two hands.

Orchardists exercise superior care. The orchard is planted in good soil, and
widely spaced rows provide enough room for the plants to breathe. Vining shrubs
are tied to wires, giving easy access to fruit pickers. We stand under the fruit trees
or bend over the strawberry plants to pick the fruit. The orchardist had farmed
his land well and hopes for the best crop, but the best crop is not up to him. He
depends on God for ample rain alternating with sunshine to produce the crop.

Our lives produce a harvest too. The effort we put into our lives shows the
degree of care we give to living. Others can recognize the quality of our lives by
the words that come out of our mouths. Words express attitudes, and God takes
us at our word. We may say anything we like, but the outcome is not within our
control. Whatever choices we make, God controls the outcome; He produces
fruit in accordance with those choices in our lives.

Cut to the Quick

And he came to Nazareth, where he had been brought up: and, as
his custom was, he went into the synagogue on the sabbath day,
and stood up for to read ... And he closed the book, and he gave
it again to the minister, and sat down. And the eyes of all them
that were in the synagogue were fastened on him. And he began
to say unto them, This day is this scripture fulfilled in your ears.
And all bare him witness, and wondered at the gracious words
which proceeded out of his mouth. And they said, Is not this
Joseph's son? ... And he said, Verily I say unto you, No prophet
is accepted in his own country ... And all they in the synagogue,
when they heard these things, were filled with wrath, And rose up,
and thrust him out of the city, and led him unto the brow of the
hill whereon their city was built, that they might cast him down
headlong. But he passing through the midst of them went his way.
—Luke 4:16, 20–22, 24, 28–30

For the Word of God is quick, and powerful, and sharper
than any twoedged sword, piercing even to the dividing
asunder of soul and spirit, and of the joints and marrow, and
is a discerner of the thoughts and intents of the heart.
—Hebrews 4:12

The words of Jesus Christ are life-changing; they pierce our fleshly armor like
a sharp sword. The words of truth make us aware that we have spiritual lives
and that the spiritual side of life matters even more than the physical side of life.
His words penetrate our psyches like twisted ligaments send pain around the joint.

God's Word is true, so it judges our attitudes, preconceptions, misconceptions,
hearts, and minds—all that we are. When Jesus Christ began His ministry, He
spoke in the hometown synagogue. Wonderful reports had preceded Him from
the other synagogues where he had already preached, so Nazareth expected
another good message. Yes, they were blown away by the "gracious words" that
came out His mouth. They could hardly believe that the carpenter's son could
speak so eloquently. When the tone of the message changed, the attitudes of the
congregation changed. Jesus, their hometown hero boy, seemed to affront and
insult them. Those who heard only eloquence became furious; they had heard
enough! Those who heard the truth reacted differently.

When Jesus Christ speaks to us, either we love what He says because we
live with the intention of obeying Him, or we hate what He says because we live
with the intention of rebelling against Him. His words cut us to the quick, no
matter what we choose.

APRIL 28

How to Figure Out the Truth

Many of the people therefore, when they heard this saying, said,
Of a truth this is the Prophet. Others said, This is the Christ. But
some said, Shall Christ come out of Galilee? Hath not the scripture
said, That Christ cometh of the seed of David, and out of the town
of Bethlehem, where David was? So there was a division among
the people because of him. And some of them would have taken
him; but no man laid hands on him. Then came the officers to the
chief priests and Pharisees; and they said unto them, Why have ye
not brought him? The officers answered, Never man spake like this
man. Then answered them the Pharisees, Are ye also deceived?
Have any of the rulers or of the Pharisees believed on him? But this
people who knoweth not the law are cursed. Nicodemus saith unto
them, (he that came to Jesus by night, being one of them,) Doth our
law judge any man, before it hear him, and know what he doeth?
—John 7:40–51

Some of us are more gregarious than others, but none of us can equal the
communication skills or the number of personal contacts Jesus made in a few
short years of effective ministry. Jesus Christ spoke with multitudes, individuals,
and groups of people. Everyone had something to say about Him, but opinions
varied widely.

Some people thought He was a prophet; others thought He was the Messiah
come to save them. They were spiritually minded, so they were trying to place
what they had been taught with the person who faced them personally. The
temple guards never heard anyone speak like Jesus, so they had not yet made
up their minds about Jesus. They were more practical-minded, but they felt the
human need for a Savior, just like everyone else. The Pharisees viewed Jesus as
a deceiver of conscientious religious people. They were religion-minded, so they
discounted the truth, even when it stared them in the face.

The Pharisee Nicodemus was the only one who knew how to figure out the
truth about Jesus. He said they should let Jesus speak for Himself before deciding
who He was. It does not matter which perspective or training or learning we
possess when we are trying to figure out the truth. The advice of Nicodemus is
still valid today. Read the Bible to figure out the truth about Jesus Christ. Then,
make up your mind about Him.

Marriage

And the Lord God said, It is not good that the man
should be alone; I will make him an help meet for him …
Therefore shall a man leave his father and his mother, and
shall cleave unto his wife: and they shall be one flesh.
—Genesis 2:18, 24

And did not he make one? Yet had he the residue of the
spirit. And wherefore one? That he might seek a godly
seed. Therefore take heed to your spirit, and let none
deal treacherously against the wife of his youth.
—Malachi 2:15

For the woman which hath an husband is bound by the
law to her husband so long as he liveth; but if the husband
be dead, she is loosed from the law of her husband.
—Romans 7:2

Marriage is honourable in all, and the bed undefiled:
but whoremongers and adulterers God will judge.
—Hebrews 13:4

The meaning of marriage, the concept of marriage, and the definition of marriage
have been called into question in our time because people have forgotten how
the first marriage came about. God established marriage in the Garden of Eden
between Adam and Eve, the first man and the first woman. We may think of Adam
and Eve as the grand parents of us all, who set the example for their progeny.

Marriage is the idea of God; it is not the idea of mere humans, so it is
important to stay true to the original meaning of the institution of marriage.
Marriage is meant to be a lifelong commitment because ultimately, all of us belong
to God. This means that it is always possible for husbands and wives to get along
with each other permanently. Divorce and worse marital behaviors displease the
God who established marriage. Marriage is meant to last throughout this life; it
does not continue into the next. This means that we must work at it in this life. All
people are strong-willed because of the sinful nature, so it is important to submit
to one another in love and strengthen the marriage bond instead of destroy it. This
goes against the grain of human behavior, but it is possible to live in love anyway.

Marriage is an exclusive relationship—one to another—in love—honoring
God—preserving the family structure—passing on a godly heritage to children.

Discipline

Blessed is the man whom thou chastenest, O Lord, and teachest
him out of thy law; That thou mayest give him rest from the
days of adversity, until the pit be digged for the wicked.
—Psalm 94:12–13

And ye have forgotten the exhortation which speaketh unto you
as unto children, My son, despise not thou the chastening of the
Lord, nor faint when thou art rebuked of him: For whom the
Lord loveth he chasteneth, and scourgeth every son whom he
receiveth. If ye endure chastening, God dealeth with you as with
sons; for what son is he whom the father chasteneth not? But if
ye be without chastisement, whereof all are partakers, then are ye
bastards, and not sons. Furthermore we have had fathers of our
flesh which corrected us, and we gave them reverence: shall we
not much rather be in subjection unto the Father of spirits, and
live? For they verily for a few days chastened us after their own
pleasure; but he for our profit, that we might be partakers of his
holiness. Now no chastening for the present seemeth to be joyous,
but grievous: nevertheless afterward it yieldeth the peaceable
fruit of righteousness unto them which are exercised thereby.
—Hebrews 12:5–11

None of us likes to be disciplined, but we do acknowledge that discipline is
good for us. Learning how to discipline ourselves in basic ways is perhaps the
most overriding feature of our educational experience as children. Learning to tell
clock time in order to begin and end our subjects on time, learning how to engage
in team sports and follow the rules, learning how to do the chores at home without
grumbling—all of these and many more basic disciplines filled the time of childhood.

Now that we have entered the college world, we must transfer the skills
that were forced upon us as children into self-motivation that makes us do the
tasks ourselves as young adults. We should be able to motivate ourselves without
prompting from anyone else. Another aspect of the adult world is that our parents
no longer tell us what to do. This means that God now takes over as the primary
disciplinarian of our lives.

The goals of godly discipline differ from the goals of human training. God
wants us to be whole and complete people, so He sends us disciplinary experiences
to engage our wills and develop our holiness. God wants us to be more like Him,
and there is no one better to accomplish the task than the one who made us.

MAY 1

Folly or Caution?

Fools because of their transgression, and because of their iniquities,
are afflicted. Their soul abhorreth all manner of meat; and they
draw near unto the gates of death. Then they cry unto the Lord in
their trouble, and he saveth them out of their distresses. He sent his
word, and healed them, and delivered them from their destructions.
—Psalm 107:17–20

The fear of the Lord is the beginning of knowledge:
but fools despise wisdom and instruction.
—Proverbs 1:7

Reality television, newspapers, and popular magazines frequently portray the folly of those who think erroneously about a situation and then act upon their misunderstandings. We have seen mountain bikers unexpectedly topple off treacherous trails. We have read about mountain climbers who are suddenly overtaken by blizzards.

We probably know the careless person who drove off the road because of texting while driving. We understand the human side of such folly because we share in the same fallible human nature. What seems at first to be logical turns out to be folly, and much suffering ensues as a result of personal choice. Because all of us are subject to the same impulses, we see ourselves at our worst in these shows.

Do we understand that the origin of human folly is the sinful nature that breeds rebellion toward God? It is only when we acknowledge the futility of our reasoning and cry out to God that He uses His Word to heal us. Instead of trusting to our own judgment, we should always remember that only the Truth is true. Our thoughts are not true unless they agree with what the Bible already says. Before we hurtle ourselves into a situation unthinkingly, we need to stop and consider how much help we need and how much help is available to us—every time we need it.

Temptations

Then was Jesus led up of the Spirit into the wilderness to be tempted
of the devil. And when he had fasted forty days and forty nights,
he was afterward an hungred. And when the tempter came to him,
he said, If thou be the Son of God, command that these stones be
made bread. But he answered and said, It is written, Man shall not
live by bread alone, but by every word that proceedeth out of the
mouth of God. Then the devil taketh him up into the holy city,
and setteth him on a pinnacle of the temple, And saith unto him,
If thou be the Son of God, cast thyself down: for it is written, He
shall give his angels charge concerning thee: and in their hands
they shall bear thee up, lest at any time thou dash thy foot against a
stone. Jesus said unto him, It is written again, Thou shalt not tempt
the Lord thy God. Again, the devil taketh him up into an exceeding
high mountain, and sheweth him all the kingdoms of the world, and
the glory of them; And saith unto him, All these things will I give
thee, if thou wilt fall down and worship me. Then saith Jesus unto
him, Get thee hence, Satan: for it is written, Thou shalt worship
the Lord thy God, and him only shalt thou serve. Then the devil
leaveth him, and, behold, angels came and ministered unto him.
—Matthew 4:1–11

The writer of the book of Hebrews tells us that Jesus was tempted in every
imaginable way just as the rest of us are, but Jesus never sinned like all of us
do. So what can we learn about temptation from the experience of Jesus?

First of all, Jesus was tempted in the wilderness, and this location represents
the sinful world in which we live—the wild and uncertain territory of sin. It
surrounds us on every side, and we always need help from God to travel through
it. Second, Satan tempted Jesus with food when He was hungry. Wilderness
experiences can cause us to desire the comforts we have foregone, but we can still
choose to imitate the Savior. We can learn that living according to God's Word
matters more than fulfilling immediate physical desires. Third, Satan tempted
Jesus to presume upon the power of God to save Him from certain harm and
death. The mind-set that presumes upon God's grace tells us that we can live on
the edge without suffering any consequences. Jesus reminds us that God protects
the obedient, not the daredevils.

Finally, Satan tempted Jesus with power, but Jesus knows that only God
has power, so He is not enticed to capitulate. His humility reminds us to humble
ourselves and submit our desires to the mighty hand of God.

Future Plans

The preparations of the heart in man, and the answer of the tongue,
is from the Lord. All the ways of a man are clean in his own eyes;
but the Lord weigheth the spirits. Commit thy works unto the Lord,
and thy thoughts shall be established. The Lord hath made all things
for himself: yea, even the wicked for the day of evil ... A man's
heart deviseth his way: but the Lord directeth his steps ... The lot
is cast into the lap; but the whole disposing thereof is of the Lord.
—Proverbs 16:1–4, 9, 33

We all dream about the future and what it holds for us. Human thoughts imagine only the best, never the worst, but the truth is that we really do not know what tomorrow holds for us, do we? Is it possible for us to know what God wants us to do for the rest of our lives? It seems like this passage is telling us that we probably have some idea and hope to flesh it out in the next few years. It also reminds us that God directs our thoughts and our courses of action according to His purposes, not ours.

It seems that we understand ourselves, our world, and our skill set one way, but God understands them another way. The difference in perspective has to do with the fact that God sees reality from beginning to end whereas we only know the reality of the present moment. The obscurity of human vision prevents us from knowing more.

When we focus on the Lord and commit our plans and ideas to Him, He may reformulate the human plans we have formulated so clearly in our minds. His ends serve His purposes. We plan, but God always directs our steps unfailingly.

Honing and Sharpening

Iron sharpeneth iron; so a man sharpeneth the countenance of his
friend … As in water face answereth to face, so the heart of man
to man … Happy is the man that findeth wisdom, and the man
that getteth understanding. For the merchandise of it is better than
the merchandise of silver, and the gain thereof than fine gold.
—Proverbs 27:17, 19; 3:13–14

For the Word of God is quick, and powerful, and sharper than
any twoedged sword, piercing even to the dividing asunder of
soul and spirit, and of the joints and marrow, and is a discerner
of the thoughts and intents of the heart. Neither is there any
creature that is not manifest in his sight: but all things are naked
and opened unto the eyes of him with whom we have to do.
—Hebrews 4:12–13

Some of our parents used carbon steel cutlery in the kitchen, and they probably sharpened the knives on a honing rod. Some of us had jackknives as children, and we probably also had a whetstone to keep the blade sharp. Many ordinary experiences help us to understand that the harder implement hones the softer tool. When the implement becomes dull, it must be sharpened in order to maintain its usefulness.

There is only one way to sharpen a hard object—to use force against the implement for its own good, you might say. But there are two ways to sharpen a person—to use force from external circumstances or to look within and figure out what must change. Self-reflection, such as in a mirror or water, can cause us to spruce ourselves up and hone our best features. Friends and relatives can hone us simply because their different qualities make us self-aware and cause us to change. Coworkers and other less familiar people can hone us is a rasping sort of way because they are not as sympathetic as our closer companions.

The method is not as important as the process, for honing helps us find wisdom from God. He controls the process and brings out the best in us.

MAY 5

Waiting for God

Now the sojourning of the children of Israel, who dwelt in Egypt,
was four hundred and thirty years. And it came to pass at the end of
the four hundred and thirty years, even the selfsame day it came to
pass, that all the hosts of the Lord went out from the land of Egypt.
It is a night to be much observed unto the Lord for bringing them out
from the land of Egypt: this is that night of the Lord to be observed
of all the children of Israel in their generations ... Thus did all the
children of Israel; as the Lord commanded Moses and Aaron, so did
they. And it came to pass the selfsame day, that the Lord did bring
the children of Israel out of the land of Egypt by their armies.
—Exodus 12:40–42, 50–51

Who does not like to watch prominent people? The personal lives of athletes,
politicians, entertainment stars, and local heroes intrigue us because we
see clearly that they are doing something larger than life—at least larger than the
lives we live. Such people seem to move effortlessly through life—they find jobs
when they need them, they get promotions when desired, they get married when
they like, they even have children according to their own timetable. Their lives
exemplify the upward mobility that a democratic society idolizes.

If life is a journey, we all want a pleasant trip, but this is not realistic for a lot
of us. When we look at the Israelites, we know they wanted to get out of slavery
as much as anyone could desire anything in life, but the reality of the exodus was
arduous and life changing; it did not occur according to any human plan.

Just like the enslaved Israelites, we wait on God to move us up and out of an
unpleasant situation. Hindsight sees clearly that God was in charge back then, but
current reality often finds it impossible to see past the troubles of the moment.
When we obey God's commandments, we will eventually see and experience
the personal deliverance He brings about in the ordinary circumstances of our
daily lives.

Sphere of Influence

> And it came to pass at the end of seven days, that the word of
> the Lord came unto me, saying, Son of man, I have made thee
> a watchman unto the house of Israel: therefore hear the word at
> my mouth, and give them warning from me. When I say unto the
> wicked, Thou shalt surely die; and thou givest him not warning, nor
> speakest to warn the wicked from his wicked way, to save his life;
> the same wicked man shall die in his iniquity; but his blood will
> I require at thine hand. Yet if thou warn the wicked, and he turn
> not from his wickedness, nor from his wicked way, he shall die in
> his iniquity; but thou hast delivered thy soul ... So thou, O son of
> man, I have set thee a watchman unto the house of Israel; therefore
> thou shalt hear the word at my mouth, and warn them from me.
> —Ezekiel 3:16–19; 33:7

Some of us come from unbelieving and godless families. In the same way, Ezekiel lived as a devout believer among an unbelieving and godless people. Being the sole believer among many unbelieving family members can weigh heavily upon our minds because we know that they should be able to turn to the Lord, just as we have done. Ezekiel felt the same concern for his national family that we feel for our immediate families.

It is a fact of life that we cannot make people do what they do not want to do, but as Christians, we know that we (and others) should obey God. So how can we influence the family God has placed within our immediate sphere of influence? We can think of ourselves like Ezekiel did.

It may be that God has made the sole believer as the watchman for the spiritual welfare of the extended family. Watchful care involves many tasks, but it will always include praying for them and presenting the gospel to them. If the family members refuse the truth, at least they know what they do not want. We cannot run away from them or never speak to them again unless we want God to hold us to some degree accountable for their spiritual poverty.

Real Worship or Phony Worship?

> Now when Jesus was born in Bethlehem of Judaea in the days
> of Herod the king, behold, there came wise men from the east
> to Jerusalem, Saying, Where is he that is born King of the Jews?
> for we have seen his star in the east, and are come to worship
> him. When Herod the king had heard these things, he was troubled,
> and all Jerusalem with him ... Then Herod, when he had privily
> called the wise men, enquired of them diligently what time the
> star appeared. And he sent them to Bethlehem, and said, Go and
> search diligently for the young child; and when ye have found him,
> bring me word again, that I may come and worship him also. When
> they had heard the king, they departed; and, lo, the star, which
> they saw in the east, went before them, till it came and stood over
> where the young child was. When they saw the star, they rejoiced
> with exceeding great joy. And when they were come into the house,
> they saw the young child with Mary his mother, and fell down,
> and worshipped him: and when they had opened their treasures,
> they presented unto him gifts; gold, and frankincense and myrrh.
> And being warned of God in a dream that they should not return
> to Herod, they departed into their own country another way.
> —Matthew 2:1–3, 7–12

Sometimes churchgoers become disenchanted with the church because they hear people saying the right words, while at the same time, they observe them doing the wrong deeds. While it is possible to walk away from ordinary people and avoid them forever, when the hypocritical person holds great power, it seems impossible to escape the harm they always seem to intent upon perpetrating.

The three wise men, so familiar to us, were also caught between the two sides of real and phony worship. Herod the Great was a man who feigned an interest in the Savior, but he really wanted to safeguard his own position of power. They had no reason to disbelieve the king, so God safeguarded His Son by warning them in a dream to avoid returning by the same route. In retaliation for being tricked, Herod ordered the slaughter of baby boys under the age of two in the vicinity of Bethlehem. We know that his plan was an utter failure and a needless slaughter of innocent life. No one needs to run away from a person in order to avoid a problem.

The best decision to make is to inquire of the Lord what He wants you to do. Then, go and obey God. The Magi obeyed God.

Light along my Path

The people which sat in darkness saw great light; and to them
which sat in the region and shadow of death light is sprung up.
—Matthew 4:16

In him was life; and the life was the light of men ... That
was the true Light, which lighteth every man that cometh
into the world ... Then spake Jesus again unto them, saying,
I am the light of the world: he that followeth me shall
not walk in darkness, but shall have the light of life.
—John 1:4, 9; 8:12

Thy word is a lamp unto my feet, and a light unto my path.
—Psalm 119:105

Take heed therefore that the light which is in thee be not
darkness. If thy whole body therefore be full of light,
having no part dark, the whole shall be full of light, as when
the bright shining of a candle doth give thee light.
—Luke 11:35–36

Children usually perceive that adults know everything about life—how to live it, where to work in it, how to behave through it, how to talk about it. This is only true when the parents teach their children according to the precepts of God's Word. The Bible teaches life-affirming principles by which we may all live. As maturity increases, the false perception of children may change into a more tremulous and wavering fog of indecision.

Older teenagers often ask questions like: What shall I do? Where shall I go to college? What type of work will be mine? Who will hire me? Should I move? Should I change my major? What about getting married and having children? The uncertainties are endless and confusing unless we turn to the Word of God. Just before Jesus began His earthly ministry, John the Baptist told people that illumination was at hand. Jesus Christ reminds us that He is the Light we seek.

When we commit our way to Him who is the Light, when we look at Him as the Light instead of at our fears, when we follow the Light of His leading, He puts the light of life in us—and we will see where to go and what to do. We will become the happiest and most satisfied creatures we can be—in the light of God's Word!

Problems with Work

Then the word of the Lord came unto me, saying, Before I formed
thee in the belly I knew thee; and before thou camest forth out
of the womb I sanctified thee, and I ordained thee a prophet
unto the nations. Then said I, Ah, Lord God! behold, I cannot
speak: for I am a child. But the Lord said unto me, Say not, I
am a child: for thou shalt go to all that I shall send thee, and
whatsoever I command thee thou shalt speak. Be not afraid of
their faces: for I am with thee to deliver thee, saith the Lord.
—Jeremiah 1:4–8

Do we enjoy every job we work at? Have we ever wished the tasks of the job
were easier? How can we meet the incessant demands of the job? Jeremiah
the prophet was given a job from God that was a bit unusual. God appointed him
from before he was born to speak a message of repentance to his nation if they
wanted to avoid the punishment that would surely follow. It was an extremely
important task, yet it was also an unpopular and unrewarding sort of position to
hold in a nation who had strayed from obedience to God.

We can easily imagine that Jeremiah did not relish the job God assigned
to him. He offered a lame excuse to God to get out of the job, but he failed to
convince God to let him off the hook. Instead, God recognized his human fear
of the situation. The Lord put him at his ease and empowered him for a lengthy
but thankless task.

Whatever job God gives us to do, we should remember that He has chosen
us for the task. He will enable us to overcome the problems we face in that
position because He has appointed us to it. When God is with us in the job
situation, we will always have that loving sense of help and rescue that comes
from Him.

From Tryouts to Trying

Cast thy bread upon the waters: for thou shalt find it after many
days … As thou knowest not what is the way of the spirit, nor
how the bones do grow in the womb of her that is with child:
even so thou knowest not the works of God who maketh all.
In the morning sow thy seed, and in the evening withhold
not thine hand: for thou knowest not whether shall prosper,
either this or that, or whether they both shall be alike good.
—Ecclesiastes 11:1, 5–6

The wind bloweth where it listeth, and thou hearest the
sound thereof, but canst not tell whence it cometh, and
whither it goeth: so is every one that is born of the Spirit.
—John 3:8

Parents delight to let their children try out for many activities. They participate
in sports practices, music lessons, scout meetings, church youth group,
summer camp, ballet lessons, and library activities. These activities teach children
many nonacademic skills. They enable children to find out on their own what
they are good at.

The skills acquired from childhood activities carry into the many peripheral
skills of adulthood. It does not matter whether children have excelled at an
activity or whether other factors limited participation. Children benefit from
every learning effort, and it seems like God treats the adult world in the same way.

At first, it seems like any type of job will be all right. Then, it seems that
a particular professional path is the right one to follow, so students choose the
college major accordingly. Students are not idle, but sometimes, success eludes
them. God is still in charge. He may have different plans for our skills that our
best planning and effort can presently imagine. When we keep on trying, we will
learn what God wants us to do.

Hanging in There

This second epistle, beloved, I now write unto you; in both which
I stir up your pure minds by way of remembrance: That ye may
be mindful of the words which were spoken before by the holy
prophets, and of the commandment of us the apostles of the Lord
and Saviour: Knowing this first, that there shall come in the last
days scoffers, walking after their own lusts, And saying, Where
is the promise of his coming? for since the fathers fell asleep, all
things continue as they were from the beginning of the creation.
For this they willingly are ignorant of, that by the Word of God the
heavens were of old, and the earth standing out of the water and
in the water ... Seeing then that all these things shall be dissolved,
what manner of persons ought ye to be in all holy conversation
and godliness ... Wherefore, beloved, seeing that ye look for
such things, be diligent that ye may be found of him in peace,
without spot, and blameless. And account that the longsuffering
of our Lord is salvation; even as our beloved brother Paul also
according to the wisdom given unto him hath written unto you.
—2 Peter 3:1–5, 11, 14–15

College students sometimes face bad roommate situations, and it seems
impossible to live above the difficulties of the current circumstances. The
dormitory room assignments are full, and the best advice from the counselor is
to wait until next term, when someone withdraws and frees up another space.
Maybe the bad situation occurs at work, at home, or in the classroom, and we
wonder whether living for God can really make a dent in the difficult situation.

Yes, God can intercede for us, and it does not matter what others do as
much as it matters what we do. God's standards of holy, set-apart living extend
to every situation. Our lives bear witness of Christ to others whether or not we
speak a single word because human behavior indicates the intention of the brain.

While we are cringing about how to avoid the difficulties of the situation,
others wonder at why we are living a godly life. Sometimes God's patience means
that others need to see a godly life in action before they can entertain the concept
that they are sinners who need salvation.

Doing What God Wants

And the angel of the Lord appeared unto him, and said unto him,
The Lord is with thee, thou mighty man of valour. And Gideon said
unto him, Oh my Lord, if the Lord be with us, why then is all this
befallen us? and where be all his miracles which our fathers told
us of, saying, Did not the Lord bring us up from Egypt? but now
the Lord hath forsaken us, and delivered us into the hands of the
Midianites. And the Lord looked upon him, and said, Go in this thy
might, and thou shalt save Israel from the hand of the Midianites:
have not I sent thee? And he said unto him, Oh my Lord, wherewith
shall I save Israel? behold, my family is poor in Manasseh, and I am
the least in my father's house. And the Lord said unto him, Surely
I will be with thee, and thou shalt smite the Midianites as one
man. And he said unto him, If now I have found grace in thy sight,
then shew me a sign that thou talkest with me ... And Gideon said
unto God, If thou wilt save Israel by mine hand, as thou hast said,
Behold, I will put a fleece of wool in the floor; and if the dew be on
the fleece only, and it be dry upon all the earth beside, then shall I
know that thou wilt save Israel by mine hand, as thou hast said. And
it was so: for he rose up early on the morrow, and thrust the fleece
together, and wringed the dew out of the fleece, a bowl full of water.
—Judges 6:12–17, 36–38

Most of us belong to the countless billions who get up every day, go to work, and drive back home again. This is the story of our ordinary lives. If this is what God wants us to do, then this is the best life to live. But sometimes, God asks the ordinary worker, like a farmer threshing wheat, to perform an incredible task.

Even though Gideon was doing an ordinary task of farming, he was doing it in an unusual way. He was threshing the wheat secretly—in a winepress—to keep the Midianites from stealing it. Country life is at its worst when a farmer cannot work openly or safely on his own land. Perhaps the knowledge of the evil times in which he lived was enough to cause Gideon to believe God's Word to him, but he had no illusions of grandeur about doing great deeds by himself.

He asked God for help, and God gave him His presence, His strength, and His favor. The dry fleece that became wet over one night and dry the next night was the visible sign Gideon needed to apply God's presence, strength, and favor to his behavior. He, and 300 fighting men, went out and defeated the Midianites in the power of the Lord.

Children and God

> Hear, O Israel: The Lord our God is one Lord: And thou shalt love
> the Lord thy God with all thine heart, and with all thy soul, and
> with all thy might. And these words, which I command thee this
> day, shall be in thine heart: And thou shalt teach them diligently
> unto thy children, and shalt talk of them when thou sittest in thine
> house, and when thou walkest by the way, and when thou liest down,
> and when thou risest up. And thou shalt bind them for a sign upon
> thine hand, and they shall be as frontlets between thine eyes. And
> thou shalt write them upon the posts of thy house, and on thy gates.
> —Deuteronomy 6:4–9

Parents should always be concerned about passing on a godly faith to their children, and God desires this outcome as well. God has given a formulaic prayer to accomplish this task. Some people take offense at rote learning, but for the sake of quick and concise summation of important concepts, memorization is a time-honored way to learn.

So what do children need to learn about God? The Creator God is one God. He is not a pantheon of idols; He is not a group of ideals that represent Him. He is not a philosophical concept. Statues do not portray His likeness. Symbols do not represent him accurately. We should love God completely—heart, soul, and strength—the idea is that our entire being loves God, not just the holier parts of us, and we can let the more ordinary parts be ordinary. Whatever we endeavor, wherever we go, remember how much He loves us; and we should love Him back.

God is a personal God who can love and be loved in return. We can learn the Ten Commandments and other commandments God wants us to follow. When we have a question in mind, we can ask God to direct us to His Word about it. We can memorize memorable verses—all Scripture is profitable to us. When they become part of us, the very words we speak will begin to reflect the more God-centered way of life we live. If we did not grow up in a believing home and do not even know the Ten Commandments, Exodus 20 is a good place to begin living the Christian life.

Receive the Grace of God

Therefore if any man be in Christ, he is a new creature: old things
are passed away; behold, all things are become new. And all things
are of God, who hath reconciled us to himself by Jesus Christ, and
hath given to us the ministry of reconciliation; To wit, that God
was in Christ, reconciling the world unto himself, not imputing
their trespasses unto them; and hath committed unto us the word of
reconciliation. Now then we are ambassadors for Christ, as though
God did beseech you by us: we pray you in Christ's stead, be ye
reconciled to God. For he hath made him to be sin for us, who knew
no sin; that we might be made the righteousness of God in him ...
We then, as workers together with him, beseech you also that ye
receive not the grace of God in vain. (For he saith, I have heard thee
in a time accepted, and in the day of salvation have I succoured thee:
behold, now is the accepted time; behold, now is the day of salvation.)
—2 Corinthians 5:17–21; 6:1–2

The message of salvation is simple. Jesus Christ died on the cross to save
us from our sins. The sinful human nature has been dealt with, once and
for all, by the death of Jesus Christ on the cross. Because we are sinners, we
are naturally against God, and we need forgiveness from Him. In spite of our
wickedness, Jesus Christ took upon Himself all our evil, wickedness, and sin so
that we might become righteous and holy, like Him. The grace of God changes
our fundamental nature.

When we belong to Christ, we are not ourselves anymore—this is a
wonderful truth! The grace of God turns us into ambassadors for Christ—we
represent Him in the foreign country of this world. We are tactful and polite so
that foreigners (those who do not know Him yet) will not misunderstand what it
means to live for Christ. We should never receive God's grace in vain. We should
not repent, get saved, and then never go to church. We should not continue to
live a life of sin and act like the Bible doesn't govern our behavior.

When God approaches us to ask us to accept Him, we should do it
unreservedly and wholeheartedly. Take salvation today, and keep it forever.

MAY 15

Building Right from the Start

Is it time for you, O ye, to dwell in your cieled houses, and this house
lie waste? Now therefore thus saith the Lord of hosts; Consider your
ways. Ye have sown much, and bring in little; ye eat, but ye have not
enough; ye drink, but ye are not filled with drink; ye clothe you, but
there is none warm; and he that earneth wages earneth wages to put
it into a bag with holes ... Ye looked for much, and, lo it came to
little; and when ye brought it home, I did blow upon it. Why? saith
the Lord of hosts. Because of mine house that is waste, and ye run
every man unto his own house. Therefore the heaven over you is
stayed from dew, and the earth is stayed from her fruit ... I smote you
with blasting and with mildew and with hail in all the labours of your
hands; yet ye turned not to me, saith the Lord ... Is the seed yet in the
barn? yea, as yet the vine, and the fig tree, and the pomegranate, and
the olive tree, hath not brought forth: from this day will I bless you.
—Haggai 1:4–6, 9–10; 2:17, 19

Most people draw a connection between pleasing God and gaining a lot of
material goods. Some churches even preach the wealth and health gospel.
According to this idea, God's blessings to us equal the same thing as God saying
that we are okay, or an alternate version of this same message—nothing goes
wrong because we are on God's side.

The logic of God is not the same as human rationalization that is sometimes
mistaken for logical thinking. We see this same erroneous reasoning in ancient
times. After Israel had lived as captives in Babylon for a while, they were doing
well enough financially. They thought that this meant that God liked what
they were doing, right?—Wrong! They still lived in the sin of ignoring God, of
putting other things first in life. God let them know He was in charge of their
professional effort and labor. He let farmers plant the crops, but God gave them
a small harvest. He gave them food and drink, but it never seemed like enough.
He gave them clothing, but the fabric was shoddy. He helped them earn money,
but they could not manage it very well.

God did this to draw their attention back to Him. The temple, the spiritual
center of life, was in ruins, just like their spiritual lives were in ruins. They needed
to get right with God in order to get God's blessing. Building right from the
beginning means building right in the heart first.

MAY 16

Clean Minds

Unto the pure all things are pure: but unto them that are defiled
and unbelieving is nothing pure; but even their mind and
conscience is defiled ... Young men likewise exhort to be sober
minded. In all things shewing thyself a pattern of good works: in
doctrine shewing uncorruptness, gravity, sincerity, Sound speech,
that cannot be condemned; that he that is of the contrary part
may be ashamed, having no evil thing to say of you ... For the
grace of God that bringeth salvation hath appeared to all men,
Teaching us that, denying ungodliness and worldly lusts, we
should live soberly, righteously, and godly, in this present world.
—Titus 1:15; 2:6–8, 11–12

We are so accustomed to the use of foul language in media portrayals that we may have forgotten that not everyone uses language we would rather not hear. Have you ever noticed in real life, that people who use a lot of bad language tend to expect the worst?—that they see only filth, even in the most innocent of situations? They think the worst of others because their minds are corrupted with sin.

The negative thought pattern created by the use of bad language is the opposite of Christian thinking created by the study of God's Holy Word. Some of us grew up in homes where bad language was the norm, and now we are believers. We need to change our minds, our thoughts, our attitudes, and our outlooks to conform to the new and positive outlook that comes from living according to the Word of God.

God helps give self-control over the tongue, and changing old habits is the place to start. When we think well of others and act with kindness and gentleness toward others, the Holy Spirit shines out of our lives, and God helps us to be more like Him. Since God is infinite, there is no limit to the amount of love and kindness we can show to others. We will always gain more of the Savior when we model our behavior on His example.

Prepare Ahead of Time

Now it came to pass, as David sat in his house, that David said to
Nathan the prophet, Lo, I dwell in an house of cedars, but the ark of
the covenant of the Lord remaineth under curtains. Then Nathan said
unto David, Do all that is in thine heart; for God is with thee. And it
came to pass the same night, that the Word of God came to Nathan,
saying, Go and tell David my servant, Thus saith the Lord, Thou shalt
not build me an house to dwell in ... And David said, Solomon my
son is young and tender, and the house that is to be builded for the
Lord must be exceeding magnifical, of fame and of glory throughout
all countries: I will therefore now make preparation for it. So David
prepared abundantly before his death. Then he called for Solomon his
son, and charged him to build an house for the Lord God of Israel.
—1 Chronicles 17:1–4; 22:5–6

We all have ideas about what we want to accomplish in life. We make plans,
we wait for the right timing, and we consult others just to confirm and
adjust our best intentions. David loved God and knew God had chosen him in
a unique way. He wanted this love to become visible by building a temple for
the ark of God. After all, he was king. He had done many types of great things,
so why not add one more project to the list?—but it wasn't God's plan for him.

Nathan the prophet was a man who spoke the truth to David, but his advice
was not infallible. The prophet initially told David to go ahead with his plans
and do whatever he wanted, but God spoke to Nathan (via a dream) to say that
David should not build the temple of the Lord. David was not disappointed; now,
he now understood his role differently. To build a temple would take many years
of effort, so King David assembled the materials, the plans, and the craftsmen
before his death. He tasked his son Solomon with the actual building of it.

When thinking about our own lives, we might want to consider who has
preceded us and made a lot of preparations for us to be able to do a specific job
or go to a specific college. Will we be the ones who complete the big plans, or will
we be the ones to pass on the big plans to another? We cannot know this right
now, but we can be aware that God uses our skills whatever way He decides to,
and the outcome will be all right with us.

Words and Deeds

And whatsoever ye do in word or deed, do all in the name
of the Lord Jesus, giving thanks to God and the Father by
him ... And whatsoever ye do, do it heartily, as to the Lord,
and not unto men; Knowing that of the Lord ye shall receive
the reward of the inheritance: for ye serve the Lord Christ.
Let your speech be always with grace, seasoned with salt,
that ye may know how ye ought to answer every man.
—Colossians 3:17, 23–24; 4:6

The grace of our Lord Jesus Christ be with you. Amen.
—1 Thessalonians 5:28

God gives us such a renewal of mind and body when we repent of our sins that every aspect of life alters dramatically. The transformation of a human life from self-centered everyday interests to God-centered spiritual interests brings about immediate and noticeable differences. Our knowledge reflects the first changes of the new life in Christ. Instead of relying on individual preferences as personal truth, we accept the unchanging truth of the Word of God.

When we accept God's offer of salvation, God enables us to pass on the good news on to others, even in ordinary conversations with others. Our motivations have changed. Instead of selfish personal pursuits, we remember to call upon the name of the Lord Jesus. He now helps us to speak and behave in the way that honors Him. Our incentives have changed. Instead of temporal goals, we pursue eternal goals.

God honors those who honor Him, so any type of work can glorify God. Whatever we do or whatever we say can now reflect the One who lives in us. The fullness or well roundedness of our new lives testifies to the efficacy of God's work in us and displays our faith and trust in Him. The grace of God renders our lives beautiful to Him.

Doing What Is Easy

Now Naaman, captain of the host of the king of Syria, was a great man
with his master, and honourable, because by him the Lord had given
deliverance unto Syria: he was also a mighty man in valour, but he
was a leper ... And he brought the letter to the king of Israel, saying,
Now when this letter is come unto thee, behold, I have therewith
sent Naaman my servant to thee, that thou mayest recover him of his
leprosy ... And Elisha sent a messenger unto him, saying, Go and
wash in Jordan seven times, and thy flesh shall come again to thee,
and thou shalt be clean. But Naaman was wroth, ... And his servants
came near, and spake unto him, and said, My father, if the prophet had
bid thee do some great thing, wouldest thou not have done it? how
much rather then, when he saith to thee, Wash, and be clean? Then
went he down, and dipped himself seven times in Jordan, according to
the saying of the man of God: and his flesh came again like unto the
flesh of a little child, and he was clean. And he returned to the man
of God, he and all his company, and came, and stood before him: and
he said, Behold, now I know that there is no God in all the earth, but
in Israel: now therefore, I pray thee, take a blessing of thy servant.
—2 Kings 5:1, 6, 10–11a, 13–15

Many people think that God's commands are so unusual or difficult that they put
off thinking about them and obeying them. They remain in an unsaved state
unless God sends an affliction into their lives that causes them to seek out God. The
army commander Naaman, from the country of Aram, was just such an unbeliever.

When he contracted the dreaded disease of leprosy, a contagious and crippling
disease, he realized he wanted to live instead of die. He did not yet understand
that spiritual life was intrinsically more important than physical life, but he knew
that the end of his physical life was staring him in the face. A young Israelite maid
who waited on his wife told him that Elisha the prophet could heal him of leprosy.

A formal communication was sent from Naaman's king to the Israelite king
to ask for healing for the valued commander Naaman. Elisha was not overawed
by getting a letter from any king because he knew that Naaman could be healed
of leprosy by washing seven times in the Jordan River. Moreover, Elisha did not
need to go to Naaman; he just sent a messenger to him detailing the cure. Such a
simple solution enraged Naaman because he was used to more complicated battle
strategies. His servants pleaded with him. They made him realize that God asks
us to do simple tasks; it is easy to please God.

Once Naaman understood the simplicity and beauty of obedience to God,
he believed the truth. He did the truth. The truth healed him when Naaman
turned to God in humility and thanks.

The Book? Or the Books?

And I saw a great white throne, and him that sat on it, from whose
face the earth and the heaven fled away; and there was found no
place for them. And I saw the dead, small and great, stand before
God; and the books were opened: and another book was opened,
which is the book of life: and the dead were judged out of those
things which were written in the books, according to their works.
And the sea gave up the dead which were in it; and death and hell
delivered up the dead which were in them: and they were judged
every man according to their works. And death and hell were cast
into the lake of fire. This is the second death. And whosoever was
not found written in the book of life was cast into the lake of fire.
—Revelation 20:11–15

A day will come—no one knows exactly when—when the earth will be
gone—although it is impossible to imagine it now. At that time, God will
sit on an enormous, white throne of judgment. The earth, the sky, and all that is
familiar to us now will act according to the command of God. They will know
enough to flee from God and let Him get on with the show.

All people—both the living and the dead alike—will stand before God, the
supreme judge of the human race. Those who have lived in rebellion to God will
be judged according the books that have recorded all their sins. Many volumes
belong to those books. Only shame belongs to those who must listen to what is
written about them in those numerous books.

Those who have turned to God in repentance will be judged according the
book of life. The one book records only names in it—no sins are recorded in the
book of life. God has forgotten to record our sins because Jesus Christ has paid
the price for them. Those sins are eradicated forever. What elation belongs to
those who hear only their names spoken! As long as we live on this earth, we have
the hope of eternal life through the repentance for our sins. No one needs to face
the volumes of books that have recorded our sins on judgment day. Repentance
means that God erases the bad pages in the books and records only the name in
the book of life. Everyone may come to the One who writes a name only in the
book of life. Don't hesitate any longer to come to Jesus for forgiveness of sins.

MAY 21

Low Times in Life

I will extol thee, O Lord; for thou hast lifted me up, and hast not
made my foes to rejoice over me. O Lord my God, I cried unto
thee, and thou hast healed me. O Lord, thou hast brought up my
soul from the grave: thou hast kept me alive, that I should not go
down to the pit. Sing unto the Lord, O ye saints of his, and give
thanks at the remembrance of his holiness. For his anger endureth
but a moment; in his favour is life: weeping may endure for a night,
but joy cometh in the morning. And in my prosperity I said, I shall
never be moved. Lord, by thy favour thou hast made my mountain
to stand strong: thou didst hide thy face, and I was troubled.
—Psalm 30:1–7

Some of us are more prone to gloomy and depressing states of mind than
others, but all of us experience low times in life. Because most of David's life
was spent in eluding Saul who wanted to kill him, and fighting enemies of hostile
nations who wanted to overthrow him, David experienced his share of low times.

When we think of him tending sheep, we remember that David killed a
lion and a bear with only a slingshot because they were predators upon his flock
of sheep. We may think that facing wild animals that maul and kill is akin to
protecting self and country against forces of evil; perhaps David thought the
same. The challenges of shepherding seem like the kind of experiences that
would prevent him from falling into low times in his life, but they didn't.

Even though David knew what God wanted him to do overall, he recognized
his lack of power to prevail against his enemies. David prayed frequently and
vociferously for help, but when God did not answer him quickly, he sometimes
became despondent. Emotionally, he felt that God was angry with him at such
times, but theologically, he knew he was wrong. When God answers prayers as
quickly as David could pray them, David felt complacent. He felt he could no
longer be assailed. When God delayed to answer the prayer, David increased his
supplication to God. He came to realize that God sometimes withdraws His
favor to help us recognize how much we need God to sustain us every moment
for the task ahead.

Paralysis

And again he entered into Capernaum after some days; and it
was noised that he was in the house … And they come unto him,
bringing one sick of the palsy, which was borne of four. And when
they could not come nigh unto him for the press, they uncovered
the roof where he was: and when they had broken it up, they let
down the bed wherein the sick of the palsy lay. When Jesus saw their
faith, he said unto the sick of the palsy, Son, thy sins be forgiven
thee … And immediately when Jesus perceived in his spirit that they
so reasoned within themselves, he said unto them, Why reason ye
these things in your hearts? Whether is it easier to say to the sick
of the palsy, Thy sins be forgiven thee; or to say, Arise, and take
up thy bed, and walk? But that ye may know that the Son of man
hath power on earth to forgive sins, (he saith to the sick of the
palsy,) I say unto thee, Arise, and take up thy bed, and go thy way
into thine house. And immediately he arose, took up the bed, and
went forth before them all; insomuch that they were all amazed,
and glorified God, saying, We never saw it on this fashion.
—Mark 2:1, 3–5, 8–12

Jesus healed the paralysis of the man who lived with long-term and genuine physical limitations. In the days when universal design for public buildings did not exist, handicapped people could not press a button to open a heavy door any more than they could maneuver around in electric wheelchairs. To live a somewhat normal life, friends and relatives carried paralytics everywhere, if anywhere. Specialized nursing, such as organized home health care, did not exist.

The physical paralysis of the handicapped man can also represent the emotional, psychological, or spiritual paralyses that stunt the growth of any of us. When we cannot do ordinary things because of a personal paralysis, we need to go to the Lord, or we need to let others take us to the Lord and ask on our behalf. The paralytic knew why he could not walk, but he had heard about the man named Jesus who healed people.

We do not always know why we cannot do something, but we know that God helps us in every difficulty. This healing seems to be linked to spiritual disease because Jesus forgave the man's sins before He healed his body. For puzzling problems in life, God alone has the answers for us.

Heavenly Wonders

And there shall come forth a rod out of the stem of Jesse, and a
Branch shall grow out of his roots: And the spirit of the Lord shall
rest upon him, the spirit of wisdom and understanding, the spirit
of counsel and might, the spirit of knowledge and of the fear of
the Lord ... Behold, God is my salvation; I will trust, and not be
afraid: for the Lord Jehovah is my strength and my song; he also
is become my salvation ... Sing unto the Lord; for he hath done
excellent things: this is known in all the earth ... O Lord, thou art
my God; I will exalt thee, I will praise thy name; for thou hast done
wonderful things; thy counsels of old are faithfulness and truth.
—Isaiah 11:1–2; 12:2, 5; 25:1

The prophetic portion of the Old Testament tells us in metaphorical terms
here about the birth of Jesus Christ—the rod from the stem of Jesse. The
purpose of metaphors is to convey a grander, deeper meaning so as to impress
readers with the immensity of the concept. In human terminology, Jesus Christ
belongs to the house and lineage of King David; David's father was Jesse.

Because the Bible is the Word of God, we can understand the grandeur
in many ways on many levels. We gain a sense of the perfection of Jesus Christ
here. God's plan is fulfilled when the family of Jesse of Bethlehem bears fruit in
the birth of the Savior. The power and counsel of the Holy Spirit rest on Him
perfectly and give Jesus Christ great delight in the fear of God. He is endowed
with perfect wisdom, perfect power, and perfect knowledge.

What God has done for sinners is surpassingly marvelous. He planned it so
long ago, yet He sticks to the plan and makes salvation happen. Salvation from
God is truly wonderful, glorious, and delightful. Sometimes we just need to think
about the wonders of heaven that God has given to us. Words do not do them
justice, but we know the day will come when all the superlatives become our
constant and continuing reality.

The One True God

Ye are my witnesses, saith the Lord, and my servant whom I have chosen: that ye may know and believe me, and understand that I am he: before me there was no God formed, neither shall there be after me. I, even I, am the Lord; and beside me there is no saviour. I have declared, and have saved, and I have shewed, when there was no strange god among you: therefore ye are my witnesses, saith the Lord, that I am God. Yea, before the day was I am he; and there is none that can deliver out of my hand: I will work, and who shall let it? ...
Thus saith the Lord the King of Israel, and his redeemer the Lord of hosts; I am the first, and I am the last; and beside me there is no God.
—Isaiah 43:10–13; 44:6

I f we believe everything we read, we may gain the idea that religion is a matter of personal choice, no more, no less. Like a lot of popular ideas, this is partly true because every individual chooses what or who to believe. Unfortunately, the idea that comes across to us is that we may choose from a smorgasbord of any religion, any god, any idol, any path, any belief, or any philosophy. Whatever we choose, we call it our own. This type of thinking elevates both personal emotion and human reasoning above any other consideration.

If we have learned anything at all about human nature, we must admit to many failures where unrestrained emotion or skewed logic determines the course. If we are interested in archeology and ancient cultures, we may have learned that idolatry in multifarious forms dominated many ancient civilizations, no matter how advanced they were. The vulgarity of these objects of worship remains offensive, even today.

When we read the Old Testament, we learn that God severely punished and sometimes destroyed entire cultures who lived in pagan rebellion to Him. The Bible tells us that in ancient times, people knew who He was, even when they chose to live in rebellion and idolatry. This passage reveals the indignation of God that humans could think less of Him when they know better.

Strong Fortress

And he said, The Lord is my rock, and my fortress, and my deliverer.
—2 Samuel 22:2

Bow down thine ear to me; deliver me speedily: be thou my strong
rock, for an house of defence to save me. For thou art my rock and
my fortress; therefore for thy name's sake lead me, and guide me.
—Psalm 31:2–3

To many of us, a fortress is no more than a historical site where we may inspect a battlefield, replete with battlements and defense walls, lined with cannons, and built with enough barracks to house the militia who once used the property during a time of conflict. When national defense was less secure than it is today, the fortress might also have housed an enclosure where local residents could take refuge when the area was overrun with enemies who would slaughter any locals who got in their way.

The Bible uses the fortress imagery to assure us that our lives are an unseen but real, spiritual battlefield. God is still our strong fortress today. David learned, just like we can learn, that God protects us and delivers us from evil. We can run to Him when we are in danger and fear for our lives. God doesn't just protect us (from the negative things in life), but He also leads us (to the positive things in life)—to place us exactly where He wants us to be.

When we trust in God, he also strengthens us in Him—to make us as strong as He is. God our fortress has three dimensions to it: the evil He protects us from, the good He leads us to, and the likeness of Him that He gives to us as we surrender to Him. Who does not want to be bigger and better and stronger than they are right now?

The Extremes of Life

He hath put my brethren far from me, and mine acquaintance are
verily estranged from me. My kinsfolk have failed, and my familiar
friends have forgotten me. They that dwell in mine house, and my
maids, count me for a stranger: I am an alien in their sight. I called
my servant, and he gave me no answer; I intreated him with my
mouth. My breath is strange to my wife, though I intreated for the
children's sake of mine own body. Yea, young children despised
me; I arose, and they spake against me. All my inward friends
abhorred me: and they whom I loved are turned against me. My
bone cleaveth to my skin and to my flesh, and I am escaped with
the skin of my teeth … Oh that my words were now written! oh
that they were printed in a book! That they were graven with an
iron pen and lead in the rock for ever! For I know that my redeemer
liveth, and that he shall stand at the latter day upon the earth: And
though after my skin worms destroy this body, yet in my flesh
shall I see God: Whom I shall see for myself, and mine eyes shall
behold, and not another; though my reins be consumed within me.
—Job 19:13–20, 23–27

The life of Job illustrates the extreme changes that can occur to anyone
unexpectedly. Job was a fabulously wealthy rancher. But one day, all his
livestock were either stolen or burned to a crisp. Job enjoyed a large family
life. And on the same day, all his children died under one roof while they were
celebrating a family feast. Job was healthy. He was unpredictably afflicted with
incurable sores from head to foot. Instead of respect for the neighborhood rich
guy, the locals loathed him. Instead of family gatherings, the remaining relatives
shunned him, even his wife. Instead of dutiful servants, they treated their master
like an alien. Instead of smelling good, Job reeked from his sores, and children
taunted him. Instead of good looks, he was a gaunt bag of bones.

The only desire of his misery was that others would know how bad it was
for him—and today we have the Word of God to tell us. The only knowledge
Job could cling to was faith in his Redeemer. When God afflicts us, He is the
only certainty we can cling to.

Job's confident faith in God in spite of overwhelmingly horrible
circumstances is also recorded for posterity, just as he hoped. We hope we never
face the enormous tragedies of Job's life, but if we do, we have an example of
how to trust God in that extremely difficult situation.

MAY 27

A Firm Foundation

And why call ye me, Lord, Lord, and do not the things which
I say? Whosoever cometh to me, and heareth my sayings, and
doeth them, I will shew you to whom he is like: He is like
a man which built an house, and digged deep, and laid the
foundation on a rock: and when the flood arose, the stream
beat vehemently upon that house, and could not shake it: for it
was founded upon a rock. But he that heareth, and doeth not,
is like a man that without a foundation built an house upon
the earth; against which the stream did beat vehemently, and
immediately it fell; and the ruin of that house was great.
—Luke 6:46–49

And it came to pass, when Jesus had ended these sayings,
the people were astonished at his doctrine: For he taught
them as one having authority, and not as the scribes.
—Matthew 7:28–29

People who live along the shoreline have most likely witnessed the destruction
that one severe storm, at high tide and full moon, can wreak. Parking lots
and paved roads disappear during the winter storm. The following summer,
rock-sized pieces of tar mixed among the natural pebbles and seashells of the
beach are all that is left.

When storms breach a sandbar that protects an inner harbor, the incoming
tide will erode the beach first, the septic tank second, and the house third. It
is shocking to see that a house that appeared so substantial for decades has
completely disappeared! Its broken pieces become the flotsam and jetsam of
the ocean, subject to tidal forces. Sometimes, our lives seem as unstable as the
shifting sands and rising tides of ocean storms that come upon us.

Our lives require a foundation, and obedience to God's Word is the only sure
substructure for our spiritual lives. Any other foundation upon which we build
our lives is subject to the vagaries of storm season. Every life will have its storm
season, some sooner, some later. Television and movies may portray every type
of human folly, but it is more beneficial to believers to read about how Christians
live so that they may learn how to weather the storms of their lives. No two lives
are exactly the same, but we want to learn the practical applications from God's
Word for daily use to build up a firm foundation for our own lives.

Who Is at Fault?

And as Jesus passed by, he saw a man which was blind from his
birth. And his disciples asked him, saying, Master, who did sin,
this man, or his parents, that he was born blind? Jesus answered,
Neither hath this man sinned, nor his parents: but that the works
of God should be made manifest in him. I must work the works of
him that sent me, while it is day: the night cometh, when no man
can work. As long as I am in the world, I am the light of the world.
—John 9:1–5

Most of us hold to the belief that God rewards or punishes human beings
according to the deeds of their lives. We are quick to judge the situations
of others by this notion. We also pat ourselves on the back that we are exempt
from the punishment that others clearly deserve. This assumption explains
why so many religions can require their adherents to follow numerous rules of
conduct and behavior. The false religions flourish as long as the members find
the specific rules tolerable.

People in the time of Jesus were subject to the same misunderstanding as
today, so Jesus took pains to explain the inaccuracy of this false assumption.
The reward or punishment theory is inaccurate because it does not adequately
explain why natural disasters occur. It does not explain why babies die. It does
not explain why young children become terminally ill. It does not explain why
horrible events occur in untimely ways. Humans always seek the satisfaction of
an explanation, but we do not always find it.

We can hold on to our inaccurate belief, or we can change our minds. In
every situation we face, we need to remember that God will share His glory with
no one else. In any situation, no matter how serious, no matter how trivial, the
glory of God will be displayed.

Training to Win the Prize

Know ye not that they which run in a race run all, but one receiveth
the prize? So run, that ye may obtain. And every man that striveth
for the mastery is temperate in all things. Now they do it to obtain
a corruptible crown; but we an incorruptible. I therefore so run, not
as uncertainly; so fight I, not as one that beateth the air: But I keep
under my body, and bring it into subjection: lest that by any means,
when I have preached to others, I myself should be a castaway.
—1 Corinthians 9:24–27

I press toward the mark for the prize of the
high calling of God in Christ Jesus.
—Philippians 3:14

But refuse profane and old wives' fables, and exercise thyself
rather unto godliness. For bodily exercise profiteth little:
but godliness is profitable unto all things, having promise
of the life that now is, and of that which is to come.
—1 Timothy 4:7–8

When the Olympic games are underway, we all begin to think about the
training that top-notch athletes undergo. Some of us who are athletic
ourselves may vicariously imagine ourselves in their place, but most of us sit back
in a cushy chair and watch the elite athletes compete. Unlike the enjoyment we
get from watching the Olympic races, we cannot take an armchair attitude to the
race of the Christian life.

The Christian life involves training in righteousness (instead of running).
Training means doing specific exercises repetitively to strengthen the specific
muscle groups for a specific sport (not the haphazard walk or jog or stretch that
most of us call exercise). Training tones the specific muscles most needed for
superior performance. Training in righteousness begins first with daily Bible
reading so that we will know what the Bible says and begin to apply what it says
to our lives. Some of us are flabby physically, but we cannot afford to be flabby
spiritually.

God's goal is to make us more like Jesus, so we need to learn what the
standards are, practice those skills in order to live up to the standards, and keep
on racing to win the prize for which God has called us heavenward.

God Wastes Nothing

Thus saith the Lord, thy redeemer, and he that formed thee from
the womb, I am the Lord that maketh all things; that stretcheth
forth the heavens alone; that spreadeth abroad the earth by myself;
That frustrateth the tokens of the liars, and maketh diviners mad;
that turneth wise men backward, and maketh their knowledge
foolish; That confirmeth the word of his servant, and performeth
the counsel of his messengers; that saith to Jerusalem, Thou shalt
be inhabited; and to the cities of Judah, Ye shall be built, and I will
raise up the decayed places thereof: That saith to the deep, Be dry,
and I will dry up thy rivers: That saith of Cyrus, He is my shepherd,
and shall perform all my pleasure: even saying to Jerusalem, Thou
shalt be built; and to the temple, Thy foundation shall be laid.
—Isaiah 44:24–28

It is always important to remember that God is sovereign—He rules over the
kingdoms of this world. He created the universe and the inhabited world, and
He knows what He wants to do with them. Unlike Him, we set personal goals
and temporary goals, but God's plans have eternal goals in mind. We cannot fully
understand them, but we can trust God—that is the main point. Sometimes our
plans are foiled, sometimes our strategies go wrong, or sometimes they change
completely.

We cannot understand how or why God operates even when we know that
His purpose prevails. Sometimes we see how people who live in rebellion to God
get ahead in life when more godly people get left behind. This may bother us, but
God uses everyone in the plans He has for planet earth. God used King Cyrus
to do His will, even though it does not appear that Cyrus was a believer in God.

God directs human activity by opening doors that no one else can shut or
by closing doors that no one else can open. God is sovereign over all the affairs
of all people. He wastes no thing. He uses all people to fulfill His overarching
plan for planet earth.

Shout for Joy

Make a joyful noise unto the Lord, all ye lands. Serve the Lord
with gladness: come before his presence with singing. Know ye
that the Lord he is God: it is he that hath made us, and not we
ourselves; we are his people, and the sheep of his pasture. Enter
into his gates with thanksgiving, and into his courts with praise: be
thankful unto him, and bless his name. For the Lord is good; his
mercy is everlasting; and his truth endureth to all generations.
—Psalm 100:1–5

Then he said unto them ... Go your way ... for this day is holy unto
our Lord: neither be ye sorry; for the joy of the Lord is your strength.
—Nehemiah 8:10

Do we ever notice the faces of passersby when we are walking down the
sidewalk of a busy city, sauntering through the mall, or strolling along
a crowded beach? When we do, we perceive that most people are preoccupied
or worried or hurried. Their faces rarely reflect the joy of the Lord. Maybe we
should ask ourselves the same kind of question. Are we so happy with the Lord
in our lives that we want to shout for joy? Does He make our hearts so glad that
we sing of Him daily?

This exuberant life comes from knowing that the Lord really is the God of
heaven and earth. It means a rejection of idols and materialistic pursuits. It means
an acceptance of our small place in the huge universe. The joyful life means that
we are glad to belong to the God of heaven. At the same time, we admit that we
are no better than dumb sheep that graze in the rain, catch cold, and come close
to dying for their innate stupidity. We should shout for joy that God still wants
us dummies to belong to Him.

The happy life means that we bask in the love God showers upon us, and
we call to mind that He will always be here for us, now and later in life. The
enthusiasm we accept from the hand of God enlivens us, and we carry it into our
lives as we praise Him continually.

From Overconfidence to Love

They that go down to the sea in ships, that do business in great
waters; These see the works of the Lord, and his wonders in the
deep. For he commandeth, and raiseth the stormy wind, which lifteth
up the waves thereof. They mount up to the heaven, they go down
again to the depths: their soul is melted because of trouble. They
reel to and fro, and stagger like a drunken man, and are at their wit's
end. Then they cry unto the Lord in their trouble, and he bringeth
them out of their distresses. He maketh the storm a calm, so that
the waves thereof are still. Then are they glad because they be quiet;
so he bringeth them unto their desired haven. Oh that men would
praise the Lord for his goodness, and for his wonderful works to
the children of men! Let them exalt him also in the congregation
of the people, and praise him in the assembly of the elders.
—Psalm 107:23–32

Many of us take vicarious delight in learning about modern day adventurers.
They dive into the depths of the ocean. They climb to the top of daunting
mountain peaks. They trek across dangerous volcanic zones. They hurtle through
outer space. They descend into dark caverns. For the rest of us, their exploits
mirror the same spirit of adventure required for the more mundane tasks of life,
so we derive inspiration from them.

Nevertheless, we all feel the same need to be lifted above the daily routine,
and adventurers show us how. The opposite of such nervy people are the
daredevils who adventure carelessly and get themselves into mortal trouble
from unwarranted overconfidence. We may learn about them too, but with a lot
less enthusiasm.

Adventures occur in our lives as well, but on a more ordinary level. Whether
adventures are exciting or outright dangerous, God still cares about us when
trouble overtakes us. Sometimes, God can stir up a tempest around us that causes
courage to melt into deadly peril, leaving a hapless sense of no exit. When we cry
out to God in our peril, He alleviates our distress. He stills the storm. He guides
us to His desired haven. His activity on our behalf reveals His unfailing love—a
steadier inspiration than strangers with extraordinary human powers.

God Is with Me

O lord, thou hast searched me, and known me. Thou knowest
my downsitting and mine uprising, thou understandest my
thought afar off. Thou compassest my path and my lying down,
and art acquainted with all my ways. For there is not a word in
my tongue, but, lo, O Lord, thou knowest it altogether. Thou
hast beset me behind and before, and laid thine hand upon me.
Such knowledge is too wonderful for me; it is high, I cannot
attain unto it. Whither shall I go from thy spirit? or whither
shall I flee from thy presence? ... Search me, O God, and know
my heart: try me, and know my thoughts: And see if there be
any wicked way in me, and lead me in the way everlasting.
—Psalm 139:1–7, 23–24

The natural yearning for companionship and understanding from another
person is a very strong and genuine human requirement. We look for a soul
mate, but even when we find the person, human companionship will at times
disappoint us. God wants us to learn from everything in our lives that He alone
is the one who knows us best.

What a relief to know that God knows us both inside and out! Even when
we do not know what to say, where to go, or what to do, God guides us infallibly
by hemming us in. He stands behind us to direct us, and He stands in front of
us to illuminate the way.

What a comfort to know that the Holy Spirit is everywhere—both above and
below—in darkness and in light—in front and in back. His guidance cannot be
hindered by any impediment. What a wonder to know that God created us before
anyone knew who we would become. He has already planned out all our days
for us. We need to get on board and take the personal journey of life with Him.

JUNE 3

Leavening

> Another parable spake he unto them; The kingdom of
> heaven is like unto leaven, which a woman took, and hid in
> three measures of meal, till the whole was leavened.
> —Matthew 13:33

Everyone loves pizza or maybe focaccia or a crusty French bread, especially when it is fresh and hot from the oven. Grocery stores often display them when they are just baked and watch customers snatch them off the racks. The hungrier we are, the more we enjoy these yeasty staples. Bread is a staple food, and Jesus used simple leavened bread to teach us about the kingdom of heaven, the destination of believers.

Flour is a plentiful and inexpensive ingredient, indicating that it is easy for anyone to enter the kingdom of heaven. Only one tablespoon of yeast is needed to leaven from one to five cups of flour, a huge difference in quantity. Only about three to nine percent of the finished product is actually leavening, but the final product has doubled in size from the small amount of leavening. The leavening has worked its way throughout the entire loaf of bread, and the taste is considered unsurpassed by many who enjoy it. The leavening represents the means by which those who enter the kingdom of heaven grow in the knowledge of God.

Many of us call ourselves by the name of Christ. When the Word of God permeates our lives, like yeast in bread. We grow exponentially, apparently without effort. Others can see this growth as much as we can. When we allow the leavening of God's Word to spread throughout our lives, we grow in the way God prescribes.

Great Riches

Again, the kingdom of heaven is like unto treasure hid in a field; the
which when a man hath found, he hideth, and for joy thereof goeth
and selleth all that he hath, and buyeth that field. Again, the kingdom
of heaven is like unto a merchant man, seeking goodly pearls: Who,
when he had found one pearl of great price, went and sold all that he
had, and bought it ... Lay not up for yourselves treasures upon earth,
where moth and rust doth corrupt, and where thieves break through
and steal: But lay up for yourselves treasures in heaven, where neither
moth nor rust doth corrupt, and where thieves do not break through
nor steal: For where your treasure is, there will your heart be also.
—Matthew 13:44–46; 6:19–21

The perspectives we hold make a huge difference in our lives; many would
agree that people cannot "see" what they are not looking for. For some
young believers who grew up in an unbelieving family, this type of contradiction
may rankle in the mind for several decades: How can anyone hold onto ungodly
attitudes, behaviors, and assumptions without ever seeing the beautiful treasure
that God offers to the creatures He has formed in His image and likeness? It
seems impossible, yet it happens. Even though the nurture and care of children
is important and cannot be disregarded, the spiritual side of life is the more
important and enduring aspect of life.

When godly spirituality is overlooked, its absence creates a void that only
Jesus Christ can fill. The absence of a godly outlook also creates a blindness to
spiritual truths. Nevertheless, God can use the emptiness from this part of life
to create in young believers a lifelong appreciation of the riches of the glorious
inheritance that belongs to them.

Salvation is a precious treasure—rejected by some, gratefully accepted
by others. Salvation holds the highest value, unacknowledged by some and
appreciated by others.

Holiness

But ye are a chosen generation, a royal priesthood, an holy nation,
a peculiar people; that ye should shew forth the praises of him
who hath called you out of darkness into his marvellous light;
Which in time past were not a people, but are now the people
of God: which had not obtained mercy, but now have obtained
mercy. Dearly beloved, I beseech you as strangers and pilgrims,
abstain from fleshly lusts, which war against the soul; Having
your conversation honest among the Gentiles: that, whereas they
speak against you as evildoers, they may by your good works,
which they shall behold, glorify God in the day of visitation.
—1 Peter 2:9–12

And ye shall keep my statutes, and do them:
I am the Lord which sanctify you.
—Leviticus 20:8

What does holiness mean to a lot of people except to be weird in a way that repels others? Nothing could be farther from the truth! True holiness should attract, not repel others. True personal holiness should cause others who know us to desire what we have and they lack. Peter is trying to convey to his readers the grandeur of holiness, because holiness belongs to God.

God is holy—perfect—magnificent—far beyond the human conception of any superlative term. And furthermore, holiness is the quality that should mark the life of the believer. Holiness means that even though God is utterly unlike us, we have been made in His image, and He chooses individuals like us to visibly portray His personal qualities to others. Holiness involves obedience to God's expressed commands. Holiness means that our behavior should be above reproach because we belong to an elite group chosen by God.

Why live a holy life? To bring glory and praise to God—holiness belongs to God, and now holiness belongs to us. Holiness motivates us to live such good lives that others will recognize God in us, resulting in more glory to God, the only one who deserves such high praise.

JUNE 6

Hope for the Lost

Therefore say, Thus saith the Lord God; Although I have cast them
far off among the heathen, and although I have scattered them
among the countries, yet will I be to them as a little sanctuary in
the countries where they shall come. Therefore say, Thus saith the
Lord God; I will even gather you from the people, and assemble
you out of the countries where ye have been scattered, and I will
give you the land of Israel. And they shall come thither, and
they shall take away all the detestable things thereof and all the
abominations thereof from thence. And I will give them one heart,
and I will put a new spirit within you; and I will take the stony
heart out of their flesh, and will give them an heart of flesh ...
Then did the cherubims lift up their wings, and the wheels beside
them; and the glory of the God of Israel was over them above.
And the glory of the Lord went up from the midst of the city, and
stood upon the mountain which is on the east side of the city.
—Ezekiel 11:16–19, 22–23

Although we may not like to admit it, the Bible tells us unmistakably that
all of us have sinned and wandered far from God. Some of us have lived
such terrible lives that we would rather not mention our exploits to others lest
we alienate them from us.

Israel was in just such a state of alienation—that is why God sent them as
captives to the nation of Babylon. He knew that when they experienced personal
loss from the sins they thought were advancing them through life, they would
realize how much they needed to repent and turn back in obedience to the God
who loved them.

In any century or in any country, God gives hope to the vilest of sinners.
Even when living in complete rebellion to God, God still provides a way out,
a place of sanctuary for sinners. We may look for that sign of God's grace, if
we have been there. Look for the way God gathers us to Himself as part of a
believing community—the church—marvel at how God is now making us into
real human beings, with real hearts of love for Him. Rejoice that those filthy
images have been removed from our minds and lives. Obeying God's laws and
following His decrees is a beautiful experience!

Where Do You Come From?

But when Herod was dead, behold, an angel of the Lord appeareth
in a dream to Joseph in Egypt, Saying, Arise, and take the young
child and his mother, and go into the land of Israel: for they are dead
which sought the young child's life. And he arose, and took the young
child and his mother, and came into the land of Israel. But when he
heard that Archelaus did reign in Judaea in the room of his father
Herod, he was afraid to go thither: notwithstanding, being warned
of God in a dream, he turned aside into the parts of Galilee: And he
came and dwelt in a city called Nazareth: that it might be fulfilled
which was spoken by the prophets, He shall be called a Nazarene.
—Matthew 2:19–23

D o we think of ourselves as small town girls or big city guys? We tend to
identify ourselves with the places we have lived. We believe that some
qualities of that location, whether rural, urban, or suburban have adhered to our
personalities. We feel certain that specific characteristics of that region, whether
New England, South, West, Southwest, West Coast, or Middle Atlantic have
shaped our outlooks on life. Perhaps this is true, but even it is, locations should
not rule our lives.

Think about the facts of the life of Jesus Christ: He was born in one country
(Israel), He moved to a foreign land (Egypt) as a toddler, and He moved back
to a different part of his own country (from Bethlehem to Nazareth) as a boy.
Some of us would consider this to be too much moving around for any normal
family. When we think of Jesus of Nazareth, we never think of Him as an alien
or immigrant in Egypt.

But God carries out His unique purposes in how He arranges human lives.
Not only did God protect His Son from harm, Jesus also set an example for us
to look to God for where to go next, even if it means leaving the home country
for a while.

Reality Shows

Then said they unto him, Where is he? He said, I know not ... They
say unto the blind man again, What sayest thou of him, that he hath
opened thine eyes? He said, He is a prophet ... He answered and said,
Whether he be a sinner or no, I know not: one thing I know, that,
whereas I was blind, now I see ... If this man were not of God, he
could do nothing ... Jesus heard that they had cast him out; and when
he had found him, he said unto him, Dost thou believe on the Son
of God? ... And he said, Lord, I believe. And he worshipped him.
—John 9:12, 17, 25, 33, 35, 38

Reality shows portray dramatic transformations of human beings in an
incredibly short time span. Even when the host of the show explains that
the changes have occurred over weeks or months, the show still concludes in
an hour or less. The degree of change boggles the mind of the average viewer,
but the shows do prove that human minds, bodies, and spaces can alter quickly,
given enough impetus.

The Bible also tells of dramatic transformations that rival those produced
by human ingenuity. Consider the man, blind from birth, whose sight was
instantly restored by Jesus Christ. He experienced both physical and spiritual
transformation in one brief day. The steps of his transformation are recorded for
us today. According to his first impression, he thought of Jesus as a man, but he
didn't know where that wonderful man had disappeared to. Then, he upgraded
his opinion of Jesus; he believed that Jesus was a prophet because He healed him
from an incurable affliction. In his final transformation of thought, the formerly
blind man understood that Jesus was really a miracle worker and upgraded Jesus
to a "man from God."

When Jesus Christ confronted the newly sighted man, He asked if he believed
in the Son of Man? Clearly, the events of the day and the rapid-fire questions of
the Pharisees had caused the man to do some hard thinking. He responded to
Jesus in belief—he had found the Savior—the best reality of all.

Wrong Goals

Thus saith the Lord, What iniquity have your fathers found in me,
that they are gone far from me, and have walked after vanity, and
are become vain? ... The children gather wood, and the fathers
kindle the fire, and the women knead their dough, to make cakes
to the queen of heaven, and to pour out drink offerings unto
other gods, that they may provoke me to anger. Do they provoke
me to anger? saith the Lord: do they not provoke themselves to
the confusion of their own faces? ... Only acknowledge thine
iniquity, that thou hast transgressed against the Lord thy God,
and hast scattered thy ways to the strangers under every green
tree, and ye have not obeyed my voice, saith the Lord ... Thus
saith the Lord of hosts, the God of Israel, Amend your ways
and your doings, and I will cause you to dwell in this place.
—Jeremiah 2:5; 7:18–19; 3:13; 7:3

We are taught from many sources that when we establish goals and follow through on them, we are on the high road to achieving success. This makes sense to us, because we know that must follow through on a plan in order to accomplish a goal. We also admire those highly focused people who are great achievers in life because we think they have followed some more exacting steps to fulfill their lofty goals.

But God speaks a word about our goal-setting ways. Goals are not wrong, but when our goals omit God from our lives, we choose trash instead of treasure. When we persist in pursuit of these worthless goals, our lives become as worthless as our choices. No one can live above those choices.

Do we understand that we harm ourselves most when we choose rebellion? Nevertheless, God still waits for us to return to Him just like He waited for Israel to return to Him in the time of Jeremiah and the Babylonian captivity. When we acknowledge sin, when we humble ourselves and mend our ways, God's presence returns to us. God desires our fellowship.

JUNE 10

How This World Operates

If he set his heart upon man, if he gather unto himself his
spirit and his breath; All flesh shall perish together, and man
shall turn again unto dust ... I know that thou canst do every
thing, and that no thought can be withholden from thee.
—Job 34:14–15; 42:2

He hath made the earth by his power, he hath established the world by
his wisdom, and hath stretched out the heaven by his understanding.
—Jeremiah 51:15

Who being the brightness of his glory, and the express
image of his person, and upholding all things by the word
of his power, when he had by himself purged our sins,
sat down on the right hand of the Majesty on high.
—Hebrews 1:3

Scientists seek to discover how the systems of the earth operate: tides and
oceans, hurricanes and tsunamis, desert and mountain habitats, sunny and
stormy weather, volcanoes and eruptions. The natural forces of the earth are
mighty, and ultimately, they are beyond the complete comprehension of the
human mind. Even when we learn a lot about the systems of the earth, we realize
that quite a lot still remains unknown and perhaps unknowable.

Philosophers also make inquiry about the natural world too. Some of them
conclude that God has left us alone because they see natural forces raging out
of control; therefore, God does not care or is not there, or both. They do not
understand how this world operates.

Only the Bible tells us how this world operates—but not in a scientific or a
philosophic sense. This world operates by God's explicit intention, by His express
command, by His living breath, by His overwhelming power, according to His
infinite wisdom, according to His unfathomable understanding. The Son of God
radiates God's glory, and the Son of God sustains all things by His powerful
Word. We need to learn science and philosophy, but we also need to learn the
Word of God. Let us be glad and never cease to wonder at the marvels of this
beautiful world that God created for us.

Pure Gold

Blessed be the God and Father of our Lord Jesus Christ, which according to his abundant mercy hath begotten us again unto a lively hope by the resurrection of Jesus Christ from the dead, To an inheritance incorruptible, and undefiled, and that fadeth not away, reserved in heaven for you, Who are kept by the power of God through faith unto salvation ready to be revealed in the last time. Wherein ye greatly rejoice, though now for a season, if need be, ye are in heaviness through manifold temptations: That the trial of your faith, being much more precious than of gold that perisheth, though it be tried with fire, might be found unto praise and honour and glory at the appearing of Jesus Christ: Whom having not seen, ye love; in whom, though now ye see him not, yet believing, ye rejoice with joy unspeakable and full of glory: Receiving the end of your faith, even the salvation of your souls.

—1 Peter 1:3–9

Have you recently received a gold engagement ring? Were you recently married with a gold wedding ring? Gold is a fitting symbolic reminder of the purity and value of longevity in marriage. The precious metal remains malleable even when subjected to high heat. In the same way, marriages can endure a lot of stress. Gold lasts a long time, just like marriage is supposed to last a long time.

God gives us many things in this earthly life to remind us what the spiritual life is like. The indissoluble bond of marriage is a concrete reminder of our faith—an intangible quality we cannot touch or see. Faith is worth more than gold—an expensive and desirable metal that we feel around our fingers once we put it on. Just like the marital bond strengthens both of us when facing the onslaught of worldly difficulties, God's power shields our faith from dissolving when we face trials.

It is always helpful to think of the small things of this life to remember the joy of the salvation of our souls, which holds infinitely greater joy than the human mind can conceive.

Trusting in Your Own Strength

And the woman bare a son, and called his name Samson: and the
child grew, and the Lord blessed him ... Then went Samson to Gaza,
and saw there an harlot, and went in unto her ... That he told her
all his heart, ... And she made him sleep upon her knees; and she
called for a man, and she caused him to shave off the seven locks of
his head; and she began to afflict him, and his strength went from
him. And she said, The Philistines be upon thee, Samson. And he
awoke out of his sleep, and said, I will go out as at other times before,
and shake myself. And he wist not that the Lord was departed from
him ... Howbeit the hair of his head began to grow again after he
was shaven ... And Samson said, Let me die with the Philistines.
And he bowed himself with all his might; and the house fell upon the
lords, and upon all the people that were therein. So the dead which
he slew at his death were more than they which he slew in his life.
—Judges 13:24; 16:1, 17a, 19–20, 22, 30

The birth of Samson was announced to his sterile mother by an angel of the
Lord. Both parents had prayed for God's help to raise a godly son, and as
Samson grew, the Spirit of the Lord began to move within him. In spite of God's
hand on his life, Samson was a man who lacked basic discipline and self-control.

As a young man, he wanted to marry a Philistine woman—not just a woman
of a different faith, but a woman of no faith. Instead of living a morally pure life,
he visited houses of prostitution as well. Samson was physically strong. He tore
a lion apart with his bare hands. He caught 300 foxes, tied their tails in pairs, lit
the tails with torches, and sent them through Philistine farm fields. He broke out
of strongly tied bonds of rope. He killed 1000 men with the jawbone of a donkey.
The exploits of his life reads like the life of Superman, but Samson was a real man,
not a fictional cartoon character. Because he knew God was with him, Samson
felt he could do as he pleased. He relied on his own shrewdness every time. The
last prostitute ruined his life by shaving off his hair, the source of his strength.
The newly blinded man finally realized how ungodly his so-called religious life
had been. When his hair grew in again, he asked God for strength to defeat the
Philistines. God helped him because it is never too late to do what is right.

Samson's last act of valor was also an act of suicide. He was chained to a
pillar in the Philistine banqueting hall, so when the roof collapsed, he died with
them. Presuming upon God because you know Him always results in disaster.

Remember Where You Came From

All the commandments which I command thee this day shall ye
observe to do, that ye may live, and multiply, and go in and possess
the land which the Lord sware unto your fathers. And thou shalt
remember all the way which the Lord thy God led thee these
forty years in the wilderness, to humble thee, and to prove thee,
to know what was in thine heart, whether thou wouldest keep his
commandments, or no. And he humbled thee, and suffered thee
to hunger, and fed thee with manna, which thou knewest not,
neither did thy fathers know; that he might make thee know that
man doth not live by bread only, but by every word that proceedeth
out of the mouth of the Lord doth man live. Thy raiment waxed
not old upon thee, neither did thy foot swell, these forty years.
Thou shalt also consider in thine heart, that, as a man chasteneth
his son, so the Lord thy God chasteneth thee ... And thou say in
thine heart, My power and the might of mine hand hath gotten
me this wealth. But thou shalt remember the Lord thy God: for
it is he that giveth thee power to get wealth, that he may establish
his covenant which he sware unto thy fathers, as it is this day.
—Deuteronomy 8:1–5, 17–18

God wants us to obey Him so that we will obtain maximum blessing in this
life. He intended the same blessing for the nation of Israel, showing us that
His good intentions toward people have never changed, from ancient days to
modern times. To keep Israel focused on Him, to prevent them from yearning
after the wealth of the Egyptian land they had recently departed from, God sent
them through the wilderness for forty years.

The arid heat of the desert was hot enough to cut off the memory of wealth
and its associated sins. God knew they needed to forget about it. God fed them
manna in the wilderness. The experience of a plain and repetitive diet was enough
to cancel out the memory of all the rich food they ate in Egypt. Their clothing
and sandals did not wear out for four decades! Redirecting their affections
for a familiar place, retraining their taste buds, and relieving them from the
arduous toil of fabric weaving and garment sewing—these were three ways God
overhauled the thought processes of His people toward Him.

Their experiences reminded them that God produces wealth and bestows
it wherever and whenever He chooses. He is the same today, and we can claim
nothing as the product of our own initiative.

Sorrow for Sin

For though I made you sorry with a letter, I do not repent, though
I did repent: for I perceive that the same epistle hath made you
sorry, though it were but for a season. Now I rejoice, not that
ye were made sorry, but that ye sorrowed to repentance: for ye
were made sorry after a godly manner, that ye might receive
damage by us in nothing. For godly sorrow worketh repentance
to salvation not to be repented of: but the sorrow of the world
worketh death. For behold this selfsame thing, that ye sorrowed
after a godly sort, what carefulness it wrought in you, yea, what
clearing of yourselves, yea, what indignation, yea, what fear, yea,
what vehement desire, yea, what zeal, yea, what revenge! In all
things ye have approved yourselves to be clear in this matter.
—2 Corinthians 7:8–11

No doubt about it—*all have sinned and fall short of the glory of God*—we might like to think we are better than some, but we know that this is not really true. Sin falls into three categories: willful sins we commit, unintentional sins we commit, and accidental sins we commit. We cannot escape sin in this life. So what can we do when we fall into sin? We must repent of it, not just regret it, like Judas Iscariot did. We must be truly sorry for sin, not just rue it, like Cain did.

Worldly sorrow creates no beneficial or permanent change in the person. The sin is over, but the effects of the sin remain because *the wages of sin is death*. Judas Iscariot hanged himself. Adam's son Cain felt his punishment was more than he could humanly bear, so he wandered as far from the scene of his crime as possible. People who sin know they are doing wrong. Godly sorrow, like King David, makes a person do a complete about-face. The person is confronted with the sin. Paul confronted the Corinthians just as Nathan confronted David. The person acknowledges the grievous fault and repents of it.

Salvation brings release from the grip of sin in our lives. This means that we can repent and move on and live a life without regrets. What a much better way to live!

Worthless Idols

Thus saith the Lord, Learn not the way of the heathen, and be not
dismayed at the signs of heaven; for the heathen are dismayed at
them … For the customs of the people are vain: for one cutteth
a tree out of the forest, the work of the hands of the workman,
with the axe … They are upright as the palm tree, but speak not:
they must needs be borne, because they cannot go. Be not afraid
of them; for they cannot do evil, neither also is it in them to
do good … But the Lord is the true God, he is the living God,
and an everlasting king: at his wrath the earth shall tremble,
and the nations shall not be able to abide his indignation.
—Jeremiah 10:2–3, 5, 10

They that make a graven image are all of them vanity; and their
delectable things shall not profit; and they are their own witnesses;
they see not, nor know; that they may be ashamed. Who hath
formed a god, or molten a graven image that is profitable for
nothing? Behold, all his fellows shall be ashamed: and the workmen,
they are of men: let them all be gathered together, let them stand
up; yet they shall fear, and they shall be ashamed together.
—Isaiah 44:9–11

We live in a time of religious pluralism. This means that people can choose
to believe in anything they want to, and any kind of belief that passes for
religion is pressed upon our attention for serious consideration. We are taught
to think that all beliefs and all religions are equally valid and equally valuable to
help humans through this life. But God's Holy Word disagrees most vehemently
with this modern perspective.

From the Bible, we learn that any object or belief that is cherished and is
not the God of the Bible is really an idol, and God has let us know that idolatry
is forbidden by Him. In contrast to the one, true God, an idol is a fraud; it is a
phony; it is temporal, and it is dead. The living God who created the universe
stands in sharp and beautiful contrast to all our empty idols.

The Lord who has revealed Himself to us is true; He is alive. He is eternal.
He desires us to turn to Him instead of all the ideas or customs that others may
want us to observe. Let us allow our attention to be captivated by the One who
runs the universe and never tires of doing good toward his creatures.

Why God Saves Us

For we ourselves also were sometimes foolish, disobedient,
deceived, serving divers lusts and pleasures, living in malice and
envy, hateful, and hating one another. But after that the kindness
and love of God our Saviour toward man appeared, Not by works
of righteousness which we have done, but according to his mercy
he saved us, by the washing of regeneration, and renewing of
the Holy Ghost; Which he shed on us abundantly through Jesus
Christ our Saviour; That being justified by his grace, we should be
made heirs according to the hope of eternal life. This is a faithful
saying, and these things I will that thou affirm constantly, that
they which have believed in God might be careful to maintain
good works. These things are good and profitable unto men.
—Titus 3:3–8

Many religions teach that people must do good deeds or follow a progression
of upward steps to be accepted by God in spite of the fact that the sinful
nature shows us every day that we are never good enough to measure up to such
impossible human ideals.

The Bible is realistic because it tells us what we are really like—we are
sinners—silly, rebellious, overrun by bad desires, deceived by momentary
pleasure, malicious toward others, envious of others. We hate them, and they
hate us—fair and square! This is life.

In spite of our worst efforts, God shows His love and kindness toward the
world when He saves us. Salvation is beautiful, like coming up from the deep
water fresh and clean, like putting on clean clothes to enjoy the rest of the day.
God says we are now all right because Jesus Christ took our punishment instead.
When we trust in God to save us, we join a great company of wealthy heirs who
will gain eternal life.

Final Prayers

Wherefore David blessed the Lord before all the congregation: and David said, Blessed be thou, Lord God of Israel our father, for ever and ever. Thine, O Lord is the greatness, and the power, and the glory, and the victory, and the majesty: for all that is in the heaven and in the earth is thine; thine is the kingdom, O Lord, and thou art exalted as head above all. Both riches and honour come of thee, and thou reignest over all; and in thine hand is power and might; and in thine hand it is to make great, and to give strength unto all. Now therefore, our God, we thank thee, and praise thy glorious name.
—1 Chronicles 29:10–13

And they sing the song of Moses the servant of God, and the song of the Lamb, saying, Great and marvellous are thy works, Lord God Almighty; just and true are thy ways, thou King of saints. Who shall not fear thee, O Lord, and glorify thy name? for thou only art holy: for all nations shall come and worship before thee; for thy judgments are made manifest.
—Revelation 15:3–4

All of us know that we will come to the end of our lives, but do we ever consider to what end will we come to? Will our end be despair, suicide, and ignominy like King Saul? Will our end be one of peace and praise to God, like King David? It wasn't the material circumstances of their lives that made the difference. Both were extremely wealthy and powerful kings who had all that this world offers—indeed, everything their hearts could desire.

The difference in their final outcomes was their spiritual outlooks. King David praises God as his eternal father; he sees himself as a small drop in a boundless ocean. David acknowledges the greatness and power of God, a humble statement from such a wealthy and powerful earthly king. David says that God is glorious, majestic, and splendid, another surprising comment from a king who has enjoyed all that this world offers. David acknowledges that God owns heaven and earth; His realm is more far-reaching than the tiny land of Israel. Yet David places God first in his life instead of himself. David acknowledges that God has given him all his wealth and power.

Only the spiritually minded soul understands his position to the Creator. David cannot stop giving thanks to God, even at the end of his life. The more he believed God, the more he understood His greatness.

Waiting on God

> Now he was ruddy, and withal of a beautiful countenance, and goodly to look to. And the Lord said, Arise, anoint him: for this is he. Then Samuel took the horn of oil, and anointed him in the midst of his brethren: and the Spirit of the Lord came upon David from that day forward. So Samuel rose up, and went to Ramah.
> —1 Samuel 16:12–13

> ... Now there was long war between the house of Saul and the house of David: but David waxed stronger and stronger, and the house of Saul waxed weaker and weaker ... And David said to Joab, and to all the people that were with him, Rend your clothes, and gird you with sackcloth, and mourn before Abner. And king David himself followed the bier ... And all the people took notice of it, and it pleased them: as whatsoever the king did pleased all the people ... Then came all the tribes of Israel to David unto Hebron, and spake, saying, Behold, we are thy bone and thy flesh. Also in time past, when Saul was king over us, thou wast he that leddest out and broughtest in Israel: and the Lord said to thee, Thou shalt feed my people Israel, and thou shalt be a captain over Israel. So all the elders of Israel came to the king to Hebron; and king David made a league with them in Hebron before the Lord: and they anointed David king over Israel. David was thirty years old when he began to reign, and he reigned forty years.
> —2 Samuel 3:1, 31, 36; 5:1–4

Some of us know from an early age what we want to be or do when we grow up. We discuss our plans with our little friends as if we were grown up already. Quite often the profession is our own idea, and maybe it pans out; sometimes it is just the talk of childhood.

For the future king David, the choice of profession came from God when the prophet Samuel anointed him as king in his late teenage years. The youngest son of a well-to-do rancher was chosen by God to be a national leader.

Believers still look for such specific signs of guidance from above, but usually circumstances combine with needs to turn us in the direction God wants us to go. The most important thing is not the call but the intention. David was a man after God's own heart—he sought God's will at every decision point. He behaved with justice and kindness, depending on the situation. Most of all, he waited for God to give him the go-ahead for the plans of the Lord. Only God's signals to go ahead will lead us where God wants. God kept David occupied with many tasks before ascending the throne of Israel; they enhanced the leadership skills he would need as king.

JUNE 19

Unintentional Errors

And the sons of the prophets said unto Elisha, Behold now, the place where we dwell with thee is too strait for us. Let us go, we pray thee, unto Jordan, and take thence every man a beam, and let us make us a place there, where we may dwell. And he answered, Go ye. And one said, Be content, I pray thee, and go with thy servants. And he answered, I will go. So he went with them. And when they came to Jordan, they cut down wood. But as one was felling a beam, the axe head fell into the water: and he cried, and said, Alas, master! for it was borrowed. And the man of God said, Where fell it? And he shewed him the place. And he cut down a stick, and cast it in thither; and the iron did swim. Therefore said he, Take it up to thee. And he put out his hand, and took it.
—2 Kings 6:1–7

Most of us try to do our best, but there are times when we must face the fact that our best efforts have unfortunately turned out for the worst. This is the kind of day where everything that could possibly go wrong does go wrong. On those days, we realize that our sinful nature is acting up on us, even when we had planned otherwise.

As a prophet, Elisha ran a training school for spiritually minded young men. There were so many of them that they needed a permanent campus for their meetings and classes, like a small college campus today. They decided to build their own school facility, so they got started on the project. While they were in the preliminary building process of clearing the acreage of trees, one student prophet lost his iron axe head in the water. The necessary tool did not belong to the student; it was borrowed.

Students back then had no more money or goods than students do today, so we can imagine the tragedy of losing the borrowed implement. The student could neither return it nor repay the value of the tool to the owner. Elisha saw the loss of the tool as a teaching lesson for the company of prophets in training. He threw a stick into the water and made the iron axe head float up to the surface—an impossible task for humans, but possible to God. The floating axe head reminds us that when we commit inadvertent errors, we can turn to God because intervention from God can restore what we unintentionally lost.

Asking God for Help

The words of Nehemiah the son of Hachaliah. And it came to pass in the month Chisleu, in the twentieth year, as I was in Shushan the palace, That Hanani, one of my brethren, came, he and certain men of Judah; and I asked them concerning the Jews that had escaped, which were left of the captivity, and concerning Jerusalem. And they said unto me, The remnant that are left of the captivity there in the province are in great affliction and reproach: the wall of Jerusalem also is broken down, and the gates thereof are burned with fire. And it came to pass, when I heard these words, that I sat down and wept, and mourned certain days, and fasted, and prayed before the God of heaven … Now these are thy servants and thy people, whom thou hast redeemed by thy great power, and by thy strong hand. O Lord, I beseech thee, let now thine ear be attentive to the prayer of thy servant, and to the prayer of thy servants, who desire to fear thy name: and prosper, I pray thee, thy servant this day, and grant him mercy in the sight of this man. For I was the king's cupbearer.
—Nehemiah 1:1–4, 10–11

Some of us feel compelled to help those in trouble and severe need. As soon as we hear about a person in trouble or see groups of people in distress, we do not just sympathize or donate money, know our hour is at hand—we donate time and effort—immediately!

God gives this unique gift of helping to certain individuals, and Nehemiah, a Jewish employee of the Persian government, held this mind-set. When his brother returned to the capital city of Susa from their homeland, Hanani told Nehemiah of the destitute living conditions back in Jerusalem. The wall of the city was still broken down, and the gate had been burned, offering the residents no security against invaders.

Nehemiah had a bigger heart than most of us do. He sat down, he wept, he mourned, he fasted, and he prayed to the God of heaven. His life shows us that even when we earnestly want to help, we must get guidance from God. We cannot let emotions rule judgment, so we need to express our emotions, thus dealing with them first. Nehemiah knew that God was holy, great, and awesome, and he could never forget the situation of captivity in which the nation lived. He confessed personal sins, family sins, and national sins. He humbled himself before God in order to ask for God's help in the restoration of Jerusalem. God honored the specific request of a penitent man by letting Nehemiah lead the restoration efforts.

JUNE 21

Strength and Love

In thee, O Lord, do I put my trust; let me never be ashamed: deliver me in thy righteousness. Bow down thine ear to me; deliver me speedily: be thou my strong rock, for an house of defence to save me ... I will be glad and rejoice in thy mercy: for thou hast considered my trouble; thou hast known my soul in adversities; And hast not shut me up into the hand of the enemy: thou hast set my feet in a large room ... But I trusted in thee, O Lord: I said, Thou art my God ... My times are in thy hand: deliver me from the hand of mine enemies, and from them that persecute me ... Oh how great is thy goodness, which thou hast laid up for them that fear thee; which thou hast wrought for them that trust in thee before the sons of men! ... O love the Lord, all ye his saints: for the Lord preserveth the faithful, and plentifully rewardeth the proud doer.
—Psalm 31:1–2, 7–8, 14–15, 19, 23

Many of us have faced times when we know we cannot handle what is coming at us. We are not strong enough to fight back. We are not smart enough to know which weapon would handle the situation best. We would like to get away, but there is no space big enough where we can take our troubles.

It is at times like this that we can be glad we have already turned to the Lord. Turning to God in repentance for sins is the best decision anyone can make. God honors the soul who seeks Him by protecting him and by preventing and rescuing him from all kinds of dangers. God becomes the fortress in which the new believer is safe from the enemies. Whatever difficulties we may face, we may rejoice that God loves us beyond compare. We see His love when we realize He has given us space—space to grow, space to praise Him, and space to pray.

Seeing how God handles our lives helps us recognize that the times of our lives are truly in His hands, and whatever God does is good for us. God is always active on our behalf, to preserve us spotless for Himself.

Storms of Life

And the same day, when the even was come, he saith unto them,
Let us pass over unto the other side. And when they had sent away
the multitude, they took him even as he was in the ship. And there
were also with him other little ships. And there arose a great storm
of wind, and the waves beat into the ship, so that it was now full.
And he was in the hinder part of the ship, asleep on a pillow: and
they awake him, and say unto him, Master, carest thou not that we
perish? And he arose, and rebuked the wind, and said unto the sea,
Peace, be still. And the wind ceased, and there was a great calm. And
he said unto them, Why are ye so fearful? how is it that ye have no
faith? And they feared exceedingly, and said one to another, What
manner of man is this, that even the wind and the sea obey him?
—Mark 4:35–41

Therefore shall the strong people glorify thee, the city of
the terrible nations shall fear thee. For thou hast been a
strength to the poor, a strength to the needy in his distress,
a refuge from the storm, a shadow from the heat, when the
blast of the terrible ones is as a storm against the wall.
—Isaiah 25:3–4

What a miraculous event occurred when Jesus calmed down a raging squall to the amazement and incredulity of the disciples! Squalls are brief but intense storms that come up so quickly that no one can prepare for them ahead of time. When the squall is rain, we are drowned out. When the squall is snow, we are blinded. When the squall is wind, we are blown away.

Our lives can sometimes seem more like squalls than beautiful, calm, dry, and sunny days. When the squalls of our lives overtake us, we are apt to panic just like the disciples did. They saw that Jesus was sleeping, a sure sign of His unconcern—in their opinion. They had only just begun to trust Him, so this storm seemed inopportune. All appearances to the contrary, God is never unconcerned about believers. By bringing the situation to the attention of the Lord, Jesus immediately calmed down the storm.

Jesus Christ wants us to trust in His absolute love at all times. He will do anything to grab our attention and increase our faith in Him.

Let Someone Else Do the Work

Thou wilt keep him in perfect peace, whose mind is stayed
on thee: because he trusteth in thee. Trust ye in the Lord for
ever: for in the Lord Jehovah is everlasting strength ... The
way of the just is uprightness: thou, most upright, dost weigh
the path of the just. Yea, in the way of thy judgments, O Lord,
have we waited for thee; the desire of our soul is to thy name,
and to the remembrance of thee ... Lord, thou wilt ordain
peace for us: for thou also hast wrought all our works in us.
—Isaiah 26:3–4, 7–8, 12

Peace I leave with you, my peace I give unto you: not
as the world giveth, give I unto you. Let not your
heart be troubled, neither let it be afraid.
—John 14:27

We live in such a stress-oriented society that we cannot escape feeling
bullied, harassed, overwhelmed, or simply bothered by daily pressures.
Some people escape pressure by taking vacations in expensive resort areas—on
the beach, in the mountains, to the wilderness, or abroad. They think the external
change of scenery will change them internally. Some people escape pressure by
resorting to self-destructive habits like alcohol or worse. They think of addictive
substances as palliatives for problems. Some people escape tension by refusing
to act responsibly, so they opt out of mainstream society. They ignore and refuse
to deal with ordinary difficulties.

God understands how much stress we endure daily, and He wants to help
us live through it successfully without sinking under it. When we give our minds
to God, the peace that comes only from God comes to us. God steadies us when
we trust in Him, keeps us on an even keel. He steers our course and navigates us
through shoals and rock-strewn waters.

Perhaps the most difficult lesson of the Christian life is to learn that when
we trust God, we are letting someone else do the work for us. Yes, this is what
we all need in order to function optimally.

The Good of the Tongue

The Spirit of the Lord spake by me, and his word was in my tongue.
—2 Samuel 23:2

Come and hear, all ye that fear God, and I will declare
what he hath done for my soul. I cried unto him with
my mouth, and he was extolled with my tongue.
—Psalm 66:16–17

The preparations of the heart in man, and the
answer of the tongue, is from the Lord.
—Proverbs 16:1

Therefore did my heart rejoice, and my tongue was
glad; moreover also my flesh shall rest in hope.
—Acts 2:26

For it is written, As I live, saith the Lord, every knee shall
bow to me, and every tongue shall confess to God.
—Romans 14:11

The proliferation of cell phones has caused telephone companies to overlay area codes in more densely populated areas when the demand for telephone numbers overtakes the number of available phone numbers. Instead of one area code serving one area, now two area codes serve one area. We love to talk, so owning a landline, a cell phone, and a business phone makes sense to a lot of people.

Clearly, God created us as beings who speak—to one another in conversation, to Him in prayer, and to ourselves in internal dialogue. All forms of talking and communication may glorify the God who made the tongue. The tongue can be used to spread God's Word. We praise God with our tongues. God answers us with His tongue. Happy hearts and hopeful minds help us to rejoice in God. Everyone will eventually confess that Jesus is Lord. As believers, we want to use our tongues as part of our spiritual worship. We can decide now to refrain from slander or demeaning language.

When we speak in the way that honors God, we begin to hear a quiet voice speaking softly to us, answering us and guiding us. God's voice is beautiful to hear. We also want to bear in mind that a day will come when every tongue will acknowledge that Jesus Christ is the Lord of all.

The Great Commission

Then the eleven disciples went away into Galilee, into a mountain where Jesus had appointed them. And when they saw him, they worshipped him: but some doubted. And Jesus came and spake unto them, saying, All power is given unto me in heaven and in earth. Go ye therefore, and teach all nations, baptizing them in the name of the Father, and of the Son, and of the Holy Ghost: Teaching them to observe all things whatsoever I have commanded you: and, lo, I am with you always, even unto the end of the world. Amen.
—Matthew 28:16–20

Cast thy bread upon the waters: for thou shalt find it after many days … As thou knowest not what is the way of the spirit, nor how the bones do grow in the womb of her that is with child: even so thou knowest not the works of God who maketh all.
—Ecclesiastes 11:1, 5

The grass withereth, the flower fadeth: because the spirit of the Lord bloweth upon it: surely the people is grass. The grass withereth, the flower fadeth: but the word of our God shall stand for ever. O Zion, that bringest good tidings, get thee up into the high mountain; O Jerusalem, that bringest good tidings, lift up thy voice with strength; lift it up, be not afraid; say unto the cities of Judah, Behold your God!
—Isaiah 40:7–9

After His resurrection, Jesus commissioned His disciples to spread the gospel throughout the world. When we read those words a couple of thousand years later, we are awe-struck because we know that Word of God has gone forth throughout the known world at the time and throughout the rest of the world as it has been populated. Just a few simple sentences of the Savior show the power of God over the affairs of men. Kingdoms have arisen and fallen, but the Word of God lasts forever.

All believers today have benefitted from a small band of men who obeyed God. God still wants us to know a few things about Himself. First, only God holds all power and authority in heaven and on earth. This gives us confidence when we obey Him because God is in charge of results. We are only required to obey. Second, God wants us to teach and explain the good news of salvation to those whom He sends into our lives. Knowing the history before us motivates us to pass on what was given to us already. Jesus has sent the Holy Spirit to be with us. We need only follow His leading.

Finally, God wants us to leave the end results up to Him. We cannot understand everything that happens in this life, but we can trust God in every situation. Heaven will be the place where we learn the rest of the story we could not figure out here.

Good Fruit and Bad Fruit

For a good tree bringeth not forth corrupt fruit; neither doth a
corrupt tree bring forth good fruit. For every tree is known by his
own fruit. For of thorns men do not gather figs, nor of a bramble
bush gather they grapes. A good man out of the good treasure
of his heart bringeth forth that which is good; and an evil man
out of the evil treasure of his heart bringeth forth that which is
evil: for of the abundance of the heart his mouth speaketh.
—Luke 6:43–45

Thou hast planted them, yea, they have taken root:
they grow, yea, they bring forth fruit: thou art near
in their mouth, and far from their reins.
—Jeremiah 12:2

Blessed is the man that walketh not in the counsel of the ungodly,
nor standeth in the way of sinners, nor sitteth in the seat of the
scornful ... And he shall be like a tree planted by the rivers of
water, that bringeth forth his fruit in his season; his leaf also
shall not wither; and whatsoever he doeth shall prosper.
—Psalm 1:1, 3

Even if we are not very good at gardening and completely ignorant of the
plant world, we still know that apples grow on apple trees, corn grows on
a corn stalk, and blueberries grow on a blueberry bush. When we consider how
our childhoods have been and how different we want our adult lives to be, we
sometimes exercise the human foible of forgetting to apply an obvious natural
lesson to our spiritual lives.

If our childhoods were not oriented to God's Word (and this was the decision
of our parents, not our choice), we may worry that some old and ungodly habits
will lash out at us as adults. We worry that we will succumb to the very habit we
would like to avoid. But, Jesus always clears our heads when we look to Him—the
Bible helps us sort out such confusing thoughts. He tells us that good trees bear
good fruit. This means that when we exercise our adult freedom to obey God,
He turns our lives over to the production of good fruit. There is no possibility
of the bad fruit of childhood dragging us back down again.

Not only do we bear good fruit in our lives, others see and recognize the
good fruit of our lives. Our good friends encourage us to keep on obeying God.

Only a Partial Picture

On the next day much people that were come to the feast, when they
heard that Jesus was coming to Jerusalem, Took branches of palm
trees, and went forth to meet him, and cried, Hosanna: Blessed is
the King of Israel that cometh in the name of the Lord. And Jesus,
when he had found a young ass, sat thereon; as it is written, Fear
not, daughter of Sion: behold, thy King cometh, sitting on an ass's
colt. These things understood not his disciples at the first: but when
Jesus was glorified, then remembered they that these things were
written of him, and that they had done these things unto him.
—John 12:12–16

All of us need heroes to emulate. Our heroes may be unimportant people
from a worldly perspective; they do not need to be prominent people. We
look to those who are ahead of us to figure out how the direction of our lives
might also go. When we look at the earliest disciples, we can learn from them,
even though we may never perform the same tasks they accomplished.

The disciples of Jesus were the first pastors, missionaries, and teachers of
the gospel. We think of them in hallowed and exalted terms because they obeyed
God at great personal cost. Their names have been recorded for posterity, and we
understand in hindsight the importance of the tasks of their lives.

In spite of the human tendency to glorify the heroes of past ages, we need
to remember how vulnerable and earthly they really were. Yes, they obeyed
God. Yes, they taught the newly formed church the precepts of the Scriptures
and how to apply them to daily life, but the disciples did not fully understand
what they were doing. They could not see into the future of the spread of the
worldwide church. Their obedience and attitudes set an example for us today.
Obey God, and leave the results up to Him. Obedience is more important than
understanding.

Salvation

For all have sinned, and come short of the glory of God ... For
the wages of sin is death; but the gift of God is eternal life through
Jesus Christ our Lord ... But God commendeth his love toward
us, in that, while we were yet sinners, Christ died for us ... But
what saith it? The word is nigh thee, even in thy mouth, and in
thy heart: that is, the word of faith, which we preach; That if thou
shalt confess with thy mouth the Lord Jesus, and shalt believe in
thine heart that God hath raised him from the dead, thou shalt
be saved. For with the heart man believeth unto righteousness;
and with the mouth confession is made unto salvation. For the
scripture saith, Whosoever believeth on him shall not be ashamed.
For there is no difference between the Jew and the Greek: for
the same Lord over all is rich unto all that call upon him. For
whosoever shall call upon the name of the Lord shall be saved.
—Romans 3:23; 6:23; 5:8; 10:8–13

Why do we need to be saved?—because all of us are sinners, and our sins
prevent us from getting to know the God who created us, who loves, and
who has a plan for our lives. Are we aware that in God's sight, we are rotten to
the core? Human standards, even the highest of them, cannot measure up to
God's perfect standards, so the Creator rightly rejects us as unfit to live with
Him in heaven.

The end result of the sinful nature is physical death first and eternal death
second. So if we go through this life godlessly, we experience the loss of all the
good that God will otherwise bless us with. God wants us to have eternal life.
We cannot attain it on our own, so He makes a free gift of eternal life to us when
we repent of our sins. God did not need to save us, but He wants to. He loves us
and wants to help us out of our sinful lives into His eternal life. The decision is
easier than we think.

God is near to us because He created each one of us. We only need to confess
our sins and speak the truth that Jesus Christ is (my) Lord to be saved once and
for all and forever. It is the most important decision anyone can make. Both this
life and the next depend upon the decision made right now.

JUNE 29

Family Harmony

Behold, how good and how pleasant it is for brethren to dwell
together in unity! It is like the precious ointment upon the head,
that ran down upon the beard, even Aaron's beard: that went
down to the skirts of his garments; As the dew of Hermon, and
as the dew that descended upon the mountains of Zion: for there
the Lord commanded the blessing, even life for evermore.
—Psalm 133:1–3

Put on therefore, as the elect of God, holy and beloved, bowels of
mercies, kindness, humbleness of mind, meekness, longsuffering;
Forbearing one another, and forgiving one another, if any man have
a quarrel against any: even as Christ forgave you, so also do ye. And
above all these things put on charity, which is the bond of perfectness.
—Colossians 3:12–14

Like it or not, we will spend a lot of time thinking about our families for the
rest of our lives. We may go to work, or we may have fun in our spare time,
but we will still carry the memory of those closest to us every waking moment.
Some of us come from families where brothers and sisters fight all the time. No
one knows better than siblings how to probe a weakness, rub a sore spot the
wrong way, or humiliate the person who expects protection instead.

Those of us who come from contentious families truly desire the opposite
when we establish our own families, don't we? We do not find humor in bad
words and bad behavior—life is not a situation comedy—life involves real people
with real feelings, feelings that can easily be hurt for a very long time. All we have
to do to enjoy future family harmony is to obey God and trust Him to change
the family God has given us. Obedience to God helps us control our mouths
and behaviors, so that none of the problems brought about by the contention of
others ever arises.

The blessing of harmonious family relationships depends upon God and us
acting together. We want that slice of heavenly life in the pie of this life.

JUNE 30

Forgiveness for Sins

Come now, and let us reason together, saith the Lord:
though your sins be as scarlet, they shall be as white as snow;
though they be red like crimson, they shall be as wool.
—Isaiah 1:18

Who his own self bare our sins in his own body on
the tree, that we, being dead to sins, should live unto
righteousness: by whose stripes ye were healed.
—1 Peter 2:24

Bless the Lord, O my soul: and all that is within me, bless his holy name.
Bless the Lord, O my soul, and forget not all his benefits: Who forgiveth
all thine iniquities; who healeth all thy diseases; Who redeemeth thy life
from destruction; who crowneth thee with lovingkindness and tender
mercies; Who satisfieth thy mouth with good things; so that thy youth
is renewed like the eagle's ... He will not always chide: neither will he
keep his anger for ever. He hath not dealt with us after our sins; nor
rewarded us according to our iniquities. For as the heaven is high above
the earth, so great is his mercy toward them that fear him. As far as the
east is from the west, so far hath he removed our transgressions from
us. Like as a father pitieth his children, so the Lord pitieth them that
fear him. For he knoweth our frame; he remembereth that we are dust.
—Psalm 103:1–5, 9–14

The God who created the universe is the same God who forgives our sins
because He is personally interested in us as individuals. His oversight extends
not only to the world we are familiar with, but also to the individual self that we
call by our own name. This concept may seem unfamiliar to us because the theory
of evolution can make us think that the creation of the world belongs to the realm
of science, and topics about God belong to theology. We have sinned against the
God who created us, creating a chasm between a holy God and a sinful person.
We cannot get back to God, so God has made a way for us to get back to Him.

He sent His Son Jesus Christ to die on the cross for our sins, so that we
might be freed from the shackles of sin that now run and ruin our lives. When we
accept the fact that we are sinners, when we confess to God that we are sinners
who desire forgiveness for our sins, God forgives us. His redemption reveals His
love and compassion toward us who deserve none of it. God does not remain
angry with sinners forever because He is not vindictive.

He immediately changes our lives so that we experience the good things
that come from the forgiven life that flows out from the throne of God. The God
who created the universe is the only one who can connect the individual parts of
our lives into a cohesive and complete unit.

Happiness and Truth

The earth is the Lord's, and the fulness thereof; the world, and
they that dwell therein. For he hath founded it upon the seas,
and established it upon the floods. Who shall ascend into the hill
of the Lord? or who shall stand in his holy place? He that hath
clean hands, and a pure heart; who hath not lifted up his soul
unto vanity, nor sworn deceitfully. He shall receive the blessing
from the Lord, and righteousness from the God of his salvation.
This is the generation of them that seek him, that seek thy face,
O Jacob. Selah. Lift up your heads, O ye gates; and be ye lift up,
ye everlasting doors; and the King of glory shall come in. Who is
this King of glory? The Lord strong and mighty, the Lord mighty
in battle. Lift up your heads, O ye gates; even lift them up, ye
everlasting doors; and the King of glory shall come in. Who is this
King of glory? The Lord of hosts, he is the King of glory. Selah.
—Psalm 24:1–10

When we think about planet earth, we may feel more concerned about the
human destruction of natural habitats than we do about the natural beauty
that surrounds us. But it is good to stop and think about the attractiveness of
planet earth, especially when we compare it to the barrenness of other planetary
bodies.

When we read that God formed the earth out of the waters, we get a sense
of the holiness of God cleansing the dirtier parts of the creation. It is a reminder
that our lives should follow the same godly principle of cleansing our inner parts
to make ourselves acceptable to the Creator. Many false teachers offer ways to get
closer to God, and many devotees slavishly aim to follow their bad advice. How
do people get close to God, if not through these nonbiblical formulas?—only by
practicing holiness, cleanliness, truth, and purity of life.

This brief psalm reminds us that it is time to lift up our heads—this means
stop looking downward—to see the King of Glory and Holiness enter through
the gates of our lives. He extends blessing, happiness, and truth to the holy people
who climb the hill of faith, expecting an answer from Him.

Holiness of God

In the year that king Uzziah died I saw also the Lord sitting upon a
throne, high and lifted up, and his train filled the temple. Above it
stood the seraphims: each one had six wings; with twain he covered
his face, and with twain he covered his feet, and with twain he did
fly. And one cried unto another, and said, Holy, holy, holy, is the
Lord of hosts: the whole earth is full of his glory. And the posts
of the door moved at the voice of him that cried, and the house
was filled with smoke. Then said I, Woe is me! for I am undone;
because I am a man of unclean lips, and I dwell in the midst of a
people of unclean lips: for mine eyes have seen the King, the Lord
of hosts. Then flew one of the seraphims unto me, having a live
coal in his hand, which he had taken with the tongs from off the
altar: And he laid it upon my mouth, and said, Lo, this hath touched
thy lips; and thine iniquity is taken away, and thy sin purged.
—Isaiah 6:1–7

How can sinful beings understand the concept of the holiness of God? It
is comforting to know that long ago, the prophet Isaiah faced the same
difficulty. When he saw a vision of the Lord seated high upon a throne, he
understood that he faced the omnipotent king and unquestioned ruler of all
creation.

When Isaiah saw the train of the robe of the Lord filling the temple, he
understood that the power of almighty God permeates planet earth. When he
saw the seraphs, the angelic beings whose wings covered their faces and feet, he
understood that the holiness of God is announced with humility.

Isaiah understood that the work of God continues quietly and continuously
throughout the ages. When the seraphs announced the holiness of the Lord,
Isaiah was completely undone. Buildings shook, as if from an earthquake. Isaiah
knew how sinful he was, and he acknowledged that he lived among sinful people.
Yet his sinful being witnessed the holiness of God. No one can confuse the
holiness of God with a lesser quality.

Farming and Fishing

Another parable put he forth unto them, saying, The kingdom of
heaven is likened unto a man which sowed good seed in his field: But
while men slept, his enemy came and sowed tares among the wheat,
and went his way. But when the blade was sprung up, and brought
forth fruit, then appeared the tares also ... He answered and said
unto them, He that soweth the good seed is the Son of man; The
field is the world; the good seed are the children of the kingdom;
but the tares are the children of the wicked one; The enemy that
sowed them is the devil; the harvest is the end of the world; and
the reapers are the angels. As therefore the tares are gathered and
burned in the fire; so shall it be in the end of this world. The Son
of man shall send forth his angels, and they shall gather out of his
kingdom all things that offend, and them which do iniquity ... Again,
the kingdom of heaven is like unto a net, that was cast into the sea,
and gathered of every kind: Which, when it was full, they drew
to shore, and sat down, and gathered the good into vessels, but
cast the bad away. So shall it be at the end of the world: the angels
shall come forth, and sever the wicked from among the just.
—Matthew 13:24–26, 37–41, 47–49

Many professions depend upon instinct rather than exact knowledge. While it
may seem like intuition is a knack that some possess and others lack, this is
not really the case. Instinct belongs to the emotions, and as such, is subject to the
requisite knowledge. We might like to skip the knowledge step because it involves
a lot of hard work, but this is never a good idea. Whatever we end up doing with
our lives, we need the basic data sets of information to undergird our efforts.

Farming is an occupation that depends upon intuitive knowledge of the land,
and fishing depends upon intuitive knowledge of the water. This type of knowledge is
usually learned over a span of years. In the same way that farmers plant seed and hope
for an abundant crop, and in the same way that fishermen let down a net and hope to
catch all kinds of fish, professors troll for students who excel in the subject area they
teach. It is understood that only a few students in any given introductory course will
actually major in the subject. The required courses of the college experience makes
students think about the other types of information or voices they have been listening
to. Because the efforts of others toward us affect us, it is important to discern quality
as much as personal interest from what they have to say.

God uses many people and experiences to sift our thoughts, hone our
intellects, and shape our interests for the purpose of keeping us in His kingdom
for the day when angels will come and separate the evil from the good.

JULY 4

Banners, Flags, and Ensigns

And in that day there shall be a root of Jesse, which
shall stand for an ensign of the people; to it shall the
Gentiles seek: and his rest shall be glorious.
—Isaiah 11:10

He brought me to the banqueting house,
and his banner over me was love.
—Song of Songs 2:4

Our country loves to fly the national flag at every opportunity. The emblem
reminds us of our history. Not only are flags, banners, emblems and ensigns
colorful, they are visual, concrete representations of an abstract concept, a concept
so significant that the idea needs to be remembered continually. The red and
white stripes of the American flag, Old Glory, remind us of the thirteen original
colonies who formed the fledgling nation. The fifty stars on the blue ground
represent the fifty states now united under one government. Commemorative
flags are not a new idea.

For Moses, an altar became a banner to remind the Israelites that God
fought for them against the Amalekites at Rephidim. As long as Moses held
up his hands, they were winning; when he lowered his hands, they were losing.
Aaron and Hur propped up his hands to keep on winning. The banner of prayer
to God for deliverance needs to be remembered.

For believers, the cross of Jesus Christ the Savior, *the Root of Jesse*, becomes
a banner to remind us that salvation comes from God—for all nations. For all
of us, God places many banners over us in our lives to show His love toward us.
We should consider the banners that overarch our lives and be thankful for the
specific help we have received from the Lord.

JULY 5

Motivation

By faith Abraham, when he was called to go out into a place which
he should after receive for an inheritance, obeyed; and he went out,
not knowing whither he went. By faith he sojourned in the land
of promise, as in a strange country, dwelling in tabernacles with
Isaac and Jacob, the heirs with him of the same promise: For he
looked for a city which hath foundations, whose builder and maker
is God ... Esteeming the reproach of Christ greater riches than the
treasures in Egypt: for he had respect unto the recompence of the
reward ... Wherefore seeing we also are compassed about with so
great a cloud of witnesses, let us lay aside every weight, and the sin
which doth so easily beset us, and let us run with patience the race
that is set before us, Looking unto Jesus the author and finisher
of our faith; who for the joy that was set before him endured the
cross, despising the shame, and is set down at the right hand of the
throne of God. For consider him that endured such contradiction of
sinners against himself, lest ye be wearied and faint in your minds.
—Hebrews 11:8–10, 26; 12:1–3

Biographies of famous personages interest us because we would like to know
what made them tick. How did a specific person do a specific task that
everyone is now interested in reading about? Their lives are clearly different from
our run-of-the-mill lives, aren't they? No one is interested in writing about us,
are they? Have we ever tried to figure out what motivates us to press on, to move
forward, to succeed, or to live? The source of personal motivation provides a clue
to the foundation of our lives.

In modern terminology, the profession of the patriarch Abraham might
compare to the nomad, shepherd, farmer, rancher, or family businessman of
today. By profession, the emancipator Moses might compare to the lawyer,
teacher, professor, or governor of today. But were they motivated solely by
professional considerations in their lives? And was their source of motivation
something we can grasp today? The Old Testament is not a biography of their
lives even though it relates many details about their lives.

We can learn from Abraham and Moses that spiritual motivation does not
always mean a spiritual career, but it does mean that spiritual understanding
undergirds the best efforts of any career. We need to we learn our subject matter
thoroughly and learn how biblical precepts relate to that information.

In Spite Of ...

And it came to pass from the time that he had made him overseer
in his house, and over all that he had, that the Lord blessed the
Egyptian's house for Joseph's sake; and the blessing of the Lord was
upon all that he had in the house, and in the field ... And Joseph's
master took him, and put him into the prison, a place where the
king's prisoners were bound: and he was there in the prison ...
The keeper of the prison looked not to any thing that was under
his hand; because the Lord was with him, and that which he did,
the Lord made it to prosper ... And they said unto him, We have
dreamed a dream, and there is no interpreter of it. And Joseph
said unto them, Do not interpretations belong to God? tell me
them, I pray you ... And Joseph answered Pharaoh, saying, It is
not in me: God shall give Pharaoh an answer of peace ... And
for that the dream was doubled unto Pharaoh twice; it is because
the thing is established by God, and God will shortly bring it
to pass ... And the name of the second called he Ephraim: For
God hath caused me to be fruitful in the land of my affliction.
—Genesis 39:5, 20, 23; 40:8; 41:16, 32, 52

Some of us become faithful servants of the Lord in spite of our surroundings
and upbringings. This is half true of Joseph. He was raised by a godly father
but hated by his brothers. Some of us remain believers in spite of our situations.
This is also true of Joseph. He got a responsible job as chief manager of Potiphar's
household until the wife accused him of adultery, and the boss threw him into
prison.

Sometimes, we can only understand how blessing comes from God when we
have suffered unjustly. A few years later, Joseph became the vice regent, second
in command only to pharaoh, in the great and powerful country of Egypt. For a
former slave and prisoner, Joseph experienced an unprecedented rise to power.
It remains worthy of note that Joseph did not jockey for power, as politicians
today are accustomed to do.

Did Joseph understand the purposes of God in his young adult life? Probably
not. Did he plan to memorialize his life for generations to come? Absolutely not!
What did Joseph do? He obeyed God and let God take care of the details. So
can we.

Forgiveness Means Life

Therefore, O thou son of man, speak unto the house of Israel; Thus ye speak, saying, If our transgressions and our sins be upon us, and we pine away in them, how should we then live? ... Say unto them, As I live, saith the Lord God, I have no pleasure in the death of the wicked; but that the wicked turn from his way and live: turn ye, turn ye from your evil ways; for why will ye die, O house of Israel? Again, when I say unto the wicked, Thou shalt surely die; if he turn from his sin, and do that which is lawful and right; If the wicked restore the pledge, give again that he had robbed, walk in the statutes of life, without committing iniquity; he shall surely live, he shall not die. None of his sins that he hath committed shall be mentioned unto him: he hath done that which is lawful and right; he shall surely live.
—Ezekiel 33:10–11, 14–16

Come now, and let us reason together, saith the Lord: though your sins be as scarlet, they shall be as white as snow; though they be red like crimson, they shall be as wool ... Behold, for peace I had great bitterness: but thou hast in love to my soul delivered it from the pit of corruption: for thou hast cast all my sins behind thy back.
—Isaiah 1:18; 38:17

The inescapable fact of this world is that all of us will die someday because we are sinners. But some of us are so mired in sin right now that we think there is no hope of forgiveness from God for us. It is time to stop believing lies and believe the truth!

The Lord who created us takes no delight in punishing anyone for any reason. God is not a sadistic ruler in the sky who prides Himself on the amount of human destruction He carries out. He wants all of us to turn from all evil ways so that we may enjoy life—this earthly life and the life to come. He even goes so far as to tell us that He casts all our sins behind His back, meaning that He sees them no more.

When we do what is right, when we turn around to leave the swamplands of sin, God puts our sins behind His back. God blesses us so completely that He forgets the past. We need to put the past behind us right now.

Blessed Obedience

Then cometh Jesus from Galilee to Jordan unto John, to be baptized
of him. But John forbad him, saying, I have need to be baptized
of thee, and comest thou to me? And Jesus answering said unto
him, Suffer it to be so now: for thus it becometh us to fulfil all
righteousness. Then he suffered him. And Jesus, when he was
baptized, went up straightway out of the water: and, lo, the heavens
were opened unto him, and he saw the Spirit of God descending
like a dove, and lighting upon him: And lo a voice from heaven,
saying, This is my beloved Son, in whom I am well pleased.
—Matthew 3:13–17

Some of us work at jobs that involve so many precise and specifically timed
tasks that we find it difficult to figure out how to do all of them in a cohesive
manner. The boss seems to be somewhat patient with us, but we really know that
he is just looking for an excuse to fire us for incompetency. It is human to envy
those who have an obvious, concrete kind of job to do. The tasks are clear-cut;
no one is confused about what to do next. It would be nice to live like this—so
we think.

John the Baptist, a cousin of Jesus, was a man to whom God had given a
specific task—to prepare the hearts, minds, and souls of sinners to recognize
the Lord who dwelt among them. He succeeded at this task because people came
to the Jordan River to be baptized with water for repentance and wait for the
baptism of the Holy Spirit. On the day that Jesus came to be baptized, cousin
John was taken aback because he knew who Jesus was. It just didn't seem right
for him to baptize the Son of God. But it was right to baptize Jesus—why is
that?—because God desired the baptism to fulfill all righteousness.

God's plan was precise and pre-planned. When John baptized Jesus Christ,
they both heard God's voice of commendation and blessing from heaven. Both
of them were blessed by God for obedience to His command.

Blessings to All

Hear now, O Joshua the high priest, thou, and thy fellows that sit before thee: for they are men wondered at: for, behold, I will bring forth my servant the Branch. For behold the stone that I have laid before Joshua; upon one stone shall be seven eyes: behold, I will engrave the graving thereof, saith the Lord of hosts, and I will remove the iniquity of that land in one day ... Then he answered and spake unto me, saying, This is the word of the Lord unto Zerubbabel, saying, Not by might, nor by power, but by my spirit, saith the Lord of hosts ... And speak unto him, saying, Thus speaketh the Lord of hosts, saying, Behold the man whose name is The Branch; and he shall grow up out of his place, and he shall build the temple of the Lord ... Thus saith the Lord of hosts; Behold, I will save my people from the east country, and from the west country.
—Zechariah 3:8–9; 4:6; 6:12; 8:7

And my speech and my preaching was not with enticing words of man's wisdom, but in demonstration of the Spirit and of power.
—1 Corinthians 2:4

Sitting under the branches of a shady tree on a hot summer's day gives us such a picture of rest and relaxation, a respite from the toil and drudgery of daily cares. Do we acknowledge that Jesus is the branch under whose shady boughs we may sit and rest because He saves us from the sin that wrecks our lives? For hundreds of years, people had been offering sacrifices of atonement to God for sins, but none of them were good enough to eradicate sin forever.

When Jesus Christ died on the cross—in one moment of time—God removed all sins of all peoples: past, present, and future. What a relief to know that the sin problem had been taken care of once and for all! No more need to work so hard at what we cannot accomplish anyway.

The Lord Almighty is omnipotent; the Holy Spirit acts effortlessly according to God's will. He has brought many of us from around the globe into the kingdom of God. How sensible to trust Him for the blessing of rest that lets the Holy Spirit work through us and in us.

Who Is Really in Charge?

> There was a man in the land of Uz, whose name was Job; and
> that man was perfect and upright, and one that feared God, and
> eschewed evil. And there were born unto him seven sons and three
> daughters. His substance also was seven thousand sheep, and three
> thousand camels, and five hundred yoke of oxen, and five hundred
> she asses, and a very great household; so that this man was the
> greatest of all the men of the east ... Now there was a day when the
> sons of God came to present themselves before the Lord, and Satan
> came also among them ... Then Satan answered the Lord, and said,
> Doth Job fear God for nought? Hast not thou made an hedge about
> him, and about his house, and about all that he hath on every side?
> thou hast blessed the work of his hands, and his substance is increased
> in the land. But put forth thine hand now, and touch all that he hath,
> and he will curse thee to thy face. And the Lord said unto Satan,
> Behold, all that he hath is in thy power; only upon himself put not
> forth thine hand. So Satan went forth from the presence of the Lord.
> —Job 1:1–3, 6, 9–12

The world today promotes equality among religious beliefs, as if all beliefs are equally good and valid. We don't have to look far to find satanic influence and devilish stimuli in popular culture. Literature often represents Satan as the archenemy of God, implying that a cosmic warfare exists. In philosophy classes, good and evil are presented as equal but opposite concepts, each one struggling to outperform the other.

The Bible speaks differently and identifies both God and Satan as spiritual beings, not as representative ideas or abstract concepts. The Bible clarifies who is who, and assures us which one has power and which one lacks power. The problem of good and evil is a large problem, and even believers tend to shy away from thinking about it. Even less do we care to think about supernatural interventions (whether good or evil) that occur in human lives. We do not like to think that God tests faith in various ways, but the Bible assures us that He does. Thousands of years ago, a man named Job lived as a tremendously wealthy man, well-known as the greatest man among all the peoples of the East.

It still seems incredible that God gave Satan permission to afflict Job, but He did. This permission means that God is the powerful being, not Satan. Reading the book of Job may cause us to think that the more we have, the more severely our faith will be tested, yet we don't know for sure. Nevertheless, God is in charge of every situation; Satan operates under orders from the Creator, never according to his own power. We should be very wary of those who try to allure us to join forces with superhuman powers for any reason other than biblical ones.

Prepare Your Minds

Wherefore gird up the loins of your mind, be sober, and hope to the end for the grace that is to be brought unto you at the revelation of Jesus Christ ... And if ye call on the Father, who without respect of persons judgeth according to every man's work, pass the time of your sojourning here in fear: Forasmuch as ye know that ye were not redeemed with corruptible things, as silver and gold, from your vain conversation received by tradition from your fathers ... Seeing ye have purified your souls in obeying the truth through the Spirit unto unfeigned love of the brethren, see that ye love one another with a pure heart fervently: Being born again, not of corruptible seed, but of incorruptible, by the Word of God, which liveth and abideth for ever. For all flesh is as grass, and all the glory of man as the flower of grass. The grass withereth, and the flower thereof falleth away: But the word of the Lord endureth for ever. And this is the word which by the gospel is preached unto you.
—1 Peter 1:13, 17–18, 22–25

Education places a lot of emphasis on activities and hands-on learning experiences, especially in the early grades. This practice is based upon the understanding that a connection exists between what the brain thinks and how the body behaves. Yet for any type of learning, in order to do well in school, we need to practice basic self-discipline, like attending class every day, doing all of the assignments and homework from the teacher, and taking tests before graduating from high school. The goal of the first twelve years of education is to bring us to maturity, ready to enter life and capable of moving forward in life.

Spiritual life is similar. In order to be healthy spiritually, we need to act upon what we believe. Right now, it means attending classes, studying a lot of material, doing a lot of assignments, and taking a lot of tests. It also means attending a Bible-believing church and reading the Bible. God may give us extra-curricular assignments or situations and test our faith in college. Basic self-discipline will help us in spiritual life also.

Why should we try so hard for something so intangible?—because God reminds us that we don't live forever on this earth. Only the Word of God endures forever.

Embarrassing Family Members

And Moses and Aaron went into the tabernacle of the congregation,
and came out, and blessed the people: and the glory of the Lord
appeared unto all the people. And there came a fire out from before
the Lord, and consumed upon the altar the burnt offering and the
fat: which when all the people saw, they shouted, and fell on their
faces ... And Nadab and Abihu, the sons of Aaron, took either
of them his censer, and put fire therein, and put incense thereon,
and offered strange fire before the Lord, which he commanded
them not. And there went out fire from the Lord, and devoured
them, and they died before the Lord. Then Moses said unto
Aaron, This is it that the Lord spake, saying, I will be sanctified
in them that come nigh me, and before all the people I will be
glorified. And Aaron held his peace ... And Moses said unto
Aaron, and unto Eleazar and unto Ithamar, his sons, Uncover not
your heads, neither rend your clothes; lest ye die, and lest wrath
come upon all the people: but let your brethren, the whole house
of Israel, bewail the burning which the Lord hath kindled.
—Leviticus 9:23–24; 10:1–3, 6

Most families stick together and support one another through the best and worst of times. This is usually a good practice, but it can backfire when the behavior of even one family member is so bad that neither the behavior nor the person should be supported by anyone.

Just as families maintain standards, so does God's family uphold His holy standards. When Israel was in the process of setting up the worship process, two of Aaron's sons offered fire in the wrong way. They were not little boys who made a mistake; they were responsible adults who knew what was right and chose to do it wrong. God punished them swiftly when fire consumed them on the spot.

It is always shocking when evil occurs, especially when we witness its occurrence close to home. The closest family members are stunned to think that some of their own could behave so badly. Aaron, the dad, was speechless when he realized the gravity of their error. Parents always feel responsible to some degree for their children, so this sin reflected on his parenting skills. But the worship of God still needed to go on—correctly. God told the family not to grieve the loss of their close family members, or God would take their lives as well. Sometimes, we must move forward in obedience without looking back. God is a present help for today, not a past tradition of yesterday.

God Is Good

And now, Israel, what doth the Lord thy God require of thee, but to
fear the Lord thy God, to walk in all his ways, and to love him, and
to serve the Lord thy God with all thy heart and with all thy soul,
To keep the commandments of the Lord, and his statutes, which I
command thee this day for thy good? Behold, the heaven and the
heaven of heavens is the Lord's thy God, the earth also, with all that
therein is. Only the Lord had a delight in thy fathers to love them,
and he chose their seed after them, even you above all people, as it is
this day … Thou shalt fear the Lord thy God; him shalt thou serve,
and to him shalt thou cleave, and swear by his name … Behold, I
set before you this day a blessing and a curse; A blessing, if ye obey
the commandments of the Lord your God, which I command you
this day: And a curse, if ye will not obey the commandments of the
Lord your God, but turn aside out of the way which I command
you this day, to go after other gods, which ye have not known.
—Deuteronomy 10:12–15, 20; 11:26–28

Some people think of Christianity as a negative religion, full of commands that
begin with "Don't" or "Thou shalt not." The commands seem to engender
fear more than anything else. The skeptics rightly question the kind of God who
doesn't want people doing all kinds of activities that people really enjoy. In this
perspective, there remains very little enjoyment in life, so why bother to inquire
further about God.

But God is neither a naysayer nor spoilsport like some fear-mongers imagine
Him to be. We should not hold onto this false image of our Creator. The reason
God wants us to follow His commands is because He desires to promote our
well-being and happiness. When we engage in undesirable activities, we really
do destroy ourselves—sooner or later. No one ever considers the outcomes of
sinful choices, so they rarely recognize them when they first decide to make
wrong choices.

God is both great and good. He created the universe, the world, and us. He
knows what is best for us, so He gives a choice between blessings and curses.
Surely, it is more logical to obey God and accept His blessings than to do anything
else.

JULY 14

Giving

But this I say, He which soweth sparingly shall reap also sparingly;
and he which soweth bountifully shall reap also bountifully.
Every man according as he purposeth in his heart, so let him
give; not grudgingly, or of necessity: for God loveth a cheerful
giver. And God is able to make all grace abound toward you;
that ye, always having all sufficiency in all things, may abound
to every good work: (As it is written, He hath dispersed abroad;
he hath given to the poor: his righteousness remaineth for ever.
Now he that ministereth seed to the sower both minister bread
for your food, and multiply your seed sown, and increase the
fruits of your righteousness;) Being enriched in every thing to all
bountifulness, which causeth through us thanksgiving to God.
For the administration of this service not only supplieth the
want of the saints, but is abundant also by many thanksgivings
unto God ... Thanks be unto God for his unspeakable gift.
—2 Corinthians 9:6–12, 15

Every college student is a penny pincher. No longer under the parental roof,
daily needs crop up, and there is no allowance or after school job to cover
minor expenses. Textbooks must be bought from the campus bookstore, not
borrowed from the school district's storeroom. New friends want to go out
and celebrate, and it costs money to do all these things. But God still looks for
cheerful givers.

When we are earning nothing, we owe no tithe, but even a small income can
be tithed. One-tenth of our earnings belongs to God, and we should begin to give
the tenth conscientiously and joyfully. When we tithe, we are acknowledging that
God gave us everything, including the job. He alone is able to give all we need.
We become more mindful of God when we give because tithing lessens the grip
of materialism on our lives. When we tithe, we support God's work and those in
greater need than ourselves.

Finally, tithing helps us remember that the greatest and most indescribable
gift of all is Jesus Christ the Savior. Thank God for Jesus!

Good Advice

And the word of the Lord came unto Zechariah, saying, Thus speaketh the Lord of hosts, saying, Execute true judgment, and shew mercy and compassions every man to his brother: And oppress not the widow, nor the fatherless, the stranger, nor the poor; and let none of you imagine evil against his brother in your heart ... These are the things that ye shall do; Speak ye every man the truth to his neighbour; execute the judgment of truth and peace in your gates: And let none of you imagine evil in your hearts against his neighbour; and love no false oath: for all these are things that I hate, saith the Lord. And the word of the Lord of hosts came unto me, saying, Thus saith the Lord of hosts; The fast of the fourth month, and the fast of the fifth, and the fast of the seventh, and the fast of the tenth, shall be to the house of Judah joy and gladness, and cheerful feasts; therefore love the truth and peace.
—Zechariah 7:8–10; 8:16–19

Evil men understand not judgment: but they that
seek the Lord understand all things.
—Proverbs 28:5

When God judges humans for sinful behavior, He doesn't just express His divine ill will toward them. The just judgment of God always wants what is good and right, and He tells us repeatedly what goodness means. Goodness involves right thinking in political, social, and personal decision-making.

He desires that societies uphold the same standards in their legal, social, and cultural domains. Political decisions may involve rendering sound judicial decisions by applying biblical principles to the situation at hand.

True justice means applying biblical precepts to solve societal ills. Social decisions may involve applying ethical thinking to improve the situations of others so as to show kindness to neighbors. Personal decisions may involve telling the truth, avoiding bad behavior or stemming the spreading of rumors. Do we really want to be like the God we say we serve? Then, let us love the truth, love peace, and love God wherever we go in life.

Righting a Wrong

Yet for love's sake I rather beseech thee, being such an one as Paul
the aged, and now also a prisoner of Jesus Christ. I beseech thee for
my son Onesimus, whom I have begotten in my bonds: Which in
time past was to thee unprofitable, but now profitable to thee and
to me: Whom I have sent again: thou therefore receive him, that is,
mine own bowels: Whom I would have retained with me, that in thy
stead he might have ministered unto me in the bonds of the gospel:
But without thy mind would I do nothing; that thy benefit should
not be as it were of necessity, but willingly. For perhaps he therefore
departed for a season, that thou shouldest receive him for ever; Not
now as a servant, but above a servant, a brother beloved, specially to
me, but how much more unto thee, both in the flesh, and in the Lord?
—Philemon 9–16

In older civilizations and in other societies, wealthy masters owned many slaves.
It may be impossible for us to imagine the slave mentality where slaves not only
served their masters, but they also respected and possibly loved to serve them.

Onesimus the slave did something that modern people would actually
commend him for. He ran away from a servile relationship, and we would applaud
him for his independent thinking and successful action. With this in mind, we
read a different perspective about him because the Bible records his behavior
and at the same time, acknowledges his change of heart.

Onesimus did what few of us would ever consider doing—he returned to
his master! At the urging of the apostle Paul, Onesimus returned to his original
master named Philemon. Onesimus knew it was right to return because he had
found the Lord after running away from his master. As a new believer, he knew
he had to make restitution for what he had done wrong in his life. We do not
know if his original master Philemon accepted him as a believing brother as Paul
requested, but we do know that the faith of one disobedient slave has impacted
the lives of others.

Misbehaving Sons

Now Eli was very old, and heard all that his sons did unto all Israel;
and how they lay with the women that assembled at the door of the
tabernacle of the congregation. And he said unto them, Why do
ye such things? for I hear of your evil dealings by all this people.
Nay, my sons; for it is no good report that I hear: ye make the
Lord's people to transgress. If one man sin against another, the
judge shall judge him: but if a man sin against the Lord, who shall
intreat for him? Notwithstanding they hearkened not unto the voice
of their father, because the Lord would slay them ... Wherefore
the Lord God of Israel saith, I said indeed that thy house, and
the house of thy father, should walk before me for ever: but now
the Lord saith, Be it far from me; for them that honour me I will
honour, and they that despise me shall be lightly esteemed.
—1 Samuel 2:22–25, 30

Some of us cringe with shame to think of the immoral behavior of our close relatives—they are sleeping around a lot, and we hold no influence for good over them. Eli, a father and a priest, had such immoral sons. He remonstrated with them mildly, but they could care less. They had a cushy job for life in the priestly service, or so they thought. They served as priests by virtue of their lineage. The hours were not too demanding, so they freely sinned against God, against their wives, against the job, and against God.

People who commit outright sin have no shame about it nor do they intend to change. The sons of Eli despised God instead of honoring God, so God dealt decisively with them by punishing the sinners. In this instance, Eli was a fat, old man with mature adult sons who knew better but didn't do better. They should have respected their God, their father, and their wives. They had been living wrongly for some time. When God pronounced judgment on them, it came quickly.

We should never envy those who seem to be getting away with wickedness. We do not know when God will judge those sinners, but we know He most certainly will.

Praise God

And David spake unto the Lord the words of this song in the
day that the Lord had delivered him out of the hand of all his
enemies, and out of the hand of Saul: And he said, The Lord
is my rock, and my fortress, and my deliverer; The God of
my rock; in him will I trust: he is my shield, and the horn of
my salvation, my high tower, and my refuge, my saviour; thou
savest me from violence. I will call on the Lord, who is worthy
to be praised: so shall I be saved from mine enemies.
—2 Samuel 22:1–4

O praise the Lord, all ye nations: praise him, all ye people.
For his merciful kindness is great toward us: and the truth
of the Lord endureth for ever. Praise ye the Lord.
—Psalm 117:1–2

When we are happy, do we sing to God to celebrate? King David did. Even
if we cannot write hymns and psalms like David did, our hearts can still
sing to God. David sought the Lord and trusted Him in many difficulties.

David knew God as the rock behind which he could hide because he knew
that as a human, he was inherently weak. David knew God as the fortress that
stands impregnable against enemies. David knew God as the One who could
deliver him from evil. David knew God as the shield that repels the flaming
arrows of the Devil. David knew God as the source of his salvation. David knew
God as the hidden stronghold where the weak may rest secure. David knew God
as the hiding place of safety from harm.

David fought many physical enemies. He was a man of war, a five-star
general kind of military leader in our time, but a king in his time. His life
exemplifies the spiritual battle we all face but cannot always see. David always
turned immediate situations over to God. He never underestimated the severity
of the problem any more than he overestimated the power of God to intervene.
We can trust God and praise Him too.

Working Together for God

But it was so, that in the three and twentieth year of king Jehoash the priests had not repaired the breaches of the house. Then king Jehoash called for Jehoiada the priest, and the other priests, and said unto them, Why repair ye not the breaches of the house? now therefore receive no more money of your acquaintance, but deliver it for the breaches of the house. And the priests consented to receive no more money of the people, neither to repair the breaches of the house. But Jehoiada the priest took a chest, and bored a hole in the lid of it, and set it beside the altar, on the right side as one cometh into the house of the Lord: and the priests that kept the door put therein all the money that was brought into the house of the Lord. And it was so, when they saw that there was much money in the chest, that the king's scribe and the high priest came up, and they put up in bags, and told the money that was found in the house of the Lord. And they gave the money, being told, into the hands of them that did the work, that had the oversight of the house of the Lord: and they laid it out to the carpenters and builders, that wrought upon the house of the Lord, And to masons, and hewers of stone, and to buy timber and hewed stone to repair the breaches of the house of the Lord, and for all that was laid out for the house to repair it.

—2 Kings 12:6–12

Joash is noted as one the boy kings of the Old Testament. He ascended the throne of Judah at the tender age of seven and reigned for forty years. Joash followed the Lord, doing many good deeds for the welfare of the country. When he was fourteen, he told the priests to collect the offering money and use it to repair the damaged temple, but the repairs did not take place.

Joash let this go until he was thirty years of age. The priests followed his instructions this time. The freewill offerings were used to pay the supervisors of the temple repair work and all the workmen. Carpenters, builders, masons, and stonecutters were paid a fair wage for their craftsmanship.

Churches today still follow the pattern of freewill offerings to fund the construction of a new church building. The situation of Joash and the priests and the people teaches us that everyone must agree to do the same plan in before God gives the go-ahead to make it happen.

Letting God Help

But it came to pass, that when Sanballat heard that we builded the
wall, he was wroth, and took great indignation, and mocked the
Jews. And he spake before his brethren and the army of Samaria,
and said, What do these feeble Jews? will they fortify themselves?
will they sacrifice? will they make an end in a day? will they revive
the stones out of the heaps of the rubbish which are burned? Now
Tobiah the Ammonite was by him, and he said, Even that which
they build, if a fox go up, he shall even break down their stone wall.
Hear, O our God; for we are despised: and turn their reproach upon
their own head, and give them for a prey in the land of captivity:
And cover not their iniquity, and let not their sin be blotted out
from before thee: for they have provoked thee to anger before the
builders ... So the wall was finished in the twenty and fifth day of
the month Elul, in fifty and two days. And it came to pass, that
when all our enemies heard thereof, and all the heathen that were
about us saw these things, they were much cast down in their own
eyes: for they perceived that this work was wrought of our God.
—Nehemiah 4:1–5; 6:15–16

For a person who began so enthusiastically, prayed so fervently, and planned so meticulously, we would expect that the rebuilding of Jerusalem to go quite smoothly, but it didn't. Two long-standing enemies of Israel, represented by Sanballat the Samaritan and Tobiah the Ammonite, were furious to see the progress being made. They represent those who hate God and hate God's work, a problem in any generation.

Nehemiah and the exiles were learning to trust God. After being sent into exile for sinfulness and after thinking about what had happened for seventy years, the people and leaders were happy and willing to do what God wanted, but they did not have previous experiences of faithful situations to fall back on for guidance. They prayed for His deliverance and kept on working toward the goal God had given them and blessed them to begin.

The situation reminds us of our inabilities and weaknesses. We can lay the best plans, we can line up the best materials, we can hire the best workers, but we still need God's help. When we rely on Him, He completes His task in His time.

Forgiveness

Blessed is he whose transgression is forgiven, whose sin is
covered. Blessed is the man unto whom the Lord imputeth not
iniquity, and in whose spirit there is no guile. When I kept silence,
my bones waxed old through my roaring all the day long. For day
and night thy hand was heavy upon me: my moisture is turned
into the drought of summer. Selah. I acknowledge my sin unto
thee, and mine iniquity have I not hid. I said, I will confess my
transgressions unto the Lord; and thou forgavest the iniquity
of my sin. Selah. For this shall every one that is godly pray unto
thee in a time when thou mayest be found: surely in the floods
of great waters they shall not come nigh unto him … Be ye
not as the horse, or as the mule, which have no understanding:
whose mouth must be held in with bit and bridle, lest they come
near unto thee. Many sorrows shall be to the wicked: but he
that trusteth in the Lord, mercy shall compass him about.
—Psalm 32:1–6, 9–10

Religions promote all kinds of ideas, and some religions believe that human
nature is inherently good. This belief implies that human beings do not
need forgiveness for sin, salvation for souls, or a right relationship with God. We
are already all right. When we are honest with ourselves and when we consider
human history, we know we are sinners—we do what is wrong—we offend
God—we need forgiveness.

Humans are not like dumb animals that must be controlled by bit and bridle
in order to render useful service to their human masters. People are controlled
by the exercise of free will. We can choose forgiveness. God operates by His
immutable laws, and forgiveness for sins upon repentance is one of those laws.

Forgiveness from God for sins means happiness for us. Once we have
confessed our sins, we can communicate better with others, we can function
effectively. God energizes to do what is right, resulting in praise to Him.

Who Is Jesus Christ?

And king Herod heard of him; (for his name was spread abroad:)
and he said, That John the Baptist was risen from the dead,
and therefore mighty works do shew forth themselves in him.
Others said, That it is Elias. And others said, That it is a prophet,
or as one of the prophets. But when Herod heard thereof, he
said, It is John, whom I beheaded: he is risen from the dead.
—Mark 6:14–16

When Jesus came into the coasts of Caesarea Philippi, he asked
his disciples, saying, Whom do men say that I the Son of man
am? And they said, Some say that thou art John the Baptist: some,
Elias; and others, Jeremias, or one of the prophets. He saith unto
them, But whom say ye that I am? And Simon Peter answered
and said, Thou art the Christ, the Son of the living God.
—Matthew 16:13–16

Times have not changed much over the centuries when we consider that people in ancient times were just as confused about the identity of Jesus Christ as we are today. Many of us like to read about well-known celebrities and learn the details of their personal lives. Word of mouth accomplished the same purpose in biblical times as fan clubs and blogs do today. Do we believe all we hear or see? Hopefully not, but a reliable source of information is always welcome.

One reason the Bible was written was to assure us Jesus is the Christ, the Son of the living God. King Herod felt guilty about the murder of his brother, his subsequent marriage to the sister-in-law, and his beheading of John the Baptist who had reproached him for his sinful behavior. Herod feared that John the Baptist had come back to life to haunt his guilty memory. Others, less consumed with guilt than King Herod, saw the miracles Jesus performed and heard His wise words. They pegged Jesus Christ as a prophet. It had been about 400 years since prophets had spoken to the Jews, so it was definitely about time for a fresh word from God. Some elevated Jesus above the known prophets, and others thought that Elijah had come back to earth again. Elijah had not died; God took him away, so maybe this was his time to return.

Everyone today must still decide on the identity of Jesus Christ. Peter answered correctly. His response to the piercing question confirmed His place in God's plan.

Whose Rules Do We Follow?

Let favour be shewed to the wicked, yet will he not learn
righteousness: in the land of uprightness will he deal unjustly, and
will not behold the majesty of the Lord ... For with stammering
lips and another tongue will he speak to this people. To whom he
said, This is the rest wherewith ye may cause the weary to rest; and
this is the refreshing: yet they would not hear. But the word of the
Lord was unto them precept upon precept, precept upon precept;
line upon line, line upon line; here a little, and there a little; that they
might go, and fall backward, and be broken, and snared, and taken.
—Isaiah 26:10; 28:11–13

As for God, his way is perfect: the word of the Lord is
tried: he is a buckler to all those that trust in him.
—Psalm 18:30

The Bible teaches us that the nature of God is perfect goodness, and we understand this to mean that God is good to all—believers and unbelievers alike. The common grace of God showers rain on the fields of all farmers, not just on the God-fearing farmers. The sun rises every day for every human being, not just for the ones who fear God. God disperses life skills and unique talents to all individuals, without regard to personal belief in Him.

The Bible also tells us that even though God is good to unbelievers, they have made a decision to refuse to turn to Him. They continue living in rebellion to God, as if the fact of God allowing them to live in rebellion is the same thing as God sanctioning the rebellion. They follow their own rules—the rules of the sinful nature—so God punishes them by making them follow those rules to their eventual outcomes, outcomes that lead them to their deaths.

If only we would think more logically and remember that God's rules lead us to eternal life, we might find it easier to obey Him. The alternative is not worth the price we will eventually pay.

JULY 24

Questioning the Lord

> I form the light, and create darkness: I make peace, and create
> evil: I the Lord do all these things ... Woe unto him that striveth
> with his Maker! Let the potsherd strive with the potsherds of the
> earth. Shall the clay say to him that fashioneth it, What makest
> thou? or thy work, He hath no hands? Woe unto him that saith
> unto his father, What begettest thou? or to the woman, What hast
> thou brought forth? Thus saith the Lord, the Holy One of Israel,
> and his Maker, Ask me of things to come concerning my sons,
> and concerning the work of my hands command ye me. I have
> made the earth, and created man upon it: I, even my hands, have
> stretched out the heavens, and all their host have I commanded.
> —Isaiah 45:7, 9–12

When our lives are going well, we need no assurance that God is with us. Our well-being is ample proof of His loving care. When terrible things happen in our lives, we question our faith, and we question God. When the tragedy occurs through no personal fault of our own, we really do not understand God because we know ourselves to be innocent. God knows we are innocent of this too, but He asks us not to argue with Him. He is the heavenly Father, and who can argue with Dad and win?

God asks us to remember that we are made of dust. We know how easily a pottery mug can be shattered on a hard surface. And what is pottery?—no more than hardened dust! We are equally fragile. We may question what God has done in our lives, but God reminds us that potters know how to mold the clay, and He is the master potter.

He asks us to consider the overall operation of the earth. If He can create the universe and keep it running smoothly, can God not do as much for us even when appearances go to the contrary?

The Bad of the Tongue

And the tongue is a fire, a world of iniquity: so is the tongue
among our members, that it defileth the whole body, and setteth
on fire the course of nature; and it is set on fire of hell. For every
kind of beasts, and of birds, and of serpents, and of things in
the sea, is tamed, and hath been tamed of mankind: But the
tongue can no man tame; it is an unruly evil, full of deadly
poison. Therewith bless we God, even the Father; and therewith
curse we men, which are made after the similitude of God.
—James 3:6–9

Keep thy tongue from evil, and thy lips from speaking guile.
—Psalm 34:13

If any man among you seem to be religious, and bridleth not his
tongue, but deceiveth his own heart, this man's religion is vain.
—James 1:26

On a dry summer day in a drought-ridden area, a motorist saw smoky spires
smoldering along the edge of the interstate. The driver reported the fire
at the next rest station, only to learn that several motorists had already reported
it. The local fire department was already on the way to douse the flames. When
the drought is prolonged, everyone fears the danger of forest fires from one
small spark. We live in a time when it is considered normal to use fiery, foul
language—a little bad language proves that we are human—how many of us
believe such twisted logic?

Perhaps the reason why the tongue is used to curse God, to tell lies, to
destroy innocent people, or to boast extravagantly is that we also live in a time
of drought of the Word of God. When we are no longer familiar with the Word
of God and its injunctions to curb our worst thoughts, we think speech does not
matter too much.

Guarding the words that slip off the tongue is a first defense against the
onslaught of filth that surrounds us on every side, greets us in every arena of life,
and wants to take over our lives.

Friends

A friend loveth at all times, and a brother is born for
adversity ... A man that hath friends must shew himself friendly:
and there is a friend that sticketh closer than a brother.
—Proverbs 17:17; 18:24

And the Lord spake unto Moses face to face, as a man speaketh unto
his friend. And he turned again into the camp: but his servant Joshua,
the son of Nun, a young man, departed not out of the tabernacle.
—Exodus 33:11

This is my commandment, That ye love one another, as I have loved
you. Greater love hath no man than this, that a man lay down his life
for his friends. Ye are my friends, if ye do whatsoever I command
you. Henceforth I call you not servants; for the servant knoweth
not what his lord doeth: but I have called you friends; for all things
that I have heard of my Father I have made known unto you.
—John 15:12–15

All of us need friends, and children sometimes spend a lot of time worrying about who is the best friend and who hates them. Navigating the intricacies of childish thinking can cause emotional grief, so the possibility of having a forever friend is very appealing to young adults. We hope God give us a special friend to marry, but we still value all our other friends.

As believers, we need to think about friendship from a biblical perspective. In a human friend, we desire someone who is there for us—always, and we want someone who is like a brother or sister—but isn't. We do form instantaneous and long-lasting friendships in college, and these friendships are a blessing from God. God wants to be our best friend, and He has given us the pattern for friendship. God is a friend to the obedient. Moses, the greatest and most revered leader of the Israelites, was accounted a friend of God. God spoke with Moses face-to-face, and Moses was considered the humblest man on earth.

Today, we can commune with God by reading the Bible and through prayer. Job, in the agonies of his life, knew he had a personal intercessory friend to pray for him. Today, we know clearly that Jesus Christ is that friend whom Job knew dimly.

The Light of God

No man, when he hath lighted a candle, putteth it in a secret place,
neither under a bushel, but on a candlestick, that they which come
in may see the light. The light of the body is the eye: therefore when
thine eye is single, thy whole body also is full of light; but when thine
eye is evil, thy body also is full of darkness. Take heed therefore
that the light which is in thee be not darkness. If thy whole body
therefore be full of light, having no part dark, the whole shall be full
of light, as when the bright shining of a candle doth give thee light.
—Luke 11:33–36

Thy word is a lamp unto my feet, and a light unto
my path ... The entrance of thy words giveth light;
it giveth understanding unto the simple.
—Psalm 119:105, 130

For the commandment is a lamp; and the law is light;
and reproofs of instruction are the way of life.
—Proverbs 6:23

Light dazzles us. The effect of light is to make us feel better afterward. We
depend upon electricity to light our homes for the more prosaic side of life,
but we jump at the opportunity to display lights for the more ethereal aspects
of life. Candles on the mantle for a romantic evening, fireworks displays for
Independence Day, water-lit fountains in public gardens, Christmas displays
around the neighborhood, and outdoor garden lighting feed our heartfelt need
for the brighter, lighter side of life.

Artificial lighting cannot satisfy our valid and real spiritual need for light,
but it can help us realize how much we need spiritual illumination. Jesus is the
light of the world, so when we come to Him in repentance and trust, it is as if
our physical bodies are alight with Him. He overtakes our beings as much as we
allow Him to.

Because all people are subject to the same desires, we know how much others
want to see the light of the Lord, not just the pretty and temporary lights, but
the eternal light of the gospel—Jesus Christ living in us—shining forth through
the witness of our lives.

The Best Kind of Friend

Then was kindled the wrath of Elihu the son of Barachel the
Buzite, of the kindred of Ram: against Job was his wrath kindled,
because he justified himself rather than God. Also against his three
friends was his wrath kindled, because they had found no answer,
and yet had condemned Job. Now Elihu had waited till Job had
spoken, because they were elder than he ... I will speak, that I may
be refreshed: I will open my lips and answer ... Surely thou hast
spoken in mine hearing, and I have heard the voice of thy words,
saying, I am clean without transgression, I am innocent; neither
is there iniquity in me ... Behold, in this thou art not just: I will
answer thee, that God is greater than man. Why dost thou strive
against him? for he giveth not account of any of his matters. For
God speaketh once, yea twice, yet man perceiveth it not ... Lo, all
these things worketh God oftentimes with man, To bring back his
soul from the pit, to be enlightened with the light of the living.
—Job 32:2–4, 20; 33:8–9, 12–14, 29–30

We remember Job as a man who suffered more than anyone can possibly
imagine, yet he lived to tell the tale. He lost all his livestock (thousands of
animals) and ten children in a single day. His wife remained alive, but she ranted
at him in bitterness of heart, giving him no comfort. Most of his friends were
afraid to talk to him, but four friends sort of sympathized with Job. They sat for
a week in silent mourning with Job before daring to speak.

The first three friends were sure that Job must have caused the calamity,
pain, and suffering of his life, only they just couldn't really figure out how.
Job insisted upon his innocence. He knew his blameless life did not cause his
tragedies. He wanted answers from God, but none were forthcoming. The fourth
friend Elihu, hung back until the first three finished speaking their minds. He
had deeper spiritual insight even though he was much younger. He urged Job to
stop thinking of himself as a blameless victim because all of us are sinners and
subject to the effects of sin in this world.

God is still sovereign and owes no explanation to anyone. Sometimes, God
asks us to be silent before Him so we can learn to discern His voice from myriad
other noises. God desires our spiritual well-being so much that He sometimes
uses drastic events to grab our everlasting attention. Elihu was the best kind
of friend because he told the truth about God. We know this for a fact because
God did not condemn his words like He did the words of the first three friends.

Judging Others

Therefore thou art inexcusable, O man, whosoever thou art that
judgest: for wherein thou judgest another, thou condemnest thyself;
for thou that judgest doest the same things. But we are sure that the
judgment of God is according to truth against them which commit
such things ... Or despisest thou the riches of his goodness and
forbearance and longsuffering; not knowing that the goodness
of God leadeth thee to repentance? But after thy hardness and
impenitent heart treasurest up unto thyself wrath against the day
of wrath and revelation of the righteous judgment of God; Who
will render to every man according to his deeds: To them who
by patient continuance in well doing seek for glory and honour
and immortality, eternal life: But unto them that are contentious,
and do not obey the truth, but obey unrighteousness, indignation
and wrath ... For there is no respect of persons with God.
—Romans 2:1–2, 4–8, 11

When we have close relatives who are not believers, especially when they live
in flagrant sin or commit self-destructive habits on a continual basis, we
find it very difficult to know what to say or how to treat them. Should we even talk
to them? Should we ever visit them? We cannot judge them because we are fellow
sinners. At the same time, we know they did not need to do what they are doing.

It is good to know that judgment belongs to God. We need to keep in mind
that not long ago, we were acting as unbelievers, but God was kind to us in spite
of our sins. He was tolerant toward our bad habits. He exercised patience with
our ignorant notions of Him, even if we thought about Him at all. God wants
us now to exercise the same godly kindness, tolerance, and patience toward our
unbelieving relatives. We do not know whom God will save, but we can trust
Him to help us live up to His name as we witness to them.

God begins our spiritual growth on the home front, the same place where
He began our physical growth. Everyone will certainly grow up and mature, but
to what end? Leave the end results to God.

God Wants Our Companionship

For thus saith the Lord that created the heavens; God himself
that formed the earth and made it; he hath established it, he
created it not in vain, he formed it to be inhabited: I am the
Lord; and there is none else. I have not spoken in secret, in
a dark place of the earth: I said not unto the seed of Jacob,
Seek ye me in vain: I the Lord speak righteousness, I declare
things that are right ... Look unto me, and be ye saved, all the
ends of the earth: for I am God, and there is none else.
—Isaiah 45:18–19, 22

Yea, I have loved thee with an everlasting love:
therefore with lovingkindness have I drawn thee.
—Jeremiah 31:3

How do we know whether or not someone truly loves us?—there are two
qualities matter a lot to most of us when it comes to true love. We experience
true love when the person wants to spend a lot of time with us, and we experience
love when the person tells the truth. We cannot love a person who tells lies yet
wants to spend time with us because we know we will get hurt. We cannot love
someone who never sees us yet professes true love because the words and the
behavior contradict each other.

What a security and stability we get from true love, from fellowship based
upon the truth. This is exactly what God has done for us already. In creating the
heavens and the earth, God created a beautiful place for us to live, grow, and
worship Him in. He never wanted an empty earth. He always wanted more of
us to live here—for His pleasure, for His companionship, and for our delight.

Because of what God has done for us, we know we can rely on Him to tell
us what is best. His love will guide us with certainty.

Living the Right Way

Wherewithal shall a young man cleanse his way? by taking heed
thereto according to thy word. With my whole heart have I
sought thee: O let me not wander from thy commandments. Thy
word have I hid in mine heart, that I might not sin against thee.
Blessed art thou, O Lord: teach me thy statutes ... I will delight
myself in thy statutes: I will not forget thy word ... Teach me,
O Lord, the way of thy statutes; and I shall keep it unto the end.
Give me understanding, and I shall keep thy law; yea, I shall
observe it with my whole heart. Make me to go in the path of
thy commandments; for therein do I delight ... Behold, I have
longed after thy precepts: quicken me in thy righteousness.
—Psalm 119:9–12, 16, 33–35, 40

College can be likened to a traveler who journeys from familiar scenery to
an unknown territory, one that will become home for a long time to come.
Travelers have prepared for the trip as best as they could, and they think they
know to expect, but the new place is so utterly different from what they imagined
that a type of culture shock sets in. Travelers meet many new faces, and these new
acquaintances have a lot to say that must be digested while the newbie assimilates
into the new environment.

Similarly, college students face many unexpected decisions, and college is a
time when wrong decisions can quite easily be made on the spur of the moment.
It is important to take a personal faith to college and to practice it in the new
environment. Stay in touch with God's Word by reading it daily and put into
practice its precepts. Knowledge of the Bible can keep students from making
decisions that are later regretted.

College seems like everything in life while it is happening, but in the long
term, college is only a brief (but exciting) part of life. The easiest and most
successful way to complete the college years is to stay focused on the Lord, who
directs life and decisions better than any person can do.

AUGUST 1

Consecration

Then flew one of the seraphims unto me, having a live coal in his
hand, which he had taken with the tongs from off the altar: And
he laid it upon my mouth, and said, Lo, this hath touched thy
lips; and thine iniquity is taken away, and thy sin purged. Also I
heard the voice of the Lord, saying, Whom shall I send, and who
will go for us? Then said I, Here am I; send me ... But yet in it
shall be a tenth, and it shall return, and shall be eaten: as a teil
tree, and as an oak, whose substance is in them, when they cast
their leaves: so the holy seed shall be the substance thereof.
—Isaiah 6:6–8, 13

When we first turn to the Lord, we come to the realization that God now
has a different design for our lives than we had previously planned. This is
an exciting time in life because we wait expectantly for direction from the Lord.
One aspect of serving God that we might like to keep in mind is that God uses
those whose hearts, souls, and minds are completely focused on Him. In other
words, God looks for personal holiness in the individual whom He will use.

We can learn a little about holiness from Isaiah the prophet. When Isaiah
was confronted with the presence and holiness and majesty of God, he realized
he had a decision to make. He wanted to answer the call from God, but he knew
how wickedly sinful he was, and that no unholy human being could stand in
the presence of a holy God. God sent the seraph with the coal fire of cleansing
to purify Isaiah, to remove his guilt, to atone for his sins, and to enable him to
hear God's voice.

We understand from the experience of Isaiah that when God touches the
life of a person, He enables the person to respond to Him at the same time as
He enables the person to obey God's will. It is both frightening and humbling
to meet the Lord.

Family Problems

And Joseph knew his brethren, but they knew not him ... And they
said one to another, We are verily guilty concerning our brother, in
that we saw the anguish of his soul, when he besought us, and we
would not hear; therefore is this distress come upon us ... And he
turned himself about from them, and wept; and returned to them
again, and communed with them, and took from them Simeon, and
bound him before their eyes ... And Joseph said unto his brethren,
Come near to me, I pray you. And they came near. And he said, I
am Joseph your brother, whom ye sold into Egypt. Now therefore
be not grieved, nor angry with yourselves, that ye sold me hither:
for God did send me before you to preserve life. For these two years
hath the famine been in the land: and yet there are five years, in
the which there shall neither be earing nor harvest. And God sent
me before you to preserve you a posterity in the earth, and to save
your lives by a great deliverance. So now it was not you that sent
me hither, but God: and he hath made me a father to Pharaoh, and
lord of all his house, and a ruler throughout all the land of Egypt.
—Genesis 42:8, 21, 24; 45:4–8

Some of us come from family situations so difficult that we never want to see
Mom or Dad or brothers or sisters again—at least, not for a very long time.
We cannot explain the difficulties easily to others because they are too personal,
too hurtful, and still too close to our daily experiences. We frequently think about
those family members who are absent from our lives, and we may always wish
that our family relationships could be otherwise, but they are not.

Joseph lived with this tortured state of mind for a couple of decades, but
God brought his murder-minded brothers into Joseph's now royal presence. God
placed those brothers completely under the power of their little brother Joseph.
Although he was now unrecognizable to his older brothers, Joseph wondered
whether their characters had changed. Had they been thinking about what had
happened, like he had? Joseph tested their behavior and learned that they had
suffered decades of guilt for their bad treatment of him.

The reunion of that family reminds us that God can alter the most unyielding
of hearts and that all family members can receive the grace of God, no matter
how bad the deeds they have committed.

AUGUST 3

Unbelieving Friends and Family

> The word of the Lord came again unto me, saying ... And I will
> execute judgments upon Moab; and they shall know that I am
> the Lord ... And I will lay my vengeance upon Edom by the
> hand of my people Israel: and they shall do in Edom according
> to mine anger and according to my fury; and they shall know my
> vengeance, saith the Lord God ... Therefore thus saith the Lord
> God; Behold, I will stretch out mine hand upon the Philistines, and
> I will cut off the Cherethims, and destroy the remnant of the sea
> coast ... Therefore thus saith the Lord God; Behold, I am against
> thee, O Tyrus, and will cause many nations to come up against thee,
> as the sea causeth his waves to come up ... Again the word of the
> Lord came unto me, saying, Son of man, set thy face against Zidon,
> and prophesy against it. Son of man, set thy face against Pharaoh
> king of Egypt, and prophesy against him, and against all Egypt.
> —Ezekiel 25:1, 11, 14, 16; 26:3; 28:20–21; 29:2

Does it bother us to think about the success of unbelieving friends and
family? They live according to the law of sin, yet they have succeeded
tremendously in life! Sometimes it seems like the worst behaved people get the
best out of life. Fortunately, whenever we question anything, we can always look
farther into the Bible to find the answers. The Bible is the truth, and we cannot
rely on our own understanding of superficial appearances. We should always
remember that long ago, God made Himself known to the world in various ways.
No living human is unaware of God's presence in this world, so God takes every
human decision quite seriously.

God spoke harshly and judgmentally against the nations of Ammon, Moab,
Edom, Philistia, Tyre, Sidon, and Egypt—to name a few. Why did God speak like
this?—because even though those nations exhibited superior skills and earned
great wealth and international prominence, they lived according to the law of
sin. They lived in deliberate rebellion to God. Because nations are comprised of
individuals, we can see more personal situations in more national arenas.

Sometimes, God lets sin mature before He punishes it, but don't ever be
misled into thinking that God ignores sinful behavior or does not deal with sinful
lives. The final word about anyone or any nation belongs to the Lord.

Anger Management

But I say unto you, That whosoever is angry with his brother
without a cause shall be in danger of the judgment: and whosoever
shall say to his brother, Raca, shall be in danger of the council: but
whosoever shall say, Thou fool, shall be in danger of hell fire.
—Matthew 5:22

But the fruit of the Spirit is love, joy, peace, longsuffering, gentleness,
goodness, faith, Meekness, temperance: against such there is no law.
—Galatians 5:22–23

The precepts of psychology have permeated every aspect of our society to the point where we all feel we can understand other people without any particular professional expertise. The problem with psychological insight is that we tend to analyze the problems of others very clearly but forget about applying the same precepts to our own lives. Anger is a topic that psychology textbooks deal with, but are we aware that God has an opinion about anger too?

Some of us have grown up in homes with a lot of bickering, quarrelling, screaming, shouting, and swearing. If this home was ours, we must understand that we learned a lot about anger but nothing at all about anger management. Psychology wants us to believe that we are most prone to behave in the way we have been taught, but psychology is not the same thing as the truth, like the Bible, is it?

God does judge anger, so it is time to leave the anger and the angry people at home when we leave home for college. We do not need to take them and their influences with us to the new environment of the college campus. On campus, we alone are now responsible to God to exercise self-control and kindliness toward others. It is not difficult when we accept the help of the Holy Spirit, the third person of the Trinity. When we remember that Jesus Christ promised that He would send the comforter to believers, we can relax and let the Holy Spirit change us into the likeness of the Savior.

AUGUST 5

Devotion or Confusion?

Grace be to you and peace from God the Father, and from our Lord
Jesus Christ, Who gave himself for our sins, that he might deliver us
from this present evil world, according to the will of God and our
Father: To whom be glory for ever and ever. Amen. I marvel that
ye are so soon removed from him that called you into the grace of
Christ unto another gospel: Which is not another; but there be some
that trouble you, and would pervert the gospel of Christ. But though
we, or an angel from heaven, preach any other gospel unto you than
that which we have preached unto you, let him be accursed. For do
I now persuade men, or God? or do I seek to please men? for if I yet
pleased men, I should not be the servant of Christ. But I certify you,
brethren, that the gospel which was preached of me is not after man.
—Galatians 1:3–8, 11

What do we need most in this life? A lot of us are in college working toward
a degree, so education seems like an obvious and accurate answer to this
question. But is education God's answer for all our needs? Not according to the
apostle Paul, and he had the finest education of his time. What we need most is
to be rescued from the evils of the age in which we live.

Some college campuses try to distract students from the real purpose of
college, which is studying, by alluring them to many forms of evil behavior that
God condemns. The promotion of evil behavior on campuses stands in glaring
contrast to the lofty ideals that colleges espouse. It is understandable that college
students can quickly become confused and walk away from the God of their
youth.

Paul reminds us that because Jesus Christ died for our sins, we receive grace
and peace from God the Father to deal with situations in life. God's grace and
peace override other considerations at the same time as they undergird all our
efforts. We can accept the help of the Holy Spirit to stay on track in our spiritual
races to the end of college life and to the end of this life.

Negatives or Positives in Life?

Thus saith the Lord; Cursed be the man that trusteth in man,
and maketh flesh his arm, and whose heart departeth from the
Lord ... Blessed is the man that trusteth in the Lord, and whose
hope the Lord is ... The heart is deceitful above all things, and
desperately wicked: who can know it? I the Lord search the heart,
I try the reins, even to give every man according to his ways, and
according to the fruit of his doings ... Heal me, O Lord, and I shall
be healed; save me, and I shall be saved: for thou art my praise.
—Jeremiah 17:5, 7, 9–10, 14

How do we approach situations in life? Most of us feel confident enough to figure out most of life on our own, but the Bible uses strong contrasts to highlight the differences between human-based thinking and God-based reasoning. We feel strong in ourselves when we feel physically fit, when life plans go our way, and when we are still on good terms with all our friends. Our plans are in place, and we know where we are headed.

When we trust others for all the good things in life—the good things that God has really given us—without ever acknowledging that God is the giver of every gift—God curses us for turning away from Him. We cannot call ourselves believers yet follow our own way in life. We must acknowledge that we are sinners and that our hearts are inclined to think in this wrong way.

When we let God sift through our desires and goals, we can be sure that He will sort out the trash and throw out the junk that should not stay in our lives. God gives us confidence when we turn to Him. His goals for us are best.

AUGUST 7

The Earth Belongs to God

For he maketh small the drops of water: they pour down rain
according to the vapour thereof: Which the clouds do drop and
distil upon man abundantly. Also can any understand the spreadings
of the clouds, or the noise of his tabernacle? Behold, he spreadeth
his light upon it, and covereth the bottom of the sea. For by them
judgeth he the people; he giveth meat in abundance ... At this
also my heart trembleth, and is moved out of his place ... God
thundereth marvellously with his voice; great things doeth he,
which we cannot comprehend. For he saith to the snow, Be thou
on the earth; likewise to the small rain, and to the great rain of his
strength. He sealeth up the hand of every man; that all men may
know his work ... Where wast thou when I laid the foundations
of the earth? declare, if thou hast understanding. Who hath laid
the measures thereof, if thou knowest? or who hath stretched the
line upon it? Whereupon are the foundations thereof fastened?
or who laid the corner stone thereof; When the morning stars
sang together, and all the sons of God shouted for joy?
—Job 36:27–31; 37:1, 5–7; 38:4–7

Consider how much care and effort the Lord has put into the long-term
operation and continuous functioning of planet earth. Every natural
phenomenon speaks to His love and care for the earth and the humans who
inhabit it. We have studied science in school, so we are somewhat familiar with
the cycles of the natural habitats of our world.

We know that water is the source of life for all living creatures. But when we
tensely await the approach of a torrential downpour and cringe at every deafening
crack of thunder and lightning, we tend to think the opposite. When we stock up
on candles and blankets to await a powerful blizzard, we hope to live through it
without losing the electricity.

Storms seem indiscriminate and unplanned, but the Creator has an overall
plan of which we remain unaware. Perhaps we should also see in the storm the
same overall plan of God to govern the world and look at thunder as a sign of
the all-encompassing care of God for this world.

Paying the Price of Sin

And when he hath made an end of reconciling the holy place, and
the tabernacle of the congregation, and the altar, he shall bring the
live goat: And Aaron shall lay both his hands upon the head of the
live goat, and confess over him all the iniquities of the children of
Israel, and all their transgressions in all their sins, putting them
upon the head of the goat, and shall send him away by the hand
of a fit man into the wilderness: And the goat shall bear upon him
all their iniquities unto a land not inhabited: and he shall let go the
goat in the wilderness. And Aaron shall come into the tabernacle
of the congregation, and shall put off the linen garments, which
he put on when he went into the holy place, and shall leave them
there: And he shall wash his flesh with water in the holy place, and
put on his garments, and come forth, and offer his burnt offering,
and the burnt offering of the people, and make an atonement for
himself, and for the people … And he that let go the goat for the
scapegoat shall wash his clothes, and bathe his flesh in water, and
afterward come into the camp … And he that burneth them shall
wash his clothes, and bathe his flesh in water, and afterward he
shall come into the camp … And this shall be an everlasting statute
unto you, to make an atonement for the children of Israel for all
their sins once a year. And he did as the Lord commanded Moses.
—Leviticus 16:20–24, 26, 28, 34

In Old Testament times, the high priest Aaron made atonement for the sins of
the people once a year. He laid hands on the head of the goat and confessed
all of Israel's sins upon the animal; figuratively speaking, he placed all their
sins upon the scapegoat. The scapegoat carried the sins of the people out to
the desert where the goat was then released. After getting rid of the sins of the
people, Aaron cleansed himself with water and made sacrifices to the Lord. One
fact about the atonement for sin is clear—sin carries a hefty price tag, and sin
must be paid for.

In the New Testament, we learn that Jesus Christ has made the atonement
for our sins, once for all. The goat was not good enough; only a perfect human
life is capable of the task.

When we enter a relationship with Jesus through repentance, He gets rid of
our sins and removes them far away from us. This carrying away of sins cleanses
us from all unrighteousness. Baptism represents the spiritual cleansing of our
souls. We are able to offer our lives to God, and He is pleased with us.

AUGUST 9

Blameless Living

Thou shalt not plant thee a grove of any trees near unto the altar of
the Lord thy God, which thou shalt make thee. Neither shalt thou
set thee up any image; which the Lord thy God hateth ... When
thou art come into the land which the Lord thy God giveth thee,
thou shalt not learn to do after the abominations of those nations.
There shall not be found among you any one that maketh his son
or his daughter to pass through the fire, or that useth divination,
or an observer of times, or an enchanter, or a witch. Or a charmer,
or a consulter with familiar spirits, or a wizard, or a necromancer.
For all that do these things are an abomination unto the Lord: and
because of these abominations the Lord thy God doth drive them
out from before thee. Thou shalt be perfect with the Lord thy God.
—Deuteronomy 16:21–22; 18:9–13

No one has to look very far today to see that people are engaging in behavior
that God hates. For example, people set up Buddha idols in their homes
and gardens, sometimes on the front porch or lawn, for all to see as they drive
by. They probably bought the idol a stylish home decorating store or at an amply
stocked garden supply center. When we purchase items of idolatry from a type
of store that primarily sells other types of merchandise, the evil nature of the
purchase is lessened.

As another example, some women cannot decide which perfume to buy,
so they take the stones out of their purses, turn them to and from in order to
make a simple decision. When people turn to lifeless objects for guidance, they
turn to idolatry. Mediums set up business signs on busy streets to attract men
and women into fortune telling. When people can advertise boldly and stay in
business, we must understand that wickedness grips a significant segment of
society. Thoughtless parents can buy satanic board games and play them with
their children to introduce them to sorcery. They incorporate and condone evil
practices as they raise their children.

Do we still understand that God hates these detestable practices? We need
to live according to the truth in order to live a blameless life. God is happy
with nothing less. If any of these activities have been part of our childhood
experiences, we need to identify them for what they are. We need to decide right
now to forego such evil practices for the rest of our lives.

Bad Leadership

I have loved you, saith the Lord. Yet ye say, Wherein hast thou
loved us? Was not Esau Jacob's brother? saith the Lord: yet I loved
Jacob ... And your eyes shall see, and ye shall say, The Lord will be
magnified from the border of Israel. A son honoureth his father,
and a servant his master: if then I be a father, where is mine honour?
and if I be a master, where is my fear? saith the Lord of hosts unto
you, O priests, that despise my name. And ye say, Wherein have we
despised thy name? ... And now, I pray you, beseech God that he
will be gracious unto us: this hath been by your means: will he regard
your persons? saith the Lord of hosts ... For the priest's lips should
keep knowledge, and they should seek the law at his mouth: for he
is the messenger of the Lord of hosts ... Then they that feared the
Lord spake often one to another: and the Lord hearkened, and heard
it, and a book of remembrance was written before him for them that
feared the Lord, and that thought upon his name. And they shall be
mine, saith the Lord of hosts, in that day when I make up my jewels;
and I will spare them, as a man spareth his own son that serveth
him. Then shall ye return, and discern between the righteous and the
wicked, between him that serveth God and him that serveth him not.
—Malachi 1:2, 5–6, 9; 2:7; 3:16–18

When prospective college students fill out applications forms, they invariably
check a box that say they are leaders, not followers. Attending college is a
wake-up call that should remind us that most of us are really followers.

Think about it! Students follow a prescribed course toward the completion
of a degree. Students follow others who know the way to the next class. Students
follow the syllabus and other instructions from the professors. God holds leaders
to greater accountability than followers. He faulted the priesthood for losing
respect and promoting contempt for His holy name.

Times have not changed in more than two thousand years. When leaders go
wrong, they teach followers to go wrong. Because we cannot see God, we think
that words or actions do not matter very much, but they do. Most people rely on
teachers for accurate information; they don't bother to check it out themselves.
Even among a group that is mostly going wrong, some still believe and obey God.
They often need to separate themselves, pray to God, and ask for help. God will
listen and spare them from the punishment that belongs to those who go astray.

How Temptation Occurs

Let no man say when he is tempted, I am tempted of God: for God cannot be tempted with evil, neither tempteth he any man: But every man is tempted, when he is drawn away of his own lust, and enticed. Then when lust hath conceived, it bringeth forth sin: and sin, when it is finished, bringeth forth death. Do not err, my beloved brethren.
—James 1:13–16

Wherefore let him that thinketh he standeth take heed lest he fall. There hath no temptation taken you but such as is common to man: but God is faithful, who will not suffer you to be tempted above that ye are able; but will with the temptation also make a way to escape, that ye may be able to bear it.
—1 Corinthians 10:12–13

Watch and pray, that ye enter not into temptation: the spirit indeed is willing, but the flesh is weak.
—Matthew 26:41

When we were younger and got into trouble, we probably blamed it on someone else. He made me do it. She made me do it. The Devil made me do it. God didn't stop me, so it must be all right. These are all lame excuses for bad behavior. Good parents are not fooled by the childish excuses of their offspring. God is not fooled either. So why should we fool ourselves?

We need to understand the nature of temptation so we can learn to recognize it and avoid it. The rest of our lives depends upon how we make decisions today. First of all, God does not tempt anyone to do evil. He is the author of good, and He does not violate His holy nature. Second of all, we are sinners, and sinful desires live within us. It almost seems like they are talking to us, enticing us to think about them continually.

Finally, when we continue to entertain these alluring thoughts, we will eventually act upon those them—such is the nature of human behavior. One small sin seems insignificant, but we sin frequently, and the final outcome of sin is death.

Giants in Our Lives

And there went out a champion out of the camp of the Philistines, named Goliath, of Gath, whose height was six cubits and a span. And he had an helmet of brass upon his head, and he was armed with a coat of mail; and the weight of the coat was five thousand shekels of brass. And he had greaves of brass upon his legs, and a target of brass between his shoulders. And the staff of his spear was like a weaver's beam; and his spear's head weighed six hundred shekels of iron: and one bearing a shield went before him. And he stood and cried unto the armies of Israel, and said unto them, Why are ye come out to set your battle in array? am not I a Philistine, and ye servants to Saul? choose you a man for you, and let him come down to me ... And David said to Saul, Let no man's heart fail because of him; thy servant will go and fight with this Philistine ... And all this assembly shall know that the Lord saveth not with sword and spear: for the battle is the Lord's, and he will give you into our hands.
—1 Samuel 17:4–8, 32, 47

When children are small, it appears to them that the world is peopled by giants. Bigger children bully younger children and taunt them with bad words. They shake their fists at them to tell them how weak they are. They make faces that scare them and make them cry.

Goliath, a man over nine feet tall, behaved like this to the army of Israel. Not one, but thousands of trained, strong, adult soldiers were afraid of the Philistine giant. Only one young man, not thousands of older men, was not afraid of Goliath. The shepherd boy David—the youngest son of eight brothers—stood against the giant Goliath. His father had sent him on an errand to bring food supplies to his older brothers who were soldiers for King Saul. David did not come to the battlefield planning to slay the giant. He simply intended to do the errand of his father.

Fortunately, David knew more than the soldiers. He understood that godless people are no better than animals, so he used animal tactics to dispatch the giant Goliath to his death. God had prepared David ahead of time, even though he did not know it until the moment arrived. David had killed bears and lions while tending sheep for his father, so he knew how to slay the giant who roared his defiant words at Israel. God never acts without a purpose nor does He consign anyone to desperation. He uses every event in life to His advantage. When we think of what God has already done for us, we can take heart that He is preparing us for the future giants in our lives.

Obedience or Defiance

And it came to pass, when Solomon had finished the building of the
house of the Lord, and the king's house, and all Solomon's desire
which he was pleased to do, That the Lord appeared to Solomon
the second time, as he had appeared unto him at Gibeon. And the
Lord said unto him, I have heard thy prayer and thy supplication,
that thou hast made before me: I have hallowed this house, which
thou hast built, to put my name there for ever; and mine eyes and
mine heart shall be there perpetually ... Then did Solomon build an
high place for Chemosh, the abomination of Moab, in the hill that is
before Jerusalem, and for Molech, the abomination of the children of
Ammon. And likewise did he for all his strange wives, which burnt
incense and sacrificed unto their gods. And the Lord was angry with
Solomon, because his heart was turned from the Lord God of Israel,
which had appeared unto him twice, Wherefore the Lord said unto
Solomon, Forasmuch as this is done of thee, and thou hast not kept
my covenant and my statutes, which I have commanded thee, I will
surely rend the kingdom from thee, and will give it to thy servant.
—1 Kings 9:1–3; 11:7–9, 11

Solomon stands out today as a genius among men. He understood politics and
philosophy. He wrote thousands of proverbs and songs. He wrote a botany
book about trees and wildflowers. He taught others about animals, birds, reptiles,
and fish. Unfortunately, the Bible does not record the activities of his childhood
education, which might have given us some insight into how he learned so much.
The Bible just tells us God gave Solomon wisdom and very great insight, and
a breadth of understanding as measureless as the sand on the seashore. Great
responsibilities often accompany tremendous talent.

God also gave this gifted and talented man the throne of his father David,
even though he was not the oldest son. God expected Solomon to stay faithful
to the one true God, and Solomon did so for a while. Solomon loved so many
foreign women who worshiped idols that his devotion to them caused him do evil
in God's eyes. Once Solomon had built a high place for two prominent idols, he
capitulated to idolatry and built idols to every other idol of every other wife. God
was angry because He had spoken personally to Solomon twice, a rare privilege.

Solomon's life shows us that a spiritual life must be active, present, and
ongoing if it is to be effective and lasting. Believers must always guard their spirits
and souls from spiritual predators, no matter who or what they are.

Changing Our Ways

Josiah was eight years old when he began to reign, and he reigned
thirty and one years in Jerusalem. And his mother's name was
Jedidah, the daughter of Adaiah of Boscath. And he did that which
was right in the sight of the Lord, and walked in all the way of David
his father, and turned not aside to the right hand or to the left ... And
Hilkiah the high priest said unto Shaphan the scribe, I have found
the book of the law in the house of the Lord. And Hilkiah gave the
book to Shaphan, and he read it ... And it came to pass, when the
king had heard the words of the book of the law, that he rent his
clothes ... Thus saith the Lord, Behold, I will bring evil upon this
place, and upon the inhabitants thereof, even all the words of the
book which the king of Judah hath read: Because they have forsaken
me, and have burned incense unto other gods, that they might
provoke me to anger with all the works of their hands; therefore my
wrath shall be kindled against this place, and shall not be quenched.
But to the king of Judah which sent you to enquire of the Lord, thus
shall ye say to him, Thus saith the Lord God of Israel, As touching
the words which thou hast heard; Because thine heart was tender,
and thou hast humbled thyself before the Lord, when thou heardest
what I spake against this place, and against the inhabitants thereof,
that they should become a desolation and a curse, and hast rent thy
clothes, and wept before me; I also have heard thee, saith the Lord.
—2 Kings 22:1–2, 8, 11, 16–19

Most of us would agree that change is beneficial, and change is most
noticeable when we have gone so far wrong that we can only change for
the better. This is what happened when Josiah became the boy king of Judah. The
temple had finally been repaired. This meant that proper worship of God could
now resume, except for the fact that it had been so long since proper worship
had occurred that no one remembered how to run a worship service anymore.

After sorting through the accumulated stuff in the storerooms of the newly
renovated temple, the high priest found the Book of the Law and read it to King
Josiah. The young king tore his clothing in two when he learned that God planned to
destroy the nation because they had forsaken Him. The nation was now worshipping
idols and now giving the same respect to false priests as to godly priests.

Because the boy king Josiah responded in repentance and humility to God,
the Lord relented from destroying them. The Lord blessed Josiah and gave him
many years of fruitful service to the nation. King Josiah reminds us that we are
never too young to follow the Lord and His ways.

AUGUST 15

When Disaster Strikes

God is our refuge and strength, a very present help in trouble.
Therefore will not we fear, though the earth be removed,
and though the mountains be carried into the midst of the
sea; Though the waters thereof roar and be troubled, though
the mountains shake with the swelling thereof. Selah ... Come,
behold the works of the Lord, what desolations he hath made in
the earth. He maketh wars to cease unto the end of the earth; he
breaketh the bow, and cutteth the spear in sunder; he burneth
the chariot in the fire. Be still, and know that I am God: I will
be exalted among the heathen, I will be exalted in the earth.
—Psalm 46:1–3, 8–10

Before the days of live-streaming videos or televised news immediately following a catastrophic event, disasters like volcanoes, hurricanes, tsunamis, floods, and earthquakes that occur around the world seemed very remote. Unless we actually knew someone who lived near the affected area, we did not pay much attention or attach any importance to them.

Modern media makes global events now appear extremely real to the average viewer. Visual representations are so graphic that we may fall subject to irrational fears brought on by the images we have seen. Natural disasters can also cause us to turn to God for help, and bad news can help us want to help others in severe distress.

God uses natural disasters to remind us that He is in charge of everything in this world: creation and destruction, salvation and damnation. He cannot be moved even when the earth moves. His sovereignty extends from the natural world to the world of men. He can cause nations to come to terms of peace with each other as much as He can bring about a national disaster upon an area. God's purpose is always to exalt His name. This is extremely difficult to understand in times of disaster, but we must reckon with the fact that God is ultimately in charge of planet earth and of all human lives.

AUGUST 16

Growing in the Lord

And he said, Whereunto shall we liken the kingdom of God? or
with what comparison shall we compare it? It is like a grain of
mustard seed, which, when it is sown in the earth, is less than all the
seeds that be in the earth: But when it is sown, it groweth up, and
becometh greater than all herbs, and shooteth out great branches;
so that the fowls of the air may lodge under the shadow of it.
—Mark 4:30–32

Let's think about the biggest tree we have ever seen. Is it a sequoia? A maple?
An oak? An ash? A pine? A spruce? In the time of Jesus, we might have
called to mind the mustard tree. In that location and time, an immense tree grew
from a small seed just like a large oak tree grows from a small acorn where we
may currently live. But the mustard seed is smaller than the oak seed or acorn,
so the size of the mature tree is proportionally greater for the mustard tree than
for the oak tree.

Nevertheless, the idea is still the same—something huge comes from
something tiny. It seems impossible, but with God, nothing is impossible, is it?
Once the tree is growing in the soil, it reproduces new cells in only a few places.
The meristems—the locations for cell division—become areas of intense activity.
Meristems at branch tips grow the height of the tree. Meristems at the root tips
extend the root system of the tree. The vascular cambium is the meristem that
increases the girth of the tree, creating more meristems, allowing the tree to
grow further.

It may be helpful to think about ourselves as young believers who are firmly
rooted in the soil of God's Word. God stretches us in different directions and
through unique situations to help us grow. We remain the same person, yet our
understanding increases. We become able to shelter or help others because of
the maturity the Word of God has produced in our lives. If we love big trees, we
can also love our big God.

Our Great God

I will praise thee with my whole heart: before the gods will I sing praise unto thee. I will worship toward thy holy temple, and praise thy name for thy lovingkindness and for thy truth: for thou hast magnified thy word above all thy name. In the day when I cried thou answeredst me, and strengthenedst me with strength in my soul ... Though the Lord be high, yet hath he respect unto the lowly: but the proud he knoweth afar off. Though I walk in the midst of trouble, thou wilt revive me: thou shalt stretch forth thine hand against the wrath of mine enemies, and thy right hand shall save me. The Lord will perfect that which concerneth me: thy mercy, O Lord, endureth for ever: forsake not the works of thine own hands.
—Psalm 138:1–3, 6–8

Do we ever think about the fact that we are taking a stand against all other (false) deities when we obey the one true God by praising Him? It is important to do the easy and simple tasks that God requires of believers. In this way, we strengthen our faith, and God honors us for it. When we praise God wholeheartedly, it is understood that we are defying the gods of this world. When we attend church, we hear stories of God's love and faithfulness to His people. Both of these activities cause us to recall that the name of God and the Word of God are more precious than anything else this world.

Banking on the truth gives us the courage to make requests of God and the confidence to know that God answers prayer. It is good to know that even though God is so far above us, He still cares for us who live down here. He cares for us personally. He steadies us as we walk through troubled times. He fights for us because we are too weak.

Best of all, God has a specific purpose for us. He never lets go of us. He always guides and directs us where He wants us to go. He brings to completion everything that concerns me.

True Understanding

And straightway he constrained his disciples to get into the ship,
and to go to the other side before unto Bethsaida, while he sent
away the people. And when he had sent them away, he departed into
a mountain to pray. And when even was come, the ship was in the
midst of the sea, and he alone on the land. And he saw them toiling
in rowing; for the wind was contrary unto them: and about the fourth
watch of the night he cometh unto them, walking upon the sea, and
would have passed by them. But when they saw him walking upon
the sea, they supposed it had been a spirit, and cried out: For they all
saw him, and were troubled. And immediately he talked with them,
and saith unto them, Be of good cheer: it is I; be not afraid. And he
went up unto them into the ship; and the wind ceased: and they were
sore amazed in themselves beyond measure, and wondered. For they
considered not the miracle of the loaves: for their heart was hardened.
—Mark 6:45–52

Human frailty trips us up every time! After the disciples had witnessed the miraculous feeding of five thousand people from two loaves and five fish, we might expect them to have so much faith in Jesus that they would be the most steadfast of believers for the rest of their lives. Their increase of belief and faith did not even last for one day!

To get away from the crowd of thousands, Jesus sent his disciples into a boat onto the Sea of Galilee. The disciples who were fishermen knew the lake well, so it seemed quite sensible to let them go ahead of their master. Perhaps they did not know exactly when Jesus would catch up with them, but they were still shocked to see Him walking across the lake to meet up with them in the boat. The wind had picked up, and they were having difficulty controlling the boat. Jesus Christ saw their distress, so He came to help them, walking on the water! Jesus comforted their fears and subsided the waters too.

He knew the disciples needed another faith-strengthening experience. Instead of being buffeted about by the winds of storm and changes in life, we can turn to Jesus and let Him handle those problems.

Seasons of Work

Give ye ear, and hear my voice; hearken, and hear my speech. Doth
the plowman plow all day to sow? doth he open and break the
clods of his ground? When he hath made plain the face thereof,
doth he not cast abroad the fitches, and scatter the cummin,
and cast in the principal wheat and the appointed barley and the
rie in their place? For his God doth instruct him to discretion,
and doth teach him ... This also cometh forth from the Lord of
hosts, which is wonderful in counsel, and excellent in working.
—Isaiah 28:23–26, 29

Human nature prefers variety. A change of pace from the dull daily routine is always welcome because it prevents stagnation. We don't mind working summer jobs because we know they are seasonal. We know will not always work at a gas station, department store, fast food chain, or teenage boutique. God is very aware of our proclivities, so He oversees our lives to give us exactly what suits our needs and interests.

In this passage, He has told us to consider how farmers operate. They plow for planting. They scatter one kind of seed, not more than one kind, in the same field. They plant certain crops in succession, planting the second one after the first one is harvested. In between the seasons of work, there are leisure times, when farmers rest a little and wait for the fruit of their labors. God runs our lives in the same way. We may wish to be more energetic, but God knows it is good to pace out our time and effort.

We will accomplish more when we alternate strong effort-filled times with seasons of rest. Many college courses follow a pattern that helps the student work hard, and then relax a little while students apply knowledge learned to an end-of-term project. This pattern for fruitful living comes from God.

The Meaning of Truth

Jesus saith unto him, I am the way, the truth, and the
life: no man cometh unto the Father, but by me.
—John 14:6

I have chosen the way of truth: thy judgments have I laid before me.
—Psalm 119:30

And ye shall know the truth, and the truth shall make you free.
—John 8:32

Lead me in thy truth, and teach me: for thou art the
God of my salvation; on thee do I wait all the day.
—Psalm 25:5

What does the word "truth" mean? Is truth just a noun, a definition in the dictionary? Is truth a philosophical construct, open to many interpretations? Is truth a feeling that we have when we sense something is right for us?

When we read the Bible, we learn that truth is a person, the person of Jesus Christ. What a surprising statement, but all of a sudden, truth becomes tangible. We can learn more of the truth by learning more about Jesus Christ. This means that when we read the Bible, the book of truth tells us about the person who is the truth. We are on the right track when we follow the way of the God of truth.

When we seek the truth, we are set free. Truth has a way of slicing thorough confusion, error, misinformation, and lies. The freedom of the truth is a relief, a respite from the world. God's truth is powerful enough to guide us. Because the Bible is the truth, we can rely on it completely.

AUGUST 21

The Good Shepherd

He shall feed his flock like a shepherd: he shall gather
the lambs with his arm, and carry them in his bosom,
and shall gently lead those that are with young.
—Isaiah 40:11

The Lord is my shepherd; I shall not want.
—Psalm 23:1

To him the porter openeth; and the sheep hear his voice:
and he calleth his own sheep by name, and leadeth them
out ... And when he putteth forth his own sheep, he goeth
before them, and the sheep follow him: for they know his
voice ... I am the door: by me if any man enter in, he shall
be saved, and shall go in and out, and find pasture.
—John 10:3–4, 9

Now the God of peace, that brought again from the dead our
Lord Jesus, that great shepherd of the sheep, through the blood of
the everlasting covenant, Make you perfect in every good work to
do his will, working in you that which is wellpleasing in his sight,
through Jesus Christ; to whom be glory for ever and ever. Amen.
—Hebrews 13:20–21

We may be familiar with a childhood portrayal of Jesus as the good shepherd,
carrying a lamb in His arms. But unless we raise sheep for a living, we may
relegate the pastoral image to the forgotten days of childhood. It is easy to forget
and thereby lose the meaning of Jesus as the good shepherd when we become
adult thinkers.

Nevertheless, we should not forget that sheep are easy prey for larger
carnivores; they need protection from the shepherd. David mentions killing a bear
and a lion when he was a shepherd tending the flock. Jacob, his forebear, also knew
God as the shepherd of his life. The knowledge gained from shepherding and
caring for sheep enabled them to care for larger groups of people, the extended
family and the populous nation. Sheep give no forethought to a potentially
dangerous situation, so they need the gentle guidance of the shepherd. He cares
for them in their ignorance. Once David was anointed king, he faced many
dangerous situations, and he knew he could turn to God as his personal shepherd.

David, Jacob, and others in the Old Testament knew God as the shepherd
of their souls. In New Testament times—today—we know that Jesus Christ is
the gate of the sheepfold. When we turn to Jesus, we walk through the gateway
that leads into the fold of God—our shepherd.

Don't Worry; Be Happy

And he said unto his disciples, Therefore I say unto you, Take no thought for your life, what ye shall eat; neither for the body, what ye shall put on. The life is more than meat, and the body is more than raiment. Consider the ravens: for they neither sow nor reap; which neither have storehouse nor barn; and God feedeth them: how much more are ye better than the fowls? And which of you with taking thought can add to his stature one cubit? If ye then be not able to do that thing which is least, why take ye thought for the rest? Consider the lilies how they grow: they toil not, they spin not; and yet I say unto you, that Solomon in all his glory was not arrayed like one of these. If then God so clothe the grass, which is to day in the field, and to morrow is cast into the oven; how much more will he clothe you, O ye of little faith? And seek not ye what ye shall eat, or what ye shall drink, neither be ye of doubtful mind. For all these things do the nations of the world seek after: and your Father knoweth that ye have need of these things. But rather seek ye the kingdom of God; and all these things shall be added unto you.

—Luke 12:22–31

Living the Christian life is completely different from living any other kind of life that excludes God from it. Jesus tried to explain the nature of this life by saying that it is a life free from worry. Can this really be true? We eagerly look forward to getting a real, full-time job when we graduate from college, and when that occurs, we also feel obligated to begin worrying about how to pay all of the bills—the car, the college, the house, etc.

Jesus assures us that we need not spend our mental capacities in worrying about all our human needs, and He is always right. He refers us to the natural world. It seems that God created the natural world to serve as an object lesson for the spiritual world that we also inhabit. What we can observe in nature often reveals what lies beyond our sight. In the natural order, God provides plants for food and material for shelter for birds and other creatures. God provides nutrients in the soil and rain and sun for growth for plants.

The natural world exists in beauty and abundance because God cares for the flora and fauna even though they do not know Him. We do know God, so we ought to cease striving to let God care for us. We will never lack for any good thing when God provides for us.

AUGUST 23

What We Believe

> Moreover, brethren, I declare unto you the gospel which I preached
> unto you, which also ye have received, and wherein ye stand; By
> which also ye are saved, if ye keep in memory what I preached
> unto you, unless ye have believed in vain. For I delivered unto
> you first of all that which I also received, how that Christ died for
> our sins according to the scriptures; And that he was buried, and
> that he rose again the third day according to the scriptures: And
> that he was seen of Cephas, then of the twelve: After that, he was
> seen of above five hundred brethren at once; of whom the greater
> part remain unto this present, but some are fallen asleep. After
> that, he was seen of James; then of all the apostles. And last of
> all he was seen of me also, as of one born out of due time.
> —1 Corinthians 15:1–8

Finding a church home is important to college students because these four years are a unique opportunity and an irreplaceable time in life. The local body of believers (the church) frequently reaches out to students and their unique needs. Churches with college ministries play a formative role in guiding students through the college years. They may become a home away from home where students can meet like-minded peers who do not attend the same classes.

College is also a time for students to begin evaluating what they believe and identify the basic tenets of the Christian faith. The simple facts of the gospel cannot be stated more simply: We are sinners. Jesus died for us sinners. Jesus was buried in a tomb, like a man. Jesus came to life again because He is God. He appeared to numerous witnesses who testified to the veracity of His life, death, and resurrection.

It is a good idea to find a church home that honors the gospel, preaches it, and explains it. Drink in the message of the gospel. Let it become part of life in college.

We Have All We Need

I thank my God always on your behalf, for the grace of God which
is given you by Jesus Christ; That in every thing ye are enriched by
him, in all utterance, and in all knowledge; Even as the testimony
of Christ was confirmed in you: So that ye come behind in no
gift; waiting for the coming of our Lord Jesus Christ: Who shall
also confirm you unto the end, that ye may be blameless in the
day of our Lord Jesus Christ. God is faithful, by whom ye were
called unto the fellowship of his Son Jesus Christ our Lord.
—1 Corinthians 1:4–9

And seek not ye what ye shall eat, or what ye shall drink,
neither be ye of doubtful mind. For all these things do the
nations of the world seek after: and your Father knoweth that
ye have need of these things. But rather seek ye the kingdom
of God; and all these things shall be added unto you.
—Luke 12:29–31

When we walk down the aisles of our high school auditoriums on graduation
day, it seems like twelve years of education have suddenly been compressed
into a distant memory in one instant of time. For the longest time, school seemed
like it was a lot of effort; now, the thought of four more years of education can
seem like a heavy burden.

College is a time when we try very hard to reach a final goal. College is also
a new place where we lose the social and academic standing we once had in high
school. For a few, this means improvement, but for most, it means struggle.
Even in college where the competition can seem overwhelming, it is comforting
and relieving to remember that God has given us all we need to survive and
succeed—Jesus Christ the Son of God.

Ask Him for help: when you are tired, when you cannot understand the text,
when you must complete an assignment, when you must prepare for a test, when
you need to get to class on time. Take Jesus Christ to college with you.

From Effort to Achievement

Study to shew thyself approved unto God, a workman that
needeth not to be ashamed, rightly dividing the word of truth.
—2 Timothy 2:15

For bodily exercise profiteth little: but godliness is
profitable unto all things, having promise of the life
that now is, and of that which is to come.
—1 Timothy 4:8

Why are students required to take so many introductory courses? A parallel may be drawn from athletics. Some students attend college with ROTC scholarships, but first, they must qualify for the scholarship. At least one qualification area involves physical ability. Prospective ROTC candidates are given specific exercises to practice, and on an assigned date, they must take the physical fitness test.

One hopeful candidate did more than was required on all of the exercises—except one. He had practiced this one exercise incorrectly. He also noticed that some high school football players had not even practiced the exercises because they thought of themselves as athletic and very fit. Unfortunately, football season was long over, and none of the football players were able to pass the physical fitness test for ROTC.

Clearly, repetitive practice helps improve basic skills, and more importantly, correctly practicing basic skills helps the learner to perform above what is required. Freshman college courses play the important role of giving students the repetitive practice in basic skills that will help them perform at or above the level required to succeed academically throughout the coming college years.

Freedom of Choice

The word of the Lord came unto me again, saying, What mean
ye, that ye use this proverb concerning the land of Israel, saying,
The fathers have eaten sour grapes, and the children's teeth are
set on edge? As I live, saith the Lord God, ye shall not have
occasion any more to use this proverb in Israel. Behold, all souls
are mine; as the soul of the father, so also the soul of the son
is mine: the soul that sinneth, it shall die ... Therefore I will
judge you, O house of Israel, every one according to his ways,
saith the Lord God. Repent, and turn yourselves from all your
transgressions; so iniquity shall not be your ruin. Cast away from
you all your transgressions, whereby ye have transgressed; and
make you a new heart and a new spirit: for why will ye die, O house
of Israel? For I have no pleasure in the death of him that dieth,
saith the Lord God: wherefore turn yourselves, and live ye.
—Ezekiel 18:1–4, 30–32

Young adults frequently resolve to be different from their parents, but
only time will tell whether or not this actually happens. It is commonly
understood that children take after their parents in many ways, so when we say
that the apple doesn't fall far from the tree, we really mean that sons are a lot
like their fathers, and daughters are a lot like their mothers. Ancient Israel spoke
a similar proverb, using sour grapes as a metaphor, and we still agree, although
we would phrase it differently.

God desires us to know that family patterns never determine final outcomes
in adult lives. Individual human choices matter most. God has given life to every
human soul, and this implies freedom of choice. The parable of three generations
in Ezekiel, chapter 18 assures us that the ungodly son can reject the teachings of
a godly father as much as the godly son can reject the legacy of an ungodly father.

Children see how their parents live, but individuals always make their own
choices. Even when God assures us that soul who sins will die, He assures that He
takes no pleasure in anyone's death. God wants us to live! Repentance, a matter
of personal choice, comes first!

Friendship

A brother offended is harder to be won than a strong city: and
their contentions are like the bars of a castle ... Death and life
are in the power of the tongue: and they that love it shall eat
the fruit thereof ... A man that hath friends must shew himself
friendly: and there is a friend that sticketh closer than a brother.
—Proverbs 18:19, 21, 24

I am a companion of all them that fear thee,
and of them that keep thy precepts.
—Psalm 119:63

A friend loveth at all times, and a brother is born for adversity.
—Proverbs 17:17

The adjustment from high school to college begins the process of mature self-reflection in the adult life of a young person. The memory of best friends, bad friends, long-term friends, short-term friends, neighborhood friends, school friends, sports friends all form a finished image in the mind of the mind of the first-year college student. It is a time to escape with relief from the sorer memories of childhood and recall with fondness the sweeter memories of childhood.

College is also a great time to make many significant and lasting changes that carry us into a better future. In the new environment, academic experiences can help us find the time to develop the power of the tongue and its words, always remembering the potency of language in individual lives. We all want the best out of life, and this includes the best words.

Good friends, better friends, and best friends empower us to live the best life possible, and we may return the favor in kind. When we remember that Jesus is our eternal friend, we can find the confidence to move forward in any circumstance.

Avoid Sexual Immorality

Know ye not that the unrighteous shall not inherit the kingdom
of God? Be not deceived: neither fornicators, nor idolaters,
nor adulterers, nor effeminate, nor abusers of themselves with
mankind, Nor thieves, nor covetous, nor drunkards, nor revilers,
nor extortioners, shall inherit the kingdom of God. And such
were some of you: but ye are washed, but ye are sanctified, but
ye are justified in the name of the Lord Jesus, and by the Spirit
of our God ... Flee fornication. Every sin that a man doeth is
without the body; but he that committeth fornication sinneth
against his own body. What? know ye not that your body is the
temple of the Holy Ghost which is in you, which ye have of God,
and ye are not your own? For ye are bought with a price: therefore
glorify God in your body, and in your spirit, which are God's.
—1 Corinthians 6:9–11, 18–20

Those of us who attend a secular college campus will probably be asked if we
would like a sleeping partner within the first week of the first semester—
because we are new, because we are expected to want one, because everybody
does it, because ... any reason will do.

The first week on campus is a week of enormous changes because it delineates
the change from childhood to adulthood. When that pleasant, friendly person
asks that particular question, just say, "No!" and run in the opposite direction!
We cannot live according to the law of sin and the law of God at the same time.
If we choose one way, we are rejecting the other way.

God has cleansed us from every impurity so that we may enjoy His friendship
forever. When we commit sexual sin, we harm ourselves a lot because we are
turning against our own bodies—the body God has given us. When God dwells
in us through the Holy Spirit, our behavior should reflect true love, which is pure
and holy. God paid the price of His life for our sins, so we don't have to. If we
commit sexual sin, we will regret it.

Freedom or Licentiousness?

What shall we say then? Shall we continue in sin, that grace may abound? God forbid. How shall we, that are dead to sin, live any longer therein? Know ye not, that so many of us as were baptized into Jesus Christ were baptized into his death? Therefore we are buried with him by baptism into death: that like as Christ was raised up from the dead by the glory of the Father, even so we also should walk in newness of life ... Likewise reckon ye also yourselves to be dead indeed unto sin, but alive unto God through Jesus Christ our Lord. Let not sin therefore reign in your mortal body, that ye should obey it in the lusts thereof. Neither yield ye your members as instruments of unrighteousness unto sin: but yield yourselves unto God, as those that are alive from the dead, and your members as instruments of righteousness unto God. For sin shall not have dominion over you: for ye are not under the law, but under grace.
—Romans 6:1–4, 11–14

Some Christians believe that they are free to do anything they want to because Jesus has clearly saved them from their sins. Their answer to the question, "Shall we go on sinning so that grace may abound?" is an unequivocal, "Of course! Why not? Isn't that why I got saved in the first place?" We seem to have forgotten that freedom and licentiousness are opposite qualities, not synonyms for the same quality.

The freedom we enjoy in Christ means freedom to obey God, freedom to do good, and freedom from the clutching grasp of sin. Licentiousness means an abuse of freedom, a lack of restraint over moral behavior, and an inability to discern the difference between right and wrong.

Most people today believe that freedom is really what would more accurately be termed as licentiousness. Words can have several meanings, so we need to pay attention to what goes on around us. We should exercise discernment about meaning in order to truly understand what others and our culture are telling us all the time.

Equality

For while one saith, I am of Paul; and another, I am of Apollos; are
ye not carnal? Who then is Paul, and who is Apollos, but ministers
by whom ye believed, even as the Lord gave to every man? I have
planted, Apollos watered; but God gave the increase. So then
neither is he that planteth any thing, neither he that watereth; but
God that giveth the increase. Now he that planteth and he that
watereth are one: and every man shall receive his own reward
according to his own labour. For we are labourers together
with God: ye are God's husbandry, ye are God's building.
—1 Corinthians 3:4–9

Think about any workplace you are familiar with. Think about the echelons of employees from the owner to the managers to the hourly paid workers. During the high school and college years, most of us work at the lowest rung of the corporate ladder of importance. This satisfies us when we are young workers at our first job, but we will soon expect more when we get a "real" job.

The best work places, where people experience the highest level of satisfaction, are places where the upper levels of employees make the lower levels of employees feel valued for the jobs they do. This is true because the Bible gives a model for organizational structure within the church that church members can apply to the business world. Human nature is the same, wherever it operates. In the church, we do many tasks, and every task is important to the overall operation of the church body and the furtherance of the gospel.

The body is healthiest when we all appreciate what everyone else is doing. God has designed human nature to be interdependent. When we follow God's plan, we allow the best and most successful outcomes to occur.

Sleep in Peace

Lord, how are they increased that trouble me! many are they that
rise up against me. Many there be which say of my soul, There
is no help for him in God. Selah. But thou, O Lord, art a shield
for me; my glory, and the lifter up of mine head. I cried unto
the Lord with my voice, and he heard me out of his holy hill.
Selah. I laid me down and slept; I awaked; for the Lord sustained
me. I will not be afraid of ten thousands of people, that have
set themselves against me round about. Arise, O Lord; save me,
O my God: for thou hast smitten all mine enemies upon the
cheek bone; thou hast broken the teeth of the ungodly. Salvation
belongeth unto the Lord: thy blessing is upon thy people. Selah.
—Psalm 3:1–8

The reasons for sleeplessness are many. Sometimes we cannot stop thinking
about the argument we had with the coach or the roommate. Sometimes
we are such tightly wired people that we find it difficult to unwind enough to fall
asleep easily. Insomnia is not a modern problem created by an overstressed world.

King David suffered from sleeplessness when his usurping son Absalom
pursued him in an unsuccessful attempt to wrest the throne from his father the
king. David's insomnia sounds a lot like ours. At night, when we most want to
forget about the bad day, we keep replaying the scenario over and over again in
our heads. We may know that right is on our side, but we will probably not win the
argument or the battle. Ordinary people loom as gigantic enemies in our fatigued
minds. Our bodies cannot relax and sleep—how frustrating this is!

Yet for every difficulty of this life, no matter how great or small, God is
interested in helping us. And He always reminds us how. When we pray to God,
He answers us. When we trust in Him, He sustains us. When we rest in Him, He
delivers us. When we look to Him, He blesses us. The way to rest in peace every
night is to let the Lord sustain us.

Ordinary People

The words of Amos, who was among the herdmen of Tekoa, which he saw concerning Israel in the days of Uzziah king of Judah, and in the days of Jeroboam the son of Joash king of Israel, two years before the earthquake. And he said, The Lord will roar from Zion, and utter his voice from Jerusalem; and the habitations of the shepherds shall mourn, and the top of Carmel shall wither ... Then answered Amos, and said to Amaziah, I was no prophet, neither was I a prophet's son; but I was an herdman, and a gatherer of sycomore fruit: And the Lord took me as I followed the flock, and the Lord said unto me, Go, prophesy unto my people Israel. Now therefore hear thou the word of the Lord: Thou sayest, Prophesy not against Israel, and drop not thy word against the house of Isaac ... Seek good, and not evil, that ye may live: and so the Lord, the God of hosts, shall be with you, as ye have spoken. Hate the evil, and love the good, and establish judgment in the gate: it may be that the Lord God of hosts will be gracious unto the remnant of Joseph.
—Amos 1:1–2; 7:14–16; 5:14–15

It is easy to relegate trained preachers to the pulpit, but sometimes God chooses ordinary people to serve our extraordinary God. Consider the prophet Amos, who was a shepherd and an orchardist. We tend to think that training matters most, but God knows that hearts dedicated to Him matter most. Amos urged people to repent if they did not want to see the punishment God would send upon them.

How could Amos present the strong message with such conviction and assurance? Maybe the disciplines of the ordinary life he lived were enough to teach him the object lessons that apply to every human life. Taking care of livestock and fruit trees involves doing what promotes the healthy growth of the animals and plants. Amos had learned how to do good, not evil, in order to support himself. Israel had forgotten the basic structure of daily life so completely that sinning was their only option, but it was a deadly choice.

When we preserve basic goodness by living the right way in our respective realms of expertise, and when we spurn all forms of seemingly harmless evil in our professional life, we keep our true options open. We should never diminish the value of the daily routine.

Guidance

And Joshua rose early in the morning; and they removed from
Shittim, and came to Jordan, he and all the children of Israel,
and lodged there before they passed over. And it came to pass
after three days, that the officers went through the host; And
they commanded the people, saying, When ye see the ark of the
covenant of the Lord your God, and the priests the Levites bearing
it, then ye shall remove from your place, and go after it. Yet there
shall be a space between you and it, about two thousand cubits
by measure: come not near unto it, that ye may know the way by
which ye must go: for ye have not passed this way heretofore. And
Joshua said unto the people, Sanctify yourselves: for to morrow the
Lord will do wonders among you … That the waters which came
down from above stood and rose up upon an heap very far from
the city Adam, that is beside Zaretan: and those that came down
toward the sea of the plain, even the salt sea, failed, and were cut
off: and the people passed over right against Jericho. And the priests
that bare the ark of the covenant of the Lord stood firm on dry
ground in the midst of Jordan, and all the Israelites passed over on
dry ground, until all the people were passed clean over Jordan.
—Joshua 3:1–5, 16–17

To many incoming freshmen, college can seem like a road trip with a final
destination in mind, yet numerous roadside stops line up along the way.
Because these four years represent a new type of journey, college experiences can
parallel in brief the myriad decisions and choices people make throughout life.

In a similar way, the Israelites faced a crossroads at the banks of the Jordan
River when they were bound for the Promised Land. It is instructive to remember
that the lessons of the Old Testament are meant to be applied to our own current
and pressing circumstances. On this occasion, Israel was told to follow the priests
when they saw them carrying the ark of the covenant of the Lord. They had never
been on that road before, so they needed to know the way—and they needed to
know how to arrive safely. The people obeyed God. The priests obeyed God by
standing firm in the middle of the river. The river stopped flowing when they
stepped into it. The entire nation crossed the Jordan River safely with the Ark of
the Covenant going before them.

Just as it was then, so is it today. The presence of God goes with us when
we obey God. As we keep our eyes on Him, He leads us safely to the next place
He wants us to be.

SEPTEMBER 3
History Lesson?

Why do the heathen rage, and the people imagine a vain thing? The kings of the earth set themselves, and the rulers take counsel together, against the Lord, and against his anointed, saying, Let us break their bands asunder, and cast away their cords from us ... Serve the Lord with fear, and rejoice with trembling. Kiss the Son, lest he be angry, and ye perish from the way, when his wrath is kindled but a little. Blessed are all they that put their trust in him.
—Psalm 2:1–3, 11–12

Is history a favorite subject? History loves to tell us of the most well-known human achievements and exploits. Most of history relates wars, injustices, quarrels, and other events that no one would care to own up to individually. So when we study history seriously, we begin to realize that it is more than just a series of dates, places, and names.

We cannot always fathom the purposes behind the facts, but we can understand that greater purposes, larger than individual preferences, hold sway in historical situations. When we know that God created the world and everything in it, it makes sense to consider His perspective on the information we have learned. The Bible assures us that God has a plan for the history of this world, and no one can subvert it. Many nations plot against the Lord in an effort to free themselves from their perceived fetters, but God laughs at them, scoffs at them, rebukes them, and terrifies them. Why? Because God knows that true freedom is found only in Himself, the Creator and Ruler of all nations.

The best history tells of serving Him and surrendering to Him. Let us read the book that tells how we may become part of an everlasting and historical story, the best story ever known.

SEPTEMBER 4

Gardening Efforts

And he said, So is the kingdom of God, as if a man should cast seed
into the ground; And should sleep, and rise night and day, and the
seed should spring and grow up, he knoweth not how. For the earth
bringeth forth fruit of herself; first the blade, then the ear, after
that the full corn in the ear. But when the fruit is brought forth,
immediately he putteth in the sickle, because the harvest is come.
—Mark 4:26–29

I will be as the dew unto Israel: he shall grow as the lily, and cast
forth his roots as Lebanon. His branches shall spread, and his beauty
shall be as the olive tree, and his smell as Lebanon … Ephraim shall
say, What have I to do any more with idols? I have heard him, and
observed him: I am like a green fir tree. From me is thy fruit found.
—Hosea 14:5–6, 8

Gardeners may marvel at the change from a tiny seed to an edible plant, stalk, fruit, or vegetable. But really—who stops to think about it very often? Who bothers to acknowledge that more effort came from the sunshine, the rain, and the warmth than from the sower of the seeds?

Soil is easy to despise because it is dirty. Rain is easy to complain about because it spoils our plans. Temperatures can make us either love or hate the day. For those of us who view gardening as an interesting sideline or a way to get a little fresh air and exercise, the growth of a seed into a plant may not seem ultimately significant. But for more subsistence-oriented growers, good growth and healthy plants mean life and sustenance. The world of gardening teaches us about other aspects of our lives.

Our spiritual lives should reveal this same appreciation—that our personal lives can mirror the same type of growth. We can also understand how a small church grows from very few people little into a great congregation. God does more for us than we realize. The production of a harvest is His work. Human beings put out minimal effort compared to His.

248

Immigrants and Culture

And Joseph fell upon his father's face, and wept upon him, and
kissed him. And Joseph commanded his servants the physicians
to embalm his father: and the physicians embalmed Israel ... And
Pharaoh said, Go up, and bury thy father, according as he made
thee swear ... And when the inhabitants of the land, the Canaanites,
saw the mourning in the floor of Atad, they said, This is a grievous
mourning to the Egyptians: wherefore the name of it was called
Abelmizraim, which is beyond Jordan. And his sons did unto
him according as he commanded them: For his sons carried him
into the land of Canaan, and buried him in the cave of the field of
Machpelah, which Abraham bought with the field for a possession
of a buryingplace of Ephron the Hittite, before Mamre. And
Joseph returned into Egypt, he, and his brethren, and all that went
up with him to bury his father, after he had buried his father.
—Genesis 50:1–2, 6, 11–14

Some of us have immigrated to this country from a land of strikingly different
customs, habits, and practices. After living in the new land for a long time, it
becomes difficult to separate old habits from adopted customs because the nature
of culture is dynamic rather than static. Whether we intend to or not, we grow,
adapt, and therefore change our cultural patterns.

Sometimes we forget that the stories about the Israelites took place in
foreign lands, nations who practiced entirely different customs than the Israelite
nation was accustomed to follow. Israel had been living in Egypt for decades
when the patriarch Jacob died. Upon his father's death, Joseph made a request
of Pharaoh to bury his father back in the homeland of Canaan. Pharaoh agreed
to his request, perhaps because Joseph was second in command only to Pharaoh
himself. He commanded a large official Egyptian funeral cortege to make its
laborious way to the land of Canaan, to give the patriarch Jacob a funeral with
full Egyptian solemnity and ceremony. The Canaanites saw the funeral as an
Egyptian event, not a Jewish event.

Clearly, Joseph, more so than his brothers, lived at a cultural crossroads and
interpreted a personally difficult time to meet the exigencies of the situation. So
must we, who are new to this country, interpret our desires and needs to suit the
new homeland.

Going Astray Spiritually

And the word of the Lord came unto me, saying, Son of man,
prophesy against the shepherds of Israel, prophesy, and say unto
them, Thus saith the Lord God unto the shepherds; Woe be to
the shepherds of Israel that do feed themselves! should not the
shepherds feed the flocks? ... And they were scattered, because
there is no shepherd: and they became meat to all the beasts of
the field, when they were scattered. My sheep wandered through
all the mountains, and upon every high hill: yea, my flock was
scattered upon all the face of the earth, and none did search
or seek after them ... Thus saith the Lord God; Behold, I am
against the shepherds; and I will require my flock at their hand,
and cause them to cease from feeding the flock; neither shall
the shepherds feed themselves any more; for I will deliver my
flock from their mouth, that they may not be meat for them.
—Ezekiel 34:1–2, 5–6, 10

We often think that when we attain a certain level of competency, we will
be immune from further difficulties, and we apply this thinking to most
areas of our lives. Yet no one, not even Christian leaders, can take a certain level
of spirituality for granted. The relationship we have with God remains vibrant
and ongoing; it is never stagnant.

The God who created all people is a living being—this means that the
relationship must remain active in order to remain viable. God is real—this
means that everything we say, think, or do holds eternal value. God is holy—this
means that God demands high moral standards. God cares for the creation—this
means that we should be watchful how we treat others. God meets our daily
needs—this means that we should be accountable financially.

When we aspire to Christian service, we must consider how to live the life
that pleases God and brings others into the kingdom of God. God turns against
those who speak holy words yet do the exact opposite.

SEPTEMBER 7

Treasures of the Heart

Lay not up for yourselves treasures upon earth, where moth and rust
doth corrupt, and where thieves break through and steal: But lay
up for yourselves treasures in heaven, where neither moth nor rust
doth corrupt, and where thieves do not break through nor steal.
—Matthew 6:19–20

Are we familiar with the television shows that journey through antique homes with unusual details of woodwork and glasswork? Homeowners are thrilled to learn that their unique earthly goods are really some extremely valuable treasures. Most of us live in more modest circumstances, so the only experience we may ever have with earthly treasures is the stuff we buy or the stuff we inherit. When we buy new items, we place a high value on our hard-earned goods, but the thrill is only short-term.

Have we ever had the experience yet of clearing out Grandma's or Grandpa's house, cellar, closets, and attic when they moved or died? When this experience comes our way, we will realize how much stuff accumulates over a lifetime. Not only does it accumulate, it usually stinks! Old people tend to shutter themselves in as movement becomes more arduous. They refrain from dusting the house. They pile up the dirty laundry. They forget to wash the dishes, if they even bother to cook the food. When people care for their goods, they view themselves as taking care of a part of their lives. The goods seem somewhat valuable or at least useful to them. But God uses old age to remind us of the truth—stuff is worthless.

We need to set our young hearts on godliness, not on material goods. We might have to wait several decades to see the difference in outcomes between our lives from the lives of our grandparents, but we will be glad of the results.

Choosing a Profession

But when it pleased God, who separated me from my mother's womb,
and called me by his grace, To reveal his Son in me, that I might preach
him among the heathen; immediately I conferred not with flesh and
blood ... And was unknown by face unto the churches of Judaea which
were in Christ: But they had heard only, That he which persecuted
us in times past now preacheth the faith which once he destroyed.
And they glorified God in me ... And I went up by revelation, and
communicated unto them that gospel which I preach among the
Gentiles, but privately to them which were of reputation, lest by any
means I should run, or had run, in vain ... But contrariwise, when they
saw that the gospel of the uncircumcision was committed unto me,
as the gospel of the circumcision was unto Peter ... And when James,
Cephas, and John, who seemed to be pillars, perceived the grace that
was given unto me, they gave to me and Barnabas the right hands of
fellowship; that we should go unto the heathen, and they unto the
circumcision ... I am crucified with Christ: nevertheless I live; yet not
I, but Christ liveth in me: and the life which I now live in the flesh I live
by the faith of the Son of God, who loved me, and gave himself for me.
—Galatians 1:15–16, 22–24; 2:2, 7, 9, 20

What to do for the rest of life is a huge issue of concern to every college student, and four years may not be enough time to figure it out. When we look around, we see that some of our peers fall into a wonderful jobs and love them—the courses and the paths of their lives are set. Others shift in frustration or exasperation from job to job or from place to place, trying out a different job situation each time.

The apostle Paul encountered both experiences. To begin his professional life, his high quality Jewish education made him a leader and qualified him to chase down the Christian heretics who were undermining the faith. Later on, when God chose a profession for Paul, he began a more itinerant life, beset with dangers, supported by God more than by the original peer group.

How did he know that what he was doing was really God's will? Was it just the revelation from God? (Few of us can identify with such an unearthly experience.) No—the confirmation was obvious and logical to the early church leaders. Others saw that Paul had the requisite skills for a specific task, and they recognized that God had given His grace to help Paul accomplish that job. With God's help, Paul was no longer attracted to living out his own ideas for his life. We learn about Paul from a distance of a couple of thousand years of history, but God confirms professional choices for us in the same way today—as we identify them for ourselves, and as others help us confirm our choices along the way.

Molded by His Hands

And the vessel that he made of clay was marred in the hand
of the potter: so he made it again another vessel, as seemed
good to the potter to make it. Then the word of the Lord
came to me, saying, O house of Israel, cannot I do with you
as this potter? saith the Lord. Behold, as the clay is in the
potter's hand, so are ye in mine hand, O house of Israel.
—Jeremiah 18:4–6

Woe unto him that striveth with his Maker! Let the potsherd
strive with the potsherds of the earth. Shall the clay say to him that
fashioneth it, What makest thou? or thy work, He hath no hands?
—Isaiah 45:9

Anyone who has taken a pottery class knows how malleable clay is, yet clay requires consistent physical pressure to form the lumpy mass into useful shapes. Potters possess strong, muscular arms that can reshape the clay into different shapes as long as the clay is still wet and fresh. When we take an elective class to learn the manual skill of pottery, we learn in a concrete way about the effects of strong human effort to accomplish a beautiful and useful outcome.

God's Holy Word, the Bible draws a comparison between malleable clay and human lives. Without a doubt, God is the potter of our lives. He can make us into any shape He desires. He has a specific plan in mind for each individual life, and when we seek Him wholeheartedly, we find success, hope, and blessing from Him.

It is a bad idea to go through life without God. Just as clay can become dry and useless to further molding and shaping, at some point we can become unable to respond to the Lord. When we turn to God early, we avoid needless regret later on.

How to Be Better

For therein is the righteousness of God revealed from faith to faith: as
it is written, The just shall live by faith … But now the righteousness
of God without the law is manifested, being witnessed by the law
and the prophets; Even the righteousness of God which is by faith of
Jesus Christ unto all and upon all them that believe: for there is no
difference: For all have sinned, and come short of the glory of God.
—Romans 1:17; 3:21–23

The media bombards our senses almost every waking moment. Billboards, posters, ads, telephone solicitations all urge us to buy products or buy into a way of thinking in order to improve the quality of our lives. Some of us would like to live free from the influence of the media, but none of us can imagine what the world would be like without the media anymore.

There is a kernel of truth in all the barrage of the media. It is true that if we read a lot, we will eventually know a lot. It is true that if we exercise more and eat less, we will lose weight and gain energy. It is true that if we replace the windows and siding on our houses, they will look better and increase in value. It is true that if we set aside a sum of money now, we will have more to spend later. It is true that if we change our patterns of thinking, we will alter our attitudes and behavior. The barrage of media assumes that all of us want to be better.

The best way to be better is to turn to God and accept God's righteousness. It is free because it comes by faith. God's best for us is far more and far better than we can imagine. When the One who is best shines out of our lives, we look better because we look like Him.

Bad Companions

If after the manner of men I have fought with beasts at Ephesus,
what advantageth it me, if the dead rise not? let us eat and drink; for
to morrow we die. Be not deceived: evil communications corrupt
good manners. Awake to righteousness, and sin not; for some
have not the knowledge of God: I speak this to your shame ...
Watch ye, stand fast in the faith, quit you like men, be strong.
—1 Corinthians 15:32–34; 16:13

He that walketh with wise men shall be wise: but
a companion of fools shall be destroyed.
—Proverbs 13:20

When we believe that life is full of choices and that options are up to us alone, it is easy to make unwise choices and fall into the company of bad friends. Maybe our friends are not really all that bad. Maybe they are just silly, maybe they are fun loving, or maybe they are unthinking.

College is such a serious time that friends of the opposite sort seem to offer an opportunity to balance out the other, more serious parts of our lives. But when so-called friends divert us from studying, when so-called friends help us to engage in drinking or other self-destructive habits, they are most likely leading us into sin, and they are definitely leading us away from God. It seems harmless at first, but when our friends do not put God first in their lives, as God commands us to do, they are at best a first step on a downward path.

God's plan for any human life is infinitely better than any human plan for a human life. College is a time when we need to choose wisely to avoid self-destruction.

Pleasing God

For I will have respect unto you, and make you fruitful, and multiply you, and establish my covenant with you. And ye shall eat old store, and bring forth the old because of the new. And I set my tabernacle among you: and my soul shall not abhor you. And I will walk among you, and will be your God, and ye shall be my people ... But if ye will not hearken unto me, and will not do all these commandments ... And I will set my face against you, and ye shall be slain before your enemies: they that hate you shall reign over you; and ye shall flee when none pursueth you. And if ye will not yet for all this hearken unto me, then I will punish you seven times more for your sins ... If they shall confess their iniquity, and the iniquity of their fathers, with their trespass which they trespassed against me, and that also they have walked contrary unto me ... Then will I remember my covenant with Jacob, and also my covenant with Isaac, and also my covenant with Abraham will I remember; and I will remember the land ... And yet for all that, when they be in the land of their enemies, I will not cast them away, neither will I abhor them, to destroy them utterly, and to break my covenant with them: for I am the Lord their God.
—Leviticus 26:9–12, 14, 17–18, 40, 42, 44

College freshmen are sometimes asked to write essays about their personal beliefs, and they always express the thought that if they do good or right, then God will help them further their plans. It does not matter what religion they belong to, college students express the same idea.

This perspective may be age-related, but is also relates to God's Words spoken to His people a couple of millennia ago. Because God created all human beings, His law is written on the conscience of every individual. We instinctively know that someone great controls our destiny, but we do not naturally know how to get close to God and keep His blessing.

The Bible, both the Old Testament and the New Testament, tells us plainly to confess our sins in order to cease the hostility between us and God. God wants our best, and He knows that the only way to have it is to live life according to His revealed word.

Bad Times and Worse Times

Now it came to pass in the days when the judges ruled, that there was a famine in the land. And a certain man of Bethlehemjudah went to sojourn in the country of Moab, he, and his wife, and his two sons. And the name of the man was Elimelech, and the name of his wife Naomi, and the name of his two sons Mahlon and Chilion, Ephrathites of Bethlehemjudah. And they came into the country of Moab, and continued there. And Elimelech Naomi's husband died; and she was left, and her two sons. And they took them wives of the women of Moab; the name of the one was Orpah, and the name of the other Ruth: and they dwelled there about ten years. And Mahlon and Chilion died also both of them; and the woman was left of her two sons and her husband. Then she arose with her daughters in law, that she might return from the country of Moab: for she had heard in the country of Moab how that the Lord had visited his people in giving them bread.
—Ruth 1:1–6

Have you ever lost all your belongings in a fire? Has your house ever been blown to bits by a tornado or a tsunami? Has your home ever fallen into the water because the tide eroded all the ground around it? Did any of your close kin die in one of these catastrophes? Has a terrible tragedy occurred on your campus, very close to you? If not, count your blessings.

Those who have endured severe privation from circumstances beyond their control know that these images can be very real and devastating tragedies. How do faithful people live with the adverse and unexpected events in life? Here is one story of faith: when famine came to Bethlehem in Judah, Elimelech, his wife Naomi, and their two sons moved to Moab, a neighboring country across the Dead Sea on the other side of the mountains. They trusted God to lead them, to keep them holy, to get along with ungodly neighbors, to make a living, and to raise their sons in a foreign country. Then, the unthinkable happened. Dad died. The sons married local women, but ten years and zero children later, both sons died too.

Naomi the Mom was left alone. In spite of her grief, she practiced her faith. She heard that the Lord was helping out His people back home, so she made the difficult decision to return home.

This World

For though we walk in the flesh, we do not war after the flesh: (For the weapons of our warfare are not carnal, but mighty through God to the pulling down of strong holds;) Casting down imaginations, and every high thing that exalteth itself against the knowledge of God, and bringing into captivity every thought to the obedience of Christ; And having in a readiness to revenge all disobedience, when your obedience is fulfilled. Do ye look on things after the outward appearance? if any man trust to himself that he is Christ's, let him of himself think this again, that, as he is Christ's, even so are we Christ's … For we dare not make ourselves of the number, or compare ourselves with some that commend themselves: but they measuring themselves by themselves, and comparing themselves among themselves, are not wise.
—2 Corinthians 10:3–7, 12

Entering college is synonymous with entering the adult world. It is important to remember the difference between the two worlds and to start thinking about the differences between two other worlds: the earthly world and the spiritual world. The world offers so much advice that the best worldly advice is to do our own thing—get an education, get some training, get a job, or start a business—whatever suits us. Paul reminds us that the world grips our minds; it forms strongholds of desires, ideals, behaviors, and standards—and all of the world's best offerings are still superficial.

Living the Christian life means living life in a godly way, as God intends. Instead of fighting to get ahead using the weapons of this world, use the spiritual weaponry God provides. Submit all thoughts and plans to the precepts of the Bible, so that we may access true knowledge firsthand. The surface life we live is determined by the underlying assumptions we make about life.

True wisdom and guidance for this life comes from the Bible. It demolishes all other worldly ideas and systems because they fade in importance when compared to the light of Scripture.

SEPTEMBER 15

True Love

Behold, what manner of love the Father hath bestowed upon us, that
we should be called the sons of God: therefore the world knoweth
us not, because it knew him not … For this is the message that ye
heard from the beginning, that we should love one another … Hereby
perceive we the love of God, because he laid down his life for us:
and we ought to lay down our lives for the brethren … My little
children, let us not love in word, neither in tongue; but in deed and
in truth. And hereby we know that we are of the truth, and shall
assure our hearts before him. For if our heart condemn us, God
is greater than our heart, and knoweth all things … Beloved, let
us love one another: for love is of God; and every one that loveth
is born of God, and knoweth God. He that loveth not knoweth
not God; for God is love. In this was manifested the love of God
toward us, because that God sent his only begotten Son into the
world, that we might live through him. Herein is love, not that
we loved God, but that he loved us, and sent his Son to be the
propitiation for our sins. Beloved, if God so loved us, we ought
also to love one another. No man hath seen God at any time. If
we love one another, God dwelleth in us, and his love is perfected
in us … And we have known and believed the love that God hath
to us. God is love; and he that dwelleth in love dwelleth in God,
and God in him … We love him, because he first loved us.
—1 John 3:1, 11, 16, 18–20; 4:7–12, 16, 19

Through the media, modern culture gives us many glimpses of love. But to
truly understand the nature of love, we must look to God first. He created us,
so He knows the definition of love better than anyone else. According the Bible,
we deserve nothing good from God, not even love. We deserve no consideration
from Him, yet He lavished love on us anyway. He loves us more than we deserve.

True love overlooks sins, true love is not content with only itself, and true
love wants to extend love to others. We know about human love from parents,
relatives, brothers, sisters, friends, and spouses. These examples should help us
love others more and realize that love desires the best for others. Ultimate love
exchanges or gives up all, even life itself, for the beloved. Jesus Christ did this
for us. We do not need to die on a cross for our sins because Jesus did it already.
Love knows no limits. Love is active. Love is true to God.

Love and truth—it is impossible to separate them. When we belong to the
truth, our lives reflect the true love of God.

Joyfulness?

My brethren, count it all joy when ye fall into divers
temptations; Knowing this, that the trying of your faith worketh
patience. But let patience have her perfect work, that ye may
be perfect and entire, wanting nothing. If any of you lack
wisdom, let him ask of God, that giveth to all men liberally,
and upbraideth not; and it shall be given him. But let him
ask in faith, nothing wavering. For he that wavereth is like a
wave of the sea driven with the wind and tossed. For let not
that man think that he shall receive any thing of the Lord.
—James 1:2–7

It goes against the grain of human reasoning to think that trials, difficulties, and hardships can be considered joyful occurrences. We prefer good times, easy days, long stretches of relaxation, and times for celebration. God clearly has a higher purpose for our lives, and the way He accomplishes our complete spiritual maturity is to send us setbacks, difficulties, or trials. We may have another, more logical goal in mind, but God reasons differently than we do. He knows that difficulties help us to persevere, and that trials perfect our faith.

When we cannot figure out how to handle a situation or understand what to do, we can ask God, who possesses all wisdom. He is a safe person to talk to because God never makes fun of our ignorance like others do; we may trust in Him completely. When we trust, He stabilizes our lives because the focus is now on Him, not on the immediate circumstances of our trials or emotions.

We stop feeling like we are being blown about on a windy day. We lose the sensation of being tossed and pommelled by the waves. The wind dies down, the water calms down, and so do we. Joyfulness is quieter than we may have originally imagined.

Best Friends

And it came to pass, when he had made an end of speaking unto
Saul, that the soul of Jonathan was knit with the soul of David, and
Jonathan loved him as his own soul. And Saul took him that day,
and would let him go no more home to his father's house. Then
Jonathan and David made a covenant, because he loved him as his
own soul. And Jonathan stripped himself of the robe that was upon
him, and gave it to David, and his garments, even to his sword, and
to his bow, and to his girdle ... And as soon as the lad was gone,
David arose out of a place toward the south, and fell on his face to the
ground, and bowed himself three times: and they kissed one another,
and wept one with another, until David exceeded. And Jonathan said
to David, Go in peace, forasmuch as we have sworn both of us in the
name of the Lord, saying, The Lord be between me and thee, and
between my seed and thy seed for ever. And he arose and departed:
and Jonathan went into the city ... And Jonathan Saul's son arose,
and went to David into the wood, and strengthened his hand in God.
—1 Samuel 18:1–4; 20:41–42; 23:16

Friends are always important to us, and we value them for various qualities
they possess. The best kind of friend is the one who sticks closer than a
brother, who supports us through thick and thin, who understands us, and upon
whom we may call in need or in rejoicing.

Prince Jonathan and the renegade warrior David were true friends who
vowed to support one another. Their deep connection reminds us that true
friendship bridges many human obstacles. Their friendship was unusual, because
King Saul, Jonathan's father, was jealous of David, the young upstart whom God
had appointed to upstage him as king. Saul hated David, but Jonathan loved
David—talk about family problems! In contrast to his father, Jonathan was a
godly son and a humble man who knew his place in God's plan for the nation of
Israel—he had none—but he didn't mind.

His life shows us that when we have a good relationship with God, God
makes us content with who we are. Jonathan was the opposite of Saul, his father.
A good relationship with God benefits the self and extends the blessing of God
to others.

SEPTEMBER 18

God Has Chosen Us

Knowing, brethren beloved, your election of God. For our
gospel came not unto you in word only, but also in power, and
in the Holy Ghost, and in much assurance; as ye know what
manner of men we were among you for your sake. And ye became
followers of us, and of the Lord, having received the word in
much affliction, with joy of the Holy Ghost. So that ye were
ensamples to all that believe in Macedonia and Achaia. For from
you sounded out the word of the Lord not only in Macedonia
and Achaia, but also in every place your faith to God-ward
is spread abroad; so that we need not to speak any thing.
—1 Thessalonians 1:4–8

When we were in elementary school, we knew exactly how much we were
valued at recess time when choosing sides for a team came around. We
knew who was likely to be chosen captain and who was likely to be chosen last.
When we go off to college, we hope we have escaped the judgmental protocols
of childhood. Perhaps we have, perhaps not.

When we turn to God in repentance, we feel keenly aware of the decision we
have just made. While this is true, we need to understand that God has chosen
us as much as we have turned to Him. The fact that God has chosen us alters
our outlook forever. We now know indisputably that God loves us. Without a
doubt, we know that the Holy Spirit empowers us. The Holy Spirit enables us
to welcome the gospel message even when we endure suffering for it. We know
assuredly that God has convicted us of sin in order to live a life pleasing to Him.

The work of God in those who believe radiates out from our lives, like a bell
ringing out, like a model who represents a perfection of human beauty.

SEPTEMBER 19

People on the Fringe of Our Lives

And Enoch lived sixty and five years, and begat Methuselah:
And Enoch walked with God after he begat Methuselah three
hundred years, and begat sons and daughters: And all the days
of Enoch were three hundred sixty and five years: And Enoch
walked with God: and he was not; for God took him.
—Genesis 5:21–24

By faith Enoch was translated that he should not see death; and was
not found, because God had translated him: for before his translation
he had this testimony, that he pleased God. But without faith it is
impossible to please him: for he that cometh to God must believe
that he is, and that he is a rewarder of them that diligently seek him.
—Hebrews 11:5–6

And Enoch also, the seventh from Adam, prophesied of
these, saying, Behold, the Lord cometh with ten thousands
of his saints, To execute judgment upon all, and to convince
all that are ungodly among them of all their ungodly deeds
which they have ungodly committed, and of all their hard
speeches which ungodly sinners have spoken against him.
—Jude 14–15

Enoch is a man from the early days of planet earth about whom we have been given minimal information. The Bible relates selective details about his life. He was the seventh generation from Adam. He was married, and he fathered a son who lived longer than Adam. According to the New Testament, he seems to have been a prophet and preacher, well known in his day, but barely recognized today.

Enoch was faithful to God; he pleased God so much that God took him from planet earth alive instead of letting him die a natural death like the rest of us. The writer of Hebrews reminds us that Enoch believed that faith was the only way to approach God and that God really honors those who believe in Him. Today, Enoch may represent to us the kind of people who live on the fringes of our lives, people whom we don't know very well, but God uses them to convey messages to us about Him anyway. When we think about the casual conversations we have with a group of friends at lunch time or a quick word with coworkers before a meeting, when we experience a time of unplanned fellowship, we may later recall that one person spoke a sentence, perhaps once or twice, and the words still ring in our minds. Those words answer a question in our minds or settle an issue we can't figure out.

God uses every circumstance and every person in our lives to His advantage in our lives. Let us look to God for answers when we least expect it.

Do Not Forget the Lessons Learned

And Asa cried unto the Lord his God, and said, Lord, it is nothing
with thee to help, whether with many, or with them that have no
power: help us, O Lord our God; for we rest on thee, and in thy name
we go against this multitude. O Lord, thou art our God; let no man
prevail against thee ... And the Spirit of God came upon Azariah
the son of Oded: And he went out to meet Asa, and said unto him,
Hear ye me, Asa, and all Judah and Benjamin; The Lord is with you,
while ye be with him; and if ye seek him, he will be found of you;
but if ye forsake him, he will forsake you ... And at that time Hanani
the seer came to Asa king of Judah, and said unto him, Because thou
hast relied on the king of Syria, and not relied on the Lord thy God,
therefore is the host of the king of Syria escaped out of thine hand.
Were not the Ethiopians and the Lubims a huge host, with very many
chariots and horsemen? yet, because thou didst rely on the Lord,
he delivered them into thine hand. For the eyes of the Lord run to
and fro throughout the whole earth, to shew himself strong in the
behalf of them whose heart is perfect toward him. Herein thou hast
done foolishly: therefore from henceforth thou shalt have wars.
—2 Chronicles 14:11; 15:1–2; 16:7–9

Asa was generally a good king of Judah. He removed idol altars and
commanded the nation to seek God and obey His laws. He built up the
fort cities, and no one fought against him for several years. When the Cushites
decided to attach Judah, Asa cried to God for help. He followed his own advice
and humbled himself because he knew that he was powerless against the enemy.
The Lord came to his aid and struck down the enemy. A prophet cemented the
lesson learned by Asa when he reminded him that God's presence goes with
those who seek him.

Unfortunately, Asa forgot this lesson a few years later when he faced another
serious national threat. This time, he allied with a human king instead of calling
upon God for help. Another prophet called him on it, and King Asa was so
furious that he threw the prophet in jail. God punished Asa by keeping the nation
at war until his death. Asa had such a completely (bad) change of heart that at
the end of his life, when God gave him a severe foot disease, he still refused to
seek help from God.

The life of King Asa teaches us that faith in God is present and continuous,
new every day. We cannot rest on the laurels of yesterday.

Saving Our Lives

And when he had called the people unto him with his disciples also, he said unto them, Whosoever will come after me, let him deny himself, and take up his cross, and follow me. For whosoever will save his life shall lose it; but whosoever shall lose his life for my sake and the gospel's, the same shall save it. For what shall it profit a man, if he shall gain the whole world, and lose his own soul? Or what shall a man give in exchange for his soul? Whosoever therefore shall be ashamed of me and of my words in this adulterous and sinful generation; of him also shall the Son of man be ashamed, when he cometh in the glory of his Father with the holy angels.
—Mark 8:34–38

Self-preservation is a basic human instinct. It doesn't matter whether we come from a home where we had very little money or a home with a lot of wealth, we all want to grab onto some things in life and keep them. Things make us feel as though we have a life, don't they?

But if we want to live for God, we must challenge this all too human tendency. We must deal with greed and ditch it. Jesus Christ assures us that in order to save our lives, we must learn the way of self-denial. He wants us to give up ourselves, our ideas, our preferences, our things, our very souls—to Him. The loss of our lives to this world becomes the gain of our souls to God and His salvation from sin. None of us will live forever unless we have made this decision. When we come to Jesus, the Creator of our souls and the architect of our bodies is the only being capable of training our good desires and derailing our bad desires.

When we give ourselves to God for safekeeping, God helps us to follow Him. The right focus preserves our souls, and saving our lives begins with the simple decision to follow Him first.

Spiritual Revival

For thus saith the Lord God, the Holy One of Israel; In returning
and rest shall ye be saved; in quietness and in confidence shall be your
strength: and ye would not ... And therefore will the Lord wait, that
he may be gracious unto you, and therefore will he be exalted, that
he may have mercy upon you: for the Lord is a God of judgment:
blessed are all they that wait for him ... O Lord, be gracious unto
us; we have waited for thee: be thou their arm every morning, our
salvation also in the time of trouble ... For the Lord is our judge,
the Lord is our lawgiver, the Lord is our king; he will save us.
—Isaiah 30:15, 18; 33:2, 22

Many locations in the world seem to live from one crisis to another. Televised weather informs us of raging wildfires in the arid West, unexpected flash floods in the East, deadly tornadoes in the Southwest, devastating hurricanes in the Southeast, and traumatic earthquakes on the West coast. Underwater disasters occur in the ocean. Military news is often unwelcome. The larger world news likewise seems to reflect the same disastrous mode of existence.

News makes us ask a lot of hard questions. Who is to blame for all of this bad news? Do our lives also reflect in private the public disasters that occur too often? It is obvious that natural forces are beyond our control. Should we then blame God? We can blame people. We can blame governments. We don't know exactly who to blame, so we finally beg for God's mercy. The Bible tells us that some national disasters occur as punishment from God for sins, but we will never know enough to know whether or not this is true of a particular event. But—we can know with certainty that God wants us to repent as individuals (and individuals comprise a nation) so that He may show compassion to us when we are in distress.

The roles of the godhead as judge, lawgiver, and king reveal a balance of power that best enables the Lord to deal compassionately with the crises that occur without warning—but only when we turn to Him in quietness and confidence.

The Lottery

> Wherefore of these men which have companied with us all the
> time that the Lord Jesus went in and out among us, Beginning
> from the baptism of John, unto that same day that he was taken
> up from us, must one be ordained to be a witness with us of his
> resurrection. And they appointed two, Joseph called Barsabas, who
> was surnamed Justus, and Matthias. And they prayed, and said, Thou,
> Lord, which knowest the hearts of all men, shew whether of these
> two thou hast chosen, That he may take part of this ministry and
> apostleship, from which Judas by transgression fell, that he might
> go to his own place. And they gave forth their lots; and the lot fell
> upon Matthias; and he was numbered with the eleven apostles.
> —Acts 1:21–26

The lottery is a time-honored way of making an unbiased choice. In today's society, we see the lottery in action when we are called for jury duty. The names of the jurors are on cards, and the court official draws names to appoint the jury from those present. One extra juror is chosen, and the final lottery draw removes one person by chance just before the final jury deliberation.

This passage does not condemn the use of the lottery as much as it points out to us that mere human logic and traditions are fallible. They are the best we can do under the circumstances, but our best human efforts cannot supersede the will of God. God is not illogical, but He knows what He wants a better outcome than we do. History records very little about the newly appointed twelfth apostle Matthias, but history records a lot about the divinely appointed Saul. Saul was God's choice for the recently vacated position of twelfth apostle. God met Saul, a fierce persecutor of Christians on the road to Damascus. God changed his name to Paul.

Paul knew he was chosen by God to fill the position of "apostle to the Gentiles." Paul thought of himself as being born in the wrong time, doing the wrong things, completely unfit for the task, yet God chose him.

SEPTEMBER 24

The Way of the Lord

Blessed is the man that walketh not in the counsel of the ungodly,
nor standeth in the way of sinners, nor sitteth in the seat of the
scornful ... As for God, his way is perfect: the word of the Lord
is tried: he is a buckler to all those that trust in him ... The
meek will he guide in judgment: and the meek will he teach his
way. All the paths of the Lord are mercy and truth unto such as
keep his covenant and his testimonies ... Teach me thy way, O
Lord, and lead me in a plain path, because of mine enemies.
—Psalm 1:1; 18:30; 25:9–10; 27:11

Once we embark upon the Christian life, we may wonder about its differences
from any other way of life. How does God's way differ from any other way
we might have chosen? Many life choices seem nonreligious or non-moral, so
the distinction needs to be clarified.

In contrast to making decisions based upon the best of human knowledge
or the uncertain guidance of emotions, God's way offers timeless principles
that apply to life situations. When we remember that God's Word is perfect, we
understand that the application of biblical principles to a situation gives reliable
guidance. When people make decisions in life, they cannot normally know at the
beginning how the situation will turn out at the end. Most people would like to
be assured of a favorable outcome instead of otherwise. Turning to God instead
of another source for guidance indicates humility, and God lovingly guides us in
the rightness of His way, preventing us from human error.

When many paths seem to beckon, the Bible leads us in a straight line kind
of way that does not digress from God's principles of truth. Following God's way
confers safety along the path we travel.

Eternal Life

And the Lord God formed man of the dust of the
ground, and breathed into his nostrils the breath
of life; and man became a living soul.
—Genesis 2:7

The life is more than meat, and the body is more than raiment.
—Luke 12:23

For whosoever will save his life shall lose it; but whosoever shall
lose his life for my sake and the gospel's, the same shall save it.
—Mark 8:35

He that believeth on the Son hath everlasting life:
and he that believeth not the Son shall not see life;
but the wrath of God abideth on him.
—John 3:36

Technology has advanced far enough to create artificial life. Dolly, the cloned sheep, was a scientific marvel of laboratory creation. Unfortunately, she did not live a healthy life because human efforts fall far short of God's effort at creating life.

God made us, and God also made all creatures out of dust! Not even the most intelligent scientist can understand what this means or copy this act of creation. We know that God gives life to all that live and breathe, so indirectly God created Dolly, not the lab or the scientist. Unlike dumb animals, we all value our lives, and we want our lives to count for something. Even this vague desire comes from God who created us to think that way.

If we really want to gain life, Jesus Christ tells us to lose it—give it to Him—in repentance. Even during the times when life stretches out in front of us, we know that life is fleeting, not endless. God wants our moments of life to matter for Him, so He provides the way for us to have eternal life, through Jesus Christ His Son.

SEPTEMBER 26

God Loves Sinners

And he spake this parable unto them, saying, What man of you,
having an hundred sheep, if he lose one of them, doth not leave
the ninety and nine in the wilderness, and go after that which is
lost, until he find it? ... I say unto you, that likewise joy shall be
in heaven over one sinner that repenteth, more than over ninety
and nine just persons, which need no repentance. Either what
woman having ten pieces of silver, if she lose one piece, doth not
light a candle, and sweep the house, and seek diligently till she
find it? ... Likewise, I say unto you, there is joy in the presence
of the angels of God over one sinner that repenteth ... For the
Son of man is come to seek and to save that which was lost.
—Luke 15:3–4, 7–8, 10; 19:10

One result of attending primary school, middle school, and high school is that
we spend a lot of time with a lot of people we would not otherwise come
into contact with. We have also spent much of that time comparing ourselves
to them. We notice who has the best physical prowess and the best academic
abilities. We also notice personality quirks and sundry oddities. Sometimes, we
divide our classmates into categories of good kids and bad kids.

Whoever we are, we know who we are (in comparison to others), and God
uses this experience to teach us about our sinful nature. The depth of depravity
in our sinful nature should cause us to turn to the Lord in repentance. But will
God accept us, or must we hang our heads in shame forever? Jesus assures us
that He is as careful as a shepherd with a large flock of sheep. When one sheep
is lost, He tracks the wayward sheep down until He finds it and saves it from
further harm. Jesus is as tender as a woman who has labored to save ten small
coins. When one coin goes missing, she turns the house upside down until she
finds the missing coin.

Remember how much Jesus Christ loves us. Remember how often He seeks
us out. Remember that He came to earth to seek and to save sinners from eternal
death.

Spiritual Warfare

For we know that the law is spiritual: but I am carnal, sold under
sin. For that which I do I allow not: for what I would, that do I
not; but what I hate, that do I. If then I do that which I would not,
I consent unto the law that it is good. For I delight in the law of
God after the inward man: But I see another law in my members,
warring against the law of my mind, and bringing me into captivity
to the law of sin which is in my members. O wretched man that
I am! who shall deliver me from the body of this death? I thank
God through Jesus Christ our Lord. So then with the mind I
myself serve the law of God; but with the flesh the law of sin.
—Romans 7:14–16, 22–25

When we first turn to the Lord, we feel a huge sense of relief. The image
of Christian in the classic allegory *Pilgrim's Progress* portrays the relief that
all new babes in Christ feel. He climbs to the top of the hill along the highway
of salvation where he loses the burdensome backpack of sin. Knowing he has
done the right thing relaxes him. The happiness and relief can sometimes make
a new believer feel that nothing more difficult will ever happen again. This is
what Christian felt, but he soon finds out he was wrong. He takes a long nap in
the middle of the day, and when he wakes, he leaves abruptly, forgetting his scroll
(the scroll guaranteed his entry into heaven). Christian must then begin the battle
of spiritual warfare that is aimed at believers.

Likewise, we are wrong if we think like Christian did, but it is a comfort
to know that the apostle Paul was once a new believer too. When he turned his
life over to the Lord, Paul became aware of the ongoing spiritual battle between
good and evil, sin and righteousness, truth and falsehood. The war between
the heavenly forces is also the same war waged upon us within our human
faculties. Paul expresses the battle by using contrasts, and we know exactly what
he means. Turning to the Lord enables us to understand the difference between
right and wrong, so we know the right choice to make every time. But, the sinful
nature rises up against our better spiritual judgment, causing tremendous conflict
within us.

How did Paul reconcile these opposing forces within himself? He trusted
God—to the point of being a slave to God. He needed God every moment, just
like we do. From the beginning of our lives all the way to the end of them, we
need the help of Jesus, our Lord and Savior.

SEPTEMBER 28

A Solid Foundation

According to the grace of God which is given unto me, as a wise
masterbuilder, I have laid the foundation, and another buildeth
thereon. But let every man take heed how he buildeth thereupon.
For other foundation can no man lay than that is laid, which is Jesus
Christ. Now if any man build upon this foundation gold, silver,
precious stones, wood, hay, stubble; Every man's work shall be made
manifest: for the day shall declare it, because it shall be revealed by
fire; and the fire shall try every man's work of what sort it is. If any
man's work abide which he hath built thereupon, he shall receive a
reward. If any man's work shall be burned, he shall suffer loss: but
he himself shall be saved; yet so as by fire. Know ye not that ye are
the temple of God, and that the Spirit of God dwelleth in you? If
any man defile the temple of God, him shall God destroy; for the
temple of God is holy, which temple ye are. Let no man deceive
himself. If any man among you seemeth to be wise in this world,
let him become a fool, that he may be wise. For the wisdom of this
world is foolishness with God. For it is written, He taketh the wise
in their own craftiness … And ye are Christ's; and Christ is God's.
—1 Corinthians 3:10–19, 23

Every aspect of our lives is meant to glorify God. If we think we can hold on
to outdated values, outmoded standards, old ways, or timeworn ideas, we
will find out soon enough that they cannot support this new life in Christ that
we now live.

The very foundation of our lives has changed because of what Jesus Christ
did for us. Foundations for homes cost a lot of money, but the foundation of Jesus
Christ is free, because we have come to Him, and He has set up our lives for
us—in Him. Some people build their homes themselves, but they are not builders
or carpenters, so they make many structural errors. They violate building codes.
They do shoddy work. It is less expensive in the long run to let a master builder
do the work of building the home. Homeowners make a few personal choices in
the process, but the foundation, structure, and plan are best when they originate
from a qualified architect and builder of homes.

God wants us to let Jesus Christ build our lives because He is the architect
and builder of our souls—our lives. People who build their homes themselves
sometimes build junk heaps, even when they look good for a few years. In a
similar way, when we surrender to God, we prevent ourselves from wasting our
own effort.

When in Need

Ho, every one that thirsteth, come ye to the waters, and he that
hath no money; come ye, buy, and eat; yea, come, buy wine and milk
without money and without price ... Wherefore do ye spend money
for that which is not bread? and your labour for that which satisfieth
not? hearken diligently unto me, and eat ye that which is good, and
let your soul delight itself in fatness. Incline your ear, and come unto
me: hear, and your soul shall live; and I will make an everlasting
covenant with you, even the sure mercies of David ... Seek ye the
Lord while he may be found, call ye upon him while he is near: Let
the wicked forsake his way, and the unrighteous man his thoughts:
and let him return unto the Lord, and he will have mercy upon him;
and to our God, for he will abundantly pardon ... Lift up your eyes to
the heavens, and look upon the earth beneath: for the heavens shall
vanish away like smoke, and the earth shall wax old like a garment,
and they that dwell therein shall die in like manner: but my salvation
shall be for ever, and my righteousness shall not be abolished.
—Isaiah 55:1–3; 6–7; 51:6

College may be a time of excitement when many new experiences broaden
our minds and open many doors. But college is also a time when students
feel keenly aware of their financial needs, physical wants, and material deficits.

Some college students know they have one semester or one year paid for,
but after that, the future remains uncertain. God sympathizes with this human
plight, so it is good to know that our spiritual lives need not mirror our financial
lives. The salvation of the human soul is a matter of the will, not a matter of
money, culture, gender, or any other identification tag we may like to attach to
it. When we are thirsty enough to know that our souls are dry, we may turn to
God. When we are hungry enough to know that there is no more for food in our
budget or bank account, we may turn to God.

When we call to the Lord out of our deepest needs, He has mercy on us.
When we repent, He forgives our sins. The best news of the good news is that
salvation costs nothing and lasts forever. We will get physically thirsty and
hungry again, but all our spiritual desires are fully met in Jesus Christ.

SEPTEMBER 30

Talking to God

Give ear to my words, O Lord, consider my meditation. Hearken unto
the voice of my cry, my King, and my God: for unto thee will I pray.
My voice shalt thou hear in the morning, O Lord; in the morning
will I direct my prayer unto thee, and will look up ... But as for me,
I will come into thy house in the multitude of thy mercy: and in thy
fear will I worship toward thy holy temple. Lead me, O Lord, in
thy righteousness because of mine enemies; make thy way straight
before my face ... But let all those that put their trust in thee rejoice:
let them ever shout for joy, because thou defendest them: let them
also that love thy name be joyful in thee. For thou, Lord, wilt bless
the righteous; with favour wilt thou compass him as with a shield.
—Psalm 5:1–3, 7–8, 11–12

God has shown us great mercy by saving us from our sins by the finished work
of redemption through Jesus Christ, who died on the cross for human sin.
Now He shows us even greater mercy by allowing us to approach Him through
prayer.

Because the substitutionary death of Jesus Christ for our sins has opened
up the way to God for us, any place of prayer becomes a temple to God from
which we can pour out our hearts. His work has lessened the burden of our
spirits because we no longer have to try so hard to reach Him. When we have a
relationship with God, we want to talk to the Lord frequently. We don't always
have the exact words to say what we mean, but the Lord understands our sighs
and our cries. Because God is personal and because God is the king of the
universe, we expectantly await an answer.

The temple of prayer becomes a place of refuge for us and makes us very
happy. Talking to God about our life means trusting the one who leads us on the
right path and protects us as we follow it.

OCTOBER 1

The Source of Knowledge

The fear of the Lord is the beginning of knowledge: but fools
despise wisdom and instruction ... My son, if thou wilt receive my
words, and hide my commandments with thee ... Then shalt thou
understand righteousness, and judgment, and equity; yea, every good
path. When wisdom entereth into thine heart, and knowledge is
pleasant unto thy soul ... So shall the knowledge of wisdom be unto
thy soul: when thou hast found it, then there shall be a reward, and
thy expectation shall not be cut off ... Whoso loveth instruction
loveth knowledge: but he that hateth reproof is brutish ... A wise
man is strong; yea, a man of knowledge increaseth strength.
—Proverbs 1:7; 2:1; 2:9–10; 24:14; 12:1; 24:5

Where do people begin learning anything at all? We all come from homes
where we have developed a lot of rudimentary abilities and learned a lot of
formative skills, but these differ from the skills we learn at school. Most schools
place a lot of emphasis on critical thinking skills, or "wisdom" today. The task of
schooling is to unite the factual side of learning with the application of the same.

We would equate critical thinking skills with the wisdom mentioned in
the Bible, but when we consider that a lot of education omits God from the
classroom, we can see why a division has occurred between "the Lord" and
"knowledge." So how can the facts we know, or "knowledge" relate to the Lord
of all "wisdom"? Remember that God created all things, and this means that He
knows all the facts—God is omniscient. When we teach and learn holistically,
we make a disciplined and conscientious effort to rejoin these two parts that have
become separated from one another.

The discipline that students exert for academic success holds significance,
not just for the temporal goal of the degree, but also for the eternal goal, toward
which God directs all of us individually.

OCTOBER 2

Good and Evil

And the Lord God planted a garden eastward in Eden; and there
he put the man whom he had formed. And out of the ground
made the Lord God to grow every tree that is pleasant to the
sight ... and good for food; the tree of life also in the midst of the
garden, and the tree of knowledge of good and evil ... And the
Lord God took the man, and put him into the garden of Eden to
dress it and to keep it. And the Lord God commanded the man,
saying, Of every tree of the garden thou mayest freely eat: But of
the tree of the knowledge of good and evil, thou shalt not eat of
it: for in the day that thou eatest thereof thou shalt surely die.
—Genesis 2:8–9; 15–17

Can we possibly imagine what life was like in the Garden of Eden for two
perfect human beings? Probably not, but we do know that Adam and Eve
were the first two people to struggle with the same problems we experience today.
We share their nature.

Sometimes we find it difficult to distinguish good from evil, better from
worse, right from wrong, just as they did. This perplexity reveals more about us
that it does about the situation. During their early days in the Garden of Eden,
God made the nature of good and evil clear to Adam and Eve by giving them
only one rule to obey: God forbade them to eat from the tree of the knowledge
of good and evil. Good clearly means obedience to God, and evil clearly means
disobedience to God. First Eve, and then Adam, turned aside from the words
God had directly spoken to them. They sinned, and everyone knows the rest of
the story.

Nevertheless, God still wants to apply what He has told us (in the Bible)
to situations we face. This means reading the Bible, studying the Bible, and
applying its concepts directly to the situation at hand—every single time. We
cannot escape the sinful nature in this life, but we can let God direct our lives
and protect us from the danger of sinful choices.

OCTOBER 3

Diligence

And he spake many things unto them in parables, saying, Behold,
a sower went forth to sow; And when he sowed, some seeds
fell by the way side, and the fowls came and devoured them up:
Some fell upon stony places, where they had not much earth: and
forthwith they sprung up, because they had no deepness of earth:
And when the sun was up, they were scorched; and because they
had no root, they withered away. And some fell among thorns;
and the thorns sprung up, and choked them: But other fell into
good ground, and brought forth fruit, some an hundredfold, some
sixtyfold, some thirtyfold. Who hath ears to hear, let him hear.
—Matthew 13:3–9

When the growing season is rainy at first and then dry at the appropriate times for good plant growth, no one pays much attention to the weather. When the season is dry and then drought-ridden, everyone realizes the importance of the weather combined with good soil for optimal plant growth.

Some of us depend on harvesting a minimum number of bushels of corn, wheat, or soybeans per acre for a living to make ends meet. We begin to get anxious when the outlook appears otherwise. Does God relate to us? And does our knowledge about plant life pertain to the spiritual life? The parable of the four types of soil illustrates how God has planted the seed of His Word in the life-soil of this world. How can anyone receive the Word of God and walk away unchanged by it?—but we know they do. Some people exist in such perilous living situations that those around them prevent them from hearing the Word of God. Some people eagerly believe but walk away from the truth as soon as something more captivating comes along. Some people are so surrounded by sinful living that they cannot recognize truth or goodness, even when faced with it.

Still, other people accept the seed of truth or let it germinate in their lives. This is how God makes faith grow and produce a yield—one hundred times, sixty times, or thirty times the initial size. Be thankful for good soil.

OCTOBER 4

Unsaved Family Members

> But now in Christ Jesus ye who sometimes were far off are made
> nigh by the blood of Christ. For he is our peace, who hath made
> both one, and hath broken down the middle wall of partition
> between us; Having abolished in his flesh the enmity, even the
> law of commandments contained in ordinances; for to make in
> himself of twain one new man, so making peace; And that he
> might reconcile both unto God in one body by the cross, having
> slain the enmity thereby: And came and preached peace to you
> which were afar off, and to them that were nigh. For through him
> we both have access by one Spirit unto the Father. Now therefore
> ye are no more strangers and foreigners, but fellowcitizens with
> the saints, and of the household of God; And are built upon the
> foundation of the apostles and prophets, Jesus Christ himself
> being the chief corner stone; In whom all the building fitly framed
> together groweth unto an holy temple in the Lord: In whom ye also
> are builded together for an habitation of God through the Spirit.
> —Ephesians 2:13–22

Have we grown up in a family that holds to another type of belief system than the one we currently hold? General observation and psychological theory often agree that most people follow along in the footsteps of their families. But if this is universally true, then a lot of us are in spiritual trouble. God says that this observation is simply not true!

The good news is that the blood of Jesus Christ enables anyone to come close to Him through repentance for sins, even those who are and ought to remain far from God by human logic. Believers become part of the foundation that is Jesus Christ. Because Jesus leads us, because God builds us, because God now dwells in us by the Holy Spirit, we do not and cannot remain the same as we were beforehand.

If we grew up in a household of unbelief, mockery, scorn, or derision for all things holy, we need not continue to dwell on it. Remember the wonder of God's grace—that He chose us—in love—forever—in Him.

OCTOBER 5

Angels and Demons

I will therefore put you in remembrance, though ye once knew this, how that the Lord, having saved the people out of the land of Egypt, afterward destroyed them that believed not. And the angels which kept not their first estate, but left their own habitation, he hath reserved in everlasting chains under darkness unto the judgment of the great day. Even as Sodom and Gomorrha, and the cities about them in like manner, giving themselves over to fornication, and going after strange flesh, are set forth for an example, suffering the vengeance of eternal fire. Likewise also these filthy dreamers defile the flesh, despise dominion, and speak evil of dignities. Yet Michael the archangel, when contending with the devil he disputed about the body of Moses, durst not bring against him a railing accusation, but said, The Lord rebuke thee. But these speak evil of those things which they know not: but what they know naturally, as brute beasts, in those things they corrupt themselves.
—Jude 5–10

Television shows, movies, books, and video games that feature angels and demons are very popular today. Because these beings are presented to the audience as fictitious characters, most people relegate angels and demons to the world of make-believe in the harmless imaginary world of childhood thoughts.

But contrary to popular media, the Bible assures us that the spirit world is real and subject to the dominion of almighty God. At some time in the distant past, some real angels left their home in heaven and abandoned their obedience to God. God now keeps them in darkness, bound with chains, until the day He judges them. Similarly, some human beings, who have given themselves over to sexual immorality and perversion, like the inhabitants of Sodom and Gomorrah did, behave like unreasoning beasts. They destroy themselves through disobedience just like the angels did.

Some real angels still obey God, and they fight for the truth against the demons who oppose the truth. They respect and honor God enough to know that He alone fights the battle of evil, through those who always obey God without fail.

Showers of Blessing

> I will seek that which was lost, and bring again that which was
> driven away, and will bind up that which was broken, and will
> strengthen that which was sick: but I will destroy the fat and the
> strong; I will feed them with judgment ... Therefore thus saith
> the Lord God unto them; Behold, I, even I, will judge between
> the fat cattle and between the lean cattle ... And I will set up one
> shepherd over them, and he shall feed them, even my servant
> David; he shall feed them, and he shall be their shepherd. And I
> the Lord will be their God, and my servant David a prince among
> them; I the Lord have spoken it. And I will make with them a
> covenant of peace, and will cause the evil beasts to cease out of the
> land: and they shall dwell safely in the wilderness, and sleep in the
> woods. And I will make them and the places round about my hill a
> blessing; and I will cause the shower to come down in his season;
> there shall be showers of blessing ... And ye my flock, the flock of
> my pasture, are men, and I am your God, saith the Lord God.
> —Ezekiel 34:16, 20, 23–26, 31

Do we like weather, whatever it is, or do we always complain about it? Is it always too hot, too humid, too cold, or too rainy?—no matter what kind of weather we are having, we do not like it much?

An appreciation for the weather, especially rainy weather, can give us insight into the way God treats our lives when we obey Him. A blinding downpour can frighten us when we are driving on unfamiliar roads, but it can also make us thankful for necessary moisture. Have we read the Bible well enough to know that the phrase "showers of blessings" comes from the book of Ezekiel? It is not just the title of an old-fashioned hymn. Instead of overlooking the phrase because it sounds like a song Grandma probably loved to sing, we can figure out what it means for us today.

Ezekiel tells us that God is a shepherd who seeks out the lost sheep who have strayed from the flock. He is a good shepherd because He always deals fairly, justly, and equably with the flock. God also judges between the fat sheep and the lean sheep. Does this mean between laziness and inactivity?—between evil and good?—between wrong and right?—maybe all of these. He has sent His son Jesus Christ to be the only shepherd who can lead the lost to the place of blessing. God blesses obedience. He showers the obedient with His blessings.

He gives us as much as we need, and sometimes, He gives us a lot more than we need. Only a God who judges justly can know how to give exactly the right gift to each one of His own sheep. He is the one who send us "showers of blessings."

Family Upbringing

And Terah lived seventy years, and begat Abram, Nahor, and
Haran. Now these are the generations of Terah: Terah begat Abram,
Nahor, and Haran; and Haran begat Lot ... And Abram and Nahor
took them wives: the name of Abram's wife was Sarai; and the
name of Nahor's wife, Milcah, the daughter of Haran, the father
of Milcah, and the father of Iscah ... But Sarai was barren; she had
no child. And Terah took Abram his son, and Lot the son of Haran
his son's son, and Sarai his daughter in law, his son Abram's wife;
and they went forth with them from Ur of the Chaldees, to go into
the land of Canaan; and they came unto Haran, and dwelt there.
—Genesis 11:26, 29–31

Even as Abraham believed God, and it was accounted to him
for righteousness. Know ye therefore that they which are of
faith, the same are the children of Abraham. And the scripture,
foreseeing that God would justify the heathen through faith,
preached before the gospel unto Abraham, saying, In thee shall
all nations be blessed. So then they which be of faith are blessed
with faithful Abraham ... Christ hath redeemed us from the
curse of the law, being made a curse for us: for it is written,
Cursed is every one that hangeth on a tree: That the blessing
of Abraham might come on the Gentiles through Jesus Christ;
that we might receive the promise of the Spirit through faith.
—Galatians 3:6–9, 13–14

Do we come from a believing family or from a faithless family? Depending
upon personal choices we have recently made, we are either acutely
embarrassed or eternally grateful for the families we were raised in. But there
is a larger, more extensive family to which we may all belong—the family of
Abraham—the family of faith.

We might want to consider where Abraham came from: he came from a land
where idolatry was the primary religion. He followed his father and the family
business until God told him to move elsewhere. He desperately wanted a son and
heir. No one expects a husband of one hundred years of age and a wife of ninety years
of age to have a baby—yet they did! Abraham is the father of the faithful because
he believed God's Word in spite of incongruous family and social circumstances.

The extreme circumstances of his life remind us that believers must always obey
God's Word, for decades if necessary, in order to please God. When we believe God's
Word, we act by faith. Believing that Jesus Christ redeemed us on the cross brings
blessing to us. Believing in God's Word allows the Holy Spirit to actively lead our lives.

Honoring the Body God Gives Us

And the king spake unto Ashpenaz the master of his eunuchs, that
he should bring certain of the children of Israel, and of the king's
seed, and of the princes; Children in whom was no blemish, but well
favoured, and skilful in all wisdom, and cunning in knowledge, and
understanding science, and such as had ability in them to stand in
the king's palace, and whom they might teach the learning and the
tongue of the Chaldeans … But Daniel purposed in his heart that
he would not defile himself with the portion of the king's meat, nor
with the wine which he drank: therefore he requested of the prince of
the eunuchs that he might not defile himself … So he consented to
them in this matter, and proved them ten days. And at the end of ten
days their countenances appeared fairer and fatter in flesh than all the
children which did eat the portion of the king's meat … As for these
four children, God gave them knowledge and skill in all learning and
wisdom: and Daniel had understanding in all visions and dreams.
—Daniel 1:3–4, 8, 14–15, 17

I beseech you therefore, brethren, by the mercies of
God, that ye present your bodies a living sacrifice, holy,
acceptable unto God, which is your reasonable service.
—Romans 12:1

We have to admit that we live in an overweight society when we can also
readily call to mind numerous health books, fitness shows, and buff gurus
who tout stronger, healthier bodies when we follow a specific plan. Although the
food we eat does not bring us closer to God let alone save us, the way we handle
our bodies and food intake matters to God.

Daniel was a young man who lived during the Babylonian captivity. He and
three other college-aged young men were chosen to be highly trained servants of
the king of Persia, the country of their national humiliation and disgrace. These
four young men were not only handsome, they bore no physical defects, and they
were known as good students—the best of their class. At their relatively young
age, they understood the relationship between good learning and good diet. As
a result, they refused to eat the rich royal diet. Instead, they politely requested
a vegetable and water diet. How many of us have heard that this type of diet is
still the healthiest today?

God honored their choice in a difficult situation. God gave them greater
understanding to serve Him because they honored God with their bodies.

OCTOBER 9

Losses in Life

> For the wrath of God is revealed from heaven against all
> ungodliness and unrighteousness of men, who hold the truth in
> unrighteousness ... For the invisible things of him from the creation
> of the world are clearly seen, being understood by the things that are
> made, even his eternal power and Godhead; so that they are without
> excuse ... Wherefore God also gave them up to uncleanness through
> the lusts of their own hearts, to dishonour their own bodies between
> themselves ... And even as they did not like to retain God in their
> knowledge, God gave them over to a reprobate mind, to do those
> things which are not convenient ... But we are sure that the judgment
> of God is according to truth against them which commit such things.
> —Romans 1:18, 20, 24, 28; 2:2

We cannot ignore the society in which we live, a society that glorifies every form of immoral behavior. Human reasoning says that if humans do it, it must be all right—somehow. We can't really figure out how, so why not accept it and let it be?—we forget that God has holy standards for human behavior.

We forget the more logical thought that the God who created all humans should know the best way to live the life He has given us. The Bible tells us that when we live godless and wicked lives, we are really trying to pretend that the truth does not exist. God punishes humans in three distinct ways for such evil behavior. First, sinful behavior results in spiritual loss. People refuse to acknowledge the eternal qualities of God that are plain for everyone to see every day of their lives. Next, bad behavior results in physical loss. Ignorance of God's standards means that people make up their own rules of sexual behavior.

Finally, sinful behavior results in mental loss, when God allows filthy thoughts to overtake all processes of thinking and behavior. Only the truth will keep us clean and pure and help us avoid losses in life.

The Problem of Temptation

Moreover, brethren, I would not that ye should be ignorant, how
that all our fathers were under the cloud, and all passed through
the sea; And were all baptized unto Moses in the cloud and in
the sea; And did all eat the same spiritual meat; And did all drink
the same spiritual drink: for they drank of that spiritual Rock
that followed them: and that Rock was Christ. But with many
of them God was not well pleased: for they were overthrown in
the wilderness … Now all these things happened unto them for
examples: and they are written for our admonition, upon whom
the ends of the world are come. Wherefore let him that thinketh he
standeth take heed lest he fall. There hath no temptation taken you
but such as is common to man: but God is faithful, who will not
suffer you to be tempted above that ye are able; but will with the
temptation also make a way to escape, that ye may be able to bear it.
—1 Corinthians 10:1–5, 11–13

Life is a minefield through which we must march and learn to bivouac in a
safe spot. If we are adventure-minded and love to camp out, we enjoy this
migratory type of challenge. But the nation of Israel had a forty-year camping
experience, and they did not like it much at all.

For at least one generation of God's chosen people, life turned out so
unexpectedly different that they never really got used to it. They followed visible
guidance from the Lord when they crossed the Red Sea. They followed the pillar
of cloud by day and the pillar of fire by night to know when to move and when to
stay in the same place. They drank from the rock when Moses touched it. They
ate manna and quail at the daily command of the Lord. In spite of so many visible
manifestations of God's guidance, their sins of greed, idolatry, immorality, and
complaining prevented them from enjoying their salvation.

It is easy to be sidetracked by temptations that become full-blown sins in
our lives. God knows this, and He provides a way out for us. He warns us from
a distance of a few thousand years to turn our attention to Him and ask for His
ever-present help.

Human Temptations

And Jesus being full of the Holy Ghost returned from Jordan, and was led by the Spirit into the wilderness, Being forty days tempted of the devil. And in those days he did eat nothing: and when they were ended, he afterward hungered. And the devil said unto him, If thou be the Son of God, command this stone that it be made bread. And Jesus answered him, saying, It is written, That man shall not live by bread alone, but by every Word of God. And the devil, taking him up into an high mountain, shewed unto him all the kingdoms of the world in a moment of time. And the devil said unto him, All this power will I give thee, and the glory of them: for that is delivered unto me; and to whomsoever I will I give it. If thou therefore wilt worship me, all shall be thine. And Jesus answered and said unto him, Get thee behind me, Satan: for it is written, Thou shalt worship the Lord thy God, and him only shalt thou serve. And he brought him to Jerusalem, and set him on a pinnacle of the temple, and said unto him, If thou be the Son of God, cast thyself down from hence: For it is written, He shall give his angels charge over thee, to keep thee: And in their hands they shall bear thee up, lest at any time thou dash thy foot against a stone. And Jesus answering said unto him, It is said, Thou shalt not tempt the Lord thy God.
—Luke 4:1–12

For we have not an high priest which cannot be touched with the feeling of our infirmities; but was in all points tempted like as we are, yet without sin.
—Hebrews 4:15

Why do we say that Jesus was tempted just like we are tempted?—because we can read how it happened. Jesus Christ was full of the Holy Spirit—no one can be holier than that—yet, Satan still tempted Him.

Jesus Christ was initially tempted through his physical senses. He was hungry. Perhaps he remembered that Esau was once hungry and sinned, trading his birthright for food. Jesus Christ chose to obey God, not physical cravings. Next, Jesus Christ was tempted by the promise of personal power. Fortunately, He knew that Satan was a liar, incapable of telling the truth, by his own willful and wicked choice. Besides, only God is worthy of worship. Jesus was not fooled by the big and empty words of Satan. Finally, Jesus Christ was tempted to presume upon God's grace. Unlike Abraham, who presumed that God would extricate him from sticky situations (when he told the king that Sarah was his sister, not his wife; and when he let his wife convince him to father the child of promise by her maid Hagar), Jesus obeyed God. Yes, God did accomplish His divine plan through Abraham, but Abraham paid the price for presuming upon God's blessing.

Jesus Christ did not presume upon the grace of God, and He did not relent from following the Lord. He was tempted in every way, just like us, but Jesus did not give in to temptation and sin.

OCTOBER 12

What Do We Really
Want from Life?

And Naomi said unto her two daughters in law, Go, return each to
her mother's house: the Lord deal kindly with you, as ye have dealt
with the dead, and with me. The Lord grant you that ye may find rest,
each of you in the house of her husband. Then she kissed them; and
they lifted up their voice, and wept. And they said unto her, Surely we
will return with thee unto thy people ... And Ruth said, Intreat me
not to leave thee, or to return from following after thee: for whither
thou goest, I will go; and where thou lodgest, I will lodge: thy people
shall be my people, and thy God my God: Where thou diest, will I
die, and there will I be buried: the Lord do so to me, and more also,
if ought but death part thee and me. When she saw that she was
stedfastly minded to go with her, then she left speaking unto her.
Ruth 1:8–10, 16–18

Some of us grew up in ungodly homes, the kind of home where God is a swear
word, where religion is derided, where idols sit on pedestals, where church
is the last event on anyone's agenda, where family members jump in and out of
bed with anyone they please, where prescriptions drugs (or worse) dull the pain
of sinful living.

With this in mind, we can imagine how Ruth, the Moabite daughter-in-law
of Naomi, felt when she lived in an ungodly culture. Ruth knew from first-hand
experience that there is nothing to admire about people who live their lives
apart from God. She had glimpsed the beauty of holiness in the lives of her late
husband, her late brother-in-law, and her late father-in-law. She experienced the
love that accompanies holiness, and she wanted it so badly that she married a
man from another culture. We can also imagine the severity of the loss created
by their deaths. Ruth did not want to live among ungodly people any longer.

Living a holy life speaks volumes to others. Ruth exercised her freedom of
choice, and she chose the Lord. Poverty and the Lord are still worth more than
wealth and idols. When a moment of decision comes, the choice of the truth is
so obviously the best choice.

OCTOBER 13

Obnoxious People

A soft answer turneth away wrath: but grievous
words stir up anger ... A fool uttereth all his mind:
but a wise man keepeth it in till afterwards.
—Proverbs 15:1; 29:11

Wherefore, my beloved brethren, let every man be swift to hear,
slow to speak, slow to wrath: For the wrath of man worketh
not the righteousness of God. Wherefore lay apart all filthiness
and superfluity of naughtiness, and receive with meekness the
engrafted word, which is able to save your souls. But be ye doers
of the word, and not hearers only, deceiving your own selves.
—James 1:19–22

Some of us have grown up in homes where explosive, irate words are the only kind we have been accustomed to hear for eighteen years or more. Living with angry, obnoxious people can foster the idea that the rest of the world—everybody out there—hates me, is against me, and probably wants to spoil my life somehow.

Now that we are no longer in daily contact with this former way of life, we need to understand that such a false perception of others only feeds a morally filthy mind. The sewer mouth mentality that frequently results from acquiescing to this incorrect assumption needs to disappear. When we turn to the Lord out of a home life like this, the bad words can still echo in the mind. But college is a time to identify actions by their correct names, even the actions that occurred in the past. Read the Bible frequently. The beauty of its words speaks directly against the filthy words that want to rule the mind.

The humble acceptance of the Word of God means that we actively recognize that God is greater than anything else, especially bad language. We no longer passively acquiesce to wrong thinking. God has saved us, and He must grow greater. All else should lessen.

The Wrong Kind of Fear of the Lord

> Then said Saul unto his servants, Seek me a woman that hath a
> familiar spirit, that I may go to her, and enquire of her. And his
> servants said to him, Behold, there is a woman that hath a familiar
> spirit at Endor. And Saul disguised himself, and put on other raiment,
> and he went, and two men with him, and they came to the woman
> by night: and he said, I pray thee, divine unto me by the familiar
> spirit, and bring me him up, whom I shall name unto thee. ... Then
> said the woman, Whom shall I bring up unto thee? And he said,
> Bring me up Samuel ... Then said Samuel, Wherefore then dost thou
> ask of me, seeing the Lord is departed from thee, and is become
> thine enemy? And the Lord hath done to him, as he spake by me:
> for the Lord hath rent the kingdom out of thine hand, and given
> it to thy neighbour, even to David: Because thou obeyedst not the
> voice of the Lord, nor executedst his fierce wrath upon Amalek,
> therefore hath the Lord done this thing unto thee this day ...
> —1 Samuel 28:7–8, 11, 16–18

Those who want to do evil need not look too far from home. Along every strip highway in every byway of the town or city where we live, we see many small business owners. It is also quite likely that anyone may drive the same business strip and also espy a large sign in front of a fortuneteller's house.

Even in ancient Israel, Saul knew exactly where to look for a medium in his area. He had sent them out of his country into the neighboring country. He decided to consult the witch at Endor because it seemed to him that God was not answering his prayers anymore. He was right (that God was not answering his prayers), but he never once considered that he always disregarded the Word of God. He never figured out that the perceived silence of God was really his defiant silence toward God. Apart from God, people live in terror and fear, just like Saul. Apart from God, people look in wrong places and find wrong answers. Saul was trying to outsmart God by going to a medium, so God outsmarted him instead by letting the dead prophet Samuel speak to him from beyond the grave. This is the wrong way to get an answer from God. Saul learned of his rebellion, and he learned that God had rejected him as king.

Getting the answer from a wrong source made Saul even more afraid. He knew he could have waited on God for an answer. He knew he could have changed his mind and begun to obey God in any difficult situation, but Saul never did, did he?

Long-Lasting Success

> But even after that we had suffered before, and were shamefully
> entreated, as ye know, at Philippi, we were bold in our God to
> speak unto you the gospel of God with much contention. For our
> exhortation was not of deceit, nor of uncleanness, nor in guile: But
> as we were allowed of God to be put in trust with the gospel, even so
> we speak; not as pleasing men, but God, which trieth our hearts. For
> neither at any time used we flattering words, as ye know, nor a cloke
> of covetousness; God is witness: Nor of men sought we glory, neither
> of you, nor yet of others, when we might have been burdensome,
> as the apostles of Christ. But we were gentle among you, even as a
> nurse cherisheth her children: So being affectionately desirous of
> you, we were willing to have imparted unto you, not the gospel of
> God only, but also our own souls, because ye were dear unto us.
> —1 Thessalonians 2:2–8

Paul and his traveling companions visited Thessalonica on a missionary trip soon after Paul's release from prison in Philippi. Everyone would like to hear a message from such a hardy soul, if only out of curiosity, but Paul had learned the hard way that the content of the message is always more important than the personal factors that bring the messenger to the audience.

Paul's new life of faith in Jesus Christ had completed an about-face from the former Saul. Once, Paul used all the political and religious clout he could gather to do the ungodly work of chasing down believers in the new sect of Judaism. Now, Paul accepted God's help to do God's work. Once, Paul believed in the rules of the Pharisees. Now, Paul told the truth of the gospel. Now, Paul wanted to please God because he loved the truth. Now, Paul loved others instead of hating them. His single-minded devotion to the gospel gave him such an effective letter that we are still reading Paul today! Paul's change from blasphemer and persecutor to believer and preacher coupled with his suffering for the Lord humbled him.

These few verses give us a beautiful progression of the effective Christian life: tell the truth, love the truth; love others. This is how God grants success in the Christian life.

OCTOBER 16

God Knows Best

We are bound to thank God always for you, brethren, as it is meet, because that your faith groweth exceedingly, and the charity of every one of you all toward each other aboundeth; So that we ourselves glory in you in the churches of God for your patience and faith in all your persecutions and tribulations that ye endure: Which is a manifest token of the righteous judgment of God, that ye may be counted worthy of the kingdom of God, for which ye also suffer: Seeing it is a righteous thing with God to recompense tribulation to them that trouble you; And to you who are troubled rest with us, when the Lord Jesus shall be revealed from heaven with his mighty angels ... Wherefore also we pray always for you, that our God would count you worthy of this calling, and fulfil all the good pleasure of his goodness, and the work of faith with power: That the name of our Lord Jesus Christ may be glorified in you, and ye in him, according to the grace of our God and the Lord Jesus Christ.
—2 Thessalonians 1:3–7, 11–12

We may have heard people utter the cliché that difficulties shape us or that failures help us succeed or other unwelcome platitudes. Whether or not we agree is beside the point. We mostly hope to escape such difficult situations ourselves. But God is in control of our lives, and He desires us to grow in the grace and knowledge of Jesus Christ.

The church members who lived in Thessalonica had been undergoing trials for their faith. Troubles are always unwelcome and unexpected, so we can be sure they disliked the situation as much as we would today. Nevertheless, the apostle Paul commends them because he sees faith, love, perseverance, and purposeful living growing exponentially in them. He recognizes the work of God in their lives. Perhaps they did not see it that way, so his words encouraged them to press on. God knows ahead of time exactly how we will react to a stimulus, unlike psychology textbooks that can only give general guidelines and principles about human behavior.

In light of their situation, Paul tells the church members in Thessalonica that God is right and God is just, a new thought for new believers of a new religion that tells the unvarnished truth about human behavior.

OCTOBER 17

Adoptive Parents

And let the maiden which pleaseth the king be queen instead of Vashti.
And the thing pleased the king; and he did so ... So it came to pass,
when the king's commandment and his decree was heard, and when
many maidens were gathered together unto Shushan the palace, to the
custody of Hegai, that Esther was brought also unto the king's house, to
the custody of Hegai, keeper of the women. Esther had not shewed her
people nor her kindred: for Mordecai had charged her that she should
not shew it. And Mordecai walked every day before the court of the
women's house, to know how Esther did, and what should become of
her. Now when every maid's turn was come to go in to king Ahasuerus,
after that she had been twelve months, according to the manner of the
women, (for so were the days of their purifications accomplished, to
wit, six months with oil of myrrh, and six months with sweet odours,
and with other things for the purifying of the women;) ... And Esther
obtained favour in the sight of all them that looked upon her ... And
when the virgins were gathered together the second time, then
Mordecai sat in the king's gate. Esther had not yet shewed her kindred
nor her people; as Mordecai had charged her: for Esther did the
commandment of Mordecai, like as when she was brought up with him.
—Esther 2:4, 8, 10–12, 15b, 19–20

Children who grow up with adoptive parents often face a quandary about how
much to reveal to others about their true identity. The teenager Esther had
been adopted by her older cousin Mordecai when they lived as exiles, captives
in Persia. Mordecai had forbidden Esther to reveal her nationality or religion to
King Xerxes. He also made sure that a reliable eunuch was assigned to instruct
her in proper royal etiquette.

Mordecai worked in the upper echelons of palace administration, second only
to the king in prominence. He served God quietly in a place of overt idolatry. He
was highly respected by both Persians and Jews—for doing his job in an exemplary
way and for working quietly for the good of the Jews. He sounds like the soundest,
most reliable person anyone would want as a public official. At one point, Mordecai
learned of an assassination plot against the king; he reported it to Esther and she in
turn told the king, who was able to thwart it. Mordecai continued to give Esther the
good advice of a good parent even after she became part of the king's household.

Even though it is outside of our cultural context to imagine a king who
chooses a bride from a harem, the story reminds us how important parental
advice can be, that God ultimately rules over every wild situation, and that God
has a purpose, even in the most unimaginable of situations.

What Do You Want Most?

> And Solomon the son of David was strengthened in his kingdom,
> and the Lord his God was with him, and magnified him
> exceedingly … And Solomon said unto God, Thou hast shewed
> great mercy unto David my father, and hast made me to reign in his
> stead. Now, O Lord God, let thy promise unto David my father be
> established: for thou hast made me king over a people like the dust
> of the earth in multitude. Give me now wisdom and knowledge,
> that I may go out and come in before this people: for who can judge
> this thy people, that is so great? And God said to Solomon, Because
> this was in thine heart, and thou hast not asked riches, wealth, or
> honour, nor the life of thine enemies, neither yet hast asked long
> life; but hast asked wisdom and knowledge for thyself, that thou
> mayest judge my people, over whom I have made thee king: Wisdom
> and knowledge is granted unto thee; and I will give thee riches, and
> wealth, and honour, such as none of the kings have had that have
> been before thee, neither shall there any after thee have the like.
> —2 Chronicles 1:1, 8–12

When we are on the cusp of entering the adult world, the world seems to open up before us. We think about our future a lot, but we do not know which path we will walk. We must consider our abilities, interests, and circumstances. We must rely on God to take us through all the steps. We know God answers prayer, but which prayer will He be most likely to answer as we consider the lengthy list of our desires?

Long ago, Solomon was a young prince who became a king, not a profession in life that many of us will ever know. Solomon was also a young man on the brink of adult responsibilities. In addition to being very wealthy, he was of a genius mentality. He could have anything he wanted, mentally, physically, or spiritually. The world was his to choose. So what did Solomon request of God?

Solomon, the young man, asked God for wisdom and knowledge to do the job of his life. He thanked God for being kind to him. He recognized that his place in life came about by God's desire, not his or his father's. He humbled himself before the great God of heaven. God was pleased with his simple request and promised to also give him more than he could imagine. History tells us it really happened.

Submitting to God

For thus saith the Lord God, the Holy One of Israel; In returning and rest shall ye be saved; in quietness and in confidence shall be your strength: and ye would not … And therefore will the Lord wait, that he may be gracious unto you, and therefore will he be exalted, that he may have mercy upon you: for the Lord is a God of judgment: blessed are all they that wait for him. For the people shall dwell in Zion at Jerusalem: thou shalt weep no more: he will be very gracious unto thee at the voice of thy cry; when he shall hear it, he will answer thee. And though the Lord give you the bread of adversity, and the water of affliction, yet shall not thy teachers be removed into a corner any more, but thine eyes shall see thy teachers: And thine ears shall hear a word behind thee, saying, This is the way, walk ye in it, when ye turn to the right hand, and when ye turn to the left.
—Isaiah 30:15, 18–21

We face many turning points in life—these are the specific times when we must make a decision that will affect the years to come. We must make choices about which college to attend, which profession to enter, which job to accept, and which location to move to—these are momentous decisions. We want to be sure that we have chosen what is best for us.

But how do we really know what is God's best for us? When we face these decision points in life, we need to remember two things: God wants to be gracious to us, and God will definitely speak to us in a way we can understand. He is in charge of our lives, and He desires to guide us on His path. Difficulties and setbacks confuse us because we rarely see them as a way that God leads us, but in time, God will clear the pathway.

Sometimes, it will seem as if God is whispering in the ear. No one can confuse His voice with any other. God directs those who submit to Him. There is no mistake about it—His direction is both quiet and confident.

OCTOBER 20

Problems created by Others

O taste and see that the Lord is good: blessed is the man that trusteth
in him. The young lions do lack, and suffer hunger: but they that seek
the Lord shall not want any good thing. Come, ye children, hearken
unto me: I will teach you the fear of the Lord. What man is he that
desireth life, and loveth many days, that he may see good? Keep thy
tongue from evil, and thy lips from speaking guile. Depart from evil,
and do good; seek peace, and pursue it ... The Lord is nigh unto them
that are of a broken heart; and saveth such as be of a contrite spirit.
—Psalm 34:8, 10–14, 18

Moreover the light of the moon shall be as the light of the
sun, and the light of the sun shall be sevenfold, as the light
of seven days, in the day that the Lord bindeth up the breach
of his people, and healeth the stroke of their wound.
—Isaiah 30:26

Some of us have turned to the Lord even though we grew up in a family that
did not honor God. One of the delights of this new life is to find out how
good God is to believers. We cannot judge the home we come from, but we can
set new standards for the new home that we now make in the Lord.

If the godless home in which we were raised included lying, bad behavior,
or fighting, we may come out of it with a broken heart, a broken spirit, or even
broken bones. Let us remember that God has a special care for those who have
been crushed by others. What is more, God promises full restoration of all that
was lost to us (through the faults of others) when we take shelter in Him. The day
will come—we don't know when—that God will remove from us the wounds
and bruises inflicted upon us by others.

God takes full responsibility for these wounds and afflictions because He
is the only one capable of restoring us to ourselves—in His image—the way He
wanted us to be from the first.

Humility

And he came to Capernaum: and being in the house he asked
them, What was it that ye disputed among yourselves by the way?
But they held their peace: for by the way they had disputed among
themselves, who should be the greatest. And he sat down, and called
the twelve, and saith unto them, If any man desire to be first, the
same shall be last of all, and servant of all. And he took a child,
and set him in the midst of them: and when he had taken him in
his arms, he said unto them … And they brought young children
to him, that he should touch them: and his disciples rebuked those
that brought them. But when Jesus saw it, he was much displeased,
and said unto them, Suffer the little children to come unto me,
and forbid them not: for of such is the kingdom of God. Verily I
say unto you, Whosoever shall not receive the kingdom of God
as a little child, he shall not enter therein. And he took them
up in his arms, put his hands upon them, and blessed them.
—Mark 9:33–36; 10:13–16

The modern world is so oriented toward public figures, politicians, and
entertainers that the rest of us cannot escape the desire to make a name
for ourselves. The popularity of reality shows and the availability of media
for personal promotion indicate that the desire for fame and glory runs high.
Apparently, we all dream secretly of reveling in our five minutes of fame.

To live the Christian life, we must not just change our perspective just a little.
We must retrain our thinking and our outlook entirely. Jesus Christ tells us that
those who are last will be first in His world. He cites children as an example of
humility. They are small, the least accountable members of any family because
they do not know a lot. Their parents take care of them. They know they are little,
not big. Jesus Christ wants us, even as adults, to keep this same mind-set toward
God. We don't know much, we are small and insignificant compared to Him.

God loves us and takes care of us. This should be enough. Let us forget
about fame and humbly accept what God has in store for us.

The High and Holy Way

And an highway shall be there, and a way, and it shall be called
The way of holiness; the unclean shall not pass over it; but it
shall be for those: the wayfaring men, though fools, shall not err
therein. No lion shall be there, nor any ravenous beast shall go up
thereon, it shall not be found there; but the redeemed shall walk
there: And the ransomed of the Lord shall return, and come to
Zion with songs and everlasting joy upon their heads: they shall
obtain joy and gladness, and sorrow and sighing shall flee away.
—Isaiah 35:8–10

Some of us have climbed steep rocky mountain trails to the summits. We feel exhilarated from the deep breaths we take as we ascend. Some of us have hiked on trails through the salt marsh to the ocean, and the whiff of salt air invigorates us to notice every natural detail. Some of us have walked through a park to an old battlefield, and we add to our personal knowledge of historical details. Some of us have sunk in the sand of sand dune pathways as we trek down to the shore. Our tension gives way to enjoyment as the seeming quicksand gives way beneath our feet. Some of us prefer the more civilized stroll through a public garden. The orderly organization and meticulous detail make us appreciate hard work and consistent effort.

We love walking because it gives us a sense of progress as we experience both the beginning and the end of the journey. We might benefit by transferring our love of hiking to our love of God and applying it to how we walk through this life.

The Bible tells us that the highway of holiness will be the final trail we hike. All other trails in life have led us to it. God's road is the only safe way to travel. No dangers are on it, so we travel in complete safety. We will sing with joy when we hike that highway. When we hike our favorite trails, let's keep in mind that the best trail is still before us.

OCTOBER 23

Salvation

And it shall come to pass, that whosoever shall call on the name of the Lord shall be saved. Ye men of Israel, hear these words; Jesus of Nazareth, a man approved of God among you by miracles and wonders and signs, which God did by him in the midst of you, as ye yourselves also know: Him, being delivered by the determinate counsel and foreknowledge of God, ye have taken, and by wicked hands have crucified and slain: Whom God hath raised up, having loosed the pains of death: because it was not possible that he should be holden of it … Therefore let all the house of Israel know assuredly, that God hath made the same Jesus, whom ye have crucified, both Lord and Christ. Now when they heard this, they were pricked in their heart, and said unto Peter and to the rest of the apostles, Men and brethren, what shall we do? Then Peter said unto them, Repent, and be baptized every one of you in the name of Jesus Christ for the remission of sins, and ye shall receive the gift of the Holy Ghost. For the promise is unto you, and to your children, and to all that are afar off, even as many as the Lord our God shall call.
—Acts 2:21–24, 36–39

It may sound exciting to some of us to have lived in the time of Jesus, but considering the uncertain political situation of those times, we may like to change our minds. The fledgling church knew the time was exciting because Jesus had been crucified, and He came to life again. Such news could not remain unknown. Then, five hundred of them saw Jesus ascend up to heaven. Such spectacular news could not be kept from others.

Their excitement came from the truth of the message, not from a nostalgic desire to live in old-fashioned times. Then, as now, the truth of the resurrection demands a response from individuals.

What will any of us do with Jesus Christ? We should repent of our sins and get baptized for the forgiveness of sins. When we make the decision, God the Holy Spirit gives us a gift—whatever gift God wants us to have. God calls all humans to Himself. His promise of salvation is true for all of us.

297

Brilliant Light

And God saw the light, that it was good: and
God divided the light from the darkness.
—Genesis 1:4

The Lord is my light and my salvation; whom shall I fear? the
Lord is the strength of my life; of whom shall I be afraid?
—Psalm 27:1

In him was life; and the life was the light of men. And the light
shineth in darkness; and the darkness comprehended it not.
—John 1:4–5

Wherefore he saith, Awake thou that sleepest, and arise
from the dead, and Christ shall give thee light.
—Ephesians 5:14

For God, who commanded the light to shine out of
darkness, hath shined in our hearts, to give the light of the
knowledge of the glory of God in the face of Jesus Christ.
—2 Corinthians 4:6

It is unusual to find a person who prefers darkness to light. When we work in artificially lighted environments, underground in the basement of the building, or deep in the mines of the earth, we love to exit into the natural daylight and feel its sunny warmth.

Daylight can change our mood from one of gloom, like our environment, to one of cheerfulness, like the sun. After God created light, He declared it good, and we still agree with God today. We want to live in homes with a lot of natural light so we can feel a connection to the outdoors and the goodness of the light. Daylight also teaches us about the character of God and how He conducts Himself toward us. The world God created is beautiful, and light allows us to admire the handiwork of the Creator. We can praise Him for any reason.

The guidance God gives us is as clear as the sunlight. Just as the light allows us to see our way without stumbling, the Word of God informs our understanding. Let us turn to the God of light for everything.

God the Warrior

For we wrestle not against flesh and blood, but against
principalities, against powers, against the rulers of the darkness
of this world, against spiritual wickedness in high places.
—Ephesians 6:12

Plead my cause, O Lord, with them that strive with
me: fight against them that fight against me.
—Psalm 35:1

Fight the good fight of faith, lay hold on eternal life,
whereunto thou art also called, and hast professed
a good profession before many witnesses.
—1 Timothy 6:12

When our nation is engaged in a war, we are probably acquainted with soldiers who serve our country. They fight for us: to maintain the freedom we take for granted, to ensure peace where none exists, and to halt the spread of evil with deadly force when necessary. We appreciate the tasks they accomplish although they remain unseen on the home front.

We might want to remember that the Bible characterizes our lives as spiritual battlegrounds between the unseen forces of good and evil. It is good to know that our God is a warrior who fights for us. The weapons of spiritual warfare are not the same as modern day munitions; they are spiritually perceived, not physically seen. When we obey God, He takes our obedience to His credit, and God fights for us through the word that we live by.

The good fight of faith that we fight is the power of God in us who live a godly life. God gives us the stamina to endure and persevere when we remain determined to maintain a godly life.

Poverty

And he looked up, and saw the rich men casting their gifts into
the treasury. And he saw also a certain poor widow casting in
thither two mites. And he said, Of a truth I say unto you, that
this poor widow hath cast in more than they all: For all these
have of their abundance cast in unto the offerings of God: but
she of her penury hath cast in all the living that she had.
—Luke 21:1–4

If we watch a lot of media, it appears to us that most people are wealthy or at
least well to do. At the very least, they are certainly better off economically
than those of us who spend our hard-earned cash to watch them on the screen.
The false images that we mistake for reality make all of us wish we had more
disposable cash because we think cash will help us out—it won't.

We need to remember the difference between appearances and reality. The
hard truth is that most people are not very well off financially. In fact, plenty of
people have just enough money to get by. To keep the more realistic perspective
in mind, Jesus relates a story about a woman who really was dirt poor and severely
deprived economically. Her example tells us about the reality of poverty (instead
of the appearance of riches). Let us think about this widow. She had some meager
employment. If poverty marks our lives, we can still behave with integrity by
working hard. She had an attitude of giving, which means she was content with
her ability and place in life. She was happy to do what she was able to do. We
do not need to spend more time wishing for what cannot happen. She kept her
personal desires to the bare minimum in order to have an active spiritual life.

We do not need to clutter our lives with junk just because we are poor. Her
life reminds us that true poverty or true riches are spiritual, not physical.

Living Sacrifices

I beseech you therefore, brethren, by the mercies of God, that ye present your bodies a living sacrifice, holy, acceptable unto God, which is your reasonable service. And be not conformed to this world: but be ye transformed by the renewing of your mind, that ye may prove what is that good, and acceptable, and perfect, will of God. For I say, through the grace given unto me, to every man that is among you, not to think of himself more highly than he ought to think; but to think soberly, according as God hath dealt to every man the measure of faith. For as we have many members in one body, and all members have not the same office: So we, being many, are one body in Christ, and every one members one of another. Having then gifts differing according to the grace that is given to us, whether prophecy, let us prophesy according to the proportion of faith.
—Romans 12:1–6

Once we are saved, some of us wonder whether we should abandon secular professional goals for more spiritually related occupations. Sometimes this occurs, sometimes not. God leads each person individually, and He is more concerned with the spiritual condition of our minds and souls than He is with our personal interests.

Whatever choice we make, or if no choice is made, God wants us to offer ourselves to Himself unreservedly—body, mind, and soul. He captured our souls when He saved us; now He wants the rest of us. When we remember that God gave us both physical life and spiritual life, we know that this is the right decision. God takes our desires, our skills, our interests, and He transforms them into useable gifts for the kingdom of God. Maybe we will enter a Christian vocation, maybe not. But we can still glorify God in our lives by submitting all we think, all we are, and all we have to Him.

The living sacrifice of ourselves to God pleases Him and keeps us on the road of holy living—whatever we do, wherever we go. The life of God in us is more exciting than our paltry plans anyway.

Avoid Immorality

All things are lawful unto me, but all things are not expedient: all
things are lawful for me, but I will not be brought under the power
of any. Meats for the belly, and the belly for meats: but God shall
destroy both it and them. Now the body is not for fornication, but
for the Lord; and the Lord for the body ... Know ye not that your
bodies are the members of Christ? shall I then take the members
of Christ, and make them the members of an harlot? God forbid.
What? know ye not that he which is joined to an harlot is one body?
for two, saith he, shall be one flesh. But he that is joined unto the
Lord is one spirit. Flee fornication. Every sin that a man doeth
is without the body; but he that committeth fornication sinneth
against his own body. What? know ye not that your body is the
temple of the Holy Ghost which is in you, which ye have of God,
and ye are not your own? For ye are bought with a price: therefore
glorify God in your body, and in your spirit, which are God's.
1 Corinthians 6:12–13, 15–20

Since the decade of the 1960s, the free love movement has swayed countless
numbers to have sex before marriage, commit adultery after marriage, or
fornicate and never get married in the first place. Call it prostitution, call it having
a relationship, call it being together—whatever we call it, sexual immorality is a
sin in God's sight.

Think about what has happened in our society since the 1960s. Many adults
have had numerous sexual relationships and multiple marriages. About half of
the younger and middle-aged generations have never known morality or stability
within a two-parent family structure. About four dozen sexually transmitted
diseases now afflict many sexual sinners, and AIDS is only at the top of that list.
Let's get real and admit that we live only one life in one body—a body that God
has lent to us for the brief span of one life! We cannot trade in the used model
for a newer version.

God created the human body to function one way best, no matter what
aspect of human behavior is under consideration. We should never give in to
sexual immorality of any kind because God has better plans for us, for our
bodies, and for our lives.

OCTOBER 29

The Foundation of Faith

In the Lord put I my trust: how say ye to my soul, Flee as a bird
to your mountain? For, lo, the wicked bend their bow, they make
ready their arrow upon the string, that they may privily shoot
at the upright in heart. If the foundations be destroyed, what
can the righteous do? The Lord is in his holy temple, the Lord's
throne is in heaven: his eyes behold, his eyelids try, the children
of men. The Lord trieth the righteous: but the wicked and him
that loveth violence his soul hateth. Upon the wicked he shall
rain snares, fire and brimstone, and an horrible tempest: this
shall be the portion of their cup. For the righteous Lord loveth
righteousness; his countenance doth behold the upright.
—Psalm 11:1–7

Some of us have faced severe trials in our short lives, even before we entered
the college world. Extended illnesses, severe financial reversals, family break-
ups, unemployment, or homelessness rank among the most stressful of personal
challenges a youngster can face. Enormous difficulties can make us feel that
others are shooting arrows at us just as snipers hide to ambush innocent people.

The young man David, even though anointed as king, spent more than a
decade fleeing his enemies, notably King Saul and anyone Saul sent after David.
He knew the kind of trouble that comes from sources and people outside of
himself. He also knew the Savior as the one who could save him on the inside,
spiritually and physically. Because he knew that God was righteous and just,
David knew that he could trust Him in every situation. He did what anyone can
do when faith is assailed. He continued to trust the Lord of heaven.

The same Lord who protected the young David centuries ago is the same
God who protects us who flee to Him for refuge today. Whatever challenges we
have faced or will face, God is on our side.

OCTOBER 30

God Is Light

This then is the message which we have heard of him, and declare
unto you, that God is light, and in him is no darkness at all. If
we say that we have fellowship with him, and walk in darkness,
we lie, and do not the truth: But if we walk in the light, as he is
in the light, we have fellowship one with another, and the blood
of Jesus Christ his Son cleanseth us from all sin … He that saith
he is in the light, and hateth his brother, is in darkness even until
now. He that loveth his brother abideth in the light, and there
is none occasion of stumbling in him. But he that hateth his
brother is in darkness, and walketh in darkness, and knoweth not
whither he goeth, because that darkness hath blinded his eyes.
—1 John 1:5–7; 2:9–11

We may enjoy traipsing around the neighborhood or the dormitories at night
with a flashlight on Halloween night. We may know the way perfectly in
daylight, but the path is obscure and scary in the dark. For one night, it is fun
to see the same place in a different light—the outlandish costumes, the spooky
decorations, the dimly colored lights. It satisfies the human desire for excitement.
In spite of the momentary high of one night, no one really wants to walk through
life in the dark.

Guidance for every day and every night is greatly appreciated by everyone.
As believers, we have turned to the source of light—the Son of God. Saying that
God is light involves more than just physical and impermanent brightness. The
belief that God is light involves fellowship with God and others, forgiveness of
sins, purification by the blood of Christ, love for others, and telling the truth.
John was trying to convey the both enormity and the attractiveness of the
concept that God is light.

Saying true words is not the same as mouthing empty words. True words
have a present reality in our lives today. Scripture always wants us to apply what
we know so that we may experience the reality of truth, not the philosophy of
truth, in our lives.

The Visibility of Light

No man, when he hath lighted a candle, putteth it in a secret place,
neither under a bushel, but on a candlestick, that they which come
in may see the light. The light of the body is the eye: therefore when
thine eye is single, thy whole body also is full of light; but when thine
eye is evil, thy body also is full of darkness. Take heed therefore
that the light which is in thee be not darkness. If thy whole body
therefore be full of light, having no part dark, the whole shall be full
of light, as when the bright shining of a candle doth give thee light.
—Luke 11:33–36

Ye are the light of the world. A city that is set on an hill cannot
be hid. Neither do men light a candle, and put it under a bushel,
but on a candlestick; and it giveth light unto all that are in the
house. Let your light so shine before men, that they may see
your good works, and glorify your Father which is in heaven.
—Matthew 5:14–16

Do we ever wonder whether our lives shine out and reveal our identity in
Christ? Jesus assures us that the visibility of His light is indeed shining
through us, and the light is clearly seen by others.

Sometimes, the task of a believer is only to shine, not to talk, not to do
anything at all. Not always, but sometimes. The Word of God compares the
visibility of our lives to the visibility of a sprawling city. Have we ever driven in
a hilly part of the country? The view is spectacular!—and the view cannot be
hidden! We drive on the roads that run fairly straight—straight into the hills!
This is the best way to see the folded grayish green hues of the hills rising up in
front of us. When the road takes us into a city set on a hill, we become very aware
that we drive on flatter land at first and slowly rise up to meet the elevations of
the city streets.

We know we can meet the challenge (even if it is car that puts out the effort).
Following the right road with a little bit of light is enough to reveal the way to
the place where we want to go.

NOVEMBER 1

The Good Shepherd

The Lord is my shepherd; I shall not want. He maketh me to lie down in green pastures: he leadeth me beside the still waters. He restoreth my soul: he leadeth me in the paths of righteousness for his name's sake. Yea, though I walk through the valley of the shadow of death, I will fear no evil: for thou art with me; thy rod and thy staff they comfort me. Thou preparest a table before me in the presence of mine enemies: thou anointest my head with oil; my cup runneth over. Surely goodness and mercy shall follow me all the days of my life: and I will dwell in the house of the Lord for ever.
—Psalm 23:1–6

We are very familiar with the image of Jesus as the good shepherd who provides all needs for the sheep. But, do we just mouth the beautiful words, or do we try to figure out how they might apply to modern life today? Do we think that this shepherd provides for our needs and wants by giving us rest when needed? Or, do we rush about our business heedlessly?

When we let the good shepherd run our lives, we exhibit a calmness and serenity of presence that soothes us as we perform our duties. Others notice the difference too, so the blessing extends to those around us as well. Do we recognize the restorative properties of quiet-running waters? Or, do we maintain a frenzied pace? When we take time off from the daily routine and engage in completely different types of activities, we recharge ourselves when we return, equipping ourselves for more efficient effort. Do we turn to God in the dark times of life? Or, do we angrily reject Him when we need Him most? This is the time when we most need Him, so we should not spurn His offer to help us. Those closes to us may sympathize with the hard times we experience, but they also watch us to see how we will react to adverse circumstances. Do we see the rod and staff as instruments of correction or as catalysts for guidance? God does not always punish us, but He certainly directs us by shifting us from our direction to the one of His choosing. Do we understand that God makes us appear successful in front of our enemies, even when we feel like complete failures? Or, do we cower before them in mortification?

We should never overlook the power of the presence of God in the life of one individual. God causes others to perceive obedient believers as productive in spite of personal emotions. Do we see goodness and love flowing from the heart of God as easily as oil pouring out of a bottle? The overflow of God's love in our lives to others enables us to witness the beauty of holiness and godliness.

True Happiness

Blessed is the man that walketh not in the counsel of the ungodly,
nor standeth in the way of sinners, nor sitteth in the seat of the
scornful. But his delight is in the law of the Lord; and in his law doth
he meditate day and night. And he shall be like a tree planted by the
rivers of water, that bringeth forth his fruit in his season; his leaf
also shall not wither; and whatsoever he doeth shall prosper. The
ungodly are not so: but are like the chaff which the wind driveth
away. Therefore the ungodly shall not stand in the judgment, nor
sinners in the congregation of the righteous. For the Lord knoweth
the way of the righteous: but the way of the ungodly shall perish.
—Psalm 1:1–6

Where does happiness come from? Happiness is the blessedness that the
Bible mentions frequently. Our culture tells us that happiness is whatever
we make it to be, as if any good thing, any bad thing, any stupid thing, any fun
thing, any crazy thing, or anything at all possesses the ability to confer happiness
upon us.

But the Bible, the living truth, tells us otherwise. We learn from the Bible
that happiness is rooted in goodness, and goodness comes only from God. When
we deliberately avoid listening to the counsel of the wicked, the avoidance of
ungodly advice opens our minds and souls to God's true and happy way. When
we refuse to stand in the way of sinners, we deliberately choose to turn from the
contemplation of evil, perhaps bad movies or television shows, perhaps from
unhealthy friends. When we refuse to sit in the seat of scornful mockers, we
deliberately avoid hanging out with those whose values ridicule the Lord.

Remember that God will blow away everything else to achieve our happiness
in Him while He watches carefully over those who look to Him for what He
alone can give.

The Weedier Side of Life

> Another parable put he forth unto them, saying, The kingdom of
> heaven is likened unto a man which sowed good seed in his field:
> But while men slept, his enemy came and sowed tares among the
> wheat, and went his way. But when the blade was sprung up, and
> brought forth fruit, then appeared the tares also. So the servants
> of the householder came and said unto him, Sir, didst not thou sow
> good seed in thy field? from whence then hath it tares? He said unto
> them, An enemy hath done this. The servants said unto him, Wilt
> thou then that we go and gather them up? But he said, Nay; lest while
> ye gather up the tares, ye root up also the wheat with them. Let both
> grow together until the harvest: and in the time of harvest I will say
> to the reapers, Gather ye together first the tares, and bind them in
> bundles to burn them: but gather the wheat into my barn. Another
> parable put he forth unto them, saying, The kingdom of heaven is like
> to a grain of mustard seed, which a man took, and sowed in his field.
> —Matthew 13:24–31

While we are thinking about what to do for the rest of our lives, we may imagine ourselves working at a wonderful job and entering upon a fulfilling career. But the reality can sometimes fall short of the rosy vision in our heads. What a headache—why do we have to work with such unpleasant and difficult people? Wouldn't life be easier if we all thought the same, behaved the same, and got along? Perhaps, but this is so unrealistic that we know it will never happen.

God has a purpose for the weedier aspects of life. Think about how informal learning occurs. We observe others and try to analyze them as much as they do the same to us. Sometimes, God answers questions about the past through the behavior of people in the present. Sometimes, God uses others to bring about an awareness of our own habits. Sometimes, God introduces new ideas to us through the knowledge of others.

God lets nothing go unnoticed in our lives, even the weeds that grow alongside the plants. His purpose prevails for everyone.

NOVEMBER 4

Single-Mindedness

And he said unto another, Follow me. But he said, Lord, suffer
me first to go and bury my father. Jesus said unto him, Let the
dead bury their dead: but go thou and preach the kingdom of
God. And another also said, Lord, I will follow thee; but let
me first go bid them farewell, which are at home at my house.
And Jesus said unto him, No man, having put his hand to the
plough, and looking back, is fit for the kingdom of God.
—Luke 9:59–62

When we consider all the good deeds we would like to accomplish for others
and for ourselves in this life, we write up a mental list and check off the
tasks in our minds as we go along. We automatically classify the tasks from most
important to least important. We may never get around to the least important
tasks, but that is all right—in our minds anyway.

Most people feel confident that the personal list of self-imposed hierarchical
tasks is a beneficial and accurate way to live an orderly life. But, Jesus thinks
that the purpose of this life is more spiritual than temporal. When we consider
the spiritual, the academic, and the professional worlds we inhabit, we realize
that they share similar qualities. All the parts of our lives require us to follow
someone who knows more than we do. All require our undivided attention and
effort along with a willingness to let other areas of life (even though they seem
critical) slide down the scale of importance. Those who begin one way and later
change their minds lose the benefits of persistence and discipline so necessary
for accomplishment.

It is never a good idea to let the spiritual side of life slide away from us. Jesus
understood how important it is to choose Him now because the decision may
never come to us again.

NOVEMBER 5

Familiarity Breeds Contempt

> Blessed are the poor in spirit: for theirs is the kingdom of
> heaven. Blessed are they that mourn: for they shall be comforted.
> Blessed are the meek: for they shall inherit the earth. Blessed
> are they which do hunger and thirst after righteousness: for
> they shall be filled. Blessed are the merciful: for they shall
> obtain mercy. Blessed are the pure in heart: for they shall see
> God. Blessed are the peacemakers: for they shall be called the
> children of God. Blessed are they which are persecuted for
> righteousness' sake: for theirs is the kingdom of heaven.
> —Matthew 5:3–10

Familiar passages can become sort of singsong in the head and lose their meaning, so we need a way to think about them differently. One way to trick our brains into a more meaningful understanding is to turn statements into questions and ponder the difference. When we consider the blessed passages, we might ask ourselves the following questions:

- Do we understand how spiritually impoverished we are—even as honest believers? No one is perfect except the Savior Jesus Christ.
- Are we proud of ourselves as believers? Or, do we mourn the lack of spiritual depth in our lives?
- Do we accept humbly whatever God gives us?
- Do we yearn for the holiness that seems just out of reach? Do we draw closer to Jesus Christ?
- Are we able and willing to do good deeds toward others? This is a sign that we have understood God's mercy to ourselves and wish to extend it to others.
- Do we keep our minds, hearts, and souls clean? No one can understand God otherwise.
- Do we refrain from anger or creating disputes? This shows a godly character in action.
- Do others treat us badly because they know we are believers?

Only those who share the likeness of the Savior enter the kingdom of heaven. Do we truly desire to get there?

For God Alone

Therefore say unto the house of Israel, thus saith the Lord God;
I do not this for your sakes, O house of Israel, but for mine holy
name's sake, which ye have profaned among the heathen, whither
ye went. And I will sanctify my great name, which was profaned
among the heathen, which ye have profaned in the midst of them;
and the heathen shall know that I am the Lord, saith the Lord God,
when I shall be sanctified in you before their eyes. For I will take
you from among the heathen, and gather you out of all countries,
and will bring you into your own land. Then will I sprinkle clean
water upon you, and ye shall be clean: From all your filthiness, and
from all your idols, will I cleanse you. A new heart also will I give
you, and a new spirit will I put within you: and I will take away
the stony heart out of your flesh, and I will give you an heart of
flesh. And I will put my spirit within you, and cause you to walk in
my statutes, and ye shall keep my judgments, and do them … Not
for your sakes do I this, saith the Lord God, be it known unto you:
be ashamed and confounded for your own ways, O house of Israel.
—Ezekiel 36:22–27, 32

God is good to all His creatures. When life is going well, we take His goodness for granted. When times are rough, we look for God to deliver us from the problems. Whether or not our present difficulties are a direct result of our own behavior or choice is not the point. We always know that the sinful nature wreaks havoc in lives, and only God can save sinners.

God promises to remove us from the persuasive allurement of sin and cleanse us from all harm. He promises to give us new hearts and spirits so that we may love Him and obey Him. God softens us to obey Him. God prospers us where He places us.

All the while we are thinking that God does this for us, He reminds us bluntly that He does not do it for our sakes, but He does it to glorify Himself and to express the holiness of His great name—what a humbling motivation to put God first in life.

Freedom or Bondage?

Stand fast therefore in the liberty wherewith Christ hath made
us free, and be not entangled again with the yoke of bondage ...
For in Jesus Christ neither circumcision availeth any thing, nor
uncircumcision; but faith which worketh by love ... For, brethren,
ye have been called unto liberty; only use not liberty for an occasion
to the flesh, but by love serve one another. For all the law is fulfilled
in one word, even in this; Thou shalt love thy neighbour as thyself.
—Galatians 5:1, 6, 13–14

We live in a society that endorses sexual promiscuity as freedom instead
of the bondage that it actually is. The free love movement of the 1960s
promulgated this idea, but we now know that the bad idea has degenerated into
broken homes and every form of illicit sexual relationships.

When we read that Christ has set us free for freedom's sake, we may easily
confuse freedom with licentiousness. Paul makes himself clear when he reminds
us not to use freedom (meaning licentiousness) as an excuse to indulge in the
worst, most provocative, blatantly sinful behaviors. Love is not the same as
promiscuity. Licentiousness serves the needs and desires of the self. Love serves
the needs and desires of others. Instead of taking advantage of someone where
he is most vulnerable, we should show love and respect toward others. False
love destroys. If we come from a home where love has been confused with
licentiousness, we may already know about the type of destruction that Paul
mentions. When we avoid it at all costs, we also avoid the consequences of such
licentious living.

Our adult lives can be happier and more productive than the lives of our
relatives because the consequences cannot follow us any farther when we leave
all sinful behavior and practices behind—where they belong.

Powerhouse

Wherefore I put thee in remembrance that thou stir up the gift
of God, which is in thee by the putting on of my hands. For God
hath not given us the spirit of fear; but of power, and of love, and
of a sound mind. Be not thou therefore ashamed of the testimony
of our Lord, nor of me his prisoner: but be thou partaker of the
afflictions of the gospel according to the power of God; Who
hath saved us, and called us with an holy calling, not according
to our works, but according to his own purpose and grace,
which was given us in Christ Jesus before the world began.
—2 Timothy 1:6–9

Many television shows and movies portray powerful people using their physical power and prowess in astonishing ways. We know that stunt doubles perform staged scenes of powerful feats; nevertheless, these situations appeal to viewers because we all want to be more powerful than we currently are.

Would it surprise us to learn that God wants us to be powerful too? And since He made us, He knows how we can be more powerful. Through the Holy Spirit, God makes us powerful, but the power of the Holy Spirit is not entirely physical. It is at once spiritual, mental, emotional, and psychological. This type of power is more powerful than any television show or movie can portray and so much more than the human mind can imagine. The love that comes from God, the self-control that expresses our gifts appropriately, the good purposes of God, the grace we do not deserve—all of this power was given to us, in Christ Jesus—from before the beginning of time!

Television and movies may express the right generic idea, but don't let them get us off track by looking for power where it cannot be found.

Worship Idols or Worship Truth?

Nebuchadnezzar the king made an image of gold, whose height was
threescore cubits, and the breadth thereof six cubits: he set it up in the
plain of Dura, in the province of Babylon ... And whoso falleth not
down and worshippeth shall the same hour be cast into the midst of
a burning fiery furnace ... There are certain Jews whom thou hast set
over the affairs of the province of Babylon, Shadrach, Meshach, and
Abednego; these men, O king, have not regarded thee: they serve not
thy gods, nor worship the golden image which thou hast set up. Then
Nebuchadnezzar in his rage and fury commanded to bring Shadrach,
Meshach, and Abednego. Then they brought these men before the
king ... Shadrach, Meshach, and Abednego, answered and said to the
king, O Nebuchadnezzar, we are not careful to answer thee in this
matter. If it be so, our God whom we serve is able to deliver us from
the burning fiery furnace, and he will deliver us out of thine hand,
O king. But if not, be it known unto thee, O king, that we will not
serve thy gods, nor worship the golden image which thou hast set
up ... Therefore because the king's commandment was urgent, and the
furnace exceeding hot, the flames of the fire slew those men that took
up Shadrach, Meshach, and Abednego ... Then Nebuchadnezzar the
king was astonished, and rose up in haste, and spake, and said unto his
counsellors, Did not we cast three men bound into the midst of the
fire? They answered and said unto the king, True, O king. He answered
and said, Lo, I see four men loose, walking in the midst of the fire, and
they have no hurt; and the form of the fourth is like the Son of God.
—Daniel 3:1, 6, 12–13, 16–18, 22, 24–25

King Nebuchadnezzar shows us the extent of the vanity of those who worship
idols. The result of idolatry was that He transferred his idolatry of gods to
idolatry of himself. When people worship idols, they assume they are better than
others. They never consider how offensive they really appear to others.

Because Nebuchadnezzar was the king, he assumed no one would contradict
his edict to worship the statue of himself. Not only was he surprised, he was
furious at the three high-ranking Hebrews (who were actually aliens under his
reign). The vanity of Nebuchadnezzar made him think he was in charge of the
lives of the three friends, but he was not! Only God is in charge of human life,
and even kings need to know this indisputable fact.

Daniel and his friends show us an example of true worship. When God-
fearing people choose to obey God at all costs, God is with them. When we
undergo fiery trials, we should look for the One who walks with us, unbound
and unharmed, "like the Son of the God." He is Jesus Christ, the Son of God.

Happiness

Now to him that worketh is the reward not reckoned of grace, but
of debt. But to him that worketh not, but believeth on him that
justifieth the ungodly, his faith is counted for righteousness. Even
as David also describeth the blessedness of the man, unto whom
God imputeth righteousness without works, Saying, Blessed are
they whose iniquities are forgiven, and whose sins are covered.
Blessed is the man to whom the Lord will not impute sin.
—Romans 4:4–8

We all try very hard to accomplish the goals we set for ourselves, both
personal and professional. The achievement of the goal represents the
fulfillment of hard-earned effort—a source of happiness—and we know we
deserve it. This is the debt about which Paul speaks. To get happiness in life, we
persevere to the end we want to achieve. When we get there, we can rest on our
laurels briefly, but we soon set more goals and begin working again to achieve
more. Climbing the ladder of success to achieve happiness never ends.

Spiritual living is different from everyday living because the rules are
different. To get happiness in spiritual life, we exert no effort at all. We understand
that we are sinners who have ruined every chance for advancement that we may
like to achieve. The only way to overcome the spiritual deficit is to give our
bodily selves, not our deeds, to the Lord. We trust God to forgive our sins, and
He makes us happy. His happiness satisfies us now and forever; the gifts of God
are not temporal.

Not only does God forgive us, He never counts our sins against us. Our
mistakes, sins, and errors do not count! God's kind of happiness brings freedom
and joy to live in the best way possible.

Prevent Unnecessary Problems

Having your conversation honest among the Gentiles: that, whereas
they speak against you as evildoers, they may by your good works,
which they shall behold, glorify God in the day of visitation ...
Honour all men. Love the brotherhood. Fear God. Honour the
king. Finally, be ye all of one mind, having compassion one of
another, love as brethren, be pitiful, be courteous: Not rendering
evil for evil, or railing for railing: but contrariwise blessing;
knowing that ye are thereunto called, that ye should inherit a
blessing. And who is he that will harm you, if ye be followers of
that which is good? ... But sanctify the Lord God in your hearts:
and be ready always to give an answer to every man that asketh
you a reason of the hope that is in you with meekness and fear.
—1 Peter 2:12, 17; 3:8–9, 13, 15

We enter college with high excitement, but as soon as the semester gets
underway, we realize that we must put up with many aspects of daily life
that we normally prefer to avoid. The college years throw complete strangers
into close daily contact with one another. No one could imagine, before moving
into the dormitory, how different others could be—and we do not mean this in
a good way. Dormitory living is one aspect of college living that motivates us to
get through college as fast as we can.

Even in this new environment, Christian behavior still means certain things.
Roommates, dorm mates, and classmates should be able to identify us as a
Christian by our behavior, so we should not behave in the way that dishonors
our Lord.

To live harmoniously with others, we can sympathize with them, be kind to
them, respect them, and do good toward them. In this way, we will pass on the
blessing that God has already given us. God may then open up an opportunity
to explain the way of salvation to someone else who still seeks Him.

Complaining

And they first took their journey according to the commandment of the Lord by the hand of Moses ... And when the people complained, it displeased the Lord: and the Lord heard it; and his anger was kindled; and the fire of the Lord burnt among them, and consumed them that were in the uttermost parts of the camp. And the people cried unto Moses; and when Moses prayed unto the Lord, the fire was quenched ... And the mixt multitude that was among them fell a lusting: and the children of Israel also wept again, and said, Who shall give us flesh to eat? We remember the fish, which we did eat in Egypt freely; the cucumbers, and the melons, and the leeks, and the onions, and the garlick: But now our soul is dried away: there is nothing at all, beside this manna, before our eyes. And the manna was as coriander seed, and the colour thereof as the colour of bdellium ... And there went forth a wind from the Lord, and brought quails from the sea, and let them fall by the camp, as it were a day's journey on this side, and as it were a day's journey on the other side, round about the camp, and as it were two cubits high upon the face of the earth. And the people stood up all that day, and all that night, and all the next day, and they gathered the quails: he that gathered least gathered ten homers: and they spread them all abroad for themselves round about the camp. And while the flesh was yet between their teeth, ere it was chewed, the wrath of the Lord was kindled against the people, and the Lord smote the people with a very great plague.
—Numbers 10:13; 11:1–2, 4–7, 31–33

Everyone creates a mental picture of how a situation should be. The Israelites imagined an easy moving trip, like a vacation occurring between one home and another home, at some distance away. When they found themselves in the desert, they didn't realize how long and arduous the trip in between homes would be. So they complained to God.

Continual complaints are a wrong response to the God who cares for us because we have access to the Father through Jesus Christ. We can pray and ask God for help in difficulties instead of moaning about them. It is easy to "see" from a vantage point thousands of years later that Israel was wrong to complain, but do we understand that we behave exactly the same way ourselves today? Israel had seen miraculous deliverances—out of Egypt—taking great wealth with them—safely crossing the Red Sea—guidance from the pillar of cloud by day and the pillar of fire by night. How could they dare to complain after experiencing such spectacular deliverances? They were human, and they were still sinners; so are we.

The circumstances God gives us in life may be the visible pillars of guidance. They may be unexpected, but we can trust God in them anyway. Ask for help for what is difficult and incomprehensible. Don't give in to complaining.

What Does Your Life Reveal about You?

And Naomi said unto her two daughters in law, Go, return each
to her mother's house: the Lord deal kindly with you, as ye have
dealt with the dead, and with me. The Lord grant you that ye
may find rest, each of you in the house of her husband. Then she
kissed them; and they lifted up their voice, and wept. And they
said unto her, Surely we will return with thee unto thy people.
And Naomi said, Turn again, my daughters: why will ye go with
me? are there yet any more sons in my womb, that they may be
your husbands? Turn again, my daughters, go your way; for I
am too old to have an husband. If I should say, I have hope, if I
should have an husband also to night, and should also bear sons.
—Ruth 1:8–12

Ruth belonged to the nation of Moabites. She was descended from Lot, the
nephew of Abraham—this sounds like a believing family. But, she belonged
to the despised union of Lot and one of his daughters—a lineage begun by an
incestuous relationship. She was still Jewish but definitely born on the wrong
side of the blanket. Her lineage made her reception very uncertain in the region
of Judea where she moved with her mother-in-law Naomi.

Naomi also had to deal with the sting of widowhood and the deaths of both
her sons before any grandsons were born. She and Naomi were humble enough
to know they could not presume upon the kindness and goodwill of others
in mainstream society. The people of Bethlehem watched them very closely.
Boaz, a distant relation and an eligible suitor, was favorably impressed by Ruth.
Her demeanor, behavior, and character revealed her inner self. He understood
godliness as a way of faith that sees God's blessings, even amid difficult personal
circumstances. He understood the sting of public censure toward improper
people. His mother was Rahab, the former prostitute, whom God had saved with
His people, when the city of Jericho fell.

Ruth reminds us to behave in the way that pleases God and trust God to
make our lives right before others. The Old Testament teaches us that faith is
what pleases God, not lineage or family name. God looks upon the heart and
blesses those who choose Him above all else.

Truth and Love

Grace be with you, mercy, and peace, from God the Father, and
from the Lord Jesus Christ, the Son of the Father, in truth and
love. I rejoiced greatly that I found of thy children walking in truth,
as we have received a commandment from the Father. And now I
beseech thee, lady, not as though I wrote a new commandment unto
thee, but that which we had from the beginning, that we love one
another. And this is love, that we walk after his commandments.
This is the commandment, That, as ye have heard from the
beginning, ye should walk in it. For many deceivers are entered
into the world, who confess not that Jesus Christ is come in the
flesh. This is a deceiver and an antichrist. Look to yourselves,
that we lose not those things which we have wrought, but that
we receive a full reward. Whosoever transgresseth, and abideth
not in the doctrine of Christ, hath not God. He that abideth in
the doctrine of Christ, he hath both the Father and the Son.
—2 John 3–9

Once we have turned to God in repentance, the truth of God lives in us, and
the love of God fills us—body, soul, mind, and spirit. The infilling by the
Holy Spirit is so wonderful, precious, and unique that we should neither take it for
granted nor remain ignorant of its effects in our lives. Our faith matures when we
grow in truth and love, and maturity comes from obedience to God the Father.

The Bible is the truth, although many other religions, philosophies, and ways may
tell us other fine and ennobling thoughts. To continue maturing, we need to know
the Bible so well that we can discern truth from error. We should not set the Bible
aside after once believing in it. When we discard or ignore the Bible, we can lose
the blessing of obedience we have gained.

It is of the utmost importance to hold the Word of God in high esteem by
reading it, memorizing it, understanding it, and applying it to our lives today.
God extends us grace, mercy, and peace to us when we honor Him above all.

Taming the Tongue

Behold, we put bits in the horses' mouths, that they may obey us; and we turn about their whole body. Behold also the ships, which though they be so great, and are driven of fierce winds, yet are they turned about with a very small helm, whithersoever the governor listeth. Even so the tongue is a little member, and boasteth great things. Behold, how great a matter a little fire kindleth! And the tongue is a fire, a world of iniquity: so is the tongue among our members, that it defileth the whole body, and setteth on fire the course of nature; and it is set on fire of hell. For every kind of beasts, and of birds, and of serpents, and of things in the sea, is tamed, and hath been tamed of mankind: But the tongue can no man tame; it is an unruly evil, full of deadly poison. Therewith bless we God, even the Father; and therewith curse we men, which are made after the similitude of God. Out of the same mouth proceedeth blessing and cursing. My brethren, these things ought not so to be. Doth a fountain send forth at the same place sweet water and bitter? Can the fig tree, my brethren, bear olive berries? either a vine, figs? so can no fountain both yield salt water and fresh.
—James 3:3–12

The natural world gives many parallels to human experience, and God expects us to pay attention to these details in order to understand Him better. For example, a small metal bit in the horse's mouth makes him a manageable beast. In a similar way, the tongue indicates how we guide our behavior. Secondly, the small rudder of a large vessel guides the ship even in strong wind.

Similarly, the tongue is a small part of a larger body, but its words reveal how well we manage our lives. Thirdly, fickle words that change into good deeds can still alter our lives for the better, like the two sons in the parable of Matthew 21. Fourthly, one flick of a cigarette can ignite a forest fire that burns thousands of acres. Likewise, one bad word can have a damaging effect on others, such as family, friends, or coworkers. Fifthly, fresh water and salt water may mix in estuaries, but they come from different sources. It is easy to see how two kinds can get mixed up. Finally, every kind of tree bears its own kind of fruit. No one can be mistaken when the fruit is ripe.

Clearly, we cannot live both ways, good one day, bad the next. We need to make up our minds to control our tongues, no matter what our past has been, no matter how hard it seems now. The reward of a peace and wisdom from God is worth it.

Making the Right Choices

Then Samuel took a vial of oil, and poured it upon his head, and
kissed him, and said, Is it not because the Lord hath anointed thee
to be captain over his inheritance? ... And the Spirit of the Lord will
come upon thee, and thou shalt prophesy with them, and shalt be
turned into another man. And let it be, when these signs are come
unto thee, that thou do as occasion serve thee; for God is with thee.
And thou shalt go down before me to Gilgal; and, behold, I will come
down unto thee, to offer burnt offerings, and to sacrifice sacrifices of
peace offerings: seven days shalt thou tarry, till I come to thee, and
shew thee what thou shalt do. And it was so, that when he had turned
his back to go from Samuel, God gave him another heart: and all
those signs came to pass that day ... And some of the Hebrews went
over Jordan to the land of Gad and Gilead. As for Saul, he was yet
in Gilgal, and all the people followed him trembling. And he tarried
seven days, according to the set time that Samuel had appointed:
but Samuel came not to Gilgal; and the people were scattered from
him ... And Samuel came to Saul: and Saul said unto him, Blessed
be thou of the Lord: I have performed the commandment of the
Lord. And Samuel said, What meaneth then this bleating of the
sheep in mine ears, and the lowing of the oxen which I hear?
—1 Samuel 10:1, 6–9; 13:7–8; 15:13–14

King Saul is an example of how God can set apart a person for godly service,
yet the person continually ignores or disobeys God. Saul waited seven days
for the prophet Samuel to come to him after the battle was over, yet the prophet
failed to arrive on time.

Even though he knew the law, Saul was tired of waiting. As a result, the king
offered sacrifices that only the priest should have offered! The king knew it was
wrong, but he pretended not to understand what he had done or how offensive it
was to disobey the Lord. Saul had originally agreed to eradicate the Amalekites
according to God's command, but he kept their sheep and cattle anyway. On
another occasion, Saul's son Jonathan convinced his dad that David was loyal to
him, but Saul chased David to kill him anyway. Overall, Saul reigned forty-two
years, and he continued to make many wrong choices in the professional life
God gave him.

When God leads a person to a specific task, the call is not just a one-time
event. Our lives are made up of hundreds of daily decisions. Each decision is an
opportunity to reaffirm our loyalty, love, and obedience to God. We should not
pretend otherwise.

Sanctification

For this is the will of God, even your sanctification, that ye should
abstain from fornication: That every one of you should know how
to possess his vessel in sanctification and honour; Not in the lust
of concupiscence, even as the Gentiles which know not God: That
no man go beyond and defraud his brother in any matter: because
that the Lord is the avenger of all such, as we also have forewarned
you and testified. For God hath not called us unto uncleanness,
but unto holiness. He therefore that despiseth, despiseth not
man, but God, who hath also given unto us his holy Spirit.
—1 Thessalonians 4:3–8

L iving a holy life is not just a simple matter of avoiding sexual immorality,
but we need to heed the words of the apostle Paul because our culture is
permeated with an unhealthy acceptance of all forms of sexual immorality. A lot
of advertising portrays models in suggestive poses in order to sell an ordinary
product. Every television show and movie assumes that characters are or have
been sexually promiscuous to the point that sexual purity is considered laughable
or abnormal. Instead of love followed by courtship culminating in marriage,
our culture is more familiar with lust followed by living together and marriage
culminating in divorce.

Sexual sin is the gateway into every other type of misconduct. Once we turn
against our bodies by living in the wrong way with another person, we lower
our standards concerning morality. The acceptance of one kind of immorality
extends into the reasoning of every other area of our lives.

Paul's time must have been similar to today because he stresses moral
purity as a first step to sanctification (holy living before the Lord). Once our
sins have been forgiven, we should not presume upon the grace of God for extra
forgiveness for deliberate and flagrant sins. The grace of God should teach us to
avoid immorality and its certain punishment from God.

Holy Living

> But we are bound to give thanks alway to God for you, brethren
> beloved of the Lord, because God hath from the beginning
> chosen you to salvation through sanctification of the Spirit and
> belief of the truth: Whereunto he called you by our gospel, to
> the obtaining of the glory of our Lord Jesus Christ. Therefore,
> brethren, stand fast, and hold the traditions which ye have
> been taught, whether by word, or our epistle … But the Lord is
> faithful, who shall stablish you, and keep you from evil. And we
> have confidence in the Lord touching you, that ye both do and
> will do the things which we command you. And the Lord direct
> your hearts into the love of God, and into the patient waiting
> for Christ … But ye, brethren, be not weary in well doing.
> —2 Thessalonians 2:13–15; 3:3–5, 13

In order to live the Christian life to the fullest, we need to keep in mind specific truths. First and foremost, God loves us—for all eternity. He did not just love us from the day we turned to Him, but He has loved us from before the beginning of time, when He chose our parents and relatives, planned our births, moved us to our towns, and placed us in our schools. The Lord foreknew us and planned out our lives, even to the smallest detail. He knows our parentage all the way back to Adam. God chose us to be saved; we cannot claim salvation by any other means except God.

God sanctifies us, God makes us holy, God makes us more like Him—through the work of the Holy Spirit who now dwells in us. The more we yield to the Holy Spirit, the more we understand the truth of what we believe. God wants us to stand firm in what we believe, but He already knows we cannot do it in our own strength.

As He faithfully strengthens us in goodness, He protects us from evil, He guides us by His love, and He enables us to never tire of what He desires us to do. The fullest life we want to live is the life we allow God to live in us when we yield to Him.

Good Parents, Good Kids

Haman sought to destroy all the Jews that were throughout the
whole kingdom of Ahasuerus, even the people of Mordecai ... The
posts went out, being hastened by the king's commandment, and
the decree was given in Shushan the palace. And the king and
Haman sat down to drink; but the city Shushan was perplexed ...
When Mordecai perceived all that was done, Mordecai rent his
clothes, and put on sackcloth with ashes, and went out into the
midst of the city ... And they told to Mordecai Esther's words. Then
Mordecai commanded to answer Esther, Think not with thyself
that thou shalt escape in the king's house, more than all the Jews.
For if thou altogether holdest thy peace at this time, then shall
there enlargement and deliverance arise to the Jews from another
place; but thou and thy father's house shall be destroyed: and who
knoweth whether thou art come to the kingdom for such a time
as this? Then Esther bade them return Mordecai this answer, Go,
gather together all the Jews that are present in Shushan, and fast
ye for me, and neither eat nor drink three days, night or day: I also
and my maidens will fast likewise; and so will I go in unto the
king, which is not according to the law: and if I perish, I perish.
Esther 3:6b, 15; 4:1, 12–16

Queen Esther was raised by her godly cousin Mordecai because she lost her
parents at a young age. He continued to guide her, even after she became the
queen of King Xerxes. This may seem unusual, but Mordecai was a high-ranking
official in the palace and always kept his ear out for any information about Esther.

Mordecai had raised Esther well, and she remained open to his continued
guidance. She seems to have been a person who not only obeyed readily, but also a
person who understood intentionality of choices and outcomes of behaviors from
a young age. When Haman, another high-ranking official, concocted a plot to
annihilate the Jewish population in Persia, he was delighted to have his evil plan
approved. As he put his plan into action, success was almost within his grasp! The
Persian residents were bewildered, and the Jews were terrified by the edict. Because
Esther had been a good daughter to her adoptive father Mordecai, God was able
to use her position as queen to dismantle the assassination plot devised by Haman.

Her life teaches us that early influences (more than early tragedies) carry over
into adult lives. God had promised that a Savior would come from the Jews, so
Haman's plan was truly evil—he sought to overturn God's will—he could not
have been more wrong in his thinking! What happened instead was that God
overturned the evil of Haman's plan, so Haman lost his life unexpectedly. The
shocking retribution reminds us that no one gets away with anything, no matter
how high and secure his worldly position may be.

Obedience or Rebellion?

And said, O Lord God of Israel, there is no God like thee in the heaven, nor in the earth; which keepest covenant, and shewest mercy unto thy servants, that walk before thee with all their hearts: Thou which hast kept with thy servant David my father that which thou hast promised him; and spakest with thy mouth, and hast fulfilled it with thine hand, as it is this day. [1]Now when Solomon had made an end of praying, the fire came down from heaven, and consumed the burnt offering and the sacrifices; and the glory of the Lord filled the house ... Thus Solomon finished the house of the Lord, and the king's house: and all that came into Solomon's heart to make in the house of the Lord, and in his own house, he prosperously effected. And the Lord appeared to Solomon by night, and said unto him, I have heard thy prayer, and have chosen this place to myself for an house of sacrifice. If I shut up heaven that there be no rain, or if I command the locusts to devour the land, or if I send pestilence among my people; If my people, which are called by my name, shall humble themselves, and pray, and seek my face, and turn from their wicked ways; then will I hear from heaven, and will forgive their sin, and will heal their land. Now mine eyes shall be open, and mine ears attent unto the prayer that is made in this place. For now have I chosen and sanctified this house, that my name may be there for ever: and mine eyes and mine heart shall be there perpetually.
—2 Chronicles 6:14–15; 7:1, 11–16

The dedication of a new worship building is always a high point in the life of a congregation. It represents countless hours of planning, meetings, and discussions that have finally come to an end. Numerous municipal permitting procedures and setbacks have been resolved. Persistent prayer for the timely completion of the project has been offered continually to the Lord, and loads of last minute details are finally completed. A prayer of dedication that gives God credit is always appropriate.

Solomon knew this, and his prayer reflects his wholehearted devotion to the God of heaven and earth. After all the hard work, people gladly worshiped the Lord in their new space. Then, they settled down into the routines for which the building was designed. It is wonderful to experience the blessing that results from obedience. Unfortunately, the opposite is also true, and the Lord reminded Solomon of the two-way street of either obedience or rebellion to God. This street is always open to believers as they walk the path of faith.

The Lord reminded the people to pray and humble themselves at times of disaster so that God would forgive them and heal their land. These cautionary words remind us that God is in both kinds of times in our lives—either to keep us true to Him—or to return us to Him when we stray.

Should We Care?

I said, I will take heed to my ways, that I sin not with my tongue:
I will keep my mouth with a bridle, while the wicked is before
me. I was dumb with silence, I held my peace, even from good;
and my sorrow was stirred. My heart was hot within me, while
I was musing the fire burned: then spake I with my tongue,
Lord, make me to know mine end, and the measure of my days,
what it is: that I may know how frail I am. Behold, thou hast
made my days as an handbreadth; and mine age is as nothing
before thee: verily every man at his best state is altogether vanity.
Selah ... And now, Lord, what wait I for? my hope is in thee.
—Psalm 39:1–5, 7

Some of us care tremendously about the feelings, the welfare, or the health of others. We will probably enter one of the helping professions such as psychology, social work, welfare, education, nursing, or one of many other medical options. Sympathy, empathy, or the desire to help others is a gift God gives to some, but not to others.

Those who work in the helping professions find the keenest satisfaction in their work because the human interaction of helping benefits everyone: those who give help and those who receive help. Another reason we care so deeply for others is because we have a sense of the transitory nature of this life. Emotional health is fragile for some individuals. Economic and social well-being escape many hard workers. Physical health can change overnight. Learning is difficult for some students. We hope by helping others to enhance the quality of the lives they live.

Learning to view life from an eternal perspective is an asset to anyone, but it is a necessity to give complete and well-rounded help to another person. Our faith can also help us to focus on the task of the moment. This may be exactly what a needy person needs.

NOVEMBER 22

How to Gain Eternal Life

And when he was gone forth into the way, there came one running,
and kneeled to him, and asked him, Good Master, what shall I
do that I may inherit eternal life? And Jesus said unto him, Why
callest thou me good? there is none good but one, that is, God.
Thou knowest the commandments, Do not commit adultery, Do
not kill, Do not steal, Do not bear false witness, Defraud not,
Honour thy father and mother. And he answered and said unto
him, Master, all these have I observed from my youth. Then
Jesus beholding him loved him, and said unto him, One thing
thou lackest: go thy way, sell whatsoever thou hast, and give to
the poor, and thou shalt have treasure in heaven: and come, take
up the cross, and follow me. And he was sad at that saying, and
went away grieved: for he had great possessions ... And they were
astonished out of measure, saying among themselves, Who then
can be saved? And Jesus looking upon them saith, With men it is
impossible, but not with God: for with God all things are possible.
—Mark 10:17–22, 26–27

One young man, desperate to get to heaven, ran up to Jesus and fell to his
knees before asking Him how to inherit eternal life. The man understood
the concept of inheritance better than most of us because he was very wealthy.
In his experience, someone else, most likely a close relative, dies and bequeaths
a lot of wealth to another. He was half right in his understanding of salvation—
someone else gives it to you—but he did not apply what he knew to be true to
the more important spiritual situation.

The way he addressed Jesus showed that he was also half wrong. He called
Jesus "good," indicating that he was trying to figure out which good deed of his
would merit heaven. The man knew he had lived a blameless life in spite of his
riches. He thought his good deeds would give him heaven. Jesus corrected his
idea sharply by telling him to give up his goods in order to be saved.

The truth is that if we want to follow Jesus, all of us must give up whatever
we count as fundamental to our self-identity. These goods, even though they
may be good, if they prevent us from knowing God better, are not good after
all. When we let go and give up something dear, God is able to fill the vacant
space with something better, bigger, and greater. We should not be afraid to let
the greatness of God replace our smallness.

327

NOVEMBER 23

The Omniscient God

Who hath directed the Spirit of the Lord, or being his counsellor
hath taught him? With whom took he counsel, and who instructed
him, and taught him in the path of judgment, and taught him
knowledge, and shewed to him the way of understanding? ... To
whom then will ye liken God? or what likeness will ye compare
unto him? The workman melteth a graven image, and the goldsmith
spreadeth it over with gold, and casteth silver chains. He that is
so impoverished that he hath no oblation chooseth a tree that
will not rot; he seeketh unto him a cunning workman to prepare
a graven image, that shall not be moved. Have ye not known?
have ye not heard? hath it not been told you from the beginning?
have ye not understood from the foundations of the earth?
—Isaiah 40:13–14, 18–21

We create many conceptions of God in our minds, and we try to fit God
into the human mold. The trouble with thinking like this is that God is
exactly and only who He says He is. He is not who we imagine Him to be. One
of the most awe-inspiring and most difficult concepts to understand is that God
is omniscient. He knows everything. He has never learned anything. We cannot
teach Him anything, nor can He can learn anything.

We live in a time when the idols of Eastern religions have taken hold in our
society. We think that a statue of Buddha adds something to our lives. The truth
is that an idol is no more than a block of carved wood or a hollow, cast metal
piece overlaid with somewhat attractive metal plating. The idol is deaf, dumb,
and blind. It knows nothing.

It is logical and right to look to the God who is personal, the God who
knows everything, the God who guides us out of His infinite knowledge. It
makes sense to let idols take their proper place in the world: let them be burned
in a fire; let them be thrown in the dumpster; let them rust away to nothing. That
is all they are worth in the first place.

Do It Now, Not Later!

And the angel of the Lord spake unto Philip, saying, Arise, and go
toward the south unto the way that goeth down from Jerusalem
unto Gaza, which is desert. And he arose and went: and, behold, a
man of Ethiopia, an eunuch of great authority under Candace queen
of the Ethiopians, who had the charge of all her treasure, and had
come to Jerusalem for to worship, Was returning, and sitting in his
chariot read Esaias the prophet. Then the Spirit said unto Philip,
Go near, and join thyself to this chariot. And Philip ran thither to
him, and heard him read the prophet Esaias, and said, Understandest
thou what thou readest? And he said, How can I, except some man
should guide me? And he desired Philip that he would come up
and sit with him … Then Philip opened his mouth, and began at
the same scripture, and preached unto him Jesus. And as they went
on their way, they came unto a certain water: and the eunuch said,
See, here is water; what doth hinder me to be baptized? And Philip
said, If thou believest with all thine heart, thou mayest. And he
answered and said, I believe that Jesus Christ is the Son of God. And
he commanded the chariot to stand still: and they went down both
into the water, both Philip and the eunuch; and he baptized him.
—Acts 8:26–31, 35–38

At the same time that we live in an instant society, many of us are prone to
procrastination. We have the ability to turn on the television for instant
entertainment, the ability to microwave food, the ability to buy a high-tech
computer, the ability to wash clothes rapidly, the ability to purchase ready-made
food or clothing, and the ability to use an appliance instead of doing it slower
ourselves. None of us wants to live without these instant amenities.

The benefits of modern society can give us the idea that because any task
is really simple, we can put it off until a later date. It is important to remember
that the ability to do things effortlessly can also have a positive effect in our
lives by helping us desire to do more because more time is freed up in our lives.
The Ethiopian eunuch belonged to the latter persuasion. As a high-ranking
government official for Queen Candace, he had a lot of tasks done for him
instantly. Slaves were the "technology" of ancient times. But he understood the
importance of acting quickly because he had often been the one to make things
happen for others.

The meeting of Philip with the Ethiopian eunuch reminds us that salvation
and baptism are decisions that we should act upon right now, just like the
eunuch did.

A Life-or-Death Situation

Your little ones, your wives, and thy stranger that is in thy camp,
from the hewer of thy wood unto the drawer of thy water: That
thou shouldest enter into covenant with the Lord thy God, and into
his oath, which the Lord thy God maketh with thee this day: That
he may establish thee to day for a people unto himself, and that
he may be unto thee a God, as he hath said unto thee, and as he
hath sworn unto thy fathers, to Abraham, to Isaac, and to Jacob.
Neither with you only do I make this covenant and this oath; But
with him that standeth here with us this day before the Lord our
God, and also with him that is not here with us this day ... And
it come to pass, when he heareth the words of this curse, that he
bless himself in his heart, saying, I shall have peace, though I walk
in the imagination of mine heart, to add drunkenness to thirst.
—Deuteronomy 29:11–15, 19

At a time when many choices appear alluring, we need to make the right initial choice in order to enjoy the rest of our lives. Sometimes religion is tacked on to our lives as a useless appendage, but the Word of God assures us that the religious choices we make are so potent that they hold the power of life and death.

Everyone wants many good things out of life and probably has a plan in mind how to accumulate those goods or accomplish those goals. When we forget that God is the source of all goodness and prosperity, we will ultimately foil our best efforts in securing them. No one needs to live with such frustration because the Word of God is accessible to us.

If we want to live the best life possible, we need to obey God. The blessings God gives us are not just for us because God is not selfish. We can pass them on to our children and double the original good from God. Whatever choice we make for life or for death, God holds us accountable, but He wants us to choose life and live life to the fullest in Him.

What Does God Use?

> And the Lord said unto him, What is that in thine hand? And he
> said, A rod. And he said, Cast it on the ground. And he cast it on the
> ground, and it became a serpent; and Moses fled from before it.
> —Exodus 4:2–3

> And Gideon said unto God, If thou wilt save Israel by
> mine hand, as thou hast said, Behold, I will put a fleece of
> wool in the floor; and if the dew be on the fleece only, and
> it be dry upon all the earth beside, then shall I know that
> thou wilt save Israel by mine hand, as thou hast said.
> —Judges 6:36–37

> … Then he said, Go, borrow thee vessels abroad of all thy
> neighbours, even empty vessels; borrow not a few. And
> when thou art come in, thou shalt shut the door upon thee
> and upon thy sons, and shalt pour out into all those vessels,
> and thou shalt set aside that which is full … Then she came
> and told the man of God. And he said, Go, sell the oil, and
> pay thy debt, and live thou and thy children of the rest.
> —2 Kings 4:3–4, 7

In order to live the Christian life, we need the Bible for guidance, but another question may nag at us continually. Is this book all we need, or does God sometimes use, need, or want any other thing? This is not a trick question, but people sometimes give wild testimonies in church about how God has worked in their lives. When we hear these spectacular testimonies, we start poking around in our lives, wondering whether we have missed out on something vital.

To reassure ourselves, we should always remember that God created this world and everything in it. Everything, even humanly fashioned objects, have their ultimate origin in God the Creator. On one occasion, God let Moses use a staff, a long stick, shaped by human hands from a tree branch into a useful object, to work miracles in front of pharaoh, king of Egypt. Do all sticks carry magical properties?—No, but God used the staff of Moses for His own purpose, to display His glory in front of the Egyptians.

In another instance, God alternately wet the fleece of a sheep and dried the same fleece of a sheep to convince Gideon to do God's will. Can any fleece foretell the future?—No, but God can use anything in any way He wants to His own end, for His glory. At a time of critical need, God used the household staple of oil to provide enough tax money to a widow to pay her creditors. Does oil normally have the ability to pay debts?—No, but when it suits His purposes, God is not limited by anyone or any object.

331

Remembering Jesus

And he took the cup, and gave thanks, and said, Take this, and divide
it among yourselves: For I say unto you, I will not drink of the fruit of
the vine, until the kingdom of God shall come. And he took bread,
and gave thanks, and brake it, and gave unto them, saying, This is my
body which is given for you: this do in remembrance of me. Likewise
also the cup after supper, saying, This cup is the new testament in
my blood, which is shed for you. But, behold, the hand of him that
betrayeth me is with me on the table. And truly the Son of man goeth,
as it was determined: but woe unto that man by whom he is betrayed!
—Luke 22:17–22

According to the tendency of our human nature, we are forgetful people.
Even when we know that our brains and memories work better and faster
than others, we can suffer from momentary lapses at the most critical of times.
It is frustrating to be human, and Jesus Christ knows our nature—He shared it
with us.

Jesus wants us to remember two very important facts about our lives now
that our lives have been regenerated by Him. Given our human propensity for
intermittent memory loss, Jesus also has the solution to the problem. Communion
is a sacrament instituted by Jesus Christ at the Last Supper. Most churches have
a communion table in the front of the sanctuary with the words of Jesus carved
into the front of it: "Do this in remembrance of me." Jesus broke the bread with
disciples and told them to remember that His body was given for us, for our
sins. Just as physical bread sustains physical life, so the offering of one innocent,
perfect life gives spiritual life to sinners. He died so that we might live. The
sinless One removes the sins of the sinners. Jesus drank the wine and told the
disciples to remember that His blood was for our salvation too.

He did not need to surrender His lifeblood, but He voluntarily did so—
because without the shedding of blood there is no forgiveness of sins. When
we take communion, let's remember the person who died and the blood that
saved us.

NOVEMBER 28

No More Anger

Be of the same mind one toward another. Mind not high things,
but condescend to men of low estate. Be not wise in your own
conceits. Recompense to no man evil for evil. Provide things honest
in the sight of all men. If it be possible, as much as lieth in you, live
peaceably with all men. Dearly beloved, avenge not yourselves, but
rather give place unto wrath: for it is written, Vengeance is mine; I will
repay, saith the Lord. Therefore if thine enemy hunger, feed him; if
he thirst, give him drink: for in so doing thou shalt heap coals of fire
on his head. Be not overcome of evil, but overcome evil with good.
—Romans 12:16–21

Some of us were raised in homes where anger ruled the roost. Until we get away
from those angry words and angry people, we may not even realize the extent
to which anger has been a part of our formative years. Children need to leave
home for a number of reasons, and one good reason to leave home is to separate
the former life of childhood from the future life of adulthood.

We accomplish this by identifying, evaluating, and acting upon the parts of
our early years that need to change. Anger belittles others in order to build up the
self. As believers, we no longer need to do that because Christ has lifted us up to
Himself when He saved us. We can now behave with kindness to others. Anger,
whether intentional or not, hurts others a lot, sometimes permanently. When we
behave with peace and love toward others, we may speak a much-needed healing
word to a sufferer. Just like angry people at home may never know how much
their anger has hurt us, we may never learn how much a good word helps another.
It doesn't matter anyway. We no longer feel the need for payback.

The forgiveness we have received from Christ gives us the freedom to be a
better person and the ability to overcome evil with good.

NOVEMBER 29

True Love

Charity suffereth long, and is kind; charity envieth not; charity
vaunteth not itself, is not puffed up, Doth not behave itself
unseemly, seeketh not her own, is not easily provoked, thinketh
no evil; Rejoiceth not in iniquity, but rejoiceth in the truth;
Beareth all things, believeth all things, hopeth all things,
endureth all things. Charity never faileth: but whether there be
prophecies, they shall fail; whether there be tongues, they shall
cease; whether there be knowledge, it shall vanish away.
—1 Corinthians 13:4–8

Young people seek soul mates, but how can anyone tell whether the love is
real and true and lasting? This passage is the most often quoted and most
beautiful definition of love (charity) ever written. The apostle Paul wrote is as a
person who had experienced true love from the Savior he had formerly hated.

Patience means that when we experience the foibles of the beloved, we
love him anyway. Kindness means that when the beloved embarrasses himself,
embarrasses both of us, or messes up a situation, we overlook it because all
of us have sinned. Not envying means not wishing for what both of us can
never have or achieve or do. Not envying means recognizing specific strengths
and strengthening them. Not envying means not wasting emotional energy on
fruitless thinking. Not boasting or a lack of pride means recognizing that while
gifts are unique, they are not the only gifts in the world. We all have different
but equally valuable talents in the sight of God. Not being rude or self-seeking
means that sarcastic language is out, and tender words are in. True love does not
include sarcasm. Not getting angry and not keeping records of wrongs means
never holding a grudge for real or imagined slights. True love loves the truth.
Marriages based on anything less tend to founder without warning or for no
apparent reason.

True love protects the other in every way possible, places complete confidence
in the other when apart, hopes for the best in life, and keeps on trying to be the
best and do the best for the beloved.

Waiting for Answers

How long wilt thou forget me, O Lord? for ever? how long wilt
thou hide thy face from me? How long shall I take counsel in
my soul, having sorrow in my heart daily? how long shall mine
enemy be exalted over me? Consider and hear me, O Lord my
God: lighten mine eyes, lest I sleep the sleep of death; Lest
mine enemy say, I have prevailed against him; and those that
trouble me rejoice when I am moved. But I have trusted in
thy mercy; my heart shall rejoice in thy salvation. I will sing
unto the Lord, because he hath dealt bountifully with me.
—Psalm 13:1–6

We live in a society that provides instant gratification for any physical
want or need—legitimate needs as well as unlawful and illicit desires.
Unfortunately, we all possess a strong human tendency is to transfer what we see
occurring around us in the physical world to the principles of the spiritual world
that we now inhabit as believers. We think of impatience and the desire for instant
gratification as a problem unique to modern life, but the Bible tells otherwise.

David frequently complained that God was slow to answer his prayer, and
we know that David was in frequent trouble with Saul, then with other nations,
then with family members. David wanted instant answers too. In that non-
technological time, without instant telephone communication or easy travel
accommodations, in that far distant time when we imagine that life was simpler
and less demanding, David hated to wait for anything. David learned the same
lesson we also need to learn today. God loves us so much and desires our
fellowship so much that sometimes He wants us to keep turning to Him even
when we seem to get no answer from Him.

Not getting a quick answer makes us focus on God more intensely—focus
on His goal, not ours. In the end, trusting in God is really more important that
getting an answer from Him.

DECEMBER 1

Many Blessings

Blessed be the God and Father of our Lord Jesus Christ, who hath
blessed us with all spiritual blessings in heavenly places in Christ:
According as he hath chosen us in him before the foundation of
the world, that we should be holy and without blame before him in
love: Having predestinated us unto the adoption of children by Jesus
Christ to himself, according to the good pleasure of his will, To the
praise of the glory of his grace, wherein he hath made us accepted in
the beloved. In whom we have redemption through his blood, the
forgiveness of sins, according to the riches of his grace; Wherein he
hath abounded toward us in all wisdom and prudence; Having made
known unto us the mystery of his will, according to his good pleasure
which he hath purposed in himself: That in the dispensation of the
fulness of times he might gather together in one all things in Christ,
both which are in heaven, and which are on earth; even in him.
—Ephesians 1:3–10

Do we ever think about how incomparably great is the goodness of God to
sinners? We all want many good earthly things in life, yet God has blessed
us with all spiritual blessings—in Christ. The blessings of God toward us go
above and beyond the human realm. And the blessings of God hold a different
purpose than human blessings.

Human blessings fulfill human needs and desires, but God's blessings serve
God's pleasure and will. Does this sound too autocratic? It is—but let us consider
Him from whom all blessings flow. Not only has He given life to us, He lavished
the riches of His grace upon us. Let us accept God's gift, the gift that is always
more than we need. God the giver is greater than we can imagine. This is the
season of the year when we begin to think about the greatest gift God has given
to all of us in the birth of His Son, Jesus Christ.

Let us keep in mind the indescribable gift of the Savior Jesus Christ as we
go about finishing our semesters and turning our thoughts to the true meaning
of Christmas time.

Love Is Divine

And Adam gave names to all cattle, and to the fowl of the air, and
to every beast of the field; but for Adam there was not found an
help meet for him. And the Lord God caused a deep sleep to fall
upon Adam, and he slept: and he took one of his ribs, and closed
up the flesh instead thereof; And the rib, which the Lord God
had taken from man, made he a woman, and brought her unto the
man. And Adam said, This is now bone of my bones, and flesh of
my flesh: she shall be called Woman, because she was taken out
of Man. Therefore shall a man leave his father and his mother,
and shall cleave unto his wife: and they shall be one flesh.
—Genesis 2:20–24

None of us likes to be alone. All people desire to find soul mates—true
life partners who complement, understand, and relate best to them. The
climate, the topography, and the geography of the world may have changed
considerably since the Garden of Eden, but human nature and its desires remain
invariable.

All of us can relate to our grandfather Adam in his desire for a suitable
helper. But we may need to consider that society today tells us that we can
invent and determine the types of relationships we desire—homosexual, lesbian,
adultery, separation, divorce, polygamy—and these relationships will work out
just the way we imagine. This is never true because God established human
relationships in the Garden of Eden when he brought Adam and Even together
as the first father and first mother of numerous children.

We are created beings, not creators, so we cannot invent another way to live
and make it work. Let us never forget that marriage between a man and a woman
creates a unique bond established by the Creator of all humans. Marriages are
blessed by the Lord and promoted by the God of love—who loves us and wants
us to be loved and share love in return. We grow closer to God when we follow
His plan.

Do Not Presume upon the Grace of God

And the men, which Moses sent to search the land, who returned,
and made all the congregation to murmur against him, by bringing
up a slander upon the land, Even those men that did bring up the evil
report upon the land, died by the plague before the Lord. But Joshua
the son of Nun, and Caleb the son of Jephunneh, which were of the
men that went to search the land, lived still. And Moses told these
sayings unto all the children of Israel: and the people mourned greatly.
And they rose up early in the morning, and gat them up into the top
of the mountain, saying, Lo, we be here, and will go up unto the place
which the Lord hath promised: for we have sinned. And Moses said,
Wherefore now do ye transgress the commandment of the Lord? but
it shall not prosper. Go not up, for the Lord is not among you; that
ye be not smitten before your enemies. For the Amalekites and the
Canaanites are there before you, and ye shall fall by the sword: because
ye are turned away from the Lord, therefore the Lord will not be with
you. But they presumed to go up unto the hill top: nevertheless the ark
of the covenant of the Lord, and Moses, departed not out of the camp.
Then the Amalekites came down, and the Canaanites which dwelt in
that hill, and smote them, and discomfited them, even unto Hormah.
—Numbers 14:36–45

Here is a situation familiar to many believers: we are afraid to obey God
because the task at hand seems so enormous that God could not possibly
want anyone to do it—this is what we tell ourselves. The Israelites behaved in
the same way when they failed to act upon the report of Joshua and Caleb that
the Promised Land was theirs for the taking.

They believed the bad report of the other ten spies, so God became angry
with them. Moses told them their punishment—that God would not allow them
now to enter the Promised Land as originally promised. God would cause them
to wander in the wilderness as punishment. They suddenly realized that God
really meant what He said, so they decided to go ahead and do what He had
asked. Moses tried to dissuade them because God had already pronounced the
punishment. They disregarded the warning and presumed that their God would
still go with them. Wrong!—They were beaten up by their enemies because the
time of God's favor had passed.

Believers should never presume upon the grace of God but act according to
His leading the moment it is given.

DECEMBER 4

Urgent Prayer

And he said unto them, Which of you shall have a friend, and shall go
unto him at midnight, and say unto him, Friend, lend me three loaves;
For a friend of mine in his journey is come to me, and I have nothing
to set before him? And he from within shall answer and say, Trouble
me not: the door is now shut, and my children are with me in bed;
I cannot rise and give thee. I say unto you, Though he will not rise
and give him, because he is his friend, yet because of his importunity
he will rise and give him as many as he needeth. And I say unto you,
Ask, and it shall be given you; seek, and ye shall find; knock, and it
shall be opened unto you. For every one that asketh receiveth; and he
that seeketh findeth; and to him that knocketh it shall be opened.
—Luke 11:5–10

Does prayer sometimes seem inconsequential and unnecessary, like the
answer would have been just the same without praying? Think again.
When we devalue prayer as part of our spiritual lives, we miss out on learning
more about the personal God who expects to hear from us regularly—in prayer.

Here is one way to determine once and for all whether God answers the
prayers of believers. Listen to the types of prayer requests made in church, and
listen again for the answers to them from the believers who seek them. Then,
ask God to show you a similar situation, where the parties do not believe, do not
ask for prayer, or do not turn to God, yet the unbelievers desire similar good
outcomes in their lives.

Figure out from this whether or not God actively answers urgent or trivial
prayers of believers. We need to use every available means to remind ourselves
that God loves us, and He always delights to help us.

DECEMBER 5

The Salt of the Earth

And every oblation of thy meat offering shalt thou
season with salt; neither shalt thou suffer the salt of
the covenant of thy God to be lacking from thy meat
offering: with all thine offerings thou shalt offer salt.
—Leviticus 2:13

All the heave offerings of the holy things, which the children of
Israel offer unto the Lord, have I given thee, and thy sons and thy
daughters with thee, by a statute for ever: it is a covenant of salt
for ever before the Lord unto thee and to thy seed with thee.
—Numbers 18:19

Ye are the salt of the earth: but if the salt have lost his savour,
wherewith shall it be salted? it is thenceforth good for nothing,
but to be cast out, and to be trodden under foot of men. Ye are
the light of the world. A city that is set on an hill cannot be hid.
—Matthew 5:13–14

No one ever thinks twice about a commodity that is so widely available that it seems like there is too much of it. Instead, we take ordinary items for granted. We forget how necessary and important small items are to daily life.

For example, salt has many practical uses. In addition to enhancing the flavor of food, salt removes clothing stains more easily. Salt keep ants out of the house. Salt stiffens egg whites for easier frothing. Salt sets gelatin more quickly. Salt cleans discolorations from metal pots and pans. Salt kills unwanted weeds in the lawn. We get the message—salt makes life easier and cleaner. A little bit does a lot more than it might initially appear to be capable of doing. In both the Old and New Testaments, salt represents the good quality of life that belongs to believers who obey God.

When our lives are sprinkled with just a little salt, the flavor permeates all aspects of our lives—this is what salt does for a substance. God uses the salt of believing people to benefit every aspect of life on planet earth.

From Death to Life

The hand of the Lord was upon me, and carried me out in the spirit
of the Lord, and set me down in the midst of the valley which was
full of bones, And caused me to pass by them round about: and,
behold, there were very many in the open valley; and, lo, they were
very dry. And he said unto me, Son of man, can these bones live?
And I answered, O Lord God, thou knowest ... So I prophesied
as he commanded me, and the breath came into them, and they
lived, and stood up upon their feet, an exceeding great army.
—Ezekiel 37:1–3, 10

But God, who is rich in mercy, for his great love wherewith
he loved us, Even when we were dead in sins, hath quickened
us together with Christ, (by grace ye are saved).
—Ephesians 2:4–5

What a spectacular picture of the meaning of life—life comes from the
spoken Word of God and from nowhere else! Dry bones come to life at
the bidding of the Lord! The valley of dry bones reminds us of who we truly are;
we cannot flatter ourselves that our lives are important or valuable.

We are no better than dry sarcophagi until the Holy Spirit breathes the life of
God into our mortal, dusty frames. There is no question that dry bones are dead
bones. They are dead to human activity, they are dead to all human endeavors,
and they are dead to any effort in life.

We think better of ourselves than that, but God reminds us of reality. Apart
from Him, we are dead; no life exists, and no effort counts. Allowing the Holy
Spirit to indwell us because we have come to eternal life in Jesus Christ is the only
way to truly live. God breathes life into us; we cannot do it ourselves.

DECEMBER 7

Holy Living

This I say then, Walk in the Spirit, and ye shall not fulfil the lust
of the flesh. For the flesh lusteth against the Spirit, and the Spirit
against the flesh: and these are contrary the one to the other: so
that ye cannot do the things that ye would ... Now the works
of the flesh are manifest, which are these; Adultery, fornication,
uncleanness, lasciviousness, Idolatry, witchcraft, hatred, variance,
emulations, wrath, strife, seditions, heresies, Envyings, murders,
drunkenness, revellings, and such like: of the which I tell you
before, as I have also told you in time past, that they which do
such things shall not inherit the kingdom of God. But the fruit of
the Spirit is love, joy, peace, longsuffering, gentleness, goodness,
faith, Meekness, temperance: against such there is no law. And
they that are Christ's have crucified the flesh with the affections
and lusts. If we live in the Spirit, let us also walk in the Spirit.
—Galatians 5:16–17, 19–25

God wants a holy people who belong to Him, and the only way to be holy is to
live according to the Holy Spirit, not according to the sinful nature. Let us
think for a moment about where we have come from—our family backgrounds
and our personal decisions. Do we see the acts of the sinful nature there? Or, do
we see the fruit of the Spirit there? This is the time for personal honesty.

We need to identify truthfully where we have come from in order to move
forward as godly individuals. Sexual revelry, religious revelry, and social revelry
are vices and sins that ruin our lives. We should not try to mix two opposing
kinds of living in one life. We need to give up what is sinful, wrong, and harmful
to us and to those who matter to us.

When we live according to the Holy Spirit, we let Him direct our lives into
the way of love, joy, peace, patience, kindness, goodness, faithfulness, gentleness
and self-control. Then the happiness, contentment, and peace that come from
the Holy Spirit will be ours.

Who Helps Us When We Need It?

And if Christ be in you, the body is dead because of sin; but the Spirit
is life because of righteousness. But if the Spirit of him that raised up
Jesus from the dead dwell in you, he that raised up Christ from the
dead shall also quicken your mortal bodies by his Spirit that dwelleth
in you ... Likewise the Spirit also helpeth our infirmities: for we know
not what we should pray for as we ought: but the Spirit itself maketh
intercession for us with groanings which cannot be uttered. And he
that searcheth the hearts knoweth what is the mind of the Spirit,
because he maketh intercession for the saints according to the will of
God. And we know that all things work together for good to them
that love God, to them who are the called according to his purpose.
—Romans 8:10–11, 26–28

There are times in life when we require specific help from specific people—
parents who love us, teachers who train us, doctors who heal us, employers
who hire us, friends who accepts us. The helpers in our lives fulfill various
necessary and valid needs in life.

When we become believers in Jesus Christ, our needs do not disappear. Our
lives still need help, and now we have an unseen helper who is always available
to meet our daily needs. The Holy Spirit gives spiritual life to our mortal bodies,
thus enabling us to do all God wants us to do in this life. The help we receive
from the Holy Spirit does not diminish the help we have received from others.
But the third person of the Trinity puts order and perspective into our lives.

The Holy Spirit strengthens our weak spots because God's effort is always
the best. The Holy Spirit prays for us because God acts in response to prayer.
The Holy Spirit searches our hearts to help us figure out what we really want, and
then He intercedes for us in agreement with the will of God.

DECEMBER 9

Get Ahead with God

Likewise, ye younger, submit yourselves unto the elder. Yea, all
of you be subject one to another, and be clothed with humility:
for God resisteth the proud, and giveth grace to the humble.
Humble yourselves therefore under the mighty hand of God,
that he may exalt you in due time: Casting all your care upon
him; for he careth for you. Be sober, be vigilant; because your
adversary the devil, as a roaring lion, walketh about, seeking
whom he may devour: Whom resist stedfast in the faith, knowing
that the same afflictions are accomplished in your brethren
that are in the world. But the God of all grace, who hath called
us unto his eternal glory by Christ Jesus, after that ye have
suffered a while, make you perfect, stablish, strengthen, settle
you. To him be glory and dominion for ever and ever. Amen.
—1 Peter 5:5–11

Human life is so far from perfect that everyone worries about all kinds of
matters, both trivial and serious. Some worries arise from personal pride.
We inaccurately think that we ought to be able to handle the situation, but we
can't.

Some worries grow out of our own inventions. Our minds blow one small
thought completely out of proportion to its importance, and it takes over our
thinking. Some worries come upon us from Satan. We need to be wary so that
we can recognize and counteract this evil attack. Whether we are proud people,
worrywarts, or hassled by Satan, the remedy for anxiety is the same.

When we let go of our worries and admit that God knows more about the
situation than we do, we find out more about the God who always loves us. Our
worries dissipate when we rest in Him. When we become aware that we are
worrying, we can cultivate a basic habit to turn to God and wait for His strength
and restoration in the difficult situation.

Unwelcome In-Laws

> And Miriam and Aaron spake against Moses because of the
> Ethiopian woman whom he had married: for he had married an
> Ethiopian woman. And they said, Hath the Lord indeed spoken
> only by Moses? hath he not spoken also by us? And the Lord heard
> it. (Now the man Moses was very meek, above all the men which
> were upon the face of the earth.) And the Lord spake suddenly unto
> Moses, and unto Aaron, and unto Miriam, Come out ye three unto
> the tabernacle of the congregation. And they three came out … And
> the anger of the Lord was kindled against them; and he departed.
> And the cloud departed from off the tabernacle; and, behold, Miriam
> became leprous, white as snow: and Aaron looked upon Miriam,
> and, behold, she was leprous. And Aaron said unto Moses, Alas,
> my lord, I beseech thee, lay not the sin upon us, wherein we have
> done foolishly, and wherein we have sinned … And Moses cried
> unto the Lord, saying, Heal her now, O God, I beseech thee. And
> the Lord said unto Moses, If her father had but spit in her face,
> should she not be ashamed seven days? let her be shut out from
> the camp seven days, and after that let her be received in again.
> —Numbers 12:1–4, 9–11, 13–14

Miriam and Aaron, the sister and brother of Moses, took a strong and sudden dislike to their sister-in-law because she was of a different race than them. They seem to have been motivated by jealousy that Moses was the leader instead of them. Once they turned against her, they could say nothing good about her.

Her skin color was wrong. Her husband was wrong. The Lord was wrong. Do we see how quickly prejudicial assumptions twist family relationships and twist our perceptions of God? Moses and God both listened to their complaints, and God took care of this misperception—no, this sin—swiftly. He spoke directly to the three siblings to confirm the leadership of Moses. He gave Miriam the horrible skin condition of leprosy to show her and everyone else how isolating her attitude was.

The entire nation got the message because they remained in the same place for seven days while Miriam was confined outside the camp. Seven days gave them plenty of time to think about their own attitudes. Even among believers, wrong attitudes can separate us from those we love most.

345

What Does God Punish?

And it shall come to pass at that time, that I will search Jerusalem
with candles, and punish the men that are settled on their lees:
that say in their heart, The Lord will not do good, neither will he
do evil ... Therefore as I live, saith the Lord of hosts, the God of
Israel, Surely Moab shall be as Sodom, and the children of Ammon
as Gomorrah, even the breeding of nettles, and saltpits, and a
perpetual desolation: the residue of my people shall spoil them,
and the remnant of my people shall possess them. This shall they
have for their pride, because they have reproached and magnified
themselves against the people of the Lord of hosts ... This is the
rejoicing city that dwelt carelessly, that said in her heart, I am, and
there is none beside me: how is she become a desolation, a place for
beasts to lie down in! every one that passeth by her shall hiss, and
wag his hand ... I said, Surely thou wilt fear me, thou wilt receive
instruction; so their dwelling should not be cut off, howsoever I
punished them: but they rose early, and corrupted all their doings.
—Zephaniah 1:12; 2:9–10, 15; 3:7

Life appears to go on very slowly minute by minute—hour after hour—
day-in day-out—year upon year. When life does not vary, it can easily seem
as if God has left us alone on planet earth. It is easy to think that we must
rely upon ourselves to make interesting changes in life. Maybe we become
more indulgent—finer clothes—more expensive vehicles—longer vacations—
whatever suits our fancy.

When we believe in the fallacy of self-reliance, we are apt to leave God out
of our lives and go our own way instead. We become complacent, feeling that
nothing will ever change. We become proud of ourselves. We pride ourselves
on our accomplishments. We insult the Lord, we mock God, and we ridicule
believers. We live carefree lives because we feel so self-assured and independent.

We are actually corrupting ourselves when we omit God and His rules as
the standard by which we should live. God punishes sin, sometimes sooner,
sometimes later. It is both humbling and wise to turn to Him when young. It is
also the only way to avoid the certainty of shipwrecked lives.

What Does God Reward?

Hold thy peace at the presence of the Lord God: for the day of
the Lord is at hand: for the Lord hath prepared a sacrifice, he hath
bid his guests ... Seek ye the Lord, all ye meek of the earth, which
have wrought his judgment; seek righteousness, seek meekness: it
may be ye shall be hid in the day of the Lord's anger ... I will also
leave in the midst of thee an afflicted and poor people, and they
shall trust in the name of the Lord ... The Lord thy God in the
midst of thee is mighty; he will save, he will rejoice over thee with
joy; he will rest in his love, he will joy over thee with singing.
—Zephaniah 1:7; 2:3; 3:12, 17

Most of us feel we must have some music or other type of sound to accompany
every activity of life. We may call it multi-tasking when we both listen and
act at the same time. We may affirm that music relaxes us and helps us concentrate
on the other task.

Wait a minute—does this mean that we are not really listening to the music?
Is the music just a background buzz that helps us live in our own little bubble?
Does it mean that we are not really paying attention to the more important task?
God want us to figure out the answer to this question because He wants us to
live productive lives in His world.

And the best way to live dynamically is to be silent before Him. This seems
like a contradiction in terms—hearing God in the silence. But God cannot speak
to us or give us understanding unless we get rid of all distractions. He wants to
know that we desire Him above all else. When we remember that God spoke
softly to Moses from within the burning bush, we can understand that He still
speaks to us in quietness today. Deliberate quietness reveals a willingness to
humble the self before God.

The treasures of God belong to the meek. We can be elated when we hear
and understand God's voice. We may even hear Him singing over us with joy! It
is worth the wait for the blessing of times ahead.

DECEMBER 13

Secrets of Faith

For I rejoiced greatly, when the brethren came and testified of the
truth that is in thee, even as thou walkest in the truth. I have no
greater joy than to hear that my children walk in truth. Beloved,
thou doest faithfully whatsoever thou doest to the brethren, and
to strangers; Which have borne witness of thy charity before the
church: whom if thou bring forward on their journey after a godly
sort, thou shalt do well: Because that for his name's sake they went
forth, taking nothing of the Gentiles. We therefore ought to receive
such, that we might be fellowhelpers to the truth … Beloved,
follow not that which is evil, but that which is good. He that doeth
good is of God: but he that doeth evil hath not seen God.
—3 John 3–8, 11

Actions really do speak louder than words, just like our parents often told us.
Whoever we are, all of us are known by our behaviors and demeanors. We
should keep in mind that those who notice us tell others about how we handle
our lives, just like they did in the early days of the church. Even the apostle John
heard about the activities in the church where his friend Gaius attended.

John immediately recognized that this young and vibrant congregation
had converted their faith into loving actions, a sure sign to him that they were
faithfully walking in the way of the Lord.

The church had learned the secret of faith. Those who live in the way that
honors God, show how wonderful, true, loving, and kind is the Father God to
His people. By imitating God who is good, the world is drawn to the truth.

True Friendship

Ye adulterers and adulteresses, know ye not that the friendship of
the world is enmity with God? whosoever therefore will be a friend
of the world is the enemy of God. Do ye think that the scripture
saith in vain, The spirit that dwelleth in us lusteth to envy? But he
giveth more grace. Wherefore he saith, God resisteth the proud, but
giveth grace unto the humble. Submit yourselves therefore to God.
Resist the devil, and he will flee from you. Draw nigh to God, and
he will draw nigh to you. Cleanse your hands, ye sinners; and purify
your hearts, ye double minded. Be afflicted, and mourn, and weep:
let your laughter be turned to mourning, and your joy to heaviness.
Humble yourselves in the sight of the Lord, and he shall lift you up.
—James 4:4–10

The college years are a wonderful time to meet some like-minded friends.
Meeting new friends in college can bear some similarities to the experience
of newborn ducks tagging along behind their mother. They attach themselves
to the first adult they see.

We face many choices when we go to college, and many college courses
support the seemingly harmless idea that any choice—the first choice—the next
choice—is a good idea. This perspective may give rise to the idea that all choices
are of equal value, but the Bible assures us this not the case. When we meet new
people or are faced with new choices, we want to be sure that we are making the
right decisions.

The Bible simplifies our choices into two categories: friendship with the
world or friendship with God. This does not mean that every believer chooses
a religious vocation. It means that when we surrender our plans, ideas, friends,
choices to God, He draws close to us. God's presence makes Satan flee, so God
clears out our minds to do all that is best and right. God enables us by His grace
to focus on the right choices.

Changes in Life

We give thanks to God and the Father of our Lord Jesus Christ,
praying always for you, Since we heard of your faith in Christ Jesus,
and of the love which ye have to all the saints, For the hope which
is laid up for you in heaven, whereof ye heard before in the word
of the truth of the gospel; Which is come unto you, as it is in all
the world; and bringeth forth fruit, as it doth also in you, since
the day ye heard of it, and knew the grace of God in truth: As ye
also learned of Epaphras our dear fellowservant, who is for you a
faithful minister of Christ; Who also declared unto us your love in
the Spirit. For this cause we also, since the day we heard it, do not
cease to pray for you, and to desire that ye might be filled with the
knowledge of his will in all wisdom and spiritual understanding;
That ye might walk worthy of the Lord unto all pleasing, being
fruitful in every good work, and increasing in the knowledge
of God; Strengthened with all might, according to his glorious
power, unto all patience and longsuffering with joyfulness.
—Colossians 1:3–11

College is a time when we look forward to changes in our lives. We may be
aware that most of the life-changing decisions we make will occur during
approximately the next ten to fifteen years of our lives. These decisions are
momentous.

In addition to professional choices we make, the changes that occur in our
spiritual lives are equally important and significant. What happens when we
repent of our sins and put our faith in Jesus Christ? Does this decision cause us
to change?—Yes, it does. We start loving others. We come across as hopeful to
others. We start understanding the concepts of the Bible.

How do we behave in this new life of faith? We see the Bible as the only
source of hope. We grow in the grace of God because we believe in the truth.
What does God do for us? He fills us with the knowledge of His will. He helps
us lead a life worthy of the name of Jesus Christ. He empowers us in His strength
to persevere in the path of His choosing, even in the choice of a profession.

Basic Beliefs

For this cause also thank we God without ceasing, because, when
ye received the Word of God which ye heard of us, ye received it not
as the word of men, but as it is in truth, the Word of God, which
effectually worketh also in you that believe ... But I would not have
you to be ignorant, brethren, concerning them which are asleep, that
ye sorrow not, even as others which have no hope. For if we believe
that Jesus died and rose again, even so them also which sleep in Jesus
will God bring with him. For this we say unto you by the word of the
Lord, that we which are alive and remain unto the coming of the Lord
shall not prevent them which are asleep. For the Lord himself shall
descend from heaven with a shout, with the voice of the archangel,
and with the trump of God: and the dead in Christ shall rise first:
Then we which are alive and remain shall be caught up together with
them in the clouds, to meet the Lord in the air: and so shall we ever
be with the Lord. Wherefore comfort one another with these words.
—1 Thessalonians 2:13; 4:13–18

The Word of God is at work in those who believe, by helping us apply what
we learn about God to life situations. The work of the Holy Spirit in our
lives helps us to show love toward others because of the love that Jesus Christ has
already shown to us. The Holy Spirit enables us to live blamelessly, to live quietly
and mind our own business, and to earn respect from others.

Even though campus life seems to offer so many alluring alternatives,
we still need to hold on to basic beliefs as the foundation of a fruitful and
fulfilling life. Here are some of the fundamentals of the faith. Jesus Christ died
on the cross. Jesus rose from the dead. God will raise those who believe in Jesus
Christ to a life with Him. Jesus will return to earth in power. An archangel will
announce Him with a trumpet blast. Living believers will meet the Lord Jesus
in the clouds. Believers will dwell with the Lord forever.

When we remember the basic beliefs of our faith, we keep the events of
today in perspective. Knowing that God has planned a specific ending to this
world encourages us to hang in there today.

Good Laws

But we know that the law is good, if a man use it lawfully; Knowing
this, that the law is not made for a righteous man, but for the
lawless and disobedient, for the ungodly and for sinners, for
unholy and profane, for murderers of fathers and murderers
of mothers, for manslayers, For whoremongers, for them that
defile themselves with mankind, for menstealers, for liars,
for perjured persons, and if there be any other thing that is
contrary to sound doctrine; According to the glorious gospel
of the blessed God, which was committed to my trust.
—1 Timothy 1:8–11

We live in a time when a lot of people feel it is a good idea to make many activities legal that were once considered immoral, illegal, unwise, unhealthy, or foolish. Think about the history of American law.

When the law prohibited the commercial sale of alcohol, alcohol related illnesses, social problems related to alcohol consumption, and family problems associated with alcohol consumption decreased dramatically. Before 1973, abortion was rare. Since abortion was legalized, more babies have been lost to abortion than the total number of soldiers lost in all the wars the nation has fought. When states legalize gambling casinos, law enforcement agencies expect increases in crimes specifically related to the vice of gambling.

So what is the purpose of a law? Is it to allow everyone to do as they please? Or, is the purpose of a law to establish a standard of right and good conduct? We need to remember that the purpose of a law is to serve the good of all citizens. This means calling bad behavior bad and supporting good behavior with laws that conform to good codes of conduct.

Minority Efforts

On that day did the king Ahasuerus give the house of Haman the Jews' enemy unto Esther the queen. And Mordecai came before the king; for Esther had told what he was unto her. And the king took off his ring, which he had taken from Haman, and gave it unto Mordecai. And Esther set Mordecai over the house of Haman ... Wherein the king granted the Jews which were in every city to gather themselves together, and to stand for their life, to destroy, to slay and to cause to perish, all the power of the people and province that would assault them, both little ones and women, and to take the spoil of them for a prey, Upon one day in all the provinces of king Ahasuerus, namely, upon the thirteenth day of the twelfth month, which is the month Adar. The copy of the writing for a commandment to be given in every province was published unto all people, and that the Jews should be ready against that day to avenge themselves on their enemies ... And in every province, and in every city, whithersoever the king's commandment and his decree came, the Jews had joy and gladness, a feast and a good day. And many of the people of the land became Jews; for the fear of the Jews fell upon them ... Thus the Jews smote all their enemies with the stroke of the sword, and slaughter, and destruction, and did what they would unto those that hated them. And in Shushan the palace the Jews slew and destroyed five hundred men.
—Esther 8:1–2, 11–13, 17; 9:5–6

The Jews were a minority population in Persia during their exile. They had assimilated into the country well enough that most locals didn't mind them, but some Persians still held on to the racial hatred.

The high-ranking government official Haman had instituted a plan and an ordinance to (unsuccessfully) annihilate the Jewish population. The position of aliens in a foreign country is always a tricky legal matter, then as now. The possibility of Jewish extermination made permissible by the edict of the king caused the alien population to seek legal redress.

The king wrote another edict allowing the Jews to defend themselves, showing us how God cares for His people in the most desperate of situations. God can cause those who once were against us (because they captured us) to soften and sympathize with our plight. God can give strength to underdogs to meet and win the challenges from frontrunners. God is faithful to His people.

The Results of Trusting in God

And Judah gathered themselves together, to ask help of the Lord:
even out of all the cities of Judah they came to seek the Lord. And
Jehoshaphat stood in the congregation of Judah and Jerusalem,
in the house of the Lord, before the new court, And said, O Lord
God of our fathers, art not thou God in heaven? and rulest not
thou over all the kingdoms of the heathen? and in thine hand is
there not power and … And he said, Hearken ye, all Judah, and ye
inhabitants of Jerusalem, and thou king Jehoshaphat, Thus saith
the Lord unto you, Be not afraid nor dismayed by reason of this
great multitude; for the battle is not yours, but God's. To morrow
go ye down against them: behold, they come up by the cliff of
Ziz; and ye shall find them at the end of the brook, before the
wilderness of Jeruel. Ye shall not need to fight in this battle: set
yourselves, stand ye still, and see the salvation of the Lord with
you, O Judah and Jerusalem: fear not, nor be dismayed; to morrow
go out against them: for the Lord will be with you … And the fear
of God was on all the kingdoms of those countries, when they
had heard that the Lord fought against the enemies of Israel.
—2 Chronicles 20:4–6, 15–17, 29

I s it worth it to trust God, or should we prefer to go it alone? When the armies
of three nations came against King Jehoshaphat, he was alarmed, but he knew
exactly what to do. He and the nation sought the will of God. They humbly
acknowledged His sovereignty over all nations, not just theirs. They admitted
their weakness against the invading armies, and they affirmed their intention to
look to the Lord alone for help.

God responds to human admissions of fallibility, not to human declarations
of strength. He assures the nation that He will fight the battle for them. They
don't have to fight. They have to be battle-ready. The believers get in position,
stand firm, and wait to see how God delivers them. They praised God when they
saw how he acted on their behalf. They found out that it is a pleasure to trust God.

Even more surprising perhaps is that the surrounding nations also
recognized the hand of God in defending them. When God acts, no one can
mistake His effort for human effort. Yes, it is worth it to trust God.

Look for the Lord in Life

> We have heard with our ears, O God, our fathers have told us,
> what work thou didst in their days, in the times of old. How thou
> didst drive out the heathen with thy hand, and plantedst them; how
> thou didst afflict the people, and cast them out. For they got not
> the land in possession by their own sword, neither did their own
> arm save them: but thy right hand, and thine arm, and the light
> of thy countenance, because thou hadst a favour unto them ... For
> our soul is bowed down to the dust: our belly cleaveth unto the
> earth. Arise for our help, and redeem us for thy mercies' sake.
> —Psalm 44:1–3, 25–26

Most of us are familiar with the saga of the Hebrew nation in Egypt: how they suffered as slaves, how God raised up Moses as their leader, how God sent ten plagues to convince the Egyptians to let them go; how God led them across the desert, how the Lord fed them with manna and quail, how God held back the Red Sea, and how God gave them victory over many enemies. The strength of God's arm to save the nation showed them the depth of His endless love for them.

God wants us to transpose the lessons of the Old Testament into our New Testament lives. Instead of just hearing about what God did for others—long ago and far away—God wants us to look for Him in our lives today. What kind of difficulties do we face? God can help us out of them. What problems plague us? God has a purpose in them for us. How difficult is it for us to find enough money to buy food? God will provide food for us. Would we be better off if we moved somewhere else? God can move us to that place.

When we look for the Lord in our lives, we will enjoy His personal love for us. He helps us in every situation, today, just as then.

Jesus Is Coming Again

And then shall they see the Son of man coming in the clouds with great power and glory. And then shall he send his angels, and shall gather together his elect from the four winds, from the uttermost part of the earth to the uttermost part of heaven ... But of that day and that hour knoweth no man, no, not the angels which are in heaven, neither the Son, but the Father. Take ye heed, watch and pray: for ye know not when the time is. For the Son of Man is as a man taking a far journey, who left his house, and gave authority to his servants, and to every man his work, and commanded the porter to watch. Watch ye therefore: for ye know not when the master of the house cometh, at even, or at midnight, or at the cockcrowing, or in the morning: Lest coming suddenly he find you sleeping. And what I say unto you I say unto all, Watch.
—Mark 13:26–27, 32–37

It has now been over two thousand years since Jesus Christ walked on planet earth. The place where He was born, the places where He lived, the places where He walked and worked still exist, but the roads have changed. The populations have increased. It has been so long since the time of Jesus Christ that we venerate specific places that now seem to be more mythical than real locations associated with the life of the Savior.

It is good that we have the Bible, the truth, to remind us that not only was Jesus Christ a real man (and the Son of God), who lived, died, and rose again, but the Bible assures us that Jesus Christ will come again to planet earth. Instead of humbling Himself to be born of a woman, born as a baby, Jesus Christ will return in full glory and power of God the Father, King of the universe. Everyone will see Him, and no one will confuse Him with anyone else (like they did while He was alive on earth).

In the meantime, we live for Him, we wait for Him, and we keep watch for Him. This means that we guard our ways to remain faithful to the One who has been faithful to us. We want Him to be glad to see us as much as we want to be glad to welcome Him.

The Tenderness and Purpose of God

A bruised reed shall he not break, and the smoking flax shall he
not quench: he shall bring forth judgment unto truth ... I the
Lord have called thee in righteousness, and will hold thine hand,
and will keep thee, and give thee for a covenant of the people,
for a light of the Gentiles ... I am the Lord: that is my name: and
my glory will I not give to another, neither my praise to graven
images ... And I will bring the blind by a way that they knew
not; I will lead them in paths that they have not known: I will
make darkness light before them, and crooked things straight.
These things will I do unto them, and not forsake them.
—Isaiah 42:3, 6, 8, 16

God looks for servants whom He can use. He has made us the way we are,
and He calls us to live a holy and righteous life before him. If we are timid,
He will lead us gently. When our understanding falters, He will encourage us.
When we have had enough of loud voices telling us what to do, He will speak
softly to us. When we are afraid to do what God wants, He will hold our hands
to lead us along.

Whatever God does in our lives, He does to bring glory to Himself. He is
so great that He cannot and will not share His glory with others. We need a God
who is bigger than we are, who is capable of leading us—because no matter how
smart we are, we are still like blind people compared to God. He dwells in light,
and we live with a sinful nature.

Because we are unable to see the way in front of us, God guides us in His
way and enlightens us as we obey Him. God will never forsake us.

The Conversion of Saul

And Saul, yet breathing out threatenings and slaughter against the disciples of the Lord, went unto the high priest, And desired of him letters to Damascus to the synagogues, that if he found any of this way, whether they were men or women, he might bring them bound unto Jerusalem. And as he journeyed, he came near Damascus: and suddenly there shined round about him a light from heaven: And he fell to the earth, and heard a voice saying unto him, Saul, Saul, why persecutest thou me? And he said, Who art thou, Lord? And the Lord said, I am Jesus whom thou persecutest: it is hard for thee to kick against the pricks. And he trembling and astonished said, Lord, what wilt thou have me to do? And the Lord said unto him, Arise, and go into the city, and it shall be told thee what thou must do … But the Lord said unto him, Go thy way: for he is a chosen vessel unto me, to bear my name before the Gentiles, and kings, and the children of Israel: For I will shew him how great things he must suffer for my name's sake. And Ananias went his way, and entered into the house; and putting his hands on him said, Brother Saul, the Lord, even Jesus, that appeared unto thee in the way as thou camest, hath sent me, that thou mightest receive thy sight, and be filled with the Holy Ghost. And immediately there fell from his eyes as it had been scales: and he received sight forthwith, and arose, and was baptized.
—Acts 9:1–6, 15–18

The conversion of Saul teaches us a lot about how God uses all our skills in His own way. Saul clearly had other plans for his life, but he learned his first lessons about God's plan in a dramatic, once-in-a-lifetime experience.

The life of Saul been very logically and methodically planned out by others—according to his lineage, according to his education, and according to his status in society. He was highly educated, the equivalent of a college professor today. He spoke well; back then, teaching depended more on oral transmission of information than textual reading, like it does today. His Jewish education taught him to chase down believers of the new way.

God grabbed his everlasting attention with a lightning flash from heaven. God's logic supersedes human logic. God taught Paul to chase down sinners and urge them to repent. Saul had chosen to persecute Christians with zeal. God chose Paul to preach about Jesus Christ to the Gentiles. God used all of Saul's abilities, to the glory of God. Even though most of us learn more slowly over a longer span of time, when we surrender ourselves to God, He will do the same for us and change our lives to reflect His glory.

358

Happy Day

And Moses said unto the people, Fear ye not, stand still, and
see the salvation of the Lord, which he will shew to you to day:
for the Egyptians whom ye have seen to day, ye shall see them
again no more for ever. The Lord shall fight for you, and ye
shall hold your peace ... But the children of Israel walked upon
dry land in the midst of the sea; and the waters were a wall
unto them on their right hand, and on their left ... Then sang
Moses and the children of Israel this song unto the Lord, and
spake, saying, I will sing unto the Lord, for he hath triumphed
gloriously: the horse and his rider hath he thrown into the sea.
—Exodus 14:13–14, 29; 15:1

We are all moved by the story of how God sent ten plagues upon the
Egyptians to convince a hard-hearted pharaoh to let God's people go
back home. In the retrospect of a few thousand years, it seems crystal clear what
God did for them. At the time, one wonders if they felt the magnitude of God's
deliverance, or were they still caught up in remembering the fertile land from
which they had just been wrenched. Were they still craving the delicious diet they
had become accustomed to?

The book of Exodus tells us that the Israelites were so terrified that they
could not imagine anything good coming out of their plight. Even though they
had been slaves, they were a civilized and cultured people. Now they were camping
out in the open air, perhaps for the first time in their lives. It does not seem likely
that slaves took family camping vacations to prepare them for the exodus from
Egypt. Moses calmed them down and spoke words of encouragement to them.
They listened to him. They obeyed God. They experienced deliverance from the
Lord when they crossed the Red Sea on dry ground, with a wall of water on either
side of them. Moses and the Israelites sang songs of thanks to God.

Do we always remember to thank God when good things happen to us? Do
we see the hand of the Lord in the events of our lives? As we read farther, we
know the Israelites didn't always either.

DECEMBER 25

The Greatest Gift

Now the birth of Jesus Christ was on this wise: When as his
mother Mary was espoused to Joseph, before they came together,
she was found with child of the Holy Ghost. Then Joseph her
husband, being a just man, and not willing to make her a public
example, was minded to put her away privily. But while he thought
on these things, behold, the angel of the Lord appeared unto
him in a dream, saying, Joseph, thou son of David, fear not to
take unto thee Mary thy wife: for that which is conceived in her
is of the Holy Ghost. And she shall bring forth a son, and thou
shalt call his name Jesus: for he shall save his people from their
sins. Now all this was done, that it might be fulfilled which was
spoken of the Lord by the prophet, saying, Behold, a virgin shall
be with child, and shall bring forth a son, and they shall call his
name Emmanuel, which being interpreted is, God with us.
—Matthew 1:18–23

When we were children, we wrote up lists of Christmas gifts, hoping to
satisfy our cravings with them. But the greatest gift of all fulfills the
greatest human need—the need to know that God is with us, that we are not
alone, and that He alone can do more than we are able to imagine.

Let us consider Mary, the mother of our Lord—a devout believer, willing
to let God touch her physically, agreeing to let God use her for His purposes,
in spite of apparent personal disgrace and social ostracism. Let us consider
Joseph—a holy man, able to put aside his feelings about an awkward situation,
ignore his feelings, believe the word the Lord spoke to him, and live according
to God's Word.

None of us now needs angelic visitors to reveal God's will to us because
we have the complete Bible, telling us about the miraculous birth, death, and
resurrection of Jesus Christ the Savior. God proved His love for us by entering
world and dying for our sins. What a great gift to remember on this holiest of
holy days!

Why This Religion?

Forasmuch as many have taken in hand to set forth in order
a declaration of those things which are most surely believed
among us, Even as they delivered them unto us, which from
the beginning were eyewitnesses, and ministers of the word;
It seemed good to me also, having had perfect understanding
of all things from the very first, to write unto thee in order,
most excellent Theophilus, That thou mightest know the
certainty of those things, wherein thou hast been instructed.
—Luke 1:1–4

And there are also many other things which Jesus did, the which,
if they should be written every one, I suppose that even the world
itself could not contain the books that should be written. Amen.
—John 21:25

Modern times do not seem much different from ancient times when we consider the number of religions in the world and the variety of choices people feel are available to them for spiritual purposes. The Bible stands apart from all other books of religion for its accuracy.

Dr. Luke writes that he has drawn up a careful and truthful account of factual historical events. This is important because when we think about what we believe, we know we are making a lifelong decision. We should be aware that the best type of decision to make is a decision based upon the truth. It is understood that whatever we believe, we will act according to those beliefs. When we believe what is not true, the results in our lives will reflect the degree of error we have believed in. When we study the Bible, God helps us to understand the truth.

Jesus is the Son of Man who died for our sins and the Son of God who came to earth as a man to show us how to live and to save us from all sins. When we learn about the life of Jesus, we are faced with the truth about ourselves. As we read on, we begin to glimpse the grandeur of God's plan for us. Believing in the truth is the best religious decision to make. The truth never fails us.

Two Choices

And there were also two other, malefactors, led with him to be put
to death. And when they were come to the place, which is called
Calvary, there they crucified him, and the malefactors, one on the
right hand, and the other on the left ... And a superscription also
was written over him in letters of Greek, and Latin, and Hebrew,
This Is The King Of The Jews. And one of the malefactors which
were hanged railed on him, saying, If thou be Christ, save thyself
and us. But the other answering rebuked him, saying, Dost not thou
fear God, seeing thou art in the same condemnation? And we indeed
justly; for we receive the due reward of our deeds: but this man
hath done nothing amiss. And he said unto Jesus, Lord, remember
me when thou comest into thy kingdom. And Jesus said unto him,
Verily I say unto thee, Today shalt thou be with me in paradise.
—Luke 23:32–33, 38–43

The scene may be familiar to us: three crosses on a hill; on the middle
cross hangs Jesus Christ; on either side hang two convicted criminals.
The imagery is vivid and exemplifies many significant truths. The location of
the hilltop can represent many ideas: we have toiled to get to the summit, like
climbing Mount Everest; we are better than a lot of others, so we are above them;
or we have achieved something great, so we are on top of the world.

All of these concepts are true of Jesus Christ. He left heaven to become
human and live a human life. He carried His cross uphill only to be ignominiously
nailed to it. Jesus Christ is better than everyone else because He is the perfect
sinless Son of God and also the Son of man. When Jesus Christ died on the cross,
He achieved what no one else could do—He saved us from our sins.

Two criminals hung on crosses on either side of the Savior. They represent
the two true choices of every human life: the choice to ridicule and reject Jesus
Christ, the Son of God dying for our sins; or the choice to repent and be thankful
that God has provided a way for us to join Him in heaven. Which choice most
marks the life we live right now?

Service to God

And in those days, when the number of the disciples was multiplied,
there arose a murmuring of the Grecians against the Hebrews,
because their widows were neglected in the daily ministration. Then
the twelve called the multitude of the disciples unto them, and
said, It is not reason that we should leave the Word of God, and
serve tables. Wherefore, brethren, look ye out among you seven
men of honest report, full of the Holy Ghost and wisdom, whom
we may appoint over this business. But we will give ourselves
continually to prayer, and to the ministry of the word. And the
saying pleased the whole multitude: and they chose Stephen, a man
full of faith and of the Holy Ghost, and Philip, and Prochorus,
and Nicanor, and Timon, and Parmenas, and Nicolas a proselyte
of Antioch: Whom they set before the apostles: and when they
had prayed, they laid their hands on them. And the Word of God
increased; and the number of the disciples multiplied in Jerusalem
greatly; and a great company of the priests were obedient to the faith.
—Acts 6:1–7

The church is a body of spiritually minded people, but it also carries out many
practical duties. Modern churches have recreation programs and facilities,
food banks, and clothing distribution, to name a few of the varied ministries of
the church. As soon as the young church was formed, it needed to be organized
because the fledgling church performed the same functions as today, setting the
example we still follow.

One reason to separate the religious or spiritual work of the church from
the practical duties of the church is that pastors cannot do everything. Another
reason is that the church is for everyone, not just for the pastor and a few other
active people. Church members who are not preachers have other gifts to use
within the administration of the church.

The early church recognized this practical need. When the church body
became too large and unwieldy for the preachers to do all the tasks, they set apart
deacons, who were God-fearing men that could oversee the practical duties of
the church. The tasks are still God-given, and they still require the leading of the
Holy Spirit. All work done for God glorifies Him, no matter what it is.

Hospitality

And when Jesus was come into Peter's house, he saw his wife's
mother laid, and sick of a fever. And he touched her hand, and
the fever left her: and she arose, and ministered unto them.
—Matthew 8:14–15

Now it came to pass, as they went, that he entered into a certain
village: and a certain woman named Martha received him into her
house. And she had a sister called Mary, which also sat at Jesus' feet,
and heard his word. But Martha was cumbered about much serving,
and came to him, and said, Lord, dost thou not care that my sister
hath left me to serve alone? bid her therefore that she help me.
—Luke 10:38–40

And on the sabbath we went out of the city by a river side,
where prayer was wont to be made; and we sat down, and spake
unto the women which resorted thither. And a certain woman
named Lydia, a seller of purple, of the city of Thyatira, which
worshipped God, heard us: whose heart the Lord opened, that
she attended unto the things which were spoken of Paul. And
when she was baptized, and her household, she besought us,
saying, If ye have judged me to be faithful to the Lord, come
into my house, and abide there. And she constrained us.
—Acts 16:13–15

In spite of a general cultural trend to devalue the household arts, many women still
love to prepare meals, entertain company, and house overnight guests. The gift of
hospitality still undergirds the soul-winning efforts of the church, but we don't always
remember to honor the women who work tirelessly behind the scenes for the Lord.

Once Jesus began His ministry, He traveled a lot, and He depended upon
the hospitality of believers. During one visit, He came to Peter's house and saw
that his mother-in-law was in bed, very ill with a fever. Jesus healed her, and
she gladly rose to wait on Him. Jesus also enjoyed staying at the home of three
siblings: Lazarus, Mary, and Martha. We tend to remember Martha as overly
concerned with meal preparation, but we should also commend her and her
sister for consistent hospitality to Jesus. Lydia, a new believer, also recognized
the importance of hospitality. She invited Paul, Silas, and Timothy to stay with
her while they ministered in Philippi, her hometown.

The effective completion of everyday tasks still matters to God.

The Fool versus the
Righteous Person

The fool hath said in his heart, There is no God. They are corrupt,
they have done abominable works, there is none that doeth good.
The Lord looked down from heaven upon the children of men,
to see if there were any that did understand, and seek God. They
are all gone aside, they are all together become filthy: there is
none that doeth good, no, not one. Lord, who shall abide in thy
tabernacle? who shall dwell in thy holy hill? He that walketh
uprightly, and worketh righteousness, and speaketh the truth in his
heart. He that backbiteth not with his tongue, nor doeth evil to his
neighbour, nor taketh up a reproach against his neighbor ... He
that putteth not out his money to usury, nor taketh reward against
the innocent. He that doeth these things shall never be moved.
—Psalm 14:1–3; 15:1–3, 5

Items of contrast force us to think about differences and what the differences
imply. When the Bible contrasts the fool with the righteous, we have to admit
that this is not a contrast with which we readily identify. We might prefer to
contrast fools with wise men or the righteous with the ungodly.

The Bible is not a dictionary or a vocabulary textbook, but it does give
meanings we can understand. Furthermore, it tells the outcomes of two distinct
ways of living. According to biblical terminology, fools live with the initial
premise that there is no God. This is also the initial premise of the philosophy
of existentialism propounded by Jean Paul Sartre in the 1970s. According to the
Bible, fools commit only evil deeds because they have turned away from God, the
source and giver of all goodness. At the same time that fools are engaged in evil
and harming the righteous, they live with an overwhelming dread about every
aspect of life. This is what a godless philosophy does to people.

According to biblical terminology, the righteous live according to God's will,
to seek and gain an understanding of it. The righteous person wants to be close
to God, so they live blameless lives. They even tell the truth and say nice things
about others. Their lives are solid, immoveable, and unshakeable—because they
fear God.

Only by the Power of God

For the preaching of the cross is to them that perish foolishness; but
unto us which are saved it is the power of God. For it is written, I
will destroy the wisdom of the wise, and will bring to nothing the
understanding of the prudent. Where is the wise? where is the scribe?
where is the disputer of this world? hath not God made foolish the
wisdom of this world? For after that in the wisdom of God the world
by wisdom knew not God, it pleased God by the foolishness of
preaching to save them that believe. For the Jews require a sign, and
the Greeks seek after wisdom: But we preach Christ crucified, unto
the Jews a stumblingblock, and unto the Greeks foolishness ... And
I was with you in weakness, and in fear, and in much trembling. And
my speech and my preaching was not with enticing words of
man's wisdom, but in demonstration of the Spirit and of power.
—1 Corinthians 1:18–23; 2:3–4

Billboards along the highway—television advertising—magazine ads—
pop-ups on the computer screen—the world broadcasts many conflicting
messages to us today. They all promise something better in exchange for a
specific sum of money.

When we know that we will be following a specific career path, we listen
very closely to the message of how to achieve the professional goal. Whatever
professional plans we have in mind, we also need to listen to the message of how
to acquire the spiritual skill set that will underpin our lives of faith.

Paul urges people to consider the message of repentance by comparing it
with human words of wisdom. He indicates that we must appropriate the skills
of faith in order to practice our faith. This makes sense to believers because we
see the parallel between the temporal world and the spiritual world. We cannot
look to human words of wisdom for spiritual insight. This should not need to be
stated, but we live in the world that tries to convince us otherwise. The apostle
speaks the same message that we should learn to lean on the Word of God alone
because God's foolishness is still wiser than the wisdom of men.

INDEX OF SCRIPTURES

Ezekiel 33:10–11, 14–16; Isaiah 1:18; 38:17 (7/7)
Ezekiel 34:1–2, 5–6, 10 (9/6)
Ezekiel 34:16, 20, 23–26, 31 (10/6)
Ezekiel 36:22–27, 32 (11/6)
Ezekiel 37:1–3, 10; Ephesians 2:4–5 (12/6)
Ezekiel 37:19, 24, 27–28 (1/8)
Ezekiel 43:4–5, 10–11 (2/8)
Daniel 1:3–4, 8, 14–15, 17; Romans 12:1 (10/8)
Daniel 3:1, 6, 12–13, 16–18, 22, 24–25 (11/9)
Daniel 4:13–17, 28, 33 (1/10)
Hosea 1:2–4, 6, 8, 10 (1/16)
Hosea 4:1–3, 6 (2/17)
Hosea 11:1–4, 7; 12:6 (3/12)
Joel 2:12–14, 21 (3/13)
Amos 1:1–2; 7:14–16; 5:14–15 (9/1)
Amos 5:4, 14–15, 24 (4/15)
Obadiah 1:15–18 (1/17)
Jonah 1:1–3, 17; 2:10; 3:1–2, 4–5; 4:1 (2/18)
Micah 6:8, 13–14, 16; 7:18–19 (3/17)
Nahum 1:1–6 (4/16)
Habakkuk 1:2, 5, 12; 2:4, 20 (1/12)
Habakkuk 2:13–14; 2:20; Zechariah 2:13; Psalm 46:10; Job 33:32–33 (3/15)
Zephaniah 1:7; 2:3; 3:12, 17 (12/12)
Zephaniah 1:12; 2:9–10, 15; 3:7 (12/11)
Haggai 1:4–6, 9–10; 2:17, 19 (5/15)
Zechariah 3:8–9; 4:6; 6:12; 8:7; 1 Corinthians 2:4 (7/9)
Zechariah 7:8–10; 8:16–19; Proverbs 28:5 (7/15)
Malachi 1:2, 5–6, 9; 2:7; 3:16–18 (8/10)
Matthew 1:18–23 (12/25)
Matthew 2:1–3, 7–12 (5/7)
Matthew 2:19–23 (6/7)
Matthew 3:13–17 (7/8)
Matthew 4:1–11 (5/2)
Matthew 4:16; John 1:4, 9; 8:12; Psalm 119:105; Luke 11:35–36 (5/8)
Matthew 5:3–10 (11/5)
Matthew 5:22; Galatians 5:22–23 (8/4)
Matthew 6:19–21 (9/7)
Matthew 8:14–15; Luke 10:38–40; Acts 16:13–15 (12/29)
Matthew 12:33–37 (4/26)
Matthew 13:3–9 (10/3)
Matthew 13:24–26, 37–41, 47–49 (7/3)
Matthew 13:24–31 (11/3)
Matthew 13:31–32; Genesis 2:9; Psalm 92:12; Zechariah 8:12 (4/5)
Matthew 13:33 (6/3)
Matthew 13:44–46; 6:19–21 (6/4)
Matthew 22:16; John 5:24–27, 30 (3/28)

Matthew 25:14–23, 29 (2/5)
Matthew 28:16–20; Ecclesiastes 11:1, 5; Isaiah 40:7–9 (6/25)
Mark 1:1–8 (1/13)
Mark 1:9–11 (2/11)
Mark 2:1, 3–5, 8–12 (5/22)
Mark 4:13, 21–25 (3/9)
Mark 4:26–29; Hosea 14:5–6, 8 (9/4)
Mark 4:30–32 (8/16)
Mark 4:35–41; Isaiah 25:3–4 (6/22)
Mark 6:14–15; 9:7 (4/12)
Mark 6:14–16; Matthew 16:13–16 (7/22)
Mark 6:45–52 (8/18)
Mark 8:34–38 (9/21)
Mark 9:33–36; 10:13–16 (10/21)
Mark 10:17–22, 26–27 (11/22)
Mark 11:1–10 (3/25)
Mark 12:28–34 (2/25)
Mark 13:26–27, 32–37 (12/21)
Mark 14:29–31, 66–68, 70–72 (1/25)
Mark 15:25–31, 37–38 (4/24)
Luke 1:1–4; John 21:25 (12/26)
Luke 1:26–27, 31–35, 37–38 (1/27)
Luke 2:28–36, 38, 40 (2/26)
Luke 3:1a, 2b, 7–14 (3/27)
Luke 4:1–12; Hebrews 4:15 (10/11)
Luke 4:16, 20–22, 24, 28–30; Hebrews: 4:12 (4/27)
Luke 6:43–45; Jeremiah 12:2; Psalm 1:1, 3 (6/26)
Luke 6:46–49; Matthew 7:28–29 (5/27)
Luke 9:59–62 (11/4)
Luke 11:2–4; Psalm 103:1–3 (4/6)
Luke 11:5–10 (12/4)
Luke 11:33–36; Matthew 5:14–16 (10/31)
Luke 11:33–36; Psalm 119:105, 130; Proverbs 6:23 (7/27)
Luke 12:22–31 (8/22)
Luke 15:3–4, 7–8, 10; 19:10 (9/26)
Luke 21:1–4 (10/26)
Luke 22:17–22 (11/27)
Luke 23:32–33, 38–43 (12/27)
John 1:12–14, 16 (1/28)
John 3:3–8 (1/9)
John 3:12–17; Numbers 21:8 (2/27)
John 3:27, 34; 5:19, 22–23, 30 (4/9)
John 4:22–24, 39, 42 (3/6)
John 7:40–51 (4/28)
John 9:1–5 (5/28)
John 9:12, 17, 25, 33, 35, 38 (6/8)
John 12:12–16 (6/27)
John 14:6; Psalm 119:30; John 8:32; Psalm 25:5 (8/20)
John 14:15–22, 26–27 (2/28)
John 15:1–8 (4/21)

369

Printed in the United States
By Bookmasters

Printed in the United States
By Bookmasters